OXFORD HISTORICAL MONOGRAPHS

Editors

Somoza and Roosevelt

Good Neighbour Diplomacy in Nicaragua,
1933–1945

ANDREW CRAWLEY

OXFORD
UNIVERSITY PRESS

OXFORD

UNIVERSITY PRESS

Great Clarendon Street, Oxford OX2 6DP

Oxford University Press is a department of the University of Oxford.
It furthers the University's objective of excellence in research, scholarship,
and education by publishing worldwide in

Oxford New York

Auckland Cape Town Dar es Salaam Hong Kong Karachi
Kuala Lumpur Madrid Melbourne Mexico City Nairobi
New Delhi Shanghai Taipei Toronto

With offices in

Argentina Austria Brazil Chile Czech Republic France Greece
Guatemala Hungary Italy Japan Poland Portugal Singapore
South Korea Switzerland Thailand Turkey Ukraine Vietnam

Oxford is a registered trade mark of Oxford University Press
in the UK and in certain other countries

Published in the United States
by Oxford University Press Inc., New York

© Andrew Crawley 2007

The moral rights of the author have been asserted
Database right Oxford University Press (maker)

First published 2007

British Library Cataloguing in Publication Data

Data available

Library of Congress Cataloging in Publication Data

Data available

Typeset by Newgen Imaging Systems (P) Ltd., Chennai, India
Printed in Great Britain
on acid-free paper by
Biddles Ltd., King's Lynn, Norfolk

ISBN 978-0-19-921265-1

1 3 5 7 9 10 8 6 4 2

Dennis Michael Crawley
Patricia Mary Crawley
In Memory

Acknowledgements

I am indebted to several people and institutions for their help in the writing of this book. I am very grateful to the British Academy for financial support, and to the board of management of the Arnold, Bryce and Read Funds at Oxford University for a scholarship that enabled me to undertake research in the United States and Nicaragua. Elizabeth Joyce and Jacqueline Edelman provided constant advice and encouragement. William and Elizabeth Steponkus were superb hosts in Washington DC. Mazen Hanna's friendship has been priceless. In preparing the book for publication, the support of Anneke Jessen was invaluable. My greatest personal debt is to Malcolm Deas, my erstwhile supervisor at St Antony's College, Oxford. In recent years my job has taken me to many countries, most of them in Latin America. I have been made aware that there is an entire community of 'Deasians' throughout the region, and I have noticed that whenever two or more of this community are gathered together, they tend to swap tales of their supervisor with an affection and respect of which most of us can only dream.

Contents

Introduction

Franklin Roosevelt died on 12 April 1945. For the president who had guided the United States out of the Depression and to certain victory in global war, the tributes from around the world claimed a status akin to myth. Winston Churchill recalled 'the beating of that generous heart which was always stirred to anger and to action by the spectacle of aggression and oppression by the strong against the weak. It is indeed a loss, a bitter loss to humanity, that those heartbeats are stilled forever.' The *Contemporary Review* asserted unambiguously that 'the annals of the modern age may be searched without our coming upon an event to compare with the death of President Roosevelt . . . The death which makes memorable the 12th. of April has no parallel.'[1]

For the president whose inaugural address in 1933 had enshrined good neighbourism as a prime goal of foreign policy, the condolences from Latin America were equally heartfelt. In Rio de Janeiro a large crowd, hundreds strong, gathered spontaneously at the gates of the US embassy in silent tribute. In Asunción, a correspondent in *El País* told his readers that Roosevelt had 'seemed to elevate the whole moral stature of the species'. It had been thus even before his death. The policy of the good neighbour, and perhaps even more so the New Deal, nurtured in Latin America an image of Roosevelt as a man deeply concerned for the disadvantaged. His oratory, amid a world depression and a world war, proved compelling. Inaugurated an unprecedented four times, having overcome grave physical infirmity to inspire a highly activist government, he seemed a consummate *caudillo*. 'All of the America of Columbus', declared Honduras's *La Época* in 1936, 'renders him its homage and admiration'. Four years later, the *Diario de Noticias* of Brazil characterized him simply as 'the greatest citizen of the present world'.[2]

During his lifetime, Franklin Roosevelt acquired a stature in Latin America unmatched by any other US president before him. When he

---

[1] Quoted in Nicholas Halasz, *Roosevelt through Foreign Eyes* (Englewood Cliffs, NJ: Van Nostrand, 1961), 308, 310.

[2] Ted Morgan, *FDR: A Biography* (New York: Simon and Schuster, 1985), 767; press sources are quoted in Donald Dozer, *Are We Good Neighbors?* (Gainesville: University of Florida Press, 1959), 28, 87, 150.

died, that stature too became the stuff of legend. A month after his death, *El Panamá-América* declared that 'the Knight of all knights transferred himself from La Mancha to North America. He carried his lance and shield; and he placed them in the service of the ideals of humanity: the service of liberty, of justice, and of the dignity of man.' Soil from twenty countries of Latin America was flown to the United States to be scattered over Franklin Roosevelt's grave.[3]

*

In the decades since 1945, Roosevelt's image has undergone the revisions to which all presidential reputations in the United States are eventually subject. He has since been seen as a flawed man, an adulterer with a fondness for petty cruelties and a tolerance of political corruption at home.[4] A shadow, too, has fallen over his policies in Central America.

Every generation's peculiar concerns about the present prompt particular demands upon the past.[5] Four decades after Roosevelt died, his successor in the White House developed a peculiar fixation with Central America. President Reagan's policies towards Nicaragua in the 1980s provoked an intense, ideologically charged, international debate in which supporters and opponents both made their demands on history. A very large body of work on US policies towards Central America was produced in that decade. The historiography of US relations with the region up to the beginning of the 1930s was already substantial. So too was the literature on American policies in the isthmus following the onset of the Cold War. Studies dealing at length with the good neighbour period in particular countries, however, were few in number. Demands for the facts of the past were therefore frustrated.

Nevertheless, it was after Franklin Roosevelt's election that Anastasio Somoza took command of the Nicaraguan National Guard. It was in Roosevelt's time that Somoza deposed the elected government of Nicaragua and established an exceptionally long regime. It was then that the National Guard murdered Augusto Sandino, a guerrilla leader whose name was adopted by the movement that eventually ousted the government of Somoza's second son. And it was the government established by that movement, four decades after Roosevelt died, that his successor in the White House was overtly trying to overthrow.

---

[3] Dozer, *Are We Good Neighbors?*, 188; Halasz, *Roosevelt*, 314.

[4] Morgan, *FDR, passim.*

[5] Arthur M. Schlesinger, *The Cycles of American History* (London: Penguin Books, 1989), 373.

In the debate of the 1980s, as the demands were made on the past, historical judgement was coloured by the political circumstances of the present. From what was known of the pre-1930 era to what was known of the post-1945 period, some intuitive leaps were undertaken. Assumptions were made, and then published, and then cited, and in some quarters were accepted as history. Thus it could baldly be claimed that an American minister in Nicaragua, half a century earlier, under instructions from Washington, had ordered the murder of Augusto Sandino. It could be maintained that the same minister personally directed an attack on the house of Sandino's host in Managua. References to America's 'installation' of Somoza as head of the National Guard, and to Washington's creation and consolidation of the Somoza regime, could become so commonplace as to be presented as fact in international conferences on the Central American crisis of the 1980s.[6] History was hostage to politics, and at a time when much of the political debate centred on the issue of intervention.

Until the early 1930s the United States had been massively interventionist in Nicaragua, militarily, politically, and fiscally. After the revolution against the long regime of José Santos Zelaya (1893–1910) and the short-lived government of his successor José Madriz (1910), the United States had attempted to stabilize the country by brokering an agreement between the main presidential hopefuls. The results were short-lived. When the Conservative president Adolfo Díaz appealed in 1912 for US support in the face of a revolution headed by General Luis Mena, his former minister of war, the United States intervened with almost 3,000 troops to keep Díaz in office. When order was restored, 130 American marines remained as the US legation guard in Managua. They symbolized Washington's military power in a country that became, in economic terms, a virtual protectorate of the United States as military intervention was matched by fiscal intervention.[7]

The marine guard remained throughout the re-elected government of Díaz (1912–17), Emiliano Chamorro (1917–21), and that of the latter's

---

[6] Such allegations abound in the literature. See Gregorio Selser, in his introduction to William Krehm, *Democracies and Tyrannies of the Caribbean* (Westport, Conn.: Lawrence Hill & Co., 1984), p. xii; Marco Antonio Valle Martínez, *La dictadura somocista* (Leon: Comité Político Universitario UNAN, 1980), 18; César Escobar Morales, *Sandino en el panorama nacional* (Managua: *s.n.*, 1979), 132–3; Rodolfo Cerdas Cruz, 'Nicaragua: One Step Forward, Two Steps Back', in Giuseppe DiPalma and Laurence Whitehead (eds.), *The Central American Impasse* (London: Croom Helm, 1986), 175, 180–1.

[7] Dana G. Munro, *The United States and the Caribbean Area* (Boston: World Peace Foundation, 1934), 229–31.

uncle, Diego Chamorro (1921–3). The events following the presidential
succession of 1924, when a large US military force again intervened to
sustain Díaz's latest presidency, form the immediate backdrop to the
Roosevelt administration's policy in Nicaragua. Those events are
described in Chapter 1 of this book. In the late 1920s, US intervention
was such that American troops were commanding and fighting alongside
the Nicaraguan National Guard against Sandinista insurgents. By the
mid 1980s, the US government was financing the remnants of the same
military institution, now insurgents, against Sandinistas who by then
comprised the government. Intervention had changed slightly in nature
and diminished only little in extent.

For part of the intervening period, the era of the good neighbour, the
fundamental tenets of US policy in Central America had been non-
intervention and non-interference. Publicly proclaimed and constantly
reiterated at the time, non-intervention became an ethos in itself. Amid
the intense isolationism of the Depression, the silent neutrality of good
neighbourism was expounded for years by officials of the Roosevelt
administration in terms that endeavoured to elevate it to the status of
a philosophy, a set of ideals that informed US policy throughout the
western hemisphere. The speeches of Sumner Welles, assistant secretary
of state for Latin American affairs during most of the period, give some
impression of the degree to which the good neighbour policy inspired a
rhetoric of fraternal altruism and inter-American harmony. Past mistakes
were to end; good neighbourism was to be a non-interventionist, foreign
policy revolution.

From the perspective of the highly interventionist 1980s, this notion
was sometimes judged to be a hollow and hypocritical conceit. Non-
intervention, in this view, did not mean that the United States had
discontinued intervention. On the contrary, the good neighbour policy
had simply been a form of continued domination in disguise, a trap for
the unwary, in which any departures from traditional thinking were
wholly overridden by the elements of continuity with the policies that preceded good neighbourism and, by implication, with those that followed.[8]

In the end, much of the evidence for this view consisted of the undeniable fact that it was in Franklin Roosevelt's time that Anastasio Somoza took
command of Nicaragua's National Guard and deposed the Nicaraguan

---

[8] The 'unwary' reference is from Gregorio Selser, *Sandino, General of the Free*
(New York: Monthly Review Press, 1981), 184.

government, thereby establishing an exceptionally long regime; that it was during Roosevelt's presidency that the National Guard murdered a guerrilla leader whose name had been adopted by the government that the United States was trying to overthrow. In this manner the past was made to coincide with the concerns of the present.

An aim of writing history must be to present the past in the context of its own concerns, not in the context of ours. This is a study in diplomatic history. It endeavours to describe the motivations, nature, and development of US policy towards Nicaragua during the good neighbour period. It attempts to judge how and to what extent US attitudes and policies affected political developments in Nicaragua during that time, and how Nicaraguan perceptions of US strategy conditioned domestic politics. It seeks to show how such attitudes and policies altered in response to shifting conditions in Nicaragua, and to the broader and changing concerns of their context: the isolationism of the inter-war years; the Depression; the rise of an external threat; the outbreak of war in Europe; the entry of the United States into a world war; and its emergence from a war in which democracy had prevailed against dictatorship.

To these ends, this study adopts a broadly chronological approach whose phases are determined by the changing conditions in Nicaragua and the international context to which good neighbourism had to react, and to which the basic principle of non-intervention had to adapt. Throughout, therefore, the study also considers the issue of diplomatic interference in US–Nicaraguan relations and the extent to which, in the context of each phase, the United States usefully effected the proclaimed central tenet of its policy.

As a work of diplomatic history this study aims to escape its present, though it is plain that the attempt can never really meet with full success. Nevertheless, the present state of relations between the United States and Nicaragua is much calmer than it was until recently, and the current international debate is less charged. Three presidents have been elected in Nicaragua since the Sandinista National Liberation Front (Frente Sandinista de Liberación Nacional, FSLN) left office. The third, Enrique Bolaños, is now approaching the end of his mandate. The Sandinistas polled second in the November 2001 elections that brought him to the presidency. Neither of the two main parties' election campaigns, marked by frequent and negative references to their opponents' past records, involved any great discussion of concrete measures for resolving the grave problems of present-day Nicaragua. Personalities therefore assumed a fundamental significance, and the leaders of the two main parties in contention fought very much in terms of the past, on which both had very different demands. This book attempts to show what demands can reasonably be made on the history of the good neighbour policy in Nicaragua, and the true nature of diplomatic relations between the governments of Anastasio Somoza and Franklin Roosevelt.

1

Becoming Good Neighbours

In the field of world policy I would dedicate this Nation to the
policy of the Good Neighbor—the neighbor who resolutely
respects himself and, because he does so, respects the rights of others; the neighbor who respects his obligations and respects the sanctity of his agreements in and with a world of neighbors. We now
realize as we have never realized before our interdependence on each
other; that we cannot merely take, but must give as well.[1]

Franklin Roosevelt
Inaugural address
4 March 1933

Three years after Franklin Roosevelt dedicated the United States to the
good neighbour policy, Anastasio Somoza deposed the elected government of Nicaragua. He thereby established a control that endured until
his assassination in 1956, and a regime that would dominate the country
until 1979. When the Guardia Nacional finally forced the departure of
the Liberal president Juan Bautista Sacasa in the summer of 1936 there
was no shortage of accusations in the Latin American press that the
Roosevelt administration was installing Somoza as president.[2] The alle-
gation was untrue, but in the circumstances that prevailed in Nicaragua
at the time it was virtually inevitable.

Part of the manner in which Somoza and his sons consolidated their
hold on Nicaragua, however, and the perceived nature of the relationship
between the Somoza regime and the United States (a perception typified
by the historiography's interminable repetition of a single, graphic quota-
tion ascribed to Roosevelt), have given some credibility to insinuations

---

[1] Quoted in Samuel Rosenman (ed.), *Public Papers and Addresses of Franklin
D. Roosevelt* (New York: Random House, 1938), ii, 14.

[2] 817.00/8444, Corrigan (El Salvador) to Hull, 19 May 1936; 817.00/8509, Weddel
(Argentina) to Hull, 6 June 1936; 817.00/8520, Boal (Mexico) to Hull, 12 June 1936.

that persist to this day. With the triumph of the FSLN in 1979, those imputations passed into the popular mythology of the Nicaraguan revolution.

Such charges suggest on Washington's part a positively formulated policy, long-range planning, and well-defined, country-specific objectives that in reality were conspicuously absent. It is true, nonetheless, that Somoza could not have assumed and retained the presidency of Nicaragua if the US State Department had actively disapproved. Of the circumstances surrounding his rise to power, Roosevelt's good neighbour policy was to be a significant feature. That policy, as expounded throughout the Americas, was to have novel foundations. In the words of a contemporary and admiring observer, it was 'founded on complete respect on the part of the strong for the rights and independence of the weak; on cooperation, not tutelage; on hope, not fear'.[3] In Nicaragua, it took as its guiding principle the ideal of non-interference in domestic political affairs.

To argue that Somoza's ascent was directly promoted and indirectly facilitated by the practical application of this doctrine is not to suggest that his assumption of power represented, for Washington, an achieved goal. That Somoza rose to power during the infancy of good neighbourism, however, was more than coincidence. The relationship between the two countries, and between the political actors in each of them, was more complex—and certainly more interesting—than much of the received wisdom has tended to suggest.

*

Two months before Roosevelt's inaugural address, the US marine corps evacuated Nicaragua. The abandonment of a country in which the United States had maintained an almost uninterrupted military presence since 1912 was the culmination of trends that had long been evident. Throughout the 1920s, the United States was increasingly determined to maintain its freedom of action through a return to isolationism and an avoidance of any foreign commitments that might constrain such freedom. The rejection of internationalism and of collective security programmes was a posture welcome at home, where prolonged involvement in other countries' affairs enjoyed little support. In the forty-three years to 1933 there were forty-three occasions on which a US president used armed forces in Latin America without congressional approval.

---

[3] Dexter Perkins, *The United States and the Caribbean* (Cambridge, Mass.: Harvard University Press, 1947), 146.

Of these, thirty-two were in the Central American and Caribbean region. Nicaragua had seen seven of them. Such interventionism was being assailed by congressional isolationists, as well as by church groups, trade unions, academia, and much of the press. As political conditions in Nicaragua worsened in the late 1920s, US public opposition to the presence of American troops in the country increased. Following the bloody battle of Ocotal in July 1927, when a frontal engagement between Sandinista guerrillas and US marines proved catastrophic for the insurgents after they were dive-bombed by five DeHaviland biplanes, a *New York Times* leader remarked that 'the lot of an international policeman on foreign soil is not a happy one . . . When it comes to actual warfare, in which there are casualties in our marines, and a reported great slaughter among the Nicaraguans who attacked them, it seems as if ill luck were malignantly pursuing the whole venture.' President Calvin Coolidge was accused of waging a private war in Nicaragua, and the Democrats took advantage of the issue to make withdrawal part of their 1928 election campaign.[4]

With the onset of the Depression, the management of foreign policy was subject to close attention. By the time Roosevelt was elected in 1932, the United States was in crisis. As urban purchasing power collapsed, the factories started to close. Unemployment, at five million in 1930, leapt to nine million in 1931 and to thirteen million in 1932; on inauguration day in 1933 it stood at fifteen million. National income fell by almost a third, and industrial production by half. The collapse of the banking system eliminated millions of savings accounts. Americans, in their millions, lost everything—jobs, homes, and possessions. The Hooverville shanties sprouted around the cities as malnutrition became a commonplace. Perhaps two million vagabonds were roaming the United States in a futile search for work. The government seemed impotent. As self-confidence evaporated, panic set in. On 4 March 1933, Franklin

[4] T. H. Greer, *What Roosevelt Thought: The Social and Political Ideas of Franklin D. Roosevelt* (East Lansing: Michigan State University Press, 1958), 158–60; C. Neale Ronning (ed.), *Intervention in Latin America* (New York: Knopf, 1970), 29–32; F. R. Dulles, *America's Rise to World Power, 1898–1954* (New York: Harper, 1955), 144–5; Samuel Flagg Bemis, *The Latin American Policy of the United States* (New York: Harcourt, Brace and Company, 1943), 202; S. Adler, *The Uncertain Giant, 1921–1941: American Foreign Policy between the Wars* (New York: Macmillan, 1965), 94–9; Benjamin T. Harrison, *Dollar Diplomat: Chandler Anderson and American Policy in Mexico and Nicaragua, 1913–1928* (Washington: Washington State University Press, 1988), 116; *New York Times*, 20 July 1927; Tony Jenkins, *Nicaragua and the United States: Years of Conflict* (New York: F. Watts, 1989), 41; Bernard Diederich, *Somoza and the Legacy of US Involvement in Central America* (New York: Dutton, 1981), 17.

Roosevelt took the presidential oath and told his compatriots: 'The only thing we have to fear is fear itself—nameless, unreasoning, unjustified terror'.[5]

The domestic problems were immediate, more concrete than a distant conflict. Almost as pressing were the memories, or at least perceptions, of the First World War. The revisionist thinking on the war, in Congress and the media, had concluded that the United States had been dragged into it by the scheming of arms manufacturers and 'high finance'—the latter being, in the public mind during the Depression, an abomination. Pacifism and isolationism proved a powerful joint force. Domestic recovery was vital, and foreign policy was to serve that goal. Asserting the uniqueness of the American political and economic order, the prevailing philosophy insisted that undue foreign activism would ensnare the country's energies and impede internal revival.[6]

The post-war dominance of the United States in the western hemisphere, moreover, facilitated a change in policy towards Latin America. New York supplanted Europe as the region's main source of credit, and thus the prime reason for non-American encroachment (the latter being, traditionally, the ostensible reason for American encroachment) had largely disappeared. 'Does anyone believe', the Secretary of State, Frank Kellogg, asked in 1928, 'that the present governments in Europe are in any position to attack any one of the South American countries and impose their form of government?' Even if they had been in such a position, it would scarcely have been worth their while to embark on trans-Atlantic intervention in order to protect European investments.[7]

The United States was also dominant in foreign trade. From 1913 to 1929, the growth of all Central American exports to the US market was substantially greater than the increase in total exports. For Nicaragua, the figures were 100 per cent and 37 per cent respectively. By 1933, 63 per cent of Nicaragua's imports came from the United States, with just 13 per cent

[5] Cleveland Rogers, *The Roosevelt Program* (New York: G. B. Putnam's Sons, 1933), 3, 7; William E. Leuchtenburg, 'Franklin D. Roosevelt and the New Deal, 1933–1940', in Arnold A. Offner (ed.), *America and the Origins of World War II, 1933–1941* (Boston: Houghton Mifflin, 1971), 1–2, 18–19; Charles C. Alexander, *Nationalism in American Thought, 1930–1945* (Chicago: Rand McNally, 1969), 2; Hugh Brogan, The *Pelican History of the United States of America* (Harmondsworth: Penguin, 1987), 531–4.

[6] Charles A. Beard (ed.), *America Faces the Future* (Boston: Houghton Mifflin, 1932); Charles A. Beard, *The Idea of National Interest: An Analytical Study in American Foreign Policy* (New York: Macmillan 1934), *passim*; Brogan, *Pelican History*, 572.

[7] Dexter Perkins, *The United States and Latin America* (Baton Rouge: Louisiana State University Press, 1961), 109; William Everett Kane, *Civil Strife in Latin America* (Baltimore, Md.: Johns Hopkins University Press, 1972), 97, 118–19.

coming from Britain and 7 per cent from Germany. In the same year, 50 per cent of Nicaragua's exports were sold in the US market; just 14 per cent went to Germany and 7 per cent to Britain. Throughout the Caribbean area, the United States was the main market and the main supplier.[8]

The growth of US isolationism, moreover, coincided with an upsurge of Yankeephobic nationalism in Latin America as the sister republics examined multilateral and juridical means of limiting habitual US interventionism. The agendas of the inter-American conferences among western-hemisphere governments began prominently to feature proposals for non-intervention protocols, and to consider the anti-intervention recommendations of the Inter-American Commission of Jurists.[9] Conditions in Nicaragua dominated the inter-American meeting of 1928 in Havana, where the Latin American delegations made a direct assault on US intervention policy. The Commission of Jurists presented a draft Convention on the Rights and Duties of States, whose central article proposed a doctrine of non-intervention. At the time, Washington was unwilling to accept the absolute repudiation of intervention that the convention demanded, but there was an implicit constraint on US policy in the Kellogg–Briand Pact of the same year: as the United States formally rejected the armed violation of national sovereignty under the terms of the pact, it seemed inconsistent to retain a right of intervention in one area of the world.[10] In these circumstances, the damage being caused by the Nicaraguan intervention to US prestige throughout the hemisphere could no longer be ignored. In the same year as the Kellogg–Briand Pact, the Clark Memorandum on the Monroe Doctrine rejected the [Theodore] Roosevelt Corollary and affirmed that the Doctrine embodied a sense of competition between the United States and Europe, not between the United States and Latin America.[11]

---

[8] James Dunkerley, *Power in the Isthmus: A Political History of Modern Central America* (London: Verso, 1988), 60; *New York Times*, 7 May 1934.

[9] Kane, *Civil Strife*, 114.

[10] Signed in Paris in 1928, the Kellogg–Briand Pact committed its fifteen signatory countries to renounce war as an instrument of national policy, and to agree that the settlement of all disputes should 'never be sought except by pacific means' except in the case of self-defence. Within three years, as the Japanese Kwantung Army occupied Manchuria and withstood all league pressure to withdraw, the pact would be seen as an instrument of very limited use. See Barbara W. Tuchman, *Sand Against the Wind: Stilwell and the American Experience in China, 1911–1945* (London: Macmillan, 1991), 130–9; Kane, *Civil Strife*, 118–19.

[11] Written by the under-secretary of state J. Reuben Clark in 1928 (and published by the State Department in 1932), the memorandum did not renounce the right of intervention

By the early 1930s, anti-Americanism was central to nationalism in much of Latin America. At the same time, isolationist sentiment in the United States was finding expression as a severe anxiety about overseas entanglements. Hence the marine evacuation of Nicaragua in 1933 was greeted with approval by the US public and Congress, and opposition came almost exclusively from US investors. Contrary, however, to the impressions inherent in the notion of the colonial economies of 'banana republics', US investment in Nicaragua had always been relatively low. US agricultural investment in the country slumped from $11.3 million in 1929 to only $2.4 by 1935. When the marines left in 1933, total US investment in Nicaragua stood at just $13 million. This was the lowest US investment figure for any of the Latin American republics except Paraguay.[12] At less than one third of 1 per cent of total US investment in the whole region, it was practically negligible. It certainly did not warrant risking the lives of American marines. By the spring of 1931, Washington had decided that it would no longer deploy troops even to save endangered American lives in Nicaragua: a State Department press release made clear that if US citizens did not feel safe, they should leave.[13]

In pursuit of the broader national interest through more cordial relations with an entire continent, little heed was paid to the objections of relatively minor private interests in a small country. As early as November 1927, the assistant secretary of state, Francis White, had devised a simple equation for US policy in Nicaragua:

To have peace and order we must have a proper constabulary; to have a proper constabulary we must have money; and to have money we must have an agreement with the bankers. The bankers, not unnaturally, are a pretty hard-boiled lot and want to see profits . . . [But] the department of state's solicitude in this matter is for Nicaragua; the bankers can take care of themselves.

There were, moreover, other financial considerations. The cost of keeping American forces in Nicaragua was $1.5 million above the marines'

---

but it did undermine Theodore Roosevelt's corollary that the United States had an obligation to ensure that Latin American nations behaved responsibly towards European countries. See William Kamman, *A Search for Stability: United States Diplomacy toward Nicaragua, 1925–1933* (Notre Dame, Ind.: University of Notre Dame Press, 1968), 198–9.

[12] US Department of Commerce, *A Balance of International Payments of the United States in 1933* (Washington DC: US Government Printing Office, 1934); H. Gerald Smith, 'Economic Ties Linking the United States and Latin America', *Commercial Pan America*, 45 (Feb. 1936), 7; Harrison, *Dollar Diplomat*, 118.

[13] Kamman, *A Search for Stability*, 202–3.

normal expenses; in the midst of the Depression, Congress was unwilling to allocate further funds to keep them there.[14]

By 1933, therefore, the intellectual underpinnings of US policy in Nicaragua had ceased to seem valid. Intervention no longer served Washington's interests. It has been persuasively argued that national interests may be located in two categories: vital interests which, if lost or clearly imperilled, will cause a nation to resort to war; and secondary interests that countries will seek to uphold non-violently. The latter may be political, economic, or 'psychological' issues related to national identity and prestige.[15] In the nineteenth century and early twentieth century, Washington had defended both sets of interests in Central America in the same manner. Hence the automatic reaction to dispatch armed forces when conditions in the region became unsettled. By 1933, with no external threat and the domestic interests of American 'high finance' suffering profound public discredit, the Roosevelt administration was able to preserve a clearer distinction between national and private concerns, and perceptions of the best means to protect US secondary interests changed.[16] American prestige had been damaged by intervention in Central America, and would now be upheld by non-intervention.

The policy of disengagement, moreover, and its subsequent evolution into good neighbourism under the Roosevelt administration, was conceived partly on the idea of reciprocity: the notion that if the United States refrained from interference in the domestic politics of Latin America, the sister republics would strive to curb activities—such as constant civil strife—that were detrimental to US interests.[17] In Nicaragua, successful reciprocity would need support if it was to ensure the broader US objectives of peace and stability. By the Tipitapa Agreement of May 1927, therefore, the US government had undertaken to create a Nicaraguan National Guard in order to protect those interests.

*

The US marine evacuation of January 1933 was not an unprecedented event in Nicaragua. The last remnant of the 1912 intervention—the 130-man marine guard at the US legation in Managua—had been withdrawn just eight years earlier, in August 1925. A much larger force was to return within a month. In August 1925 the departing US troops had left behind

[14] Ibid. 221; *New York Times*, 18 Apr. 1928.

[15] Robert D. Crassweller, *The Caribbean Community: Changing Societies and US Policy* (London: Pall Mall Press, 1972), 37.   [16] Ronning (ed.), *Intervention*, 14.

[17] Bryce Wood, *The Making of the Good Neighbor Policy* (New York: Columbia University Press, 1961), 309.

a precarious coalition government headed by a Conservative president, Carlos Solórzano, and a Liberal vice-president, Juan Bautista Sacasa.[18] Both parties had split before the 1924 elections. The 'Nationalist Liberals' nominated Sacasa for the presidency; the 'Republican Liberals' advanced Luís Corea. The mainstream Conservatives nominated Emiliano Chamorro, while a breakaway faction of 'Republican Conservatives' proposed Bartolomé Martínez, the incumbent vice-president. Martínez was constitutionally ineligible to accept the nomination, and the State Department informed him that the United States would be unable to recognize the next Nicaraguan government if he were heading it.[19]

Martínez therefore reached an agreement with the Nationalist Liberals whereby Carlos Solórzano, one of his Conservative supporters, was chosen as presidential candidate while Sacasa, the Liberal presidential candidate, agreed to be renominated for the vice-presidency. This coalition united the larger Liberal faction with the smaller Conservative one. The coalition ticket had the backing of the incumbent government and unsurprisingly won the elections. Solórzano and Sacasa took office on 1 January 1925 and were accorded US recognition.[20]

The majority Chamorrista Conservatives would not concede the legitimacy of the Solórzano government, and their antagonism grew when Conservative congressmen were summarily expelled from Congress and replaced by Liberal Nationalists. Conditions nonetheless remained calm until August. Then, with the US marines gone, disturbances erupted throughout the country; martial law was declared; the railway was closed. On 10 September, a month after they left, US troops were back at the ports of Corinto and Bluefields. The disturbances ceased; the American cruisers were withdrawn on 21 September. On 25 October, Chamorrista troops seized the presidential mansion and took over Managua with ease. Solórzano, uncertain of the loyalties of his armed forces, had refused to give them sufficient ammunition to quell an uprising. Chamorro then compelled Solórzano to sign an agreement in which the president agreed to appoint Chamorro as the army commander,

---

[18] Chester Lloyd Jones, *The Caribbean since 1900* (New York: Prentice Hall Inc., 1936), 381.

[19] US Department of State, *The United States and Nicaragua: A Survey of the Relations from 1909–1932*, Latin American Series, 6 (Washington DC: US Government Printing Office, 1932). Repr. in Henry Lewis Stimson, *Henry L. Stimson's American Policy in Nicaragua: The Lasting Legacy*, with introduction and afterword by Paul H. Boeker, plus essays by Andrés Pérez and Alain Brinkley (New York: M. Wiener Publishers, *c*.1991), 181.

[20] Ibid. 182.

and to pay him $10,000 for the expenses he had incurred in staging the coup.[21]

Facing death threats against himself and his family, Vice-President Sacasa left Nicaragua in November. On 12 January 1926 a Chamorrista-dominated Congress impeached him. On 14 January Solórzano resigned and Chamorro assumed the presidency. US recognition was withheld under the terms of the 1923 Treaty of Peace and Amity.[22] An east-coast Liberal uprising against Chamorro began in early May, and Liberal forces soon controlled much of the coast. The USS *Cleveland* was ordered to Bluefields, where marines and sailors were landed to protect American lives and property. During the summer, US ships were patrolling both coasts as the revolution expanded. In August, General José María Moncada joined the fight on Sacasa's behalf. In the south-west of the country, around San Marcos, the husband of Sacasa's niece was also fighting for the Liberal cause.[23] This *sobrino político* was Anastasio Somoza García.

The Coolidge administration faced a difficult choice. On the one hand, the Chamorro regime was plainly unconstitutional and US recognition of it, at least as a matter of precedent, was proscribed by the 1923 treaty. On the other hand, the American business community in Nicaragua backed Chamorro, apparently persuaded that US investment in the country was most secure when the Conservatives were in power. The State Department, however, feared that recognition might spur further Liberal violence.[24]

The concerns of American business were therefore considered, but it was alarm about Mexican 'bolshevism' that eventually shaped US policy in Nicaragua as the Calles administration interfered in favour of Sacasa.

[21] Ibid. 187–8.

[22] On 7 Feb. 1923, a US-organized Conference on Central American Affairs in Washington ended with a Treaty of Peace and Amity which reaffirmed the principles of recognition agreed at a similar meeting in 1907. These established that the countries of the isthmus (Panama excluded) would not recognize any Central American government which came to power as the result of a revolution or coup, or which was headed by an individual who was ineligible to exercise the presidency under the terms of his country's constitution. The United States was not a signatory to the agreement, but announced in June 1923 that its recognition policy would be guided by the accord. Washington's motivations appear to owe much to concern about revolutionary nationalism in the isthmus inspired by the Mexican revolution. See Jones, *The Caribbean*, 427; Donald C. Hodges, *Intellectual Foundations of the Nicaraguan Revolution* (Austin: University of Texas Press, 1986) 124; Dana C. Munro, *The United States and the Caribbean Area* (Boston: World Peace Foundation, 1934), 209–11.

[23] Neill Macaulay, *The Sandino Affair* (Chicago: Quadrangle Books, 1967), 25–6; Munro, *The United States*, 249. [24] Harrison, *Dollar Diplomat*, 103.

It was only a decade since Woodrow Wilson's military intervention in Mexico, and the country's relations with the United States remained strained. Washington saw Mexican support for Nicaragua's Liberal rebels as a strategy to control the isthmus. The United States refused to recognize Chamorro (and, indeed, urged his resignation throughout the year), but Mexican arms deliveries to the Liberals posed the danger of a Sacasa victory and an attendant expansion of Mexico's influence.[25] On 10 January 1927, Coolidge told a joint session of Congress that he had conclusive evidence of large Mexican arms shipments to the Liberal revolutionaries: 'The United States cannot fail to view with deep concern any serious threat to stability and constitutional government in Nicaragua . . . especially if such a state of affairs is contributed to or brought about by outside influence or by a foreign power.'[26] President Chamorro, nevertheless, was still under US diplomatic pressure to step down. The State Department had instructed Lawrence Dennis, chargé d'affaires at the Managua legation and head of mission in the absence of a minister, to exert all politic pressure to oblige Chamorro to resign. Taking his instructions very seriously, Dennis waged a remarkable campaign. This included 'urgent' telephone calls to the president in the middle of the night, demanding his resignation.[27]

By August 1926 the Liberal revolutionaries controlled most of the east-coast ports, and more US marines and sailors were landed at Bluefields. Unwilling to recognize Chamorro, but perturbed at the possibility of heightened Mexican influence in Central America in the event of a Sacasa victory, the United States strove for a negotiated settlement that denied the presidency to both of them. Washington imposed an arms embargo to curb the supply of weapons to both sides and, from 16 to 24 October, arranged a peace conference on the USS *Denver* in Corinto harbour. President Chamorro's nemesis, the US chargé d'affaires Lawrence

[25] Macaulay, *The Sandino Affair*, 26; Gordon Connell-Smith, *The Inter-American System* (London: Oxford University Press, 1966), 76; 817.00/5854, Memorandum, Robert E. Olds (Assistant Secretary of State), Jan. 1927, quoted in Kamman, *A Search for Stability*, 227.

[26] Quoted in John J. Tierney Jr, 'Revolution and the Marines: The United States and Nicaragua in the Early Years', in Belden Bell (ed.), *Nicaragua: An Ally under Siege* (Washington DC: Council on American Affairs, 1978), 8–23; Macaulay, *The Sandino Affair*, 25.

[27] Harrison, *Dollar Diplomat*, 104, 105. An account of Dennis's crusade against Chamorro is told with relish by the *New York Times* correspondent Harold N. Denny in his *Dollars for Bullets: The Story of American Rule in Nicaragua* (New York: L. MacVeagh, The Dial Press, 1929).

Dennis, presided. The talks soon reached an impasse and ended without agreement. On 31 October, hostilities resumed.[28]

The previous day, Chamorro had finally succumbed to Dennis's crusade and resigned. Congress elected another Conservative, Adolfo Díaz, to the presidency on 11 November and he was accorded prompt US recognition. Returning to Nicaragua on 1 December, Sacasa proclaimed himself head of a 'constitutional government' at Puerto Cabezas and named Moncada as his minister of war. Mexico recognized Sacasa's 'government'; the State Department informed Sacasa that he would not be recognized by the United States. This was a matter of prestige for Washington, part of an implicit contest with Mexico for supremacy in Central America.[29]

As Sacasa's Constitutionalist Liberals made military gains in late 1926, the prospects seemed bright that the Díaz government would fall without Washington's direct support. In the winter of 1926–7, therefore, the intervention escalated. On 24 December, US marine forces declared Puerto Cabezas a 'neutral zone', ordering Sacasa to evacuate the Constitutionalist army within forty-eight hours. Further marine landings on both coasts initially penned the Constitutionalists inland and disrupted supply lines. In January 1927, US forces declared all the ports neutral zones. In February, the entire Granada–Managua–Corinto railway was declared neutral. By March there were over 2,000 US marines in Nicaragua, and Washington was openly arming the Díaz government. By then, however, Moncada was leading troops across the country to the western cities, and at the end of the month General Augusto Sandino won Jinotega for Sacasa's Liberals, allowing the rebels to threaten Matagalpa and Managua. Díaz seemed doomed.[30]

Reluctant to see Díaz ousted, but unwilling to commit US marines to more direct combat against the Liberals, in May 1927 the Coolidge administration dispatched Henry Stimson, former Secretary of War in the Taft government, to mediate the civil war. Stimson reached an agreement with Díaz whereby the latter was to remain in office until the 1928 elections, which were to be supervised by the United States. An amnesty was to be declared, and all weapons were to be surrendered to American forces. The old Nicaraguan constabulary was to be disbanded, and a new

[28] Connell-Smith, *The Inter-American System*, 76–7; Harrison, *Dollar Diplomat*, 111; Stimson, *Stimson's American Policy*, 195; Munro, *The United States*, 249.

[29] Macaulay, *The Sandino Affair*, 25–8; Jones, *The Caribbean*, 388–98; Stimson, *Stimson's American Policy*, 192, 197–8; Kamman, *A Search for Stability*, 229; Munro, *The United States*, 250.

[30] Tierney, 'Revolution and the Marines', 17–18; Hodges, *Intellectual Foundations*, 124; Stimson, *Stimson's American Policy*, 192, 203; Macaulay, *The Sandino Affair*, 28–9.

National Guard was to be organized, trained and commanded by US officers. Sufficient numbers of US troops were to remain in the country to
enforce the provisions of this agreement. Stimson, meeting Moncada and
Sacasa's other representatives in Tipitapa on 4 May, threatened to use
more direct force against them if they failed to concur; Moncada did so.
Another 800 US marines were landed, bringing the total to over 3,000,
and the Constitutionalist forces were demobilized and decommissioned.

As his army was disbanded, Sacasa departed for Costa Rica. Alone
among Liberal military leaders, Augusto Sandino refused to abide by the
provisions of the Stimson agreement. As the US marines received from
the Constitutionalists 11,600 rifles, 303 machine guns, and over five million rounds of ammunition, Sandino and his followers set out for the
Nicaragua–Honduras border region to embark on guerrilla war. On 22
December 1927, an agreement was signed for the establishment of the
National Guard under the auspices of the US navy and marine corps.[31]

Some five thousand American marines supervised Nicaragua's
elections of 1928, probably the first in the country's history whose
outcome was not determined by the incumbent government. José
María Moncada, Sacasa's revolutionary 'Minister of War', was the victor.
Sacasa himself, identified by the United States as an agent of Mexican
subversion, was named ambassador to Washington. Four years later, on
6 November 1932, he won the presidency in elections again supervised
by the United States. US marine forces began to embark for home on
1 January 1933, the day of his inauguration.

*

For the State Department, the marine evacuation signified 'the realization of
the commitment which the United States had assumed at Tipitapa to organize and train a non-partisan constabulary'. More broadly it marked 'the termination of the special relationship which has existed between the United
States and Nicaragua'. Henceforth, US relations with Nicaragua were to be
on exactly the same basis as Washington's relations with any other country.
As far as the United States was concerned, the withdrawal of American forces
indicated the fulfilment of all obligations, legal and moral, it had assumed by
virtue of the intervention.[32] This point proved to be moot.

[31] Macaulay, *The Sandino Affair*, 29; Jones, *The Caribbean*, 388–91; Stimson, *Stimson's American Policy*, 205; Munro, *The United States*, 254–5.
[32] 817.1051/808, Welles to Lane, 28 December 1933; US Department of State, *Press Releases* (Washington DC: US Government Printing Office), 2 Jan. 1933.

From Washington, events were depicted as charting a new and more hopeful course. In Managua, circumstances seemed less promising. In five years of guerrilla war against the Sandinistas, the National Guard's counter-insurgency campaigns had been directed by American officers. Plans for the marine evacuation therefore demanded that Nicaraguan officers be trained. The Americans recruited rapidly, rushing civilians through the Guardia academy in an effort to make them military officers. In March 1931 the National Guard's *jefe director*, General Calvin Matthews of the US marine corps, admitted that by the time of the withdrawal the higher ranks would not be filled. A year later, less than nine months before the marines' scheduled departure date, the Guardia had just thirty-five Nicaraguan officers, all of them lieutenants. The US–Nicaraguan agreement of December 1927 had provided for a corps of ninety-three officers. According to the State Department, 178 officers was the lowest number considered essential for the Nicaraguan government.[33]

The failure to provide an adequate military leadership was compounded by an incapacity to create an apolitical Guardia. The United States was supposed to establish a politically impartial armed force. To that end, each recruit took an oath renouncing all political affiliation; punishment was threatened for any man displaying 'overt expression of preference for one party'.[34] This procedure was wholly ineffective. President Moncada, who had to approve the candidates for the military academy, naturally favoured Liberals. More specifically, he favoured what the US electoral mission's (that is, the marines') intelligence division termed 'known henchmen of President Moncada'. The entry requirements, moreover, made it likely that most recruits would be from the traditional Liberal-supporting backgrounds of the middle-class and artisan sectors.[35]

Less than two months before the evacuation, the State Department made a final effort to secure a neutral Guardia. On 20 October and 3 November respectively, General Matthews and the American minister

[33] Marvin Goldwert, *The Constabulary in the Dominican Republic and Nicaragua* (Gainesville: University of Florida Press, 1962), 38–9, 42; Richard Millet, *Guardians of the Dynasty* (Maryknoll, NY: Orbis Books, 1977), 125–32; US Department of State, *Press Releases*, 9 Apr. 1932; Stimson, *Stimson's American Policy*, 234.

[34] Millet, *Guardians*, 125.

[35] RG 38 C-10-d 6473-E, US Electoral Mission, intelligence section, intelligence report, 1 Dec. 1932; Millet, *Guardians*, 126–7.

to Managua, Matthew Hanna,[36] sent to the leaders of both political parties a written plan, approved in Washington, which endeavoured to secure an apolitical National Guard by dividing the officer positions equally between Liberals and Conservatives. The two presidential candidates, Sacasa and Díaz, were to present a list of thirty names, each composed equally of members of the two parties, from which Nicaraguan officers might be selected to replace the departing Americans in the higher ranks. Immediately after the elections, the outgoing president was to take the victorious candidate's list and appoint the men on it to the Guardia's senior posts. Sacasa and Díaz, with their vice-presidential running mates Rodolfo Espinosa and Emiliano Chamorro, were asked to sign an agreement to this effect at the US legation in the presence of Hanna, which they did on 5 November, the eve of the election.[37]

By its very nature this plan was a contradiction in terms, since it endeavoured to establish an apolitical National Guard on the basis of the appointees' political inclinations. After witnessing the direct consequences of this arrangement, a later US minister to Managua would point out the obvious: that in itself it simply underlined the National Guard's political composition. Three of the four signatories to the agreement later jointly testified that they had strong reservations about the procedure and that they expressed their apprehensions to Hanna. The minister, they claimed, stated categorically that they should rest assured that the US government would morally guarantee the accord, whereupon they signed it. It was Hanna, moreover, who wrote to Sacasa on 3 November to point out that the post of the National Guard's first Nicaraguan *jefe director* could not be subject to the provisions of the agreement.[38]

When Sacasa and Moncada were leading the Constitutionalist revolution of 1926 they had been assisted by the husband of Sacasa's niece, Anastasio Somoza García. Thirty-six years old in 1932, Somoza had been born in San Marcos and educated in the United States. There he had acquired fluent English and met his future wife, Salvadora Debayle,

---

[36] US diplomatic missions in Central America in this period were legations, each headed by a minister. The Nicaragua legation was not elevated to the status of embassy until Apr. 1943, when James Bolton Stewart presented his credentials as ambassador.

[37] The letters from Matthews and Hanna to Sacasa are reproduced in full in Juan Bautista Sacasa, *Cómo y por qué caí del poder* (León, Nicaragua: *s.n.* 1946), 14–15, 59–64.

[38] Adolfo Díaz, Emiliano Chamorro, and Juan Sacasa to Hull, 30 Nov. 1936, reproduced in Sacasa,*Cómo y por qué*, 159–60; RG 38 C-10-d 6473-E, US Electoral Mission, intelligence section, intelligence report, 1 Dec. 1932; RG 38 C-10-d 6473, commander, Special Service Squadron, to chief of naval operations (director of naval intelligence), 24 June 1936.

daughter of one of Nicaragua's most prominent families. In 1926, with Sacasa and Moncada in revolt, Somoza and some neighbours decided to take San Marcos for the Liberals. Somoza emerged from this venture with the rank of general and became a favourite of Moncada, his second cousin. Because of his command of English, and what by all accounts was an innate facility for dealing with Americans, he was selected as a translator at the Tipitapa conference. Henry Stimson was very impressed by Somoza's manners and disposition, as well as his command of English. Under Moncada's presidency the general was successively Nicaraguan consul in Costa Rica, under-secretary of foreign affairs, and foreign minister. He was widely considered to be highly competent.[39]

The United States had no official candidate for *jefe director* of the National Guard, but the US minister, Matthew Hanna, and his wife found Somoza charming and efficient, and the minister's clear preference for him could not have been easily disregarded.[40] In October 1932 he had informed the State Department of his preference in unequivocal terms: 'I look upon him as the best man in the country for the position.' Somoza's candidacy was similarly backed by General Matthews and other American officers. In the end, it fell to Somoza's friend Hanna and Somoza's cousin Moncada to revise the list of candidates prepared by Somoza's uncle, the president-elect, Sacasa. On the day when the first US troops embarked for home, Anastasio Somoza was confirmed as *jefe director* of the National Guard.[41]

It was evident to both of Nicaragua's political parties that a bipartisan agreement on the nature of the country's military establishment would

---

[39] Macaulay, *The Sandino Affair*, 236–7; William Krehm, *Democracies and Tyrannies of the Caribbean* (Westport, Conn.: Lawrence Hill & Co., 1984), 108–9; Shirley Christian, *Nicaragua: Revolution in the Family* (New York: Vintage Books, 1986), 9, 19; *Newsweek*, 13 June 1936, 17.

[40] Since Somoza's appointment as *jefe director* in Nov. 1932 was so pivotal in all that followed, it is worth noting the most persistent rumour surrounding it. This holds that Matthew Hanna was dominated by his much younger wife, and that Mrs Hanna was having an affair with Somoza. Gregorio Selser quotes a manifesto by Sandino: 'The unhappy Hoover regime has sent to Nicaragua as minister an old wreck by the name of Matthew Hanna, whose wife—a German as it happens—now runs the Yankee legation in Managua . . . [and] is addicted to young National Guard officers' (*Sandino, General of the Free* (New York: Month Review Press, 1981), 145). Similar stories are repeated by many other sources. William Krehm, *Time* correspondent in Nicaragua, puts the matter more graciously: 'Mrs. Hanna, considerably her husband's junior, adored dancing, and Tacho danced so very, very well.' (*Democracies and Tyrannies*, 109).

[41] 817.1051/701½, Hanna to White, 28 Oct. 1932; Millet, *Guardians*, 130; Diederich, *Somoza*, 2. Somoza's son, Anastasio Somoza Debayle, believed that it was his father's family connections that ensured his appointment. See Debayle, *Nicaragua Betrayed* (Boston: Western Islands, 1980), 89.

be insufficient to guarantee a smooth transition in 1933. They had been seeking means of ensuring that the departure of the marines would not prompt the same fiasco as when US forces had left in 1925. On 30 June 1932, therefore, the presidential candidates, Sacasa and Díaz, signed an agreement to accept minority representation in the government after the 1932 elections. In a second accord on 3 October they set out specific steps to be taken after the polls. These included the establishment of a bipartisan commission to negotiate peace with Sandino; minority party representation in the executive branch; at least a third of each party's lists for municipal elections to consist of individuals of the rival party; and constitutional reform to enshrine these two latter provisions in the national charter.[42] Sacasa was duly elected a month later.

By the time of the US marine withdrawal, then, the two political parties had agreed on a programme of national unity; a legitimate president had been elected in polls generally considered to have been relatively honest; a supposedly apolitical armed force was in place under a reportedly efficient *jefe director*; and Sandino's activities could reasonably be expected to diminish. In Washington, the diplomats in the State Department's Latin American division were washing their hands. The department issued a press release referring to 'an entirely new and non-partisan force, the *Guardia Nacional*' and disclaiming any responsibility for future events in Nicaragua. In New York, the leader writer at the *Times* recast the press release to praise the undoubted efficiency of the National Guard and to express the conviction that Sacasa would be equal to any problems that the situation presented.[43] This, it transpired, was wishful thinking.

Nine months earlier Laurence Duggan, chief of the Latin American division, had foreseen other possibilities in a memorandum intended for a more restricted circulation than the press release on which the *New York Times* editorial was based: 'upon the withdrawal of the Marine Officers in the *Guardia* next fall, the forces of disintegration will be set into action'.[44] The last US troops departed Nicaragua on 2 January 1933, and the country was left to govern itself.

*

Duggan was entirely right. In the decades since 1933, much has been made of Somoza's position as 'the last marine', a notion that contrives to

[42] Knut Walter, *The Regime of Anastasio Somoza, 1936–1956* (Chapel Hill: University of North Carolina Press, 1993), 27–8.

[43] US Department of State, *Press Releases*, 2 Jan. 1933; *New York Times*, 3 Jan. 1933.

[44] 817.1051/613½, Memorandum, Duggan to Wilson, 23 Mar. 1932.

make the Roosevelt administration a willing partner in his relentless rise to power. Less forthright (but more graphic) expressions of this link continue to assign the blame: Somoza, it has been said, 'was a time bomb, planted in Managua by the Hoover administration, and Franklin Roosevelt allowed it to explode'.[45]

Apportioning blame is a benefit of hindsight. In reality, it was impossible at the end of 1932 to predict what might happen even in the short term. The only likelihood, as Duggan was saying, was that something drastic would occur. It required no great foresight to predict this, and Duggan's assessment is remarkable only inasmuch as it stands out against a background of official and semi-official pronouncements averring that tranquillity would prevail.[46] This was indifference applied as diplomacy, since it was clear at the time that the new Nicaraguan government could scarcely have come to power in less favourable conditions.

First, the personality of the new president was a basic problem. Juan Sacasa, a revolutionary of very timid temperament, proved to be a remarkably weak chief executive in highly unstable circumstances. He was, according to Hanna's successor Arthur Bliss Lane, incapable of acting in a strong and determined manner. In a political system that judged personality as fundamental to authority, Sacasa was inadequate. Matthew Hanna's personal distaste for the president's weakness was manifest in his dispatches to the State Department. Even Lane, who would later work assiduously to protect Sacasa against Somoza's remorseless ascent, commented frequently in his own dispatches on what he saw as the president's striking ineptness.

Second, Sacasa was politically handicapped from the outset. In a country where there persisted the perception that the United States was a chief arbiter of executive power, it became a matter of fundamental political significance that Sacasa's attainment of the presidency was largely what the most recent US intervention had been designed to avert. Even if a policy of non-interference had not been adopted, Sacasa's authority would have been hampered by a widespread perception in Nicaragua that he was not quite what the State Department wanted in Managua's presidential mansion.

Third, in a tradition in which the removal of presidents had come to be seen as much a military as a political problem, the US marines left Sacasa

---

[45] Macaulay, *The Sandino Affair*, 258.

[46] The comments of the Secretary of State, Cordell Hull, in his instructions to the US delegation to the Montevideo conference are typical in this regard: 710G/731, Hull to the American delegates at Montevideo, 10 Nov. 1933. See the final paragraph of this chapter.

with in army which, in Lane's words, comprised 'an instrument to blast constitutional procedure off the map'. At the beginning of 1933 that instrument consisted of 4,000 men with 259 machine guns, 54 sub-machine guns, 23 automatic rifles, and 4,474 standard rifles. Even before the marine evacuation, US intelligence reports had been stressing the widespread uneasiness about what would happen after the American officers were withdrawn from the National Guard. In December 1932, one such report accurately predicted that 'the American-trained, junior native officers will refuse obedience to the political appointees of the higher ranks, and [they] . . . will cause an attitude of passive resistance to the orders of such civilian appointees to spread throughout the *Guardia* personnel.'[47]

The National Guard was hopelessly politicized, soon divided into Sacasistas, Somocistas, Moncadistas, and Chamorristas. To balance Somoza's influence, Sacasa was cultivating an alliance with General Gustavo Abaunza, the Chief of Staff. Abaunza shuffled the commands in an effort to neutralize *somocista* and *chamorrista* officers, spurring Somoza's conviction that Abaunza was fomenting military unrest in order to oust him as *jefe director*. Somoza also had to contend with what Hanna termed 'machinations and intrigues' on the part of the ministers of finance and the treasury. Chamorro, for his part, outraged at the manner in which Somoza and Sacasa were ignoring the pre-election pact for neutral armed forces, fought for a reduction in the military budget.[48]

Fourth, in a party political system traditionally marked by personalist factionalism, the divisiveness that had plagued the 1932 election campaign became highly schismatic. To succeed Moncada, who was constitutionally ineligible for a second term, no fewer than four Liberal pre-candidates had appeared in 1932: Juan Sacasa, Vice-President Enoc Aguado, the former foreign minister Leonardo Arguello, and the former minister to Washington Rodolfo Espinosa. At the beginning of 1932, Moncada had proposed calling a convention to frame a new constitution. The charter would have given the Guardia a proper legal basis and conferred constitutional validity on the Bryan–Chamorro Treaty of 1914, which accorded the United States the right to build a Nicaraguan canal.

---

[47] Vladimir Petrov, *A Study in Diplomacy: The Story of Arthur Bliss Lane* (Chicago: H. Regnery Co., 1971), 31; Walter, *The Regime*, 30; Millet, *Guardians*, 136; RG 38 C-10-d 6473-E, US Electoral Mission, intelligence section, intelligence report, 1 Dec. 1932.

[48] 817.1051/778, Hanna to State Department, 23 Mar. 1933; Eduardo Crawley, *Dictators Never Die: A Portrait of Nicaragua and the Somoza Dynasty* (London: C. Hurst, 1979), 79–81; Millet, *Guardians*, 145–50; Petrov, *A Study in Diplomacy*, 30–2; Walter, *The Regime*, 29.

These two proposals were designed to induce Henry Stimson (by then Hoover's Secretary of State) to accept the plan. Moncada sent a mission to Washington to persuade the State Department to postpone the 1932 polls, and to supervise instead elections for a constituent assembly. If the latter had been held, it would have been impossible to elect a new president in November 1932 to assume office in January 1933. The alternative would have been an extension of Moncada's term.[49]

Convinced that Moncada was planning to perpetuate his mandate, the four Liberal presidential hopefuls formed an anti-Moncada branch of the party. In March 1932 the two factions, each claiming to represent the true party, held separate conventions. On 3 April, following their Managua convention, one sector nominated Leonardo Arguello as the party's candidate for the November elections. Moncada, disconcertingly, seemed to back the Arguello faction. The US electoral mission under Admiral Clark Woodward[50] failed to recognize the Managua convention; a later gathering, held in Sacasa's home city of León, nominated him and Espinosa as the Liberal ticket. The split in the Liberals raised the possibility that a minority candidate might win the November elections. The Conservatives had nominated Adolfo Díaz, whose presidency the United States had intervened to protect in 1912 and 1926–7.[51]

If Díaz had won the presidency in 1932, few would have believed that his election had not been dictated by Washington. Sandino's activities after the marine evacuation, far from slowing, might have intensified. In a manifesto of January 1932 urging Nicaraguans to boycott the polls, the guerrilla leader had proclaimed: 'Let those affiliated with the Liberal Party not fear a victory of the Conservative platform, because that platform will not last longer than the people take to nullify it with their Defending Army of National Sovereignty'—that is, the Sandinistas.[52] Coupled with the minority position of Conservatives in the Guardia, this circumstance might have made civil war an immediate prospect. Sacasa's election delayed a breakdown in constitutional procedure, but some crisis was probably inevitable.

[49] *The Nation*, 13 July 1932.

[50] Woodward was appointed chairman of the National Electoral Board by the Nicaraguan Supreme Court.

[51] *The Nation*, 13 July 1932; RG 38 C-10-d 6473, commander, Special Service Squadron, to chief of naval operations (director of naval intelligence), 24 June 1936.

[52] In a letter to General Pedro Altamirano on 9 Nov. 1932, Sandino advised that, if the Conservatives won the election, the Sandinistas would settle the issue with bullets. Both references are from Hodges, *Intellectual Foundations*, 143.

With the departure of the marines, this intra-party factionalism reemerged abruptly as the apparent unity imposed by the pre-election pacts began to disintegrate. The Nicaraguan Senate held fifteen Liberals and eight Conservatives; twenty-nine Liberals and fourteen Conservatives sat in the Chamber of Deputies. The apparent preponderance of Liberal strength should have facilitated Sacasa's task, but the reality was different. At the end of December, Hanna had noted substantial dissension in the Liberal ranks, the result not least of Moncada's natural influence and overt lobbying. Hanna identified the vice-president of Congress and the second vice-secretary as Moncadistas. The second vice-secretary of the Senate was also a Moncadista, as were the president of the Chamber, the vice-president, and the first and second vice-secretaries. It would shortly become apparent that Sacasa's own vice-president, Rodolfo Espinosa, was working against him.[53]

Fifth, Sacasa faced an alarming series of extra-parliamentary challenges to the stability of his government. Moncada's retirement had prompted the return of many Nicaraguan exiles whom he had expelled, and who promptly resumed the activities that had led to their departure. Initially, this amounted simply to the normal propagandizing activities of disgruntled political 'outs', but the trend was disconcerting and Hanna predicted that in time it might become dangerous.[54] Conditions were exacerbated by the presence in the Segovias region of large numbers of Honduran revolutionaries who had sought refuge in Nicaraguan territory. This complicated an already difficult military situation, since Sandino controlled part of that area with armed guerrillas, a force that Sacasa would have to contain by deploying an army whose officer corps, it became evident in the first week of his administration, was plotting against him.[55]

Finally, the US presence in Nicaragua had become so dominant in the previous period that, in the words of one contemporary observer, Washington had ruled the country 'more completely than the American Federal Government rules any state in the Union'.[56] In these circumstances the abrupt removal of US influence (as the main manifestation of such influence boarded ships for home) was bound to prompt some

---

[53] 817.032/127, Hanna to Stimson, 27 Dec. 1932; 817.00/7917, Lawton to Hull, 19 Dec. 1933; 817.00/7917, memorandum, Beaulac to Wilson, 2 Jan. 1934; 817.00/7927, military intelligence report, 28 Dec. 1933.

[54] 817.00/7713, Hanna to Stimson, 16 Jan. 1933.

[55] Ibid.; 817.00/7698, Hanna to Stimson, 17 Jan. 1933.

[56] Denny, *Dollars for Bullets*, 9.

degree of political turbulence. Sacasa, however, would find little sympathy at the US legation.

Notwithstanding the State Department's public assertions to the contrary, political stability in Nicaragua was the least likely scenario at the start of 1933. Very hard to predict at the time, however, was how the inevitable short-run instability might resolve itself in the longer term, or which of the contending forces might emerge ascendant. That Anastasio Somoza—an apparently efficient and amiable 37-year-old with no military training and a fondness for dirty jokes—might have been 'planted' by the Hoover administration as part of some long-term US policy objective was a possibility of which the Roosevelt State Department seemed to be blissfully unaware.

*

In Managua, Hanna noted that the US marine withdrawal produced surprisingly little comment and was met by demonstrations of neither regret nor rejoicing on the part of the people. Hanna, evidently bemused that an event of such magnitude in Nicaragua's political life should be received with apparent indifference, offered a tentative explanation: 'Pretty much everybody whose personal interests and welfare were benefited by the presence of the marines contemplated their withdrawal with anxiety for the future . . . There is joy, of course, that the country is free from foreign troops but it is so mixed with fear of what the consequences may be that few have seen fit to proclaim their satisfaction.'[57]

The fears were justified. In circumstances that corresponded closely to the conditions attendant on the 1925 withdrawal, the tenuous stability that had been a symptom of the marines' presence began to fall apart very fast in January 1933. There were, however, two significant differences from 1925. First, this time Washington was determined not to be dragged back into Nicaragua's instability; and second, that determination had found concrete expression in the establishment of a well-armed, politically divided, ill-officered National Guard. For the State Department, the absolute need to uphold the former circumstance demanded the absolute denial of the latter. In Managua, even the department's own representatives found this contradiction hard to swallow. Lane would later write:

The people who created the National Guard had no adequate understanding of the psychology of the people here . . . Did it ever occur to the eminent statesmen who

[57] 817.00/7713, Hanna to Stimson, 16 Jan. 1933; 817.00/7705, Hanna to Stimson, 13 Jan. 1933.

created the [National Guard] that personal ambition lurks in the human breast, even in Nicaragua? In my opinion, it is one of the sorriest examples of our part, of our inability to understand that we should not meddle in other people's affairs.[58]

The bitterness of Lane's hindsight coincided with the clarity of Duggan's foresight. Just six days after the marines left, a plot against Sacasa was uncovered among the Guardia's officer corps. The crash recruiting programme among civilians, who had been promoted over serving officers, had become a source of mutinous discontent even before the evacuation. It seems likely that Somoza was not behind the conspiracy, and that he was alarmed at this early demonstration of the Guardia's innate instability. The emergence of the plot, however, and the fact that it was he who eventually brought the situation under control by appealing to the patriotism of the officer corps, were indications of his personal influence and boded ill for the future. The spirit of insubordination continued to border on incipient mutiny; both Somoza and Sacasa expected further trouble from the Guardia.[59]

With the removal of the US marines, the actual business of domestic policy-making was wholly overshadowed by the intensity of the political volatility. Sandinista–Guardia clashes were continuing; unemployment was severe; business activity was sharply depressed; political dissensions had abruptly re-emerged; subversive propaganda was circulating; and there prevailed a general belief that Sacasa lacked the character to govern under these conditions. As reflected in reports emanating from the US legation, the political atmosphere was entirely one of imminent disaster. The legation detailed the tortuous manoeuvrings of each faction, emphasizing that the Sacasa administration would probably be incapable of maintaining domestic peace, and that the instability was aggravated by the various cliques' inability to devise any coherent strategy to address the country's problems.

'The sum total of all this', Hanna told his chiefs in Washington, 'has been to create a profound anxiety concerning the future and a situation of doubt and uncertainty which arouses a lack of confidence in the government at its very inception and strengthens the forces that are not in sympathy with it.' As President Sacasa was aware, the forces not in sympathy with his government included almost everybody who mattered. On 19 January 1933, nineteen days after his inauguration and

---

[58] Quoted in Diederich, *Somoza*, 16.
[59] Goldwert, *The Constabulary*, 43; 817.00/7713, Hanna to Stimson, 16 Jan. 1933; 817.00/7709, Hanna to Stimson, 22 Jan. 1933; *New York Times*, 22 Jan. 1933.

eighteen days after the last US troops left, Sacasa declared martial law and placed the entire country under a state of siege.[60]

Juan Bautista Sacasa had reached political maturity in a context that measured the potential for political control as a twofold matter: the attitude of the United States and the availability of weapons. He therefore viewed the immediate elements of instability—the intra-party factionalism, the insurgent Sandinistas, the Honduran revolutionaries, the returning exiles, and the mutinous Guardia—as a military problem dependent on the policy of the United States. Hanna was summoned to the presidential mansion on Tiscapa Hill to hear a request for US arms. The minister was convinced that the situation warranted their supply. He informed the State Department,

> I believe that President Sacasa has not overstated the dangers of the situation or his needs if a crisis occurs and I think we should make every effort to help him ... The existing spirit of unrest with so many dangerous elements unrestrained can develop very quickly into widespread revolt. It would be impossible for this government to pay cash for the military supplies it needs.[61]

The US War Department refused to loan arms to the Sacasa administration for the purposes of defence. It further refused to sell arms on credit, on the grounds that Nicaragua remained indebted to the United States for former credits extended for armaments in 1922, 1923, and 1927. Sacasa looked elsewhere. Talks with the Ubico regime in Guatemala produced a tentative agreement to provide arms, until the State Department pointed out to Guatemala that a loan of weapons to Nicaragua would contravene article 3 of the Convention for the Limitation of Armaments.[62] It was against the background of this daunting array of challenges that Sacasa was trying to settle six years of guerrilla war in a manner acceptable to every group, and to keep the country afloat in the midst of the Depression.

The Depression had a catastrophic effect on Nicaragua. The country's GDP, which had expanded by 6.4 per cent between 1925 and 1929, contracted by 4.9 per cent between 1930 and 1934. World prices for coffee, the main source of foreign exchange and accounting for 46 per cent of

[60] 817.00/7713, Hanna to Stimson, 16 Jan. 1933; 817.00/7709, Hanna to Stimson, 22 Jan. 1933; 817.00/7820, Hanna to Stimson, 16 May 1933; 817.00/7714, military intelligence report, 31 Jan. 1933; *New York Times*, 22 Jan. 1933.

[61] 817.00/7698, Hanna to Stimson, 17 Jan. 1933.

[62] RG 94 AG 470-Nicaragua, Maj. Gen. Callahan (assistant chief of staff) to Chief of Staff; 817.00/7698, White to Secretary of War, 19 Jan. 1933; 817.00/7698, Stimson to Hanna, 26 Jan. 1933; 817.00/7701, Whitehouse to Stimson, 18 Jan. 1933.

exports, had slumped sharply in January 1932. The price of Nicaraguan coffee fell from 46¢ per kilo in 1926 to 16¢ by 1933. Between 1929 and 1933 the value of coffee exports dropped from $5.9 million to $2.2 million, despite an increase in export volumes. Indeed, the value of all Nicaraguan exports collapsed from $10.9 million in 1929 to $4.9 million in 1933 and did not stabilize until the mid 1930s. Imports were cut drastically to maintain a positive balance of trade. The Exchange Control Commission had taken direct control of imports in September 1932 and thereafter gave preference to imports of essential goods and raw materials for the export sector. Between 1929 and 1933, import values fell from $11.8 million to $3.8 million. The decline entailed a sharp drop in revenue, since tariffs on trade accounted for almost two-thirds of government income. Costa Rica, El Salvador, and Guatemala were able to boost imports and revenue via debt default. Nicaragua, however, did not default on its obligations; the country merely suspended amortization payments. Thus government spending was severely curtailed, with an attendant sharp decline in services.[63]

Facing economic catastrophe, deprived of US backing, obstructed in his search for arms to ensure self-defence, and justifiably apprehensive about his own army, Sacasa attempted to secure an alternative source of military support. Sandino was the leader of the only available armed force that might counteract an insubordinate Guardia. He had also been a general in Sacasa's Liberal army during the Constitutionalist war. Sandino, for his part, now had reason to make peace. With the US marines gone, the main motive for his insurrection had disappeared. Moncada, whom he saw as a traitor for agreeing to the Tipitapa Agreement, was no longer president; the National Guard was now controlled by the Liberals, to whom he avowed loyalty; and his ties to Central American communists were broken. In late November 1932, a joint meeting of the executive committees of both main parties had agreed to send a delegation to mediate with Sandino.[64]

On 19 January 1933, the day on which he declared martial law, Sacasa made arrangements to confer with the guerrilla. On 23 January, the president's envoy returned to Managua with a peace proposal; a fifteen-day armistice was agreed. On 2 February, Sandino went to Managua and signed a peace agreement with Sacasa. As a result, some 1,800 guerrillas surrendered their arms and were granted control of almost 37,000 square

---

[63] Dunkerley, *Power in the Isthmus*, 91–2; Victor Bulmer-Thomas, *The Political Economy of Central America since 1920* (Cambridge: Cambridge University Press, 1987), 49, 308; Walter, *The Regime*, 36–7.

[64] Dunkerley, *Power in the Isthmus*, 71; Walter, *The Regime*, 30–1.

kilometres of territory in the Segovias region to establish an agricultural commune. Sacasa also pledged to begin a series of public works projects in the area and to give the Sandinistas preference in employment. The guerrillas were to be amnestied for all political and criminal offences committed since May 1927. Finally, Sandino was allowed to retain a security force of 100 armed men for a year after the signing of the agreement.[65]

Sacasa's successful attempts at pacification gave rise to significant problems. First, although Somoza accompanied Sandino in the car from the airport to the presidential mansion, Guardia dissatisfaction at this turn of events was substantial; it was also understandable. For six years the Nicaraguan National Guard had borne the brunt of a sometimes vicious guerrilla war. As the US marines had gradually wound down their own combat activities in the field, ceding the risks to native troops, the Guardia had confronted the brutality for which the Sandinistas were renowned: the *corte de chaleco*, the *corte de cumbo*, and the *corte de blumers* were just some of the more gruesome techniques of Sandinista mutilation practised on those deemed to be enemies. That the rebels should now be allowed to settle an agricultural community at government expense could not but prompt Guardia discontent. It was also apparent that the Sandinistas were not fully disarmed. The 1,800 guerrillas demobilized at San Rafael del Norte on 22 February surrendered just 337 rifles, 2 machine guns, and 16 automatic rifles.[66]

Second, peace with the Sandinistas appeared to remove a problem that had been a powerful incentive to inter-party cooperation. The re-intensification of party rivalry imperilled the pre-election pacts. The parties split over traditional Liberal and Conservative lines, and hostility re-emerged over such issues as the question of civil and church marriages and the validity of religious schools' bachelors' degrees, as well as such specific pressing matters as the politicization of the National Guard.[67] One month after Sacasa's inauguration, the prospects for his administration were looking bleak.

*

[65] 817.00/8642, State Department memorandum, chronology of events, unsigned, undated; David Harward Bain, 'The Man who Made the Yanquis Go Home', in Andrew C. Kimmens (ed.), *Nicaragua and the United States* (New York: H. W. Wilson, 1987), 33; Diederich, *Somoza*,18; Sacasa, *Cómo y por qué*, 10; Macaulay, *The Sandino Affair*, 246.

[66] Walter, *The Regime*, 31; Macaulay, *The Sandino Affair*, 247, Crawley, *Dictators Never Die*, 72.   [67] 817.00/7793, Hanna to Hull, 18 Mar. 1933.

In the United States, the president-elect, Franklin Roosevelt, was one month away from his own inauguration. He had paid little attention to foreign policy during the election campaign and seems to have had only a limited knowledge of Latin American affairs. He had opposed the Nicaraguan intervention, however, a position evident in his 1928 *Foreign Affairs* article 'Our Foreign Policy', and was a proponent of multilateral action in Latin America rather than unilateral US intervention. He was to hint at such a hemisphere strategy in his first speech to the Pan American Union on 12 April 1933, when he stressed intra-regional cooperation and pledged to build regionalism on a spirit of mutual respect.

Roosevelt chose Cordell Hull as his Secretary of State. A former senator from Tennessee with no experience of diplomacy, Hull was an austere and opinionated man who was easily upset by criticism and whose knowledge of Latin American issues was minimal. The president appointed Sumner Welles as his assistant secretary of state for Latin American affairs. An old friend of Roosevelt, Welles had become chief of the State Department's Latin American Division in 1921, at the age of 28, and was an experienced diplomat in regional matters.[68]

Welles's appointment created a potentially difficult situation in the State Department. His background and temperament were very different from Hull's, and from the outset their relationship was poor. It soon deteriorated into keen personal acrimony. Welles was often insubordinate. Hull, a true Democrat but evidently no liberal, referred to his assistant secretary as 'my fairy'. Their conflict reflected bureaucratic rivalry in the State Department that would eventually affect Washington's policies in Latin America. Two camps were starting to be established. The 'Latin Americanists', led by Welles and Duggan, were career diplomats who had been working on the region for years. Jealous of their expertise, they viewed broader international developments from a western-hemisphere perspective. The 'internationalist' camp, headed by Hull, were old Wilsonians who viewed US–Latin American relations as simply a small part of a global network of foreign links. Only superficially acquainted with Latin American politics and history, they tended to oversimplify regional issues; they, however, were the makers of general policy.[69]

[68] Irwin Gellman, *Good Neighbor Diplomacy: United States Policies in Latin America, 1933–1945* (Baltimore, Md.: Johns Hopkins University Press, 1979), 69; Joseph M. Jones, 'Good Neighbor, New Style', *Harper's Magazine*, 192 (Apr. 1946), 316; Robert Dallek, *Franklin D. Roosevelt and American Foreign Policy, 1933–1945* (New York: Oxford University Press, 1979), 60.

[69] Gellman, *Good Neighbor Diplomacy*, 13, 70; Bryce Wood, *The Dismantling of the Good Neighbor Policy* (Austin: University of Texas Press, 1985), 2; Morgan, *FDR: A*

It was this incipiently divided foreign policy establishment that confronted the challenge of Nicaragua in the spring of 1933. Sacasa lifted the state of siege at the end of March but by mid May he was obliged to reimpose martial law in the department of Managua as what Hanna termed 'the germ of decomposition' began to take hold. By the third week in May, events seemed to be drifting towards a crisis. As confidence in the government diminished, and as the Sacasa administration appeared increasingly ineffectual in its leadership, its adversaries became more outspoken. The ruling party split into five distinct groups: supporters of Arguello, Aguado, Espinosa, Moncada, and Sacasa himself. The president and his vice-president made no effort to hide their dislike of one another, and Sacasa found himself supported by only a meagre faction of the Liberals.[70]

In these circumstances, Sacasa had at least to attempt to contain the Guardia and the burgeoning influence of its new *jefe director*, Anastasio Somoza. The activities and cost of the National Guard, in fact, were significant elements in the rapid decline in Sacasa's popularity that was steadily eroding his authority. Public criticism focused on the percentage of government income and spending allotted to the Guardia. William Eberhardt, the American minister in Costa Rica and Hanna's predecessor at the Managua legation, reported a figure of $1 million for military expenses out of a total revenue of $1.5 million. Though Eberhardt was mistaken in this respect, the amount was still substantial when set against the real value of revenue for 1932 of $2.8 million.[71]

Moreover, Eberhardt's sources indicated that the Guardia treated the public 'in a most arrogant, insolent and abusive manner, so much so that it is freely predicted that it will only be a question of time when armed opposition is bound to develop'. In March, Sacasa had sent to Congress a bill calling for a reduction in the Guardia appropriation. By June, the monthly Guardia budget had fallen from 100,000 córdobas (C$) to C$75,000; further cuts seemed likely. At the end of the month, the legislature granted Sacasa the authority to reduce government expenditures further, including Guardia costs, since revenue was insufficient to meet the budget. The military spending cuts of that month coincided with

Biography (New York: Simon and Schuster, 1985), 679; Randall Bennett Woods, *The Roosevelt Foreign Policy Establishment and the 'Good Neighbor': The United States and Argentina, 1941–1945* (Lawrence: Regents Press of Kansas, 1979), 22, 25–6.

70 *New York Times*, 24 Mar. 1933; 817.00/7812, Hanna to Hull, 13 May 1933; 817.00/7823, Hanna to Hull, 19 May 1933.

71 817.00/7856, Eberhardt to Hull, 1 Aug. 1933.

a public manifesto from Sandino—whose loyalists were continuing to suffer Guardia harassment in the Segovias—declaring the Guardia unconstitutional and calling upon Sacasa to 'arm the people'.[72] Arming the people would probably have been a mistake.

In the face of public disaffection and official assaults on its manpower and budget, the National Guard appears to have attained an institutional coherence that to some extent overrode the political and personalist divisions of its early days as a force under exclusively Nicaraguan command. Many of the higher ranks, politically appointed over the heads of the junior officers in late 1932 and early 1933, were Sacasa loyalists, and the president was evidently being marginalized. The Chief of Staff, Abaunza, at Sacasa's urging, had been displacing Conservatives. The majority Moncadistas and Somocistas had a unity of purpose in view of the clear understanding between their patrons. Military *esprit de corps* was fortified by the leniency with which Sandino had been treated by civilian politicians, and most particularly by a deterioration in the troops' living conditions that cut across their political divisions. The latter circumstance reached a head in August, by which time the Guardia had not been paid for three months. Military unrest, inevitably, had reached alarming proportions.

In that light, Sacasa's concession to the Sandinistas—financing their settlement on an agricultural commune—seems to have been an act of political ineptitude. The coup of December 1931 in El Salvador, which ousted the Araujo regime and brought General Maximiliano Hernández Martínez to power, occurred very largely because the army had not been paid. Somoza estimated that he would need $80,000 from the National Bank to cancel the arrears. Though owned by the Nicaraguan government, the National Bank of Nicaragua was incorporated in the United States and had its offices and directorate in New York. Of the nine directors, four were American citizens. Somoza cabled the directors a request for $80,000. The board replied by authorizing the bank to allot $25,000.[73]

It was this context, compounded by Somoza's loyalty to Moncada rather than to Sacasa, that led Eberhardt to believe that an early overthrow of the Sacasa administration was 'a distinct possibility'. The possibility seemed to be made graphically concrete in the early hours of 1 August,

[72] 817.00/7823, Hanna to Hull, 19 May 1933; *New York Times*, 16 Mar. 1933, 4 June 1933, 23 June 1933, 29 June 1933.

[73] 817.1051/796, Hanna to Hull, 18 Aug. 1933; *New York Times*, 28 June 1933.

when a large quantity of weapons rained down on the streets of Managua. The Guardia's main arsenal at the Campo de Marte military base had exploded, sending a shower of revolvers, rifles, machine guns, and live rounds over a radius of several blocks. Sacasa declared a state of war in the department of Managua and a state of siege throughout the rest of the country. He began to arm loyal Liberals; press censorship and a curfew were imposed.[74]

Believing that the Guardia was staging a coup, Sandino offered to provide an army of 600 men to protect Sacasa. Somoza countered by advising Sacasa that if Sandino made any such move the Guardia would revolt: machine-gun emplacements were hastily assembled at all entrances to the Campo de Marte. Responsibility for the explosion was never clarified, though the recriminations were endless and for Sacasa the question was never in dispute. Two hundred Conservatives were detained in Managua and similar arrests were made in other towns throughout the country. The inter-party hostility temporarily promoted solidarity within each of the parties, but also gave rise to further proposals to break the pre-election pacts. The atmosphere in Managua was one of intense apprehension: government employees took to going to work with revolvers in their belts.[75]

From Washington, Cordell Hull urged Hanna to 'do everything you appropriately can to counsel calmness and moderation'.[76] Hanna's distaste for Sacasa, and his lack of confidence in the president's abilities to administer the country, were manifest in his dispatches to the State Department and contrasted with his equally clear admiration for Somoza, whom he had been advising on a personal basis. These impressions cannot have passed unnoticed in Washington during the months when the new officials in the State Department's Latin American division were attempting to define their Central American policy. Hanna, however, had a professional interest and a personal stake in the maintenance of stability. He had helped prepare the marine evacuation, create the officer corps, and appoint the National Guard's *jefe director*. He saw the preservation of the pre-election agreements as essential if civil war was to be avoided, and embarked on a series of meetings with Sacasa, Somoza,

[74] 817.00/7856, Eberhardt to Hull, 1 Aug. 1933; 817.00/7850, Hanna to Hull, 4 Aug. 1933; 817.48/37, Hanna to Hull, 4 Aug. 1933; 817.48/38, Hanna to Hull, 4 Aug. 1933.
[75] 817.00/7850, Hanna to Hull, 4 Aug. 1933; 817.00/7867, Hanna to Hull, 16 Aug. 1933; 817.48/38, Hanna to Hull, 4 Aug. 1933; 817.00/7861, Hanna to Hull, 9 Aug. 1933.   [76] 817.00/7850, Hull to Hanna, 7 Aug. 1933.

disaffected Liberals, and Conservative leaders in an attempt to save the pre-election pacts. By the third week of August the furore sparked off by the arrest of the Conservatives began to diminish as the prisoners were released; this was largely because of pressure on Hanna's part. According to the US military attaché, however, it was 'only a matter of time before trouble starts again'.[77]

By the autumn of 1933 the prospects of Sacasa's completing his term did not look bright in either Managua or Washington. His anxiety over the security of his government hardened into an obsession. Hanna, whose dispatches to Washington over the previous eight months had amounted to a catalogue of woe for the administration as it lurched from one crisis to the next, complained about this: '[Sacasa] is losing sight and sacrificing the favourable influences he fell heir to as a consequence of the intervention.'[78] From Sacasa's viewpoint, such influences were not readily apparent. At the end of September he indefinitely prolonged the state of siege for the whole country as reports multiplied of his government's imminent collapse. Vice-President Espinosa informed Daniels, the US legation's first secretary, of a planned coup to overthrow Sacasa and 'eliminate' Espinosa himself. The Mexican chargé also reported rumours of a military rebellion. The announcement of an early visit to Managua by Sandino, and Sacasa's indisposition with acute malaria, tended to support this view.[79]

The American minister in Guatemala was meanwhile given a letter that had come into the possession of President Ubico. Purportedly written by Vice-President Espinosa and addressed to one Rafael Lima, a Salvadorean ex-diplomat, the letter suggested that the vice-president was involved in a plot to assassinate Sacasa. Espinosa, according to the American military attaché, had been working 'clandestinely' against the president since the inauguration. In Washington, Willard Beaulac—first secretary of the Managua legation under Eberhardt, and now back at the department—made discreet investigations. He concluded that the letter was authentic, and that Espinosa and Lima were attempting to form a revolutionary movement.[80]

---

[77] 817.00/7862, Hanna to Hull, 11 Aug. 1933; 817.00/7869, Hanna to Hull, 18 Aug. 1933; 817.00/7879, military intelligence report, 18 Aug. 1933.

[78] 817.1051/796, Hanna to Hull, 18 Aug. 1933.

[79] 817.00/7892, Daniels to Hull, 3 Oct. 1933; 817.00/7901, Daniels to Hull, 1 Nov. 1933; 817.00/7903, Daniels to Hull, 2 Nov. 1833; 817.00/7927, military intelligence report, 28 Dec. 1933.

[80] 817.00/7892, Daniels to Hull, 3 Oct. 1933; 817.00/7901, Daniels to Hull, 1 Nov. 1933; 817.00/7917, Lawton to Hull, 19 Dec. 1933; 817.00/7927, military intelligence report, 28 Dec. 1933; 817.00/7917, memorandum, Beaulac to Wilson, 2 Jan. 1934.

Daniels gave credence to the probability of a coup led by Somoza as the president was leaving Managua because of his illness. He informed the department that the *jefe director* would be the predominant force in the city and that a military dictatorship might be imminent. The following day, 10 November 1933, in his instructions to the American delegation about to leave for the Seventh Inter-American Conference in Montevideo, Hull wrote: 'it is believed that [Nicaragua] has a fair chance of remaining peaceful and of retaining the benefits which have accrued to it as a result of American assistance.' President Sacasa was at that moment preparing to move himself, his family, and his entire cabinet to a coffee plantation in the hills twelve miles south of Managua, leaving Somoza as the main political force in the capital. The pattern for good neighbourism in Nicaragua during Roosevelt's first term was thereby set.[81]

[81] 817.00/7903, Daniels to Hull, 2 Nov. 1933; 817.00/7904, Daniels to Hull, 8 Nov. 1933; 710G/731, Hull to the American delegates at Montevideo, 10 Nov. 1933.

2

Good Neighbour Diplomacy and
Somoza's Rise to Power, 1934–1935

> While older nations totter under the burden of outworn ideas, cling
> to the decayed and cruel institution of war and use precious
> resources to feed cannon rather than hungry mouths, we stand
> ready to carry on in the spirit of that application of the Golden
> Rule, by which we mean the true good will of the true Good
> Neighbor.[1]
>
> Cordell Hull

The prevailing spirit for the application of Hull's Golden Rule ensured
the ascendancy of Anastasio Somoza. This was not Washington's intention; it was simply an end result. Of the circumstances that facilitated
Somoza's rise to power the domestic considerations were as significant as
the external factors, but it is upon the latter that much of the emphasis—
and much of the responsibility—has been placed. This is valid, though
without qualification its implications are not. Given the record of
US–Nicaraguan relations up to 1933, and the general orientation of
American policy in the Caribbean region after the onset of the Cold War,
the idea that the Somoza regime was an American-created and American-
sponsored institution from the outset, that it was the planned culmination of a US design for Nicaragua, has tended to furnish much of its own
momentum. In revolutionary Nicaragua, that version of events became
accepted history.

Somoza's rise was not the result of machinations on the part of the
Roosevelt administration. On the contrary, it was in large part a result of

---

[1] From an address to the Montevideo conference. Quoted in William Appleman
Williams (ed.), *The Shaping of American Diplomacy, 1914–1968*, ii: (Chicago: Rand
McNally, 1973), 196.

their absence. The elements of Hull's Golden Rule that conditioned the relevant domestic factors in Nicaragua were largely negative in nature. Those elements were the natural consequence of a policy that consisted in practice of a pledge to an entire continent not to act in one way, rather than of a guarantee to individual neighbours to act in another.

Mention has already been made of Washington's failure to meet the obligations attendant on the Tipitapa Agreement. The failure was largely unavoidable, but it did tend to contradict insistent US rhetoric on respect for such obligations, and on the sanctity of international agreements. Washington's determination to avoid further responsibilities in Nicaragua, at a time of intense domestic isolationism, entailed a failure to accept existing obligations that the United States could not inconsequentially discount. This was compounded by a more fundamental failing: a resolute unwillingness to take full account of the true nature of Washington's role in the Nicaraguan political process. The practical impact of the non-interference principle, negative in the way in which it invited misinterpretation and positive in the scope it afforded interested parties to claim US support, was complicated by good neighbourism's continental nature, a nature that could not contain effective provision for responses to the demands of particular situations. The intermittent divergence from the non-interference ideal, the changing nature of US recognition policy, and the lack of consensus within the State Department on the fundamental nature of good neighbourism completed a set of circumstances that not only made Somoza's rise to power possible, but gave it the sense of remorseless inevitability that emerges from the historical evidence.

*

On 3 December 1933 the Seventh International Conference of American States convened at Montevideo in an atmosphere of animosity. It was a difficult meeting for the US delegation. The Latin Americans were seeking debt moratoria and expressed disdain for US creditors. The Mexican foreign minister, José Manuel Puig Casauranc, proposed a moratorium and interest rate reductions in a speech that, according to Hull, 'was applauded wildly as he dramatized the distressed debtors oppressed by conscienceless corporations in Wall Street'.[2] US warships sat off the

---

[2] Irwin Gellman, *Good Neighbor Diplomacy: United States Policies in Latin America, 1933–1945* (Baltimore, Md.: Johns Hopkins University Press, 1979), 21; Cordell Hull, *Memoirs* (New York: Macmillan, 1948), i, 335.

Cuban coast as the Grau government readied itself for collapse in the face of non-recognition by Washington. Portell Vilá of the Cuban delegation bluntly denounced this: 'intervention is not only the "curse of America" but as a Cuban internationalist has said, it is the "curse of curses" of any country, the cause of all evils of the Cuban republic.' According to the leader of the Haitian delegation, the US marines still in Haiti were bringing 'indescribable anguish' to his country. The Chaco and Leticia disputes persisted, and in Uruguay itself there was a danger that the imminent presidential elections might be violent. The circumstances for the Montevideo meeting were highly inauspicious.[3]

The draft Convention on the Rights and Duties of States, whose central article banned intervention, was pending from the sixth conference. It is clear that, originally, the United States did not intend to accept the proposal without modification. According to the State Department's instructions to the US delegation, one article in the draft 'would strike directly at the Platt Amendment and our conventions with Haiti and Santo Domingo. It would also prevent the landing of troops in any country for the protection of American nationals during the frequent revolutions in Latin American countries.'[4]

At his first inter-American conference, however, Hull was surprised at the intensity of Latin American bitterness over intervention. He decided to accept the Convention, though he added a reservation referring to US rights under 'the law of nations as generally recognized and accepted'. He cabled the State Department to report that he had voted for the Convention with reservation, adding that 'the demand for a unanimous affirmative vote was very vociferous and more or less wild and unreasonable'. His reservation was not minor, since US intervention had historically made an appeal to 'the law of nations as generally recognized', but the non-intervention protocol signed at Montevideo was truly a significant development in inter-American relations. For Nicaragua, Hull's commitment in December 1933 would prove to be a milestone.[5]

---

[3] US Department of State, *Report of the Delegates of the United States of America to the Seventh Conference of American States*, Conference Series, 19 (Washington DC: US Government Printing Office, 1934), 105; Gellman, *Good Neighbor Diplomacy*, 21; Edgar O. Guerrant, *Roosevelt's Good Neighbor Policy* (Albuquerque: University of New Mexico Press, 1950), 6–7.

[4] US Department of State, *Foreign Relations of the United States* (Washington DC: US Government Printing Office, 1933), iv, 67.

[5] Ibid. 201; Gordon Connell-Smith, *The Inter-American System* (London: Oxford University Press, 1966), 90.

In the same month, Arthur Bliss Lane replaced Matthew Hanna at the Managua legation. It was his first posting as a minister. Thirty-nine years old, Lane was the youngest officer in the history of the American foreign service ever to have been appointed as chief of mission. From the outset, however, he was unhappy at the appointment. Before his arrival in Managua he had asked the under-secretary of state 'William Phillips' to transfer him to 'a better post, preferably in Europe, before too long'.[6]

Arrived at the centre of the Nicaraguan imbroglio with its high potential for widespread violence, Lane was a man with something to prove both to himself and to his chiefs in Washington. As the first minister to be appointed to Managua under the Roosevelt administration, he saw it as his mission to nurture the fledgling democracy in Nicaragua in its early days as a sovereign and unoccupied country. Very publicly, he would be seen to fail. Indeed, he would stand wrongly indicted by generations of Nicaraguans and by historians elsewhere as a principal agent in the assassination of Augusto Sandino and the installation of Anastasio Somoza.[7] That indictment is less indicative of Lane's diplomatic skills than it is of the nature of good neighbourism in Nicaragua. President Sacasa, increasingly isolated, bequeathed a situation born of intervention and beset by problems with which he was neither personally able nor professionally equipped to deal, turned almost instinctively to the Roosevelt administration through the person of Arthur Bliss Lane, with whose arrival in Managua the good neighbour policy began to be seen for what it was.

*

Historical interest in good neighbour diplomacy has focused in large part on a debate about the extent to which it did or did not represent a departure from traditional diplomacy in conception and execution. According

---

[6] Hugh De Santis, *The Diplomacy of Silence: The American Foreign Service, the Soviet Union and the Cold War, 1933–1947* (Chicago: University of Chicago Press, 1980), 46.

[7] Declarations that Lane ordered the murder of Sandino are common in the literature, where the notion of Somoza's 'installation' by the United States tends to recur. Typical is Gregorio Selser, who states flatly that 'it was in Roosevelt's time that the patriot guerrillero Augusto C. Sandino was assassinated, at the instigation of US Ambassador [*sic*] Arthur Bliss Lane' (Selser, in the introduction to William Krehm, *Democracies and Tyrannies of the Caribbean* (Westport, Conn.: Lawrence Hill & Co., 1984), p. xii). Juan Colindres claims that Lane approved Sandino's murder in revenge for the guerrilla's military campaign; see *Anastasio Somoza: Fin de una estirpe de ladrones y asesinos* (Mexico City: Editorial Posada, 1979), 47. Marco Antonio Valle Martínez goes so far as to say that the order for Sandino's murder came direct from the White House. See *La dictadura somocista* (Leon: Comité Político Universitario UNAN, 1980), 18. Such allegations tend to come unencumbered by anything but hearsay as evidence.

to one commentator: 'Here was a nation transformed into an altruistic, anti-imperialist, peace-loving neighbor whom the Latin Americans could admire and love. As the good neighbor policy was put into execution by the Roosevelt administration...Latin Americans were persuaded to soften their harsh attitudes towards the United States and to accept their powerful neighbor as a winsome and trustworthy friend.'[8]

Opinion on this central concern ranges from such positive assertions on the one hand to glib pronouncements on the other that any policy modifications were of form, not substance, that somehow nothing had *really* changed.[9] While one view insists that US political domination of Latin America had suddenly ended, the other claims that the 'friendly counsel' diplomacy of the good neighbour policy was simply interference by another name in the interests of continued control. The questions that arise are important, and should be put, but in focusing as a point of departure on acts by the United States and consequences in Latin America this line of enquiry neglects an important consideration.

Matthew Hanna, writing to the then Secretary of State, Henry Stimson, in 1933, claimed that 'the broad purpose of the intervention was to create in the Nicaraguan people a capacity for self-determination'.[10] The intervention, clearly, created precisely the opposite. Irrespective of whether Washington's friendly counsel in Nicaragua was designed to be an extension of US political control, there can be little doubt that after decades of unequivocal political and economic interference, and the debacle of the most recent military intervention, Nicaragua's political elite was virtually incapable of action wholly independent of the United States. The attitude, real or imagined, of policy-makers in Washington was a constant factor in all political equations. The American minister in Nicaragua, following the departure of the American marines, remained one of the most influential men in the country. As late as 1936, after three years of non-interference, Managua's *La Prensa* could still justifiably refer to the American legation as 'la Meca de la política Nicaragüense'.[11] Very abruptly, however, in the name of non-interference, the State Department was refusing to make any comment whatever on conditions

[8] Donald Dozer, *Are We Good Neighbors?* (Gainesville: University of Florida Press, 1959), 20.

[9] See, as one example, Amaru Barahona Portocarrero, 'Estudio sobre la historia contemporánea de Nicaragua', *Avances de Investigación*, 24 (San José, Costa Rica: Universidad de Costa Rica, Facultad de Ciencias Sociales, Instituto de Investigaciones Sociales, 1977), 23.   [10] 817.00/7769, Hanna to Stimson, 15 Feb. 1933.
[11] 817.00/8531, Long to Hull, 16 June 1936.

in Nicaragua to the Nicaraguans themselves, thereby fostering a political perplexity that underscored the incoherence in domestic politics attendant on the marine withdrawal.

Therein lay a basic problem for the good neighbour policy from its inception. As important as the extent to which US involvement in domestic politics was recommended or denounced outside Nicaragua was the extent to which, within Nicaragua, it was anticipated as a matter of course. Such thinking, alterable in theory only over a protracted period, defined a relationship between Washington and Managua that Hull wanted to change immediately and that Sacasa, given his predicament, did not want changed at all.

Good neighbourism in Nicaragua precluded any action that might be construed as interference, but the country's political elite—and, importantly, the public at large—found it very hard to accept that the United States would no longer be a leading voice in their political life. Representatives of each faction sought to elicit a comment from American officials, particularly Lane, which might indicate Washington's attitude to action taken, planned, or merely considered. Any public comment from Washington could have a direct effect on domestic politics. In the prevailing circumstances, however, the absence of any positive expression of US opinion could be equally influential.

Damned if it did something and damned if it didn't, the State Department decided it would do nothing for Sacasa. Hull instructed Lane to refrain at all times from interfering, even if he were invited to do so. The secretary was worried that charges of interference in the wake of Montevideo would damage US relations with Latin America at a time when he was planning a hemisphere-wide programme of trade agreements, and might incur for Washington a moral responsibility for the political results in Nicaragua.[12]

*

Avoidable or otherwise, Washington's failure to meet its obligations was exacerbated by the practical application of the new diplomatic thinking. Arthur Bliss Lane, like his predecessor Matthew Hanna, disliked Sacasa personally and held him in low esteem professionally. He regarded the president as weak and vacillating, unable to influence his Congress, and highly dependent on the moral support of the American legation. Somoza,

[12] 817.00/7923, Hull to Lane, 3 Jan. 1934.

on the other hand, was clearly a man in the best caudillo tradition who had reached his position of power through his friendship with Hanna. Lane had been a diplomat since 1917, having spent eight years in Europe and eight in Mexico before the Managua assignment.[13] He had been trained in a foreign service in which it was understood that Washington's representatives in Central America were powerful figures not easily ignored. At the moment of his most significant career advance to date, his first posting as minister, it would be demanded of Lane that he reject the unwritten rules of that training. For Lane, the difficulties of that course were compounded by his temperament as a pragmatist, one who found it hard to operate dogmatically within an all-embracing philosophy.

From the outset, Lane assumed that his obligation was to work in the interests of the constitutional government of Juan Sacasa. The Sacasa administration seemed so imperilled, however, that Lane's sense of obligation to it was to draw him much deeper into local politics than was consistent with a policy of non-interference. During his time in Managua, therefore, in the name of good neighbourism, his chiefs systematically deprived him of the power to strengthen Sacasa's government against Somoza's Guardia, and his persistent expression of doubts as to their judgement earned him repeated warnings from Washington. As the Sacasa government foundered at the beginning of 1934, a divergence became apparent between the aims of the State Department's diplomatic representative in Managua and the aims of US foreign policy as dictated from Washington. Lane, often ignoring instructions from the department, did all that he reasonably could to forestall Somoza. He failed.

Somoza was affronted that the Guardia had not been allowed, as he expressed it to Lane, to 'finish' Sandino. Moreover, though the troops had again remained unpaid for several months, Sacasa had spent C$20,000 from the Guardia appropriation to build a fort outside León, a clear expression of the president's lack of confidence in his own army and of his desire to strengthen the area of the country most loyal to him. As early as the previous April it was here that the first shipment of arms bought by the Sacasa government had been stored. Somoza had objected vigorously and the action had aroused widespread comment. The Guardia further believed that Sacasa would yield to Sandino if the latter refused to surrender his remaining weapons.[14]

---

[13] De Santis, *The Diplomacy of Silence*, 7; Gellman, *Good Neighbor Diplomacy*, 71.

[14] 817.00/7922, Lane to Hull, 8 Jan. 1934; 817.1051/781, Hanna to Stimson, 21 Apr. 1933.

In response to the August explosion at the Campo de Marte, Sandino—believing that the incident indicated an imminent coup—had sent Sacasa a message of support and had offered to mobilize 600 men to protect the president. Countering, Somoza had informed Sacasa that the Guardia's junior officers were incensed and that they could become mutinous if Sandino were not dealt with. Guardia–Sandinista clashes had been increasing in recent months. The American consular agent in Matagalpa reported a high level of tension between the Guardia and Sandinistas in the region, and felt that the guardsmen were seeking a pretext to attack.[15]

As the deadline for the final disarmament of the Sandinistas approached, one year after the Sacasa–Sandino agreement, Guardia units from the interior were mobilized on manoeuvres close to the Sandinista community at Wiwili. An alarmed Sandino refused to be fully disarmed until the issue of the Guardia's 'constitutionality' had been resolved, but he reaffirmed his commitment of armed support for the president in the event of any confrontation. Sacasa summoned Sandino to Managua to reach a new accord that might lessen the tension. Anticipating trouble, Lane insisted to Somoza that he should not use the guerrilla's visit as a pretext to move against Sacasa. Somoza promised the American minister that he would take no action to embarrass the government, but Lane placed little faith in Somoza's personal assurances. He informed the department that he had 'grave doubts as to the efficiency and discipline of the [National Guard] as a whole and as to whether Somoza really controls his men'.[16]

Sandino arrived in the capital on 16 February 1934. After three days of discussions at the presidential mansion, Sacasa announced a decision. In view of his political circumstances, the decision was inept. Nicaragua's northern departments—Matagalpa, Jinotega, Estelí, and Nueva Segovia—were to be placed under the control of Horacio Portocarrero, a Sandinista loyalist and Sandino's former nominee for the presidency of a 'revolutionary government'. According to Moncada, the four departments ceded to Sandino contained Nicaragua's richest gold deposits and Sacasa was guilty of treason in allowing their 'secession'. Somoza, predictably,

[15] 817.00/7935, Lane to Hull, 14 Feb. 1934; Eduardo Crawley, *Dictators Never Die: A Portrait of Nicaragua and the Somoza Dynasty* (London: C. Hurst, 1979), 84–6.

[16] Ibid. 84–6; Krehm, *Democracies and Tyrannies*, 110; Selser, *Sandino, General of the Free* (New York: Monthly Review Press, 1981), 174; Bernard Diederich, *Somoza and the Legacy of US Involvement in Central America* (New York: Dutton, 1981), 18; 817.00/7935, Lane to Hull, 14 Feb. 1934.

was similarly furious, since the National Guard units in the northern departments would now be under the jurisdiction of Sandino. He protested bitterly to Lane that the National Guard's anger at this 'insult' would be uncontainable.[17]

On the evening of 21 February, Sacasa held a farewell dinner for Sandino in the presidential mansion. At the same time, Somoza convened an emergency meeting of the General Staff. Around 11 p.m., Lane was disturbed by the sound of machine-gun fire near the legation. The house of the agriculture minister Solfonias Salvatierra, Sandino's host in Managua, had been attacked. Sandino and two of his aides, generals Juan Pablo Umanzor and Francisco Estrada, had already been detained on leaving the mansion and taken to Managua airfield. Lane tried to contact the president but his telephone lines had been cut. While he hurried to investigate the disturbance, a Guardia firing squad executed Sandino, his half-brother, and his two generals at the airfield. The next day the National Guard, which had been bearing down on the Sandinista community at Wiwili, surrounded the camp and killed the inhabitants. Congress declared a state of siege.[18]

Without reference to Somoza, Sacasa issued a public statement blaming the Guardia for Sandino's murder, pledging an immediate investigation and promising punishment for the killers.[19] Lane was busy on another track. In an urgent telephone call to Edwin Wilson, assistant chief in the State Department's Latin American division, the minister attempted to explain that the situation was worsened by the growing feeling that he, Lane, had conspired with Somoza to have Sandino murdered. In El Salvador, the press in the capital began publishing reports of imminent catastrophe in Nicaragua. In Chihuahua a mob gathered outside the US consulate and the anti-American speeches gave way to missile-throwing.[20] In Managua, clearly mortified at the events and at allegations

[17] RG 38 C-10-d 6473, commander, Special Service Squadron, to chief of naval operations (director of naval intelligence), 24 June 1936; 817.00/7939, Lane to Hull, 22 Feb. 1934; José María Moncada, *Nicaragua: Sangre en sus montañas* (San José, Calif., 1985), 298; Crawley, *Dictators Never Die*, 85.

[18] Neill Macaulay, *The Sandino Affair* (Chicago: Quadrangle Books, 1967), 255–6; Richard Millet, *Guardians of the Dynasty* (Maryknoll, NY: Orbis Books, 1977), 156, 167 n. 78; 817.00/7935, Lane to Hull, 1 Feb. 1934; 817.00/7936, Lane to Hull, 16 Feb. 1934; 817.00/7939, Lane to Hull, 22 Feb. 1934; Diederich, *Somoza*, 19.

[19] 'Manifiesto del Presidente de la República al Pueblo Nicaragüense', 23 Feb. 1934, reproduced in Juan Bautista Sacasa, *Como y por qué caí del poder* (Leon, Nicaragua: *s.n.*, 1935), 39. No Guardia officer was ever punished for the assassination.

[20] 817.00/7946, Lane to Hull, 23 Feb. 1934; 817.00/7949, McCafferty to Hull, 24 Feb. 1934.

of his involvement, Lane was doing his utmost to contain the damage. He decided that the most immediate means to check Somoza and to forestall Guardia violence would be a brief declaration from the State Department outlining US recognition policy as embodied in the 1923 Treaty of Peace and Amity. Lane expressed profound pessimism about Nicaragua's future if events were left to run what seemed to him their inevitable course and, evidently expecting some positive response, he asked the department for a public declaration of policy on the night of Sandino's death.[21]

In a cable signed by Hull, the department informed Lane that it would be 'inadvisable' to make any such statement, but allowed that Lane could 'say orally to Somoza that there has been no change in the Department's policy'. There being little practical point to this instruction, Lane simply repeated the request for a statement, which he felt would 'check any military move against the government' and might 'quiet the anti-American feeling'. The department again refused. On 24 February, Lane again telephoned Wilson at home and emphasized his conviction that 'the only possibility of restoring order and preventing anarchy' was in a declaration from the US government. 'Only a statement on our part', Lane argued, 'can save the situation now.'[22]

The official response was a refusal. Lane persisted. On the same day he cabled Hull a dispatch that made a lengthy case for a public statement and suggested that the State Department's silence was actually influencing events. 'Some people', he contended, 'think that we might look with favour on the assumption of political power by the Guardia, tending perhaps towards a military dictatorship.' The department again refused.[23] Told repeatedly that official policy remained unchanged but that he was not allowed to state this officially, Lane, exasperated, enquired:

If this be the case I fail to see why ... the people here who think our silence is a reversal of policy should remain in ignorance, with the possible effects I have already brought to the Department's attention ... It is undeniably true that Nicaragua at the present time faces a grave crisis ... Any appropriate step which might be taken to avoid disorders and bloodshed would appear to be justified.[24]

Lane's position, which required that the United States accept some of the responsibility now in order to avoid incurring all of the blame later, was

---

[21] 817.00/7941, Lane to Hull, 22 Feb. 1934.

[22] 817.00/7942, Lane to Hull, 23 Feb. 1934; 817.00/7961, memorandum, Wilson, 24 Feb. 1934.

[23] 817.00/7963, Lane to Hull, 24 Feb. 1934; 817.00/7953, Hull to Lane, 26 Feb. 1934.   [24] 817.00/7959, Lane to Hull, 28 Feb. 1934.

unacceptable to Hull—for whom blame was not an issue and responsibility was to be avoided at all costs. Lane's complaint was that a policy of non-interference was not, in the circumstances, a policy at all. Silence, requiring as it did some degree of interpretation on the part of the Nicaraguans, openly invited misinterpretation. The department's position implicitly recognized this, but with some justification made its stand on the assumption that non-interference could only ever become a reality if the principle were to be maintained from the outset with unyielding resolution over the long term, and particularly at critical periods.

In Managua, attempting to deal with each situation as it arose and with a greater insight into the immediate nature of public perception in Nicaragua, Lane felt that neither the United States nor the Sacasa administration had the time to await the enlightenment of the Nicaraguan public. If a military dictatorship were to be established now it would be seen as American-sponsored. US interference, irrespective of the nature of US intent, would be perceived to endure for at least as long as that dictatorship. These two positions were fatally irreconcilable.

*

Aside from its crucial significance in Nicaragua's later mythologies, Sandino's assassination is important for the way in which it exemplified one of the diplomatic problems with which good neighbourism in Nicaragua was fraught. Part of what Lane was failing to see was that at Montevideo the Roosevelt administration had committed itself to a policy of non-commitment in the whole of Latin America. The domestic political climate of isolationism had coincided with the culmination of a Latin American juridical campaign against intervention. At the same time, a cordial relationship with the southern continent was thought to be important to US interests. Hence the administration had (with reservation) agreed at Montevideo to the Convention on the Rights and Duties of States, thereby pledging itself to refrain from interference.

In Nicaragua, the situation had deteriorated to such a point that Lane could describe it for his chiefs in the plainest terms: 'There are two governments in this city, both fully armed. I was in the presidential palace last night and the place is full of machine guns. The president is not running the country at all. There is bound to be a showdown sooner or later.'[25] The State Department seems to have been unconcerned at the prospect of a coup in Nicaragua, particularly if—as legation reports were

[25] 817.00/7963, Lane to Hull, 24 Feb. 1934.

indicating—the likely victor was a strong and pro-American general. In the prevailing circumstances, the collapse of constitutional government in a minor republic, even if that collapse were to be initiated by an American-made organization, was less important than running the risk of increased resentment throughout the hemisphere. This contrasted sharply with previous thinking, wherein Latin American resentment had been ignored in the interests of continued US interference in Central America.

For the Nicaraguan government, this was a fundamental flaw in good neighbourism. Hull applauded 'the universal applicability of the basic principles on which that policy is premised', and claimed that it was because of such universality that the policy enjoyed universal support.[26] But in a largely well-intentioned attempt to define a policy applicable to an entire continent, the State Department blinkered itself against the practical realities of particular situations. The Convention on the Rights and Duties of States itself characterized the lack of thought that had been given to the practicalities of the policy. According to article 8 of the Convention, 'no state has the right to intervene in the internal or external affairs of another'. In practice this would have meant that if a non-American power had secured control of the external affairs of a country in the western hemisphere, no other country in the hemisphere could have reacted forcefully, irrespective of the danger posed. 'Fifth columnism' was a term not yet coined.[27]

This was the thinking behind the movement to 'outlaw' war, the movement that had led to the conclusion of the Kellogg–Briand Pact in 1928. That thinking emphasized abstractions such as peace and non-intervention, obliging its adherents to ignore the practical responsibilities that were intrinsic to the international position of the United States. At the same time, isolationist attitudes reflected an inability to appreciate that trite pronouncements about international harmony were no substitute for accepting those responsibilities. The idea of renouncing war by decree, as Henry Cabot Lodge observed, was not only absurd but dangerous, by which he meant that it created a false sense of security while giving no thought to its own implementation. It organized no concrete means of conflict-resolution, relying entirely on moral suasion to foster compliance.[28]

[26] Quoted in Bryce Wood, *The Making of the Good Neighbor Policy* (New York: Columbia University Press, 1961), 161.

[27] Julius W. Pratt, *Cordell Hull, 1933–1944*, 2 vols., The American Secretaries of State, 12–13 (New York: Cooper Square Publishers, 1964), i, 163.

[28] F. R. Dulles, *America's Rise to World Power, 1898–1954* (New York: Harper, 1955), 158–9.

Before the decade ended, the Kellogg–Briand Pact would be rendered meaningless by the outbreak of World War II. At the time, however, its function in the United States was to satisfy a vague national conscience demanding that *something* be done, without requiring any constructive action but while offering an illusory sense of security that seemed to make international engagement unnecessary.[29] So it was with Nicaragua. The Roosevelt administration based its policy on an ideal of the stance it should adopt to the rest of the hemisphere, and paid scant regard to such a policy's consequences in Nicaragua. In the mid 1930s, that policy was virtually equivalent to severing diplomatic relations with the country at a time when some positive, carefully formulated approach was most needed.

In the end, and as Lane had foreseen, by the end of February 1934 the practical result of official silence was a general conviction in Nicaragua that the United States favoured Somoza and the Guardia against the government, and that a military coup was therefore imminent. The Guardia itself, convinced of American support, was encouraged. The State Department did nothing to dispel this view. Lane continued to reiterate his views to Washington and the department continued to take its stand on a wholly negative policy of non-interference. With no official support, Lane was doing all he could on a personal basis to avert civil war.[30]

*

Sandino's murder gave greater definition to Washington's role in Nicaragua. In the aftermath, the US military attaché for Central America, Major Harris, simply abandoned hope for the Sacasa administration. He felt that the assassination had 'thrown Nicaragua into such turmoil that nothing short of complete capitulation on the part of President Sacasa can save the country from further strife and civil war'. In this view he was at odds with Lane, who felt that the State Department could save Sacasa. There were likely to be four major factions in the event of hostilities. Sacasa had a small Guardia element and part of the Liberal Party. Somoza, with Moncada, carried the bulk of the Guardia and the rest of the Liberals; this was clearly the most powerful force in the country. The third force comprised the Conservatives under Nicaragua's perennial revolutionary, Emiliano Chamorro. Additionally, the remnants of the Sandinistas were still active.[31]

[29] F. R. Dulles, *America's Rise to World Power, 1898–1954* (New York: Harper, 1955), 160.
[30] 817.00/7945, Lane to Hull, 23 Feb. 1934; 817.00/7958, Lane to Hull, 27 Feb. 1934.   [31] 817.00/7989, military intelligence report, 2 Mar. 1934.

By the beginning of March the San José press was reporting that the Somocistas and Sacasistas were digging trenches and filling sandbags for defence against each other. This was an exaggeration, but it typified the Latin American impression of conditions in Nicaragua and the genuine sense, within the country, of imminent and violent confrontation. For the US military attaché and for officials in Washington, to whom Sandino remained an anarchic (and possibly deranged) bandit who had rendered the 1927 intervention an exercise in futility, the rebel's death was hard to lament. The isthmus seemed increasingly secure. Jorge Ubico had been in power in Guatemala since 1931 and the regime showed no signs of stress. Maximiliano Hernández Martínez, having run the risk of US non-recognition, had consolidated his power in El Salvador since his coup in 1931. Amid the Nicaraguan turmoil, Somoza and Moncada seemed to be the strongest element. Hence, for the American military attaché, Sandino's assassination was 'a hopeful sign'. He could claim that the murder 'will, in the long run, be a fine thing for the future peace and tranquility of the country', all unmindful of the possibility that, in the longer run, it might not be.[32]

The danger of a Nicaraguan civil war, however, waned in importance compared with possibilities of potentially graver consequence. Major Harris noted a Salvadorean mission to Managua to offer Sacasa military aid while President Ubico of Guatemala, in the attaché's view, 'would be disposed to lend aid and assistance to any worthy opponent of President Sacasa'. Harris concluded that this alignment might not materialize, but that 'it is a possibility, and a dangerous one.'[33] It remained to be seen how firm the non-interference principle would hold if this situation were ever to be realized.

For Arthur Bliss Lane, professionally interested in the maintenance of peace and personally involved in the situation, the value of the principle was beginning to seem dubious. Throughout the continent, rumours were rife that Lane had conspired with the Guardia in Sandino's assassination. This is understandable. The United States had created, trained, and armed the Guardia; US marines had fought alongside native guardsmen in the war against the guerrillas; and Sandino—a continental symbol of anti-Americanism—had despised the Guardia to the last. The most significant factor in fostering such a belief, however, was American silence. The murder and the silence, moreover, bound Somoza to the Roosevelt administration. Though reports of US involvement spurred

[32] Ibid.   [33] Ibid.

further anti-American sentiment, they simultaneously strengthened Somoza's hand. Left undenied, the very suggestion that he and US officials had conspired in murder appeared to indicate Washington's complete commitment to him.[34]

Lane understood that the good neighbour policy had no practical answer to the damage that accusations of US involvement were doing to American prestige throughout the hemisphere. He came to see that his own endeavours, despite persistence or the strength of his argument, would bear little fruit. He had decided on two forms of action. First, he wanted an official State Department demand that Sandino's killers be severely punished. This request had been denied. Second, he wanted an official declaration reaffirming US support for the legitimate government. Somoza objected to this request and it was in any case denied. Hence Lane was trying to induce a change in policy through personal contacts with Wilson in the department's Latin American division. Lane repeated his requests in telephone conversations with Wilson, who affected to believe that it would somehow be sufficient, in order to prevent a coup, to 'tell Somoza straight from the shoulder' that he did not have Washington's support. Lane had been doing precisely this for some time, to no effect since the statement was not public. Wilson again refused Lane permission to repeat it to anyone else. Responding to Lane's protests that to continue this course was not only futile but dangerous, Wilson advised the minister to stress to Somoza that the information 'comes straight from the Secretary'.[35]

Outraged at the apparent indifference to his position—and to Nicaragua—that this line of reasoning betrayed, Lane appeared to give up hope of constructive action from Washington, though in doing so he too was forced to abdicate what he saw as his responsibility: 'What you want me to do I will do,' he told Wilson, 'but I want you to know, and to tell the Secretary, that I assume no responsibility for the consequences . . . If nothing is done we will probably have anarchy here . . . It is not for me to say what the policy shall be, but you are inviting a military dictatorship.'[36]

In the end, however, Lane was too honourable a man to disavow what he saw as his commitments in Nicaragua. Convinced that the good neighbour policy was inadequate to prevent Somoza from overthrowing

---

[34] 817.00/8020 Hull to Lane, 13 Apr. 1934; Vladimir Petrov, *A Study in Diplomacy: The Story of Arthur Bliss Lane* (Chicago: H. Regnery Co., 1971), 42.

[35] 817.00/7941, Lane to Hull, 22 Feb. 1934; 817.00/7942, Hull to Lane, 23 Feb. 1934; 817.00/7945, Lane to Hull, 23 Feb. 1934; 817.00/7947, Hull to Lane, 23 Feb. 1934; Petrov, *A Study in Diplomacy*, 48.   [36] Petrov, 48.

Sacasa, he tried to do on a personal basis what the department was refusing to do officially. He informed Washington of this course and attempted to forestall Somoza through personal influence. The department told him that 'we desire not only to refrain in fact from interference, but also from any measure which might give the appearance of such interference.'[37] This was a clear warning to Lane but he chose to ignore it. He endeavoured to establish a truce between the government and the Guardia by urging the Sacasas to curb their efforts to dominate Somoza by humiliating him, and through repeated appeals to Somoza that he do nothing to disturb the peace.[38]

Lane's main task in Nicaragua became that of an intermediary between Somoza and the government. The trend, however, was against Sacasa. By the end of February he had transformed the presidential mansion into an armed camp. Lane insisted that he normalize the defensive arrangements, since they were provocative to the Guardia and served to detract still further from public confidence in the administration. In the face of an official US detachment, however, Lane's personal efforts were of limited effect. At the end of February he and the rest of the diplomatic corps were forced to witness a further government attempt to humiliate Somoza, when Sacasa summoned the *jefe director* and his general staff to the mansion and obliged them to renew their oath of allegiance to him.[39]

Sacasa was also attempting to undermine Somoza's influence on a more practical level. On 1 March he issued a decree that severely restricted the authority previously vested in the National Guard's *jefe director*. The new regulations empowered Sacasa to issue orders to Guardia officers without consulting Somoza; gave the president the exclusive right to approve military transfers and promotions; obliged the Guardia to make no arms transfers without executive approval; and forced Somoza to give daily reports to the president on the state of the Guardia.[40] Even more practically, on 21 March Sacasa increased the presidential guard by another 100 men.[41]

He now found further cause for alarm in the apparent alliance of two previously bitter opponents. With the approach of the Liberal primaries for the congressional elections of October 1934, Moncada announced his intention to run for senator in the department of Rivas with the support

37 817.00/7953, Hull to Lane, 28 Feb. 1934.
38 817.00/8025, Lane to Hull, 12 Apr. 1934; Petrov, *A Study in Diplomacy*, 50, 52.
39 817.00/7971, Lane to Hull, 5 Mar. 1934.
40 Decree no. 358, *La Gaceta* (Managua), 1 Mar. 1934.
41 817.00/7991, Lane to Hull, 21 Mar. 1934.

of Emiliano Chamorro and the Conservatives. The president extended the state of siege indefinitely and, in an effort to prevent further splits within the Liberals, completely reorganized the cabinet with the exception of the foreign minister, Leonardo Arguello, and the undersecretary of finance, to give greater representation to localities and sectors previously accorded little recognition.[42]

There can be little doubt that Moncada's candidacy in Rivas sprang from a desire to be named first designate to the presidency, so that when his protégé Somoza removed Sacasa the ex-president could take over the reins of government. 'The situation', Major Harris averred, 'is complicated and full of dynamite... Moncada is the greatest obstacle to the peace and tranquility of Nicaragua at the present time.'[43] It is interesting that Harris appears to have viewed Somoza, the untested young Guardia commander, wholly as an instrument for furthering the ambitions of Moncada, the experienced old caudillo. The major does not seem to have considered the possibility that Somoza might have been acting on his own account. This reflected standard thinking on US recognition policy. Harris was assuming that Somoza would not become president on ousting Sacasa because a Somoza government would not be recognized by the United States. If Moncada were first designate at the time of Sacasa's resignation, however, he could claim constitutional legitimacy.

Doubtless Moncada was a hostile individual who had made way for Sacasa only with great reluctance, but Somoza's own activities could hardly be gainsaid. The general had begun serious political campaigning in his own right and was using Guardia resources to finance a new daily, *La Nueva Prensa*, which was highly critical of the Sacasa administration.[44] This campaigning was not yet explicitly for the presidency, but Somoza was clearly positioning himself for the 1936 presidential race. He had thirty months before the polls to secure enough popular support to be able to demand the necessary changes to the constitution.[45] Sacasa's actions, or lack of them, did nothing to help. The president appears to have been incapable of acting with any self-reliance or strength of purpose, and opted instead for a heavy dependence on Lane's activities.

---

[42] 817.00/8033, Lane to Hull, 24 Apr. 1934; 817.00/8035, Lane to Hull, 26 Apr. 1934; 817.00/8038, Lane to Hull, 4 May 1934.

[43] 817.00/8041, military intelligence report, 24 Apr. 1934.

[44] 817.00/8054, Lane to Hull, 25 May 1934.

[45] The constitution prohibited the election of anyone who had held a military command within six months of the polls, and of anyone within four degrees of blood relationship to the incumbent. Somoza was ineligible on both counts.

The administration lost control of Congress through its own apathy. It should at least have been able to dominate the various committees but its paralysis in the face of US indifference gave management of those committees to hostile elements. By May the administration was controlled not only by Congress but by the Guardia, acting through Congress as well as on its own account.[46]

*

Quite apart from the direct consequences of a negative attitude on the part of the State Department, another aspect of that stance—one that the department had apparently failed to anticipate—brought the Roosevelt administration directly onto Nicaragua's political stage. Having opted for a policy that could not but define itself in terms of renunciation, expressed as an absence of constructive action, the department could not justifiably object if the Roosevelt administration were to be allotted a role in the Nicaraguan political process by any of the factions within Nicaragua.

In the absence of official and specific expressions of policy at a time of crisis, US strategy naturally became subject to an interpretation based on the historical record. The perceived veracity of such statements—alleged or otherwise—as did gain currency within Nicaragua became dependent on the number of people who believed them. This process tended to be self-generating. By the summer of 1934 it was accepted as fact in Nicaragua that the United States was supporting Somoza for the presidential elections of November 1936. In the short term, this conviction was the inevitable result of the Roosevelt administration's silence in Nicaragua and US recognition of the Martínez Hernández regime in El Salvador, which was interpreted as a reversal of established recognition policy. Somoza alone had been informed that the policy remained unchanged.

The diplomacy of silence was a rich source of political capital for Somoza, who used his personal contacts and his own newspaper to spread the word that, as Washington's man, he had ordered Sandino's murder under instructions from the State Department. The political turmoil that these reports created raised questions in Lane's mind as to the value of good neighbourism in general and of non-interference in particular, and prompted him to put some basic questions to the department. Was a hands-off policy compatible with a good neighbour policy? What steps should be taken to prevent disaster in a neighbour's home? Such questions arose in several of his dispatches to the department and in a personal letter

[46] 817.00/8052, Lane to Hull, 23 May 1934.

to Welles. In his reply, Welles ignored the basic question but commented strangely that 'our hands off attitude has been productive, in my judgement, of good results.'[47]

The good results in Nicaragua took the form of a dire political instability that lasted throughout the summer of 1934. Maintaining a high profile, Somoza embarked on a series of banquets throughout the country, ostensibly spontaneous demonstrations of affection on the part of the people of each locality but clearly sponsored by the general and financed from Guardia funds. The fetes were unmistakably political in intent. Somoza was persistent in inviting Lane and other members of the legation staff to these functions, but the minister prohibited participation because of the political nature of the festivities. On 17 June, during a banquet in Granada, a drunken Somoza announced publicly that the murder of Sandino had been carried out under his orders and that Lane was furnishing the motive power for his ambitions. Specifically, he said that his tank would annihilate anyone who got in his way and that, though he was driving it, Lane was supplying the gasoline.[48]

Appalled, Lane resumed insistent requests for some specific, official statement from Washington. Two days before the Granada incident he had told Somoza emphatically that 'this general impression of support must be counteracted', clearly to no avail. In an urgent telephone call to Welles, Lane stressed that his personal efforts at mediation were lacking in force or purpose without official backing. He noted the virtually complete control that Somoza was exercising over the president, as well as Somoza's growing influence in Congress, and emphasized again that the political activities of the Guardia were motivated in large part 'by the general belief that we are supporting them'.

Lane's plan was for a statement from the legation on Somoza's activities and on his recent speech in particular, coupled with a general statement from the department. Welles was unhappy with this suggestion and rejected out of hand the idea of a department statement which was, in Lane's view, entirely the point. In the event, it was only with obvious reluctance that the department allowed Lane to prepare a legation press statement in response.[49]

[47] 817.00/8073, Lane to Hull, 14 June 1934; Crawley, *Dictators Never Die*, 87; 817.00/8037, Lane to Hull, 4 May 1934.

[48] 817.00/8075, Lane to Hull, 20 June 1934.

[49] 817.00/8076, Lane to Hull, transcript of telephone conversation, Lane and Welles, 22 June 1936.

Even here, however, the department severely limited Lane. His original draft made specific references to Somoza. The final version, revised in Washington, eliminated all such references, made a vague reaffirmation of general principles and transformed Lane's original into a weak denial that the minister 'was in any way endeavouring to influence political developments'. Quite apart from the fact that such a statement was manifestly untrue (Lane had been trying constantly to influence political developments) its front-page publication in all newspapers did nothing to counteract the rumours. Somoza, claiming American backing, began lobbying Liberal members of Congress to frustrate the government's legislative programme.[50]

Championing the adoption of the non-interference principle in a speech to the Woodrow Wilson Foundation in December 1933, Roosevelt had suggested that if he had 'been engaged in a political campaign in some other American republic, I might have been strongly tempted to play upon the fears of my compatriots of that republic by charging the United States of North America with some form of imperialistic desire for selfish aggrandizement'.[51] Those sentiments rightly justified non-interference, but they paid no heed to the consideration that the adoption of a policy of absolute non-interference might encourage certain factions to play upon their compatriots' fears by alleging US support. Deprived of official backing, Lane could only make personal requests to Somoza that he stop making such allegations. But with the Guardia and the public firm in their belief that Washington supported the general, and with Sacasa feeling unable to take any positive action without US cooperation, the political tensions were undiminished. Aware that nothing would be done, Somoza went to comical lengths to imprint the image of the *jefe director* and the State Department together on the public mind: in August, *La Nueva Prensa* published a statement defending both Somoza and Lane; it was purported to have been written by Sandino's mother.[52]

*

US non-interference in Nicaragua, then, in both its positive and its negative aspects, had a marked influence on the country's politics. Yet the

[50] 817.00/8071, Hull to Lane, 22 June 1934; 817.00/8082, Lane to Hull, 28 June 1934; Crawley, *Dictators Never Die*, 87.

[51] Quoted in Thomas H. Greer, *What Roosevelt Thought: The Social and Political Ideas of Franklin D. Roosevelt* (East Lansing: Michigan State University Press, 1958), 159.

[52] 817.00/8113, Lane to Hull, 6 Aug. 1934.

stated aim of the Roosevelt administration was to refrain from interference and to cease influencing domestic politics. Hull, turning noninterference into a sacrament, insisted on his ministers' 'religious adherence' to the principle.[53] Was this contradiction inevitable?

The issue of military and political intervention is probably the most emotive in the history of inter-American relations. The intervention in Nicaragua had been a turning point, since it gave focus to Latin American bitterness and spurred the first serious efforts in the United States to reassess the issue. The war against the Sandinistas, criticized domestically and embarrassing internationally, seems to have imbued US policymakers with a bleak pessimism as to Washington's ability to reinvent the nature of Central American politics.[54]

Overtly political rather than purely protective, military intervention gave rise to military occupation. Complicated political responsibilities, such as electoral supervision, were incurred. War against a guerrilla army proved expensive, fruitless, and ever harder to justify. US prestige was at stake. Press editorials were suggesting that what the United States was doing in Central America was little different from what the Japanese were doing in China. The US government called the Sandinistas 'bandits', the same label applied by Japan to its opponents in Manchuria. By the autumn of 1931, when Henry Stimson was attacking Japanese intervention in China, the aerial bombardment of Nicaraguan rebels by US marines was frankly embarrassing.[55]

As isolationism continued to mount in the United States and the worst effects of the Depression began to be felt, complete withdrawal—graceful or not—became the prime goal. The United States 'nicaraguanized' the war, created and trained an army to help resolve the military problems, oversaw an honest election to help address the political problems, and then left, never to return. This development was immediately portrayed as unquestionably preferable for both the United States and Nicaragua to the conditions that had previously obtained. Always implicit, however, was the suggestion of altruism, the notion that the United States had surrendered a right for the betterment of others. Nicaragua was to receive the benefits of American self-denial.

This is understandable. The pursuit of self-interest must generally be illuminated in the best possible light, and in this case the pursuit was not

---

[53] Cordell Hull, *Memoirs*, i, 310.

[54] Connell-Smith, *The Inter-American System*, 76.

[55] Raymond Leslie Buell, 'Getting out of Central America', *The Nation*, 135/3479 (13 July 1932), 32; Connell-Smith, *The Inter-American System*, 76–7.

exclusive. Good neighbour diplomacy was indeed marked by a genuine desire to modify the worst features of previous policy and to establish more cordial relations with Latin America. That in its turn was a self-interested objective but self-interest, after all, is the function of foreign policy. As the rhetoric of good neighbourism began to furnish the policy's own momentum, however, spokesmen for the Roosevelt administration appropriated the highly emotional issue of intervention, announced its passing, and used 'non-intervention' with abandon as a magic word, a part of Hull's near-mystical Golden Rule. The problem therein was that intervention might have been an emotive issue, but it had very firm roots. Intervention and its antithesis were legal concepts whose acceptance by the United States the jurists of Latin America had been struggling to attain for years, and their free rhetorical use as magic formulas simply confused the legal issue.

Hull's written reservation to the Convention on the Rights and Duties of States expressed his concern that the Montevideo conference had had insufficient time to draw up a precise definition of such basic terms as 'intervention'. It is unlikely that there would ever have been enough time to arrive at definitions on which all the signatories could agree. A consensus on the matter was then, and would remain, elusive. Hull nevertheless signed a document whose implications he did not really understand, and that document became a milestone in inter-American relations.[56]

Hull was aware that in Central America any comment by the US government or its representatives could influence events, that any US minister's statement, public appearance or arrangement of a meeting could change a situation, that even changes in protocol would be subject to discussion. Surveying this minefield, the State Department decided that the best course was to say and do absolutely nothing. Hull, a Wilsonian internationalist whose global outlook was of a world order founded on a system of legal restraints and economic harmony, apparently failed to appreciate the problems involved in such a policy in terms of day-to-day and year-to-year diplomatic relations.

When rumours of US sponsorship began to take hold in the aftermath of Sandino's murder, the Guardia was encouraged. The Roosevelt administration's refusal to comment in order to disabuse this notion further emboldened the Guardia and was taken as tacit approval not only of the assassination but also of the general trend of events. Somoza made this

---

[56] Connell-Smith, *op.cit.* 90; William Everett Kane, *Civil Strife in Latin America* (Baltimore, Md.: Johns Hopkins University Press, 1972), 124.

process a positive one and strengthened his own hold over the situation by publicly claiming that US support provided impetus to his ambitions. In this sense, non-interference influenced events to as great an extent as interference. The process was simply less direct.

This is not to suggest, at least in the Nicaraguan context, that application of the non-interference principle constituted interference, which is how these events (with the benefit of hindsight) have occasionally been read. It is perhaps more reasonable to identify interference by intent rather than by consequence. Given the power relations between the United States and Nicaragua, the two—intention and result—would generally be intimately related. The period of the good neighbour policy, however, has shown how distant they could be. If the 'interference' label is applied only where the two coincide, there was very little of it in the period 1933–6. The main aim was the contrary, not to become involved.

That non-interference could and did enhance Somoza's prospects is not of itself an accusation. The Roosevelt administration cannot be held ultimately and solely 'accountable' for his presidency and subsequent excesses without an unrealistically austere interpretation of the chain of causality, whereby a US minister had a limited say in the appointment of a military officer in another country who subsequently overthrew the incumbent government. Specific accountability is in any case hard to identify, simply inasmuch as the second intervention was initiated under Coolidge, the National Guard was trained and Somoza appointed under Hoover, and the *jefe director* took power while Roosevelt was in the White House. To blame 'the US government' suggests a consistency of policy objectives among different Washington administrations that is belied by the evidence.

While the Roosevelt State Department cannot be charged with ultimate accountability, however, some measure of responsibility is incontestable. Elements of good neighbourism between 1933 and 1936 are easily identifiable as having played a role in the outcome of that period in Nicaragua. Significant among these are the use and abuse of the notion of non-intervention. It has rightly been said that 'in an interdependent world it is inevitable and desirable that states be concerned with and try to influence the actions and policies of other states.'[57] In such a world, wherein a country like Nicaragua is in a certain relationship to a country like the United States, and given a certain historical record of their

[57] Edward McWhinney, 'The "New" Countries and the "New" International Law', *American Journal of International Law*, 60 (Jan. 1966), 23.

relations, the very existence of diplomatic ties can entail 'intervention' by one upon the other. In its strictest interpretation, the idea that 'no state has the right to intervene in the internal or external affairs of any other state', as embodied in law at Montevideo, was an impossibility for US–Nicaraguan relations: it could begin to be complied with only if the political, economic, cultural, and military influence of the United States were equivalent to that of Nicaragua, and probably not even then.

Taken literally, it was a treaty obligation (upon which basis the United States partly founded an entire policy) that existed to be broken. It was 'literally', however, that US assurances of non-intervention were taken in Latin America. The struggle for acceptance of non-intervention was fought in juridical terms for commitment to a legal concept based on principles that were enduring. This raised two problems: first, that the legal commitment was subsequently expounded by officials of the Roosevelt administration in the much less precise language of political rhetoric; and second, that governments do not endure, and one administration's adherence to or interpretation of such principles would not necessarily coincide with (and in Central America might very possibly controvert) its predecessor's.

Weaning is not always painless, but in Nicaragua the process need not have become so bitter. The attitude of the Roosevelt administration, justifiable as an effort to satisfy Latin American demands for non-interference and to avoid the assumption of new responsibilities at a time of strong isolationism, necessarily involved the abdication of responsibilities that the United States already bore. It indicated, moreover, a fundamental misjudgement on Washington's part and the uneasy blend of cynicism and naïvety that underlay US policy. Instructions from the State Department to the Managua legation continued to express surprise that the new diplomacy was not immediately comprehensible and joyously welcomed. Dispatches from Nicaragua reflected disappointment that this was not the case. Washington would nevertheless cling to the principle and would consistently refuse to accept the suggestions of American representatives on the spot.

In 1933, American political influence in Nicaragua could not simply be declared away as a thing of the past, as the State Department affected to believe it could. It was central to local politics. As far as Washington was concerned, the whole issue of its relations with Nicaragua centred on the policy of intervention, and the only alternative it saw to that policy was an entirely negative aloofness. American influence, however, was inherent. It could alter in nature, but it could not immediately diminish in extent. In Nicaragua, the future and stability of Sacasa's government was perceived to be no less dependent on the attitude of the State Department than had been his predecessors'.

From the outset the Nicaraguan government simply did not want a policy of non-interference applied to it, at least not a policy of the nature implied by good neighbourism, since such a policy contributed to its disintegration. Unsurprisingly, the policy was never supported by the governments of those countries in which US intervention favoured the incumbent. Even amid the intensely anti-American atmosphere of the Havana conference, the head of the Cuban delegation had declared: 'The word "intervention" has everywhere a glorious past. How much nobility and grandeur there has been in some interventions!... If we declare in absolute terms that intervention is under no circumstances possible, we will be sanctioning all the inhuman acts committed within determined frontiers.' This statement is not to be disregarded. Latin American jurists agreed on the rightness of non-intervention, but Latin American governments could diverge on the matter.[58]

In this connection three former presidents of Nicaragua, a Liberal and two Conservatives whose loyalists had waged actual war against each other, sent a personal letter to Hull from which it is worth quoting at length:

El principio de no intervención, caro a todos los pueblos latinoamericanos y en el que descansa la prestigiada política del 'buen vecino'... no debe excluir la cooperación amistosa que ha de practicarse entre los países de América, ya que la indiferencia ante los conflictos o desgracias de la nación hermana, de ninguna manera puede marcar una buena voluntad hacia ella... En el caso de Nicaragua, esa cooperación del Gobierno de los Estados Unidos fluye como una consecuencia del origen de la Guardia Nacional... Por nuestra calidad de ex-Presidentes de aquella República, conocemos perfectamente el valor efectivo de esa influencia amistosa en Centro-América y lo mucho que puede alcanzarse con ella firmamente dirigida hacia el bien, sin desdoro para la autonomía de nuestra patria, ni desprestigio para la política continental americana.[59]

[58] C. Neale Ronning (ed.), *Intervention in Latin America* (New York: Knopf, 1970), 65; Kane, *Civil Strife*, 118.

[59] 'The non-intervention principle, which is dear to all the peoples of Latin America and on which the prestigious policy of the "good neighbor" is based... should not preclude the friendly cooperation that must be effected among the countries of the Americas, since indifference to conflicts or misfortunes in a sister nation does not in any way reveal good will towards that nation... In the case of Nicaragua, cooperation on the part of the government of the United States arises as a consequence of the origin of the National Guard... As former presidents of Nicaragua we know perfectly well the real value of such

These sentiments were fully shared by American diplomats in the isthmus. Though the State Department ignored them, US ministers in Central America—Lane outstanding among them—recognized the problems. As late as May 1936 Frank Corrigan, the minister in El Salvador, wrote to the department:

The actual facts of past [US] performance in this area seem to have made an impression so deep that its eradication will be a matter of considerable time...It is my belief that the Department has prematurely removed, too completely, its moral influence, that such influence is expected and, if prudently exerted, is not looked upon with such hostility as was evoked in the past by impolitic pressure and actual armed intervention...Complete detachment as a permanent policy of the United States is simply not accepted.[60]

For the moment, detachment was the only policy considered.

*

In Nicaragua, the end of June 1934 saw preparations for the congressional primaries of the Liberal Party scheduled for 1 July. Moncada's rival in Rivas was Constantino Sacasa Caraza, a cousin of the president. The legation's second secretary, Allan Dawson, reported that Somoza was following his usual practice of disregarding his executive superior and acting as though the Guardia were an independent entity completely separate from the ordinary administrative organization of the country. Both the president and the *jefe director* made public expressions of impartiality in the elections but, Dawson noted, 'the meaning of impartiality to a typical Nicaraguan politician is hardly the dictionary definition'.[61]

There were no disturbances on the day of the Liberal primaries. Results in the districts where there were major contests were largely favourable to the government, and Moncada was defeated by Sacasa Caraza in Rivas. Alleging widespread fraud, Moncada announced his intention to run on an independent ticket in the October congressional elections, probably with Conservative support in return for his backing of some Chamorrista candidates.[62]

---

friendly influence in Central America and how much it can attain if it is used to good ends, without undermining our country's autonomy or discrediting American continental policy.' Author's English translation of a letter in Spanish by Emiliano Chamorro, Juan B. Sacasa, and Adolfo Díaz to Hull, 30 November 1936, reproduced in Sacasa, *Cómo e por qué*, 159–64.

60 817.00/8416, Corrigan to Hull, 14 May 1936.
61 817.00/8053, Dawson to Hull, 29 June 1934.
62 817.00/8087, Dawson to Hull, 3 July 1934.

Lane continued to hold interviews with all parties, urging Somoza to subordinate himself to the president, but he made little headway. Throughout the summer the *jefe director* continued to organize and address political meetings disguised as social functions, often unmindful of party division. In mid July another political ball was held in his honour, this time at Managua's Conservative Club. With the apparent understanding between Moncada and Chamorro, this was particularly alarming for the president.[63]

On 16 July a Captain Castillo, chief of the Guardia barracks at Estelí, was arrested on charges of treason and conspiracy to murder both Sacasa and Somoza. Said to be a protégé of Moncada, Castillo was tried by court martial and sentenced to twenty-five years' imprisonment. Somoza immediately appointed as his aides two lieutenants accused of complicity in the plot. Somewhat pointedly, Lane indicated to the department that Castillo had 'felt he could be another Batista such as in Cuba and that the United States and other countries would keep off'. The new low in Guardia discipline was a danger that Somoza himself often stressed to Lane. It seems likely that his intention was to emphasize that, while his own political activities were legitimate, the extra-constitutional and potentially violent anti-government movement of the organization he nominally controlled was something with which he could not but be swept along. While an assumption of power in this fashion would not entirely circumvent US recognition policy, it would at least be less of a challenge to that policy than a patently engineered coup. This possibility contributed to the re-examination of a policy that in any case appeared to have acquired a flexibility of interpretation.[64]

Somoza now formally confirmed to Lane that he had serious aspirations for the presidency. If he were to wait for the scheduled elections he would be constitutionally ineligible on two counts. Articles 105 and 141 of the Nicaraguan constitution prohibited the election of any individual who had held a military command within six months of the voting, and of anybody within four degrees of blood relationship to the incumbent.[65] The *jefe director* therefore had three courses of action: to resign his command and divorce his wife; to attempt to change the constitution; or

63 817.00/8098, Lane to Hull, 17 July 1934.

64 817.00/8091, Lane to Hull, 16 July 1934; 817.00/8096, Lane to Hull, 20 July 1934; 817.00/8097, Lane to Hull, 17 July 1934; 817.00/8013, Lane to Hull, 18 July 1934; 817.00/8097, Lane to Hull, 17 July 1934; 817.1051/874, Lane to Hull, 16 Aug. 1934.

65 817.00/8123, Lane to Hull, 16 Aug. 1934; 817.1051/874, Lane to Hull, 16 Aug. 1934.

to take over by force. Of these, the latter was the most immediate and the least personally inconvenient, but there was one major risk. Somoza hesitated to confront US recognition policy head-on. He must have reflected on the experience of Chamorro, who had striven to sit out non-recognition but whose presidency had lasted only ten months before US pressure forced him to step down.

Lane told his chiefs he was 'fairly certain' that Somoza believed 'that the government of the United States would not recognize a government that came into power by such means'.[66] This was, in effect, an indirect question on Lane's part because by now he must have been less convinced that such was in fact the case. He stressed that Somoza's restraint would not be indefinite, a view with which Sacasa evidently concurred. The president's fort at León was being rearmed under the supervision of his cousin Ramón Sacasa. All of Nicaragua's extra munitions were stored there. The Guardia military base at the Campo de Marte in Managua abruptly sprouted elevated concrete pillboxes with machine-gun emplacements, whereupon the presidential mansion was fortified with machine guns, bombs, and additional personnel. Somoza sent his wife and daughter to the United States for safety in the event of hostilities and, ever anxious to involve Lane, asked the minister to 'wink his eye' to indicate approval of the general's intention to change the command at the León fort without Sacasa's knowledge. Convinced again that the time had come, Lane insisted to the State Department that it do something positive immediately 'in order to be able to show that we had not in any way aided, *through inaction on our part*, any move against the constituted government'.[67]

*

Why, then, did the American representative on the spot, who had to execute policy, find himself in conflict with the diplomatic establishment in Washington that decided policy? Since Lane so persistently questioned executive judgement, it is fitting to ask how what he saw as a failure to appreciate the situation came about. Did Hull really believe, for example, that the execution of policy in Nicaragua was relatively simple, that non-interference obviated influence and thereby enabled Washington to avoid incurring responsibility?

Inter-war American policy-makers thought they were reviving the founding fathers' conception of foreign policy and appeared to believe

---

[66] 817.00/8123, Lane to Hull, 16 Aug. 1934.
[67] Ibid. Emphasis added.

that freedom from unwanted international involvement was a natural state occasionally disrupted by meddlers at home. Undisturbed, this state would persist indefinitely. The isolationist vision thus made no provision for the consideration that freedom from entanglements might be a goal that had to be pursued through action, not inaction, nor for the possibility that the attainment of such freedom might be determined more by political conditions elsewhere than by US disengagement.[68]

The United States had fought a fruitless and costly war in Nicaragua against a continental hero. Informed by domestic isolationism, withdrawal from the situation in political and military terms had, it seemed, to be absolute. This was impossible, a fact that Hull—whose knowledge of Latin American affairs was minimal—never seemed to grasp. For reasons already given, Lane questioned this policy on moral as much as on practical grounds. In this he coincided with Frank Corrigan in El Salvador, who pointed out to the State Department that implicit even in the term 'good neighbour policy' was some measure of moral responsibility.[69]

Cordell Hull, ironically, was a diplomatic moralist par excellence. His memoirs are relentless in their insistence on the moral principles underlying American foreign policy. Of themselves, the moral abstractions that fascinated Hull are hard to criticize, but they were of strictly limited use to somebody in the position of Corrigan or Lane. Like Woodrow Wilson, Hull envisaged a global system made safe from conflict by widespread international acceptance of a juridical framework of regulations governing the acceptable behaviour of sovereign countries. Diplomatic pragmatism, which Lane was obliged to display, was made secondary to the establishment of juridical criteria that would define the boundaries of relations between states. Only with difficulty could this approach make effective provision for the unruly forces of intra-state violence that might affect inter-state relations.[70]

Hence Hull's stress on the processes of the inter-American system, his emphasis on the hemispheric conferences, his insistence that all treaties be ratified by all the republics. Every problem would have its treaty, which

[68] Hans J. Morgenthau, *In Defense of the National Interest: A Critical Examination of American Foreign Policy* (New York: Knopf, 1951), 28–9.

[69] US Department of State, *Foreign Relations of the United States*, 1937, v, 523.

[70] Robert J. Bresler, 'The Ideology of the Executive State: Essays on New Deal Foreign Policy', in Leonard P. Liggio and James J. Martin (eds.), *Watershed of Empire* (Colorado Springs, Colo.: R. Myles, 1976), 3; George F. Kennan, *American Diplomacy, 1900–1950* (London: Secker & Warburg, 1952), 95–6.

nobody would violate, and the western hemisphere—indeed the world—would live at peace. This was Hull's Golden Rule. It was a substitute for diplomacy. Hull, moreover, had to reconcile his international vision with the prevailing isolationism. Thus, while his clear aim in Central America was not to become involved, he could assert in his memoirs that:

I felt that our principles could have little effect in the world unless they produced a bounteous harvest in our own neighborhood. We could not ask for closer co-operation throughout the world, we could not hope to point a better road to nations like Germany and Japan, unless we first showed that co-operation could work in the areas of the Monroe Doctrine.[71]

Hull's confusing blend of isolationism and internationalism sometimes found expression as a kind of diplomatic escapism, albeit of a highly moral form, that tended towards contradictions in foreign policy. Adherence to his 'principles' was allowed to take primacy over their effects. The secretary universalized the principles in less than modest terms in his memoirs: 'They were solid, living, all-essential rules. If the world followed them the world could live at peace forever. If the world ignored them, war would be eternal.'[72] In the Nicaragua of the mid 1930s, Hull's solid, living, all-essential rules were virtually meaningless, though it was on him—whether he liked it or not—that the continuance of constitutional government in large part depended.

Lane had been telling him insistently what might happen if the State Department failed to act. With hindsight it is evident that—as regards the imminence of a coup—Lane was crying wolf for some time, but in the end he was right. His chiefs for the most part ignored him. For Hull, it was not that events in Nicaragua were of no importance; they were simply not important enough.[73]

In this sense, the good neighbour policy appears to have been an unstructured attempt to create an integrated and hemisphere-wide bloc under US leadership and to remove policy distinctions between the Caribbean and Central America on the one hand, and South America on

---

[71] Hull, *Memoirs*, i, 309.

[72] Quoted in Norman A. Graebner (ed.), *Ideas and Diplomacy: Readings in the Intellectual Tradition of American Foreign Policy* (New York: Oxford University Press, 1964), 562.

[73] It is hard to know what was important enough for Hull. In 1934, General Hugh Johnson, head of the National Recovery Administration, said that events in Germany (he was referring to attacks on Jews) made him sick, 'not figuratively, but physically and actively sick'; Hull publicly disowned Johnson for that comment. See Hugh Brogan, *The Pelican History of the United States of America* (Harmondsworth: Penguin, 1987), 571.

the other. This contrasted sharply with previous doctrine, wherein the United States intervened in the Caribbean region almost as a reflex. Such thinking came under renewed consideration, but it was considered by Hull in less than concrete terms. Within a decade, the rise of the Axis and fears over the security of the Panama Canal would show that an attempt to establish political relationships with Central America on the same terms as relationships with the republics to the south was, at best, premature. Equally premature was the assumption that the revitalization of inter-Americanism, the establishment of a continental framework defining national conduct, and declarations of non-interference would have the same meaning in Managua as in Buenos Aires.[74]

Hull claimed that it was his 'profound conviction at all times... that any system of international relations must deteriorate and collapse whenever moral considerations are repudiated and abandoned'.[75] He did abandon moral considerations in Nicaragua, but his policy towards the country was neither immoral nor interventionist. Throughout Roosevelt's first term it was hardly a policy at all.

*

In the summer and autumn of 1934, Somoza strove to consolidate his position. He continued his political tours around the country and Lane strove to forestall the formation of too broad a power base, activities that he justified to an apparently indifferent State Department in terms of safeguarding American prestige.[76] In August the Nicaraguan Chamber of Deputies passed a bill by thirty-three to four granting an amnesty to Sandino's murderers. Alarmed at the possibility of Guardia violence and fearful of the precedent set by Batista in Cuba eleven months earlier, Conservative voters for the bill signed a statement explaining the vote. The statement acknowledged that the Guardia was responsible for the assassination but asserted that keeping the military 'in a state of worry' over possible legal action was not conducive to public order: 'We must avoid, so far as we can, the possibility of destructive fomentation within the Army taking body, menacing us with copies of sergeants' coup d'etats

[74] Bresler, 'The Ideology of the Executive State', 66. As recently as Nov. 1930, when the then Secretary of State, Henry Stimson, was considering a new US policy statement on Latin America (which in the event was never made), he contemplated multilateralizing US policy by having Latin American countries join the United States in any intervention. But he believed that such cooperation should include only South America, not the countries of the isthmus. See William Kamman, *A Search for Instability: United States Diplomacy toward Nicaragua, 1925–1933* (Notre Dame, Ind.: University of Notre Dame Press, 1968), 199.
[75] Hull, *Memoirs*, i, 351.   [76] 817.00/8110, Dawson to Hull, 28 July 1934.

which in other countries are causing public misfortune and national destruction. Let us vote to forgive and forget.'

Quoting Goethe ('I prefer injustice to disorder'), the statement was a forceful expression of congressional weakness in the face of an armed force with as yet no place in the constitution. The Senate, similarly concerned that the Guardia might react violently against any decision prejudicial to military interests, voted for the amnesty by a large majority. The National Guard was now, in effect, a law unto itself.[77]

On 12 September there was another explosion at the Guardia's Campo de Marte base in Managua. Sacasa again declared a state of siege. The scene at Tiscapa Hill was one of complete panic. In the city, the general feeling was that the explosion was an unsuccessful attempt to eliminate Somoza. Lane's second secretary, Allan Dawson, felt that Federico and Crisanto Sacasa—the president's brother and cousin respectively—were among the most likely suspects and that the planning had been made without the president's knowledge. Both President Sacasa and Somoza were highly alarmed. Managua was covered by Guardia patrols within five minutes and machine guns were mounted at strategic points and road intersections; private telephone lines were cut. In the streets the scene was one of panic as a mass of people streamed out of the danger zone to the outskirts. The personal bodyguard squads of both Somoza and Sacasa increased. Neither would thereafter move far without a significant security detail.[78]

Sacasa again cracked down on the Conservatives. With the approach of the congressional elections, the Conservatives had already begun to arm themselves in preparation for giving some substance to their inevitable accusations of fraud. 'There is no doubt in my mind', Dawson averred, 'that the Conservatives are receiving iniquitous treatment.'[79] The manoeuvres of the Liberal strategists—notably Federico Sacasa, the real power behind the throne in the absence of the president's wife María, who was in the United States—were certainly short-sighted. Most of the

---

[77] 817.00/8126, Dawson to Hull, 24 Aug. 1934: 817.00/8127, Dawson to Hull, 5 Sept. 1934; Knut Walter *The Regime of Anastasio Somoza, 1936–1956* (Chapel Hill: University of North Carolina Press, 1993), 35.

[78] 817.00/8135, Dawson to Hull, 13 Sept. 1934; 817.00/8136, Dawson to Hull, 12 Sept. 1934; 817.00/8136, Dawson to Hull, 14 Sept. 1934; 817.24/282, Dawson to Hull, 13 Sept. 1934. Some reports suggest that the September explosion was simply part of a personal quarrel between the Managua police chief and the Guardia's quartermaster. See Millet, *Guardians*, 170 and 185 n. 12.

[79] 817.00/8145, Dawson to Hull, 27 Sept. 1934; 817.00/8174, Dawson to Hull, 5 Oct. 1934.

Nicaraguan electorate was Liberal and the party would therefore win in any case by retaining a two-thirds majority in fair elections. In tampering with the polls, the Sacasas were simply building up trouble for the future.[80]

In the event, there was little disorder on polling day. The Conservatives lost one Senate seat. In the Chamber of Deputies they lost two seats and gained one. The next Congress would therefore be composed of seventeen Liberals and seven Conservatives in the Senate, and thirty Liberals and thirteen Conservatives in the Chamber. Chamorro lost to the Liberal in Matagalpa, and Moncada withdrew his candidacy in Rivas. That these two were eliminated from the immediate parliamentary picture could not but be a source of anxiety for the president, since their extra-parliamentary activities were likely to intensify.[81]

Through contacts with 'a close relative of General Emiliano Chamorro', the US legation learned of a coup planned by Somoza for the end of December or the early part of January 1935. In view of recent developments in the Guardia—the Castillo plot and most recent arsenal explosion—Somoza had 'either to show his fangs or be rubbed out himself', by which Dawson meant that the desperation of a man who sees his power slipping might lead the *jefe director* to run the risk of non-recognition, though Washington's resumption of diplomatic ties with the Martínez regime in El Salvador must have allayed Somoza's misgivings on this point to some degree. In the final quarter of 1934 his premature presidential campaign (for elections that were two years away) began assuming proportions necessarily alarming to Sacasa and his advisers. From November, these were in violation of an executive decree prohibiting campaign activities less than ten months before the elections of December 1936.[82]

Towards the end of the year, according to Dawson, 'the rumour factory started mass production'. On 17 November the president, his family, and the entire cabinet again left Managua for León. On the following day, Somocista propaganda culminated in a mass rally of support in Managua where the speeches, which Dawson heard himself, referred to Somoza as the 'Hitler and Mussolini' of Nicaragua. The expenses were met from

[80] RG 38 C-10-d 6473-E, United States Electoral Mission, intelligence section, intelligence report, 1 Dec. 1932.

[81] 817.1051/872, Lane to Hull, 18 Aug. 1934; 817.00/8155, Dawson to Hull, 10 Oct. 1934.

[82] 817.00/8156, Dawson to Hull, 15 Oct. 1934; 817.00/8168, Dawson to Hull, 20 Nov. 1934.

Guardia funds. The strongest rumour held that Sacasa would demand the general's resignation and, in the event of a refusal, would take military action. The president, safe in his home city, could arm three thousand fellow Leonenses with arms from the local arsenal and advance on Managua.[83]

Somocista propaganda continued quite openly, and illegally, in outlying areas, and was particularly effective in Matagalpa. There were regular press reports of the meetings of the committee to organize the *jefe director*'s campaign. Activities on behalf of Espinosa and Arguello also persisted. In the meantime, attempts to elicit some statement of a political position from the US legation were becoming absurd: one member of Somoza's entourage asked for a comment on the possibility of recognition of a military government from Mr Tompkins, the legation butler.[84]

---

[83] 817.00/8167, Dawson to Hull, 17 Nov. 1934; 817.00/8168, Dawson to Hull, 20 Nov. 1934.

[84] 817.00/8173, Dawson to Hull, 4 Dec. 1934; 817.00/8175, Dawson to Hull, 11 Dec. 1934; 817.00/8177, Dawson to Hull, 28 Dec. 1934.

3

Good Neighbour Economics in Nicaragua, 1933–1936

> Business underlies everything in our national life, including our spiritual life. Witness the fact that in the Lord's Prayer the first petition is for daily bread. No one can worship God or love their neighbor on an empty stomach.[1]
>
> Woodrow Wilson
> 1912

The Depression shifted US attention from purely political matters to economics. By 1933 the country's GNP had fallen by 29 per cent from its 1929 level. Industrial production had declined by more than half. About a quarter of the labour force was unemployed. The day before Roosevelt took the inaugural oath the banking system virtually collapsed; the New York Stock Exchange suspended operations. The country's economic survival seemed imperilled.[2]

These conditions further nourished isolationist sentiment. Intense public scepticism of economic internationalism was echoed by a strongly isolationist Congress, whose support Roosevelt needed in order to implement his New Deal. In his inaugural address he dashed hopes of immediate international measures to foster internal recovery: 'our international trade relations, though vastly important, are in point of time and of necessity secondary to the establishment of a sound national economy.

---

[1] *New York Times*, 24 May 1912.

[2] Michael Grow, *The Good Neighbor Policy and Authoritarianism in Paraguay: United States Economic Expansion and Great-Power Rivalry in Latin America during World War II* (Lawrence: Regents Press of Kansas, 1981), 5–6; William E. Leuchtenburg, 'Franklin D. Roosevelt and the New Deal, 1933–1940', in Arnold A. Offner (ed.), *America and the Origins of World War II, 1933–1941* (Boston: Houghton Mifflin, 1971), 1–2.

I favour as a practical policy the putting of first things first.'[3] Domestic revival through economic nationalism therefore took priority, a programme to which the administration committed itself in the National Industrial Recovery Act and the Agricultural Adjustment Act. This stance was underlined by Roosevelt's message to the London Economic Conference in July, in which he rejected proposals for international currency stabilization and countermanded Hull's recommendations on multilateral tariff reductions.[4]

Hull, arguing that the crisis was aggravated by economic nationalism, had always advocated freer international trade on the grounds that the commercial system that emerged from the Depression no longer coincided with American interests. The methods adopted throughout the globe to attenuate the crisis tended to consist of higher tariffs or preferential bilateral and quota arrangements that regionalized trade rather than multilateralizing it as Hull urged. Bilateral agreements reduced American export trade. In 1929, the US share of world imports stood at 16.8 per cent. This fell to an average of 12.8 per cent in the period 1933–8. The decline represented a greater cut in foreign trade than that of any other major power, with US exports falling from $5,240 million in 1929 to $1,675 million in 1933.[5]

In Latin America, the barter arrangements of Britain, France, and Germany were undercutting the US position and American exporters were finding it hard to compete. The 78 per cent drop in the value of US export trade to Latin America between 1929 and 1932 was the greatest decline for any regional export market except Oceania. US imports from Latin America over the same period showed a decline of 68 per cent. Such figures gave force to Hull's insistent arguments that the United States should launch a vigorous trade programme. He had concluded after the London conference that the structure of the world's trade barriers was too complicated to allow for easy negotiation of multilateral tariff cuts, and he came to favour bilateral accords on an unconditional 'most favoured nation' basis.[6]

[3] Samuel Rosenman (ed.), *Public Papers and Addresses of Franklin D. Roosevelt* (New York: Random House, 1938), ii, 11–16; Dick Steward, *Trade and Hemisphere: The Good Neighbor Policy and Reciprocal Trade* (Columbia: University of Missouri Press, 1975), 13.

[4] S. Adler, *The Unknown Giant, 1921–1941: American Foreign Policy between the Wars* (New York: Macmillan, 1965), 150; Cordell Hull, *Memoirs* (New York: Macmillan, 1948), i, 248; Steward, *Trade and Hemisphere*, 15.

[5] Frederick C. Adams, *Economic Diplomacy: The Export-Import Bank and American Foreign Policy, 1936–1939* (Columbia: University of Missouri Press, 1976), 43–4.

[6] Francis B. Sayre, *Tariff Bargaining* (Washington DC: US Government Printing Office, 1934), 1; Paul Varg, 'The Economic Side of the Good Neighbor Policy', *Pacific*

Roosevelt's position on trade was less clear. Ill-informed on commercial matters, he tended to waver between calls for protectionism and advocacy of lower tariffs, but as the New Deal faltered during 1933 Hull's persistence began to bear fruit. His scope was widened by a disturbing decline in July and by the clear concern of private groups, notably the National Foreign Trade Council and the New York Chamber of Commerce. American exporters, used to trading mainly with a Europe now shielded by very high tariff barriers, turned their attention to potential new markets in Latin America and Asia.[7]

The State Department asked the Bureau of Foreign and Domestic Commerce to examine US trade with individual countries as a basis for future policy decisions, and by the autumn of 1933 the administration was reactivating its trade policy. In November, Roosevelt established the Executive Committee on Commercial Policy to oversee trade strategy. Concluding that the reinvigoration of export trade was essential, the committee advised that Congress should give Roosevelt the authority to alter the US tariff structure. In December, Roosevelt issued a statement that declared: 'now the time has come to initiate the second part of the recovery programme and to correlate the two parts; the internal adjustment of production with such effective foreign purchasing power as may be developed by reciprocal tariffs, barter, and other international arrangements.'[8]

During the Montevideo conference of the same month, the administration began to translate the theory into practice. On 16 December 1933 the conference accepted a Resolution on Economic, Commercial and Tariff Policy aimed at trade liberalization and pledging signatories to reduce trade barriers through bilateral reciprocal agreements based on mutual concessions. In the United States, the Reciprocal Trade Agreements Act was formulated as an amendment to the Hawley–Smoot Tariff Act in the following June. It authorized the president to raise or cut

Historical Review, 45 (Feb. 1976), 47–71; Steward, *Trade and Hemisphere*, 18; Julius W. Pratt, *Cordell Hull, 1933–1944*, 2 vols., The American Secretaries of State, 12–13 (New York: Cooper Square Publishers, 1964), i, 109; Lloyd C. Gardner, *Imperial America: American Foreign Policy since 1898* (New York: Harcourt Brace Jovanovich, 1976), 69.

[7] Harry C. Hawkins and Janet L. Norwood, 'The Legislative Basis of US Commercial Policy', in William B. Kelly (ed.), *Studies in United States Commercial Policy* (Chapel Hill: University of North Carolina Press, 1963), 69; Adams, *Economic Diplomacy*, 61–2; *Business Week*, 22 July 1933, 27.

[8] Adams, *Economic Diplomacy*, 63–5; Steward, *Trade and Hemisphere*, 19; Edgar O. Guerrant, *Roosevelt's Good Neighbour Policy* (Albuquerque: University of New Mexico Press, 1950), 104.

tariffs by up to 50 per cent, or to bind the current tariffs, in pursuit of bilateral trade agreements. Tariff-free items could not be moved to the dutiable list, and dutiable items could not be admitted free. Negotiations were to be coordinated by an inter-departmental Committee on Trade Agreements and the State Department's division of trade agreements, both bodies under the direction of the assistant secretary of state Francis Sayre. The former group produced an initial country survey before a 'country committee' was set up to undertake a detailed analysis. Lane and his colleagues at the Managua legation were to conduct the actual negotiations between the United States and Nicaragua. The reciprocal trade agreements programme was to be the heart of good neighbour economics during Roosevelt's first term.[9]

*

Nicaragua accepted the Montevideo Resolution on Economic, Commercial, and Tariff Policy against its own interests. The country's main foreign debt was the £1,250,000 Ethelburga bond issue of 1909, which had been floated for the most part in London and for which the entire customs revenue was pledged. Financial reform had been an objective of the Taft administration's Caribbean policy and, in Nicaragua, Guatemala, and Honduras, the administration had sought to refund the European debts through loans from American banks. The Knox–Castrillo Convention of 1911, by which Nicaragua was to receive $15 million under a bond issue from Brown Brothers and Seligman, looked towards refunding the Ethelburga debt. The treaty went unratified by the US Senate, but Nicaragua and the American banking interests had arranged for a loan of $1.5 million on a similar basis to the October 1910 Dawson agreements that had informed the Knox–Castrillo Convention. The loan was secured by customs revenues. A receivership was established, the office being created under the terms of the Treasury Bills Agreement of 1911 between Nicaragua and the bankers. Under this arrangement, Nicaragua could not alter tariff operations without the consent of the bankers. In December 1911 Clifford Ham, a US citizen, was appointed collector general of Nicaraguan customs.[10]

---

[9] Kenneth J. Grieb, 'Negotiating a Trade Agreement with Guatemala', *Prologue*, Spring 1973, 22–3; Pratt, *Cordell Hull*, i, 113–14; Steward, *Trade and Hemisphere*, 20; Oscar R. Strackbein, *American Enterprise and Foreign Trade* (Washington DC: Public Affairs Press, 1965), 1, 30–5; Francis B. Sayre, *Glad Adventure* (New York: Macmillan, 1957), 170–3.

[10] Thomas Dawson, the US minister in Panama, was sent to Managua in October 1910 to help establish a government following the downfall of the administration of José Santos Zelaya (1893–1909) and that of his hand-picked successor, José Madriz (1910).

In June 1912 the American bankers managed to secure an adjustment of the British claims and the customs collectorship took over the servicing of the Ethelburga loan. By 1924 Nicaragua had met all its obligations to the New York bankers but the collectorship was retained. Its maintenance afforded the country a lower rate of interest in servicing the debt. Irving Lindberg succeeded Clifford Ham as collector general in 1928.[11] From 1917 the collectorship was complemented by a high commission (the high commissioner being a US citizen selected by the Secretary of State) whose duties included supervision of the government's monthly expenditure and acting as fiscal agent for an issue of guaranteed customs bonds.[12] By the beginning of the Sacasa administration, Nicaragua's credit standing was such that the country's bonds were quoted higher than any other Latin American issue known to Lindberg. In 1932, amortization payments on the Ethelburga loan were five years ahead of schedule. On Nicaragua's only other outstanding debt—the guaranteed customs bonds of 1918—payments were seventeen years ahead of schedule. There were no outstanding obligations to American banks.[13]

Unlike Guatemala and Costa Rica, where debt default allowed growth in imports, Nicaragua continued to meet its debt commitments to the end of 1931. Thereafter, the country successfully appealed to its creditors to make amortization payments at a reduced rate and, in 1932, to suspend these. Interest payments were continued. Obliged to attempt to reduce imports as foreign exchange earnings from exports were eroded, Nicaragua suffered a severe loss of revenue from its major source, taxes on external trade. In 1933, 64 per cent of the government's total income was derived from import duties. The increase in the monthly budget deficit

---

The Dawson agreements established a mixed claims commission to arbitrate contracts and concessions granted by Zelaya, and arranged a commercial bank loan to the Nicaraguan government guaranteed by the customs receipts. See Knut Walter, *The Regime of Anastasio Somoza, 1936–1956* (Chapel Hill: University of North Carolina Press, 1993), 11; Chester Lloyd Jones, *The Caribbean since 1900* (New York: Prentice Hall Inc., 1936), 397–8; Dana C. Munro, *The United States and the Caribbean Area* (Boston: World Peace Foundation, 1934), 231–3; 817.51/2469, Memorandum, Diven, 22 Aug. 1934; US Department of State, *Nicaragua*, Information Series, 77 (Washington DC: US Government Printing Office, 1935).

[11] Jones, *The Caribbean*, 397–8.
[12] William Kamman, *A Search for Stability: United States Diplomacy toward Nicaragua, 1925–1933* (Notre Dame, Ind.: University of Notre Dame Press, 1968), 222.
[13] Collector General of Customs and High Commission, *Report for the Period of January 1, 1932 to December 31, 1932* (Managua: s.n., 1933), 3; Jones, *The Caribbean*, 403; Collector General of Customs and High Commission, *Report for the Period of January 1, 1934 to December 31, 1934* (Managua: s.n., 1935), 9; *New York Times*, 21 Feb. 1932.

throughout the year was in almost direct proportion to the reduction in the country's main source of income.[14]

While the Montevideo conference was in session to consider Hull's economic proposals, President Sacasa had attempted to explain to Lane that Nicaragua's tariffs were essential for revenue and that income could not be allowed to fall further. Largely neglecting to detail the strong financial arguments in favour of this position, the president resorted to the weaker rationale that the government's ability to reduce import duties was affected by its agreement with the bondholders, whereby Nicaragua could not alter duties without the prior approval of the customs collectorship and high commission. Sacasa evidently felt that Lindberg, who had an intimate knowledge of the country's financial situation, would not give his consent. Lane, however, had been 'authorized to express the hope' that Hull's proposals 'would meet with the sympathetic approval and support of the Government of Nicaragua', and Sacasa, desperate for US backing to his faltering government, instructed his delegation to support Hull in Montevideo. Tampering further with the Sacasa administration's tax arrangements was a prime goal of Hull's reciprocity programme in Nicaragua.[15]

Hull expounded the principles underlying his trade policy in quite distinct ways. According to the State Department document outlining the details of an agreement eventually concluded with Brazil, the aim of the programme was the expansion of

foreign markets for products of the United States (as a means of assisting in the present emergency in restoring the American standard of living, in overcoming domestic unemployment and the present economic depression, in increasing the purchasing power of the American public and in establishing and maintaining a better relationship among various branches of American agriculture, industry, mining and commerce).[16]

In testimony before the House Ways and Means Committee and the Senate Finance Committee on the Reciprocal Trade Agreements bill, Hull termed the project 'an emergency measure to deal with emergency

---

[14] Victor Bulmer-Thomas, *The Political Economy of Central America since 1920* (Cambridge: Cambridge University Press, 1987), 70; Jones, *The Caribbean*, 403; 817.51/2422, Memorandum, Orme Wilson to Duggan, 13 Apr. 1933.

[15] 710.G Economic and Financial Problems/27, Lane to Hull, 19 Dec. 1933.

[16] US Department of States, *Reciprocal Trade Agreement and Supplementary Agreement between the United States of America and Brazil,* Executive Agreement Series, 78 (Washington DC: US Government Printing Office, 1942), quoted in Guerrant, *Roosevelt's Good Neighbor Policy,* 94.

panic conditions'. Stressing its role as a recovery measure, he claimed that it was initiated 'for the express purpose of expanding our exports'.[17]

Some 63 per cent of Nicaragua's imports already came from the United States; the country had the lowest GDP in Central America. What mattered to Hull were the bigger economies. Cuba, for example, had once been among the ten best customers of the United States, buying as much as $200 million of American products. By 1932 the island's purchases in the United States had been cut to $28 million. US purchases in Brazil in 1932 ran to $82 million, but sales to the republic stood at only $29 million. From Colombia, the United States bought $60 million in goods while selling just $10 million. It was problems such as these that reciprocity, in its practical sense, was intended to tackle.[18]

As always with Hull, however, the reciprocal trade programme had its less practical dimension, which is what made it a 'programme' rather than simply a series of bilateral agreements. According to the theory, all countries would benefit from a reciprocity programme based on tariff cuts because the waning of economic nationalism would lead inevitably to a rise in the volume and value of international trade. The possibility that the theory could not make any agreement mutually profitable for its signatories was summarily dismissed by Hull as 'a shabby heresy'. Much freer multilateral trade was theoretically possible, since the inclusion in each agreement of an unconditional 'most favoured nation' clause meant that if any signatory to an accord should grant additional concessions to a third nation, the same privileges would automatically be granted to the other signatory.[19]

Another facet of Hull's vision was the notion of the 'road to peace'. Hull believed that the basic cause of war was the friction of economic forces. Everything, in the end, depended on trade: 'economic stability, financial stability, social stability, and in the last analysis political stability are all parts of an arch resting on the foundation of trade'. Five years before the outbreak of war in Europe, Hull's commercial project was, in his own immodest words, 'the only comprehensive and basic programme being

[17] William R. Allen, 'Cordell Hull and the Defense of the Trade Agreement Program, 1934–1940', in Alexander de Conde (ed.), *Isolation and Security: Ideas and Interests in Twentieth-Century American Foreign Policy* (Durham, NC: Duke University Press, 1957), 118–21.

[18] *Business Week*, 22 July 1933; Jones, *The Caribbean*, 374–5; US Tariff Commission, *Foreign Trade of Latin America*, report 146 (Washington DC: US Government Printing Office, 1942), 37, 41.

[19] Allen, 'Cordell Hull', 121; Grieb, 'Negotiating a Trade Agreement', 22.

pressed today which lays a foundation for peace'. Locating the causes of war entirely in the nature of commercial ambition ('true power', he wrote, 'became synonymous with economics'), the principles underlying Hull's economic diplomacy, like those informing the political commitments of good neighbourism, were solid, all-embracing rules that established a framework within which nations would legitimately operate on a basis of reciprocal concessions, mutual profitability, and equality of treatment.[20]

Hull instructed his legation in Managua to begin exploratory talks less than three weeks after the Montevideo Resolution on Commercial Policy. The prospects seemed bright. In 1933 the United States provided two-thirds of Nicaragua's imports and took half of the country's exports. Britain, the second most important source of imports, provided just 13 per cent. Germany, the second most important export market, took only 14 per cent of Nicaragua's foreign sales. Sacasa's clear dependence on American goodwill also seemed to offer a favourable backdrop to the talks.[21] For the foreign policy establishment concerned with Latin America the initiative seemed to give positive economic substance to political commitments that thus far had been negative. The policy statements on reciprocity emanating from Washington enshrined it as the best possible response to a dispiriting international outlook. Even Welles, whose disagreements with Hull on matters of foreign policy were often bitter, claimed that the reciprocity programme was 'one spark of sanity in a world outlook that seemed wholly and hopelessly dark'.[22] Utopian rhetoric, the curse of Hull's diplomacy, spawned an enthusiasm that rode roughshod over practical details. Circumstances seemed ideal. Lane furnished the Sacasa government with the American proposals in February 1934, and the problems inherent in their implementation in Nicaragua surfaced immediately.

*

Eight months earlier, a warning had been issued in the report of the Senate Committee on Foreign Relations to the American delegation at the London conference:

Certain foreign countries, even though willing to participate in general tariff reduction, are likely to insist on reserving the right to maintain, or even increase,

---

[20] Hull, *Memoirs*, i, 172; Allen, 'Cordell Hull', 126.

[21] US Department of State, *Nicaragua*.

[22] Cited in Allen, 'Cordell Hull', 128; Paul Varg, 'The Economic Side of the Good Neighbor Policy', *Pacific Historical Review*, 45 (Feb. 1976), 47–71.

their purely revenue duties. In some countries, certain duties intended primarily for revenue are a very important factor in total national budget and to reduce them might cause serious financial embarrassment. From the standpoint of increasing trade it would be advantageous that such duties be reduced, *but the trade advantage might be much less than the financial injury resulting.*[23]

The grave financial situation with which Nicaragua was confronted as a result of the Depression was aggravated by the high cost of the Guardia, the sudden loss of income until recently derived from US troops, and the 1931 earthquake. Coffee prices in the London market were continuing to fall. Banana exports from the Atlantic ports had fallen relative to recent years and the companies were reducing their labour force in all regions. At over a third of government spending, the Guardia appropriation represented the third highest percentage of budgetary expenditures in the world on a military establishment. Government income and debt service were dependent on customs receipts. Consequently, the Sacasa administration did not want any trade agreement with the United States based on tariff reductions and was highly reluctant even to embark on the discussions.[24]

The curious combination of self-interest and idealism underlying the policy, which had remained distinct when Hull was selling the programme to the president and to Congress, now came together in the negotiations to confront Washington's theorists with severe problems of implementation, since they were obliged from the outset of their dealings with Nicaragua to express the self-interest in terms of the idealism. The generalities of theory were simply not reconcilable with the bleak reality of the Nicaraguan economy. In the midst of the Depression the Sacasa administration was reluctant to tamper with the arrangements providing for its main source of revenue, in pursuit of an agreement that would entail a further and immediate reduction in that revenue.[25]

Another problem for good neighbour trade theorists was that a reciprocal trade agreement with Nicaragua on this basis was incompatible with existing commercial trends. Of the 1,148 items on Nicaragua's basic import schedule, only thirty-seven were admitted free. In the mid 1930s,

[23] RG 46 SEN 73A-F10, Special Memoranda Prepared for the American Delegation to the International Monetary and Economic Conference, London, June, 1933. Emphasis added.

[24] 810.50/14, memorandum, unsigned, 27 Apr. 1932; 817.51/2422, memorandum, Orme Wilson to Duggan, 13 Apr. 1933; US Department of State *Nicaragua*; 611.1731/136, Lane to Hull, 24 Aug. 1935.

[25] 611.1731/140, Warren to Hull, 1 Nov. 1935.

coffee and bananas accounted on average for over 75 per cent of the country's exports to the United States. In 1934, the total value of exports to the United States was $2,598,211, of which no less than $2,419,654 (93 per cent) consisted of coffee, bananas, and gold. All these products entered the US market free of duty. The balance of $178,557 (7 per cent), represented mostly by balsam, ipecac, and hides, either were duty-free or entered at a very low rate of duty. In fact, only 0.8 per cent of Nicaraguan exports to the United States were dutiable in 1933, making the difficulty of improving Nicaragua's position in US import trade immediately evident.[26]

It was clear from the outset that Washington was unlikely to be able to offer Managua concessions that were commensurate with those sought by the United States. US tariff cuts on exports that comprised only a small share of Nicaraguan sales to the United States would confer very minor benefits, which would be offset by the decline in revenue arising from Nicaraguan tariff cuts on imports from the United States. In essence, the State Department proposed to continue its existing tariff policy towards Nicaragua in return for Nicaraguan concessions. The idea of mutual concessions and profitability, as posited by the Montevideo resolution, never had any possibility of realization.[27] To suggest this was not, in fact, simply a shabby heresy.

The Sacasa administration realized this, as did Lane and his deputy at the Managua legation, Fletcher Warren. Whether Hull and the programme's coordinators in Washington realized it is less clear. More evident is that actual facts and figures were largely irrelevant. Given the facts, that the negotiations proceeded at all attests to the nature of the power relations between Washington and Managua, a special relationship that the Roosevelt administration had been summarily declaring away as a thing of the past. Negotiations for a trade agreement could continue only by virtue of that relationship. Highly dependent on the goodwill of the United States, the Sacasa administration could do little except stall.

Lane provided Arguello with the American proposals in February 1934. By April the foreign minister had not responded. Impatient at the delay, Lane visited him at the end of the month and was told that the matter would be discussed following Lane's return from an imminent trip

26 817.5151/121, memorandum, Beaulac to Welles, 21 June 1935.

27 611.1731/46, Department of State to the American legation in Managua, 1 Jan. 1934; US Tariff Commission, *Economic Controls and Commercial Policy in Nicaragua* (Washington DC: US Government Printing Office, 1947), 6. The same problem confronted negotiators in Guatemala; see Grieb, 'Negotiating a Trade Agreement', 25.

to El Salvador. On 11 May he visited Arguello again, but the foreign minister claimed that he had not yet had an opportunity to discuss the agreement with the finance minister, Francisco Castro. By mid July an increasingly frustrated Hull was demanding that Lane begin the talks before the beginning of September. At the same time, the Nicaraguan press began a campaign alleging that 'the United States and/or financial interests are attempting to exercise control over Nicaraguan affairs, particularly in the economic field', coupled with pleas for 'the economic and financial independence of Nicaragua' and 'the final liquidation of American intervention'.[28]

The latter was a good point. Despite the State Department statements and press releases that sought to deny responsibility, the department's Latin Americanists were patently confused as to the precise nature of US relations with Nicaragua. This problem was particularly complicated in the economic sphere. A week before the Montevideo conference, Willard Beaulac had solicited the views of personnel in the Latin American division as to whether the two governments enjoyed a 'special' relationship in view of the appointment of Lindberg, the creation of the customs collectorship and high commission, and US involvement in the financial plans of 1917 and 1920.[29]

Seven months later the question remained unresolved. Beaulac advised Wilson: 'I consider it important that the question of what obligations, if any, we still have be decided at an early date.' Definitive policy statements should not be made, he urged, 'until we are certain in our own minds of our obligations if any still exist'. A report was commissioned to clarify the position. Detailing US involvement with the arrangements that underlay Nicaragua's financial operations, the report concluded that such obligations did indeed exist since 'the circumstances surrounding the several transactions are such as justly to warrant the inference that this government not only consented to the terms of the agreements but it practically dictated them'.[30]

This was to state the obvious. The psychological impact of fiscal intervention was enormous in Nicaragua. Whatever the practical argument against a trade agreement in terms of financial arrangements and commercial trends, Managua's perception of its relations with Washington

[28] 817.0119/8 Lane to Hull, 7 July 1934; 611.1731/53a, Hull to Lane, 14 July 1934.

[29] 817.51/2469, memorandum, Beaulac, 5 Dec. 1933.

[30] 817.51/2469, memorandum, Beaulac to Wilson, 7 June 1934; 817.51/2469, memorandum, Diven, 22 Aug. 1934: 'A Note on the Relationship and Responsibility of the United States with Respect to Nicaraguan Finances'.

robbed the Sacasa administration of any bargaining leverage. As the Nicaraguan government stalled throughout the first half of 1934, that perception became Washington's best bargaining tool. Despite the rhetoric, the fundamental goals of the Hull programme were most directly informed by the immediate needs of American business. A charitable interpretation of this practical aim would be that it assumed the need for American commercial expansion, since such expansion was necessary for recovery in the United States and US recovery was a prerequisite to global stability. This raised questions about ends and means that did not occur to Hull when he resorted to threats. As the negotiations stagnated in the summer of 1934, the United States used as a bargaining weapon the threat to transfer Nicaraguan bananas and coffee, the mainstays of the economy, to the dutiable list.[31]

Lane was appalled at this threat and argued vehemently against it. The United States was not essential as a market for Nicaraguan coffee, taking only 6 per cent of the shipments in 1932. The bulk went to Europe, particularly to Germany. A threat to remove the product from the free list would be ineffective since it could have found outlets elsewhere. Bananas posed a very different problem. First, the entire crop went to the United States, and if Nicaragua were obliged at this stage of its financial crisis to begin seeking new markets the results could be disastrous. Second, the threat alone was likely to arouse enormous resentment in Nicaragua which, as Lane indicated to the department, 'would go against the idea of the good neighbour policy'. Third, all the banana distributing and exporting companies were American-owned, and a duty would therefore be detrimental to private US interests. Finally, Lane quoted chapter and verse from the Reciprocal Trade Agreements Act in an attempt to show that articles might not be transferred from the free list to the dutiable list by executive action. Lane clearly found the threat alone distasteful and felt that its implementation would probably be illegal, attitudes that he made plain to the State Department.[32]

Lane's arguments carried little weight in Washington. Even before the onset of the Depression, American investment in Nicaragua had been estimated at just $17 million for 1928. This was equivalent to half the value of US investment in any other Central American country. By 1933 the figure had fallen to $13 million, or just 0.3 per cent of total US investment in Latin America. American direct investment in Nicaragua

---

[31] 611.1731/57, Lane to Hull, 23 July 1934.
[32] Ibid.; US Tariff Commission, *Foreign Trade*, 52.

was therefore minimal, and it was explicit in the department that any damage to private interests would be offset by the potential advantages of a successful reciprocity programme throughout the hemisphere.[33] Welles, moreover, rode roughshod over the suggestion that the United States could not impose duty on duty-free items. In August he wrote to Lane stating simply that 'in the absence of any obligation to Nicaragua to retain products originating in that country on the free list, there is nothing to prevent Congress imposing duty on them if it so desires.'[34]

Lane had been mistaken in this one respect. No agreement had as yet been entered into, and the transfer to the dutiable list would therefore be proper. Lane's other arguments, however, and the spirit that informed his opposition to pressing the negotiations, were irrefutable. The United States was exploiting Nicaragua's economic weakness to force the Sacasa administration into a position that threatened its existence. In response to Welles's tetchy dismissal of his arguments, Lane defended his position at length in subsequent dispatches, doing his utmost to present a practical rationale that was specific to the Nicaraguan case.

Lane, whose position as American minister should have been to press the American advantage to the fullest extent, was doing a better job of arguing the Nicaraguan case than any official in the Sacasa government. He was in a better position to convey a view that Hull chose to ignore: that the perception of economic conditions in Nicaragua, and of the current negotiations in particular, was conditioned by the historical record of US–Nicaraguan relations. Hull, preferring to believe that a new age was dawning, chose to neglect the implications of historical continuity. He had, moreover, embarked on something that amounted to more than various trade treaties with different countries: he had launched a global 'programme' that was laying the foundations for perpetual global peace. Lane, in that light, was a pest. His objections were extraneous details.

Lane, however, seems to have been irrepressible. Citing as a base for his position 'the character of our past relations with Nicaragua, with the resultant impression here obtaining that Nicaragua's economic and financial matters are controlled by the Department or by interests in the United States', he stressed a number of points that, he felt, made it

[33] 811.503110/34, memorandum, Briggs, citing figures from Paul D. Dickens, *American Direct Investment in Foreign Countries*, US Department of Commerce, *Information Bulletin*, 731 (Washington DC, 1930) 18–19; US Department of Commerce, *A Balance of International Payments of the United States in 1933* (Washington DC: US Government Printing Office, 1934).

[34] 611.1731/57, Welles to Lane, 24 Aug. 1934.

advisable 'to defer the actual negotiations until such time as political, financial and economic conditions in this country are more stable'.

First, he thought it would be a mistake for the United States to incur responsibility for tariff concessions that reduced government revenues further unless Nicaragua were to secure comparable concessions to help offset the losses. Lane suggested an increased sugar quota. In 1927 Nicaragua had supplied 57 per cent of the dutiable sugar imported into the United States from countries other than Cuba. By 1932 this had fallen drastically.[35]

Second, wheat flour headed the list of commodities for which the State Department was seeking concessions from Nicaragua. It was the most significant import of any single commodity in 1933 and virtually all of it came from the United States. Nicaragua, however, was trying to develop the local milling of wheat; in 1934 it was in the process of building the necessary mill. Any concession granted on wheat flour would paralyse the infant industry.

Third, Lane's abiding concern was the National Guard, since it was vital that Sacasa remain solvent enough to pay the armed forces. Lane argued that any significant loss of revenue at this stage threatened the Sacasa government not only with bankruptcy but with the inability to pay a Guardia already seeking a pretext to revolt. It was in this month that Captain Castillo at the Estelí barracks tried to organize a mutiny. Lane stressed that the situation would become critical when the treasury could no longer provide funds for Guardia salaries. A week later the legation's secretary, Allan Dawson (perhaps at Lane's urging), made precisely the same point in his own dispatch to Hull. It is unlikely that any banking institution would have made a loan to Nicaragua for the purpose of having it squandered on the National Guard.[36]

Lane, quite simply, wanted the State Department to call a halt to the proceedings. He echoed the year-old warning of the Senate Foreign Relations Committee that any trade advantage for the United States might be much less than the financial damage to other countries, and he posed a basic question:

Is it worthwhile, from the point of view not only of our foreign relations but also of the possible financial gain to ourselves, to run the risk of increasing the hostile feeling towards us in Nicaragua; of being a party, even though unwittingly, to the

[35] 611.1731/57, Lane to Hull, 23 July 1934; 611.1731/59, Lane to Hull, 28 July 1934.
[36] 611.1731/59, Lane to Hull, 28 July 1934; 817.00/8103, Lane to Hull, 18 July 1934; 817.00/8110, Dawson to Hull, 28 July 1934.

financial collapse of the government here, with all the graver events which might follow in its wake; and thereby of undoing in Latin America some of the happy results accomplished as a result of the policy of the Good Neighbor?[37]

The department was not acting 'unwittingly', as Lane was fully aware. That particular parenthesis was an honourable man's concession to his chiefs. His dispatches over the previous months had been replete with figures outlining the prospect of Nicaragua's financial collapse if the American proposals were pursued. Under great pressure, however, the Sacasa administration agreed to negotiate. Six weeks after Lane suggested that his chiefs should stop, the State Department gave public notice of its intention to negotiate a trade agreement with Nicaragua.[38]

*

Having survived the threat to its main exports by agreeing to negotiate, the Sacasa administration tried the most obvious tactic. Three weeks after the formal announcement of talks, a new tariff was about to be presented to the Nicaraguan Congress. The proposed schedule made provision for raising the duties on precisely those items on which the State Department intended to seek concessions—notably wheat flour, lard, machinery, and cars. Washington's response was swift. 'The Department feels it has a right', Welles wrote to the Managua legation, 'to expect that the government of Nicaragua should refrain from increasing its import duties on products which are principally of American origin.' The legation conveyed this expectation to the foreign ministry, and Congress deferred consideration of the tariff.[39]

Obliged at least to appear to negotiate in the face of implicit threats and commercial trends that virtually ruled out anything that could be described as negotiations for mutual concessions, Nicaragua pushed its case for an increased sugar quota as the only visible means of salvaging something constructive from the negotiations. In May, Lane had informed the State Department that Nicaragua's basic aim would probably be to secure an American market for its sugar and by-products such as rum. Specifically, Managua would seek an annual quota of 10,000–15,000 tons.[40] From Lane's viewpoint, this was Washington's best bargaining tool, since it was not an excessive aim and would tend to

[37] 611.1731/57, Lane to Hull, 23 July 1934.
[38] US Department of State, *Press Releases* (Washington DC: US Government Printing Office), 7 Sept. 1934.   [39] 611.1731/161, Welles to Dawson, 28 Sept. 1934.
[40] 611.1731/52, Lane to Hull, 15 May 1934.

satisfy the government that it was securing some concession. It would, moreover, serve to promote local sugar production and would be worth about $370,000 to Nicaragua. The San Antonio plantation's warehouse at Chichigalpa was full of sugar with no outlet except to an American market.[41]

From Washington, however, the assistant secretary of state, Francis Sayre, made it clear that the United States would not grant an increased quota. A rumour began in Nicaragua that the country had been allotted a quota of 9,000 tons for 1935. In fact the US Department of Agriculture's quota regulations for the coming year had placed a ceiling of 3,000 tons on American sugar imports from Nicaragua. The State Department was anxious that these figures would further delay negotiations with Managua and informed the legation that it would be inadvisable 'to make the facts known to the public'.[42]

In the meantime the Nicaraguan government was, in the words of Lane's second secretary, Allan Dawson, 'at its wit's end to make ends meet'; Sacasa was still looking desperately for ways to increase revenue. The American threat to impose a duty on coffee, formerly of limited force, took on greater significance with Germany's introduction of regulations whereby Nicaragua would subsequently be able to sell coffee to its main market only to the extent that Nicaragua bought German goods. Sacasa wanted to boost imports from Germany and thereby increase exports, but his ideas were vague and other government officials were inclined to view the German market as lost. They were thinking about the development of new markets, particularly in the United States.[43]

Sacasa hoped to increase imports from Germany at the expense of purchases from Japan, and was therefore open to persuasion by a Mr E. C. Curtis, representative of the Textile Exporters' Association of the United States. The association had sent agents to each Central American country in an attempt to secure action to counteract the import of Japanese cotton goods, allowing US cotton exports—the most import item in American export trade with Central America as a whole—to maintain a position that was being eroded. Influenced by Curtis, Sacasa had decided to introduce a modified version of the Salvadorean

---

[41] 611.1731/57, Lane to Hull, 23 July 1934.

[42] 611.176 Sugar/40, Sayre to Dawson, 19 Oct. 1934; 611.176 Sugar/41, Welles to Dawson, 26 Nov. 1934; US Department of Agriculture, *General Sugar Quota Regulations*, ser. 1, suppl. 1, 9 Oct. 1934 (Washington DC: US Government Printing Office, 1934).

[43] 611.003/167, Dawson to Hull, 21 Nov. 1934.

preferential tariff scheme. The legation indicated to the department that no reduction in tariff rates that could plausibly be anticipated in a reciprocal trade agreement would enable American cotton exporters to compete with the Japanese in terms of price.[44]

By the following May, Sacasa was about to send the new tariff law to Congress. The measure might have led to the application of medium rather than minimum rates to American products, and Washington began to pressure the Sacasa government—with appeals to the Montevideo Resolution on Commercial Policy—'not to take any action which impairs this principle'. When these appeals failed to have the desired effect, the department again resorted to the kind of implicit threats that violated the spirit of the Montevideo resolution. The Roosevelt administration, Lane was instructed to inform Sacasa, 'cannot view with indifference such a law'. In the wake of the threat to tax Nicaraguan bananas, the Sacasa administration interpreted this as another admonition, and the Nicaraguan Congress subsequently adjourned without passing the bill. By July, Lane was able to report: 'I do not anticipate any action with regard to the passage of the three-column tariff bill.'[45]

*

Nicaragua had established exchange control in November 1931, the seventh Latin American country to do so since the onset of the Depression. The collapse of world trade, as well as commercial restrictions imposed elsewhere in attempts to promote self-sufficiency through import suppression, created grave exchange problems. Exchange shortages made it hard for the country to service its foreign obligations, or to purchase essential imports. The exchange position was particularly difficult because important enterprises such as gold and banana production were foreign-owned, so foreign exchange receipts for such exports were not commensurate with the value of the shipments. In 1931, exchange control was vested in the National Bank of Nicaragua. After January 1934, exporters were obliged to sell to the bank a percentage of the exchange derived from their exports, which the bank could then use to clear the blocked commercial balance arising from unpaid imports. Nicaragua's exchange

[44] 611.003/167, Dawson to Hull, 21 Nov. 1934.
[45] 611.003/178, Lane to Hull, 19 May 1935; 611.003/178, Hull to Lane, 25 May 1935; 611.003/180, Hull to Lane, 11 June 1935; 611.1731/107, Lane to Hull, 9 July 1935.

position, however, became increasingly acute; a growing number of unpaid claims accumulated. By the spring of 1935, claims for payment in foreign currency amounted to $1.5 million.[46] In the case of the West India Oil Company, non-payment had significant political repercussions in Nicaragua. Those developments are discussed in the next chapter.

From the beginning of 1935 the Exchange Control Commission seemed to be trying to divert part of Nicaragua's import trade from other countries to Germany, so as to secure a return on the exchange built up as a result of Nicaraguan coffee sales. Importers awaiting permits to bring in goods were informed that the necessary exchange could not be guaranteed, and that it might be several months before such exchange was available. They were then told that exchange would, however, be immediately available if they wished to import goods from Germany, on the grounds that Nicaragua had special rules governing its German trade. This was distinctly detrimental to US interests.[47]

Additionally, the National Bank of Nicaragua had entered the wholesale import business through a subsidiary, the Ultramar Corporation, and had begun importing much German merchandise. Plainly, it was easier for local importers to buy German goods when exchange was immediately available than to secure credit from American exporters to cover an eight- or nine-month delay in acquiring dollar exchange. The Central American Power Corporation had decided to make future purchases in Germany rather than in the United States because of the delay and uncertainty in securing exchange. The West India Oil Company, All American Cables, and Tropical Radio, all of them US companies, were facing similar problems.[48]

The ostensible purpose of the proposed trade agreement between the United States and Nicaragua was to stimulate trade between the two countries. Clearly, however, an increase in trade would be of little avail unless American exporters and American concerns operating in Nicaragua could obtain foreign exchange with which to transfer funds to the United States. In April the general manager of the National Bank of Nicaragua, Vicente Vita, left for Washington to secure a loan from the Export-Import Bank in order to make dollar exchange available to cover pending remittances.[49]

---

[46] US Tariff Commission, *Economic Controls*, 11; *La Gaceta* (Managua), 13 Nov. 1941; Executive Decree, *La Gaceta*, 17 Jan. 1934.

[47] 817.5151/92, Dawson to Hull, 18 Jan. 1935.

[48] 817.5151/95, Dawson to Hull, 21 Jan. 1935.

[49] 817.51/2525, Lane to Hull, 2 Apr. 1935.

In the State Department, Willard Beaulac opposed the extension of Exim credits to Nicaragua. The republic had enjoyed a good credit standing in the early 1930s. As evidenced relentlessly by Lane's dispatches, implementation of the trade agreement as the proposals now stood would make it harder for Nicaragua to meet its debt commitments. Now, one of Beaulac's prime objections was that Nicaragua was a poor credit risk. 'It is probably safe to say', he asserted, 'that no serious bank would advance a dollar to the Nicaraguan government under the conditions that obtain in Nicaragua today.'[50]

Beaulac's other main objection was another principle, that of non-interference. The State Department had threatened, in a gesture that had appalled Lane, to undermine the basis of Nicaragua's economy by taxing banana imports in order to force the republic into complete passivity in the trade negotiations. Beaulac now stated his argument, without irony, as follows: 'our entire hands-off policy would be dissipated as far as Central America is concerned.' Beaulac could conceive of 'no greater threat to our relations with the countries of Central America than the possibility that the Export-Import Bank will allow itself to become involved in the exchange situations in those countries'.[51]

George Peek, the president of Exim, was nevertheless inclined to look favourably on Nicaragua's application, and he submitted positive proposals to the State Department. Exim considered the Nicaraguan request for a loan to free blocked balances, and its Credit Committee recommended approving up to $1.5 million to liquidate American balances. These amounted to $783,531 and were divided among between three and four hundred US firms.[52]

Beaulac, however, continued to argue against the loan. Stressing that the Roosevelt administration was opposed to exchange control as a matter of principle, he argued that the Sacasa government was probably about to collapse and that economic conditions in the republic were so acute that the National Bank would probably fail or default on its obligations. The basis of his position, however, was political. Beaulac felt that he was averting accusations of dollar diplomacy because, if Exim became a creditor to the Nicaraguan government, 'instead of being a good neighbor we

[50] 817.51/2525, memorandum, Beaulac to Wilson, 19 Apr. 1935; 817.5151/107, memorandum, Beaulac to Wilson, 9 Apr. 1935.

[51] 817.5151/107, memorandum, Beaulac to Welles, 9 Apr. 1935.

[52] 811.516 Ex-Im Bank/83, meeting report, 15 May 1935; 811.516 Ex-Im Bank/99, memorandum, Heath, 27 May 1935; 817.5151/111, memorandum, Beaulac, 5 May 1935; 817.5151/114, memorandum, Beaulac, 15 May 1935.

would again be regarded as an international Shylock'. Dollar diplomacy had triggered intervention in the past, and thus Beaulac saw 'no reason to suppose that, if the Export-Import Bank became the creditor of a Central American government, or acquired a direct interest in the exchange situation in the Central American countries, there would not exist the same tendency for us to become involved in Central America'.[53]

The Latin American division split over the issue. Welles supported Peek's proposals, arguing that the non-interference principle could remain unimpaired since any other Nicaraguan government (identifying US goodwill as essential) would respect its obligations. Laurence Duggan, siding with Beaulac, opposed the Credit Committee's recommendation on the grounds that the political risks were too great and that the loan controverted a policy that asserted the inadvisability of Exim's becoming involved in the exchange situation in any Central American country as a matter of principle.[54]

There was something to be said for Beaulac's position, though neither he nor Duggan acknowledged its inherent contradictions. The United States was already a creditor to the Nicaraguan government, which was why the War Department had refused to sell arms to Sacasa. Dollar diplomacy, moreover, had simply entailed the use of US economic power to induce a change in government attitude in the Central American countries, something that the State Department had been doing since the start of the trade talks with Nicaragua. In specific cases, moreover, Beaulac's position worked against American interests and, in the particular case of the commercial programme, limited the utility of an agreement with Nicaragua from the viewpoint of American exporters.

The good neighbour policy had been based on the idea of reciprocity. Non-intervention was supposed to encourage Nicaragua to take no action detrimental to US interests. When the country did appear to take such action, as in the case of the proposed introduction of the Salvadorean tariff scheme, the State Department did intervene because that action violated a principle of the programme. It was the department itself that was here taking action that adversely affected between four and five hundred US businesses.

Finally, Beaulac himself—apparently hoping for a negative response—had commissioned a report that unfortunately had concluded that

---

[53] 817.5151/111, memorandum, Beaulac, 8 May 1935; 811.516 Ex-Im/83, memorandum, Beaulac, 15 May 1935.
[54] 812.151/107, memorandum, Duggan, 11 Oct. 1935.

US fiscal involvement in Nicaragua during the era of dollar diplomacy entailed existing, unspecified obligations. Those in his camp could not appreciate the nature of public and governmental perception in Nicaragua, where continuing economic intervention by the United States, regardless of what he believed to be the reality, was an accepted fact. Refusing to advance credit in the belief that it safeguarded the non-interference principle did nothing to counteract such thinking. On the contrary, in the light of the proposed commercial accord and Nicaragua's parlous financial situation, it reaffirmed it. Economic conditions were now so bad that in July the members of both chambers of Congress voted to reduce their own salaries by 10 per cent.[55] Beaulac, nevertheless, won the day. After considering his and Duggan's opposition during Exim meetings, the bank reversed the earlier recommendation of its Credit Committee and rejected Nicaragua's application. There was now little that the country could do but hope to obviate the worst impact of the trade agreement.

*

In Nicaragua, the treasury minister Francisco Castro continued stressing to Lane that any loss in revenue would immediately affect the government's ability to pay the Guardia, a prospect that evidently terrified the cabinet.[56] In a little over a month, as negotiations progressed and this possibility appeared increasingly likely, the Sacasa administration would be considering a pre-emptive strike against its own army through the agency of Honduran bombers.

The revenue problem arose because Nicaraguan imports from the United States covered a very broad range of commodity groups. Since the bulk of imports was accounted for by small purchases, Washington was trying to secure a total of twenty-four concessions (nine reductions and fifteen bindings), including products such as typewriters that constituted a small percentage of US exports to Nicaragua. But since the vast bulk of Nicaraguan exports to the United States covered a small product range, virtually all of which entered duty-free, a commensurate measure by Washington to compensate for the large number of concessions it sought from Managua would have to be on a single commodity—hence Nicaragua's continuing demands for an increased sugar quota and a sugar duty reduction.

55 *New York Times*, 22 July 1935.
56 611.1731/115, Lane to Hull, 24 July 1935.

Against his own wishes, Lane had informed Sacasa that a sugar quota would be ineffective since Nicaraguan sugar would be unable to compete in the US market 'because it is not completely white in colour'. In reporting to the department that he had carried out this instruction, Lane was careful to add that he had spoken to the American manager of a local sugar mill, who had informed him that a 20 per cent reduction in the duty of $1.99 per hundredweight for Nicaraguan sugar would enable the product to compete favourably in the United States.[57]

Lane believed that in the absence of a higher sugar quota a reciprocal agreement not only would damage Nicaragua's economy but ran counter to the principles of anything that could be called a good neighbour policy. He duly informed the department of the 'indefinite attitude' and 'apparent apathy' of Arguello and Castro, and of the complete lack of preparation in government circles. Eighteen months after Lane had begun talks, the Nicaraguan government still had no idea of what concessions it might ask for and was simply, in Lane's words, 'considering the advisability of asking us what we could give'.[58]

In June, Federico Sacasa visited Washington. His aim, according to Beaulac, was to secure US aid 'to assist in warding off complete financial and economic collapse'. Lane suggested that the Roosevelt administration grant a loan to Nicaragua. Beaulac, however, acknowledging that 'the natural place to look for such assistance is the United States', claimed that it was out of the question for the US government to consider advancing credit to Nicaragua or encouraging private interests to do so.[59] In the trade talks, however, Lane's persistent objections were starting to affect Beaulac. Now he admitted that there was so little the United States could give Nicaragua in a trade agreement that

grave doubt arises as to whether we should associate ourselves at this time with Nicaragua in a trade agreement which will not preserve Nicaragua from economic and financial collapse, but which may on the other hand cause us to be associated in the public mind with such a collapse if it does come . . . It is obvious that our detractors and the detractors of the trade agreements could with some appearance of justice maintain that our trade agreement, instead of helping Nicaragua, only increased its burdens and hastened economic collapse.

Beaulac himself, previously hard-line on economic relations, now suggested indefinitely delaying the negotiations.[60]

[57] 611.1731/117, Lane to Hull, 10 Aug. 1935.
[58] 611.1731/122, Lane to Hull, 17 Aug. 1935.
[59] 817.5151/121, memorandum, Beaulac to Welles, 21 June 1935.   [60] Ibid.

Hull and Sayre, however, remained adamant that the legation should continue the talks, though the Sacasa administration continued to stall. By the end of August, Castro had still not read the general provisions submitted by Lane, causing a postponement of a cabinet meeting to discuss them. He made a point of asking Lane as to whether Nicaragua would secure any advantages from the accord. Since in practical terms any honest answer to this question would have had to be in the negative, Lane was forced onto the defensive and could only attempt to assure Castro that it was not Washington's intention to reduce Nicaragua's revenues or impose an unfair treaty on the country.[61]

The matter was left untouched until October, twenty months after Lane had begun discussions, when the minister discovered that Castro had at least read half of the provisions, but those 'only casually'. The Sacasa administration, it seems, was trying to ignore Hull's trade programme for world peace in the hope that it might go away. Castro's objection now was that the foreign bonds were guaranteed by the customs receipts and that tariff reduction would not be possible without the bondholders' consent. The State Department, however, considered Nicaragua's difficulties in servicing its foreign debts to be outside the scope of the talks. Unlike the obligations of other republics in the region, the greater proportion of Nicaragua's debt—the Ethelburga bond issue of 1909—was floated in London and Paris. There were no outstanding obligations to US banks. Lindberg, moreover, assured Lane that the bondholders would follow his, Lindberg's, recommendations, rendering Castro's objection 'academic'.[62]

Lane's problems were exacerbated by the State Department's tactics. Because of the concessions granted by the Nicaraguan government to the owners of the Masaya flour mill, it was not possible for Nicaragua to reduce the duty on wheat flour; in fact there was a movement in the country to increase the duty on this product because Argentine wheat was then cheap. Wheat flour, however, was a priority for Washington. The country committee for Nicaragua had recommended 'in the circumstances' only requesting a binding on this item but the department, determined to make the agreement work in the face of the practicalities, was obliged for the sake of appearances to make pseudo-concessions. Lane was told to ask for a duty reduction on the product because it would then appear that the

61 611.1731/126, Lane to Hull, 24 Aug. 1935.
62 611.1731/134, Lane to Hull, 3 Oct. 1935; Jones, *The Caribbean*, 397; *New York Times*, 21 Feb. 1932.

United States had granted a concession to Nicaragua in subsequently withdrawing the request.[63]

As the negotiations bogged down in the winter of 1935, the gulf widened between the department's theorists in Washington and its negotiators in Managua. Lane and Warren, who were far more willing than their chiefs to give at least some measure of consideration to Nicaragua, advised the department not to proceed. Warren suggested that it was 'difficult to see what tangible advantages might accrue to Nicaragua' since sugar, the only product on which Managua might usefully seek a concession, had been excluded from the talks. He reported government officials as stating that if the United States did not make it profitable for Nicaragua to export sugar, there was simply no point in negotiating an agreement. According to Warren, the concessions sought 'would apparently not be of great benefit to us. American exporters already sell more of the articles in question than all of the other countries combined, and in many cases have a practical monopoly of the market.' He echoed Lane's suggestions that the department's persistence was aggravating the domestic political and economic problems, and concluded that 'there appear to be no real reasons for pushing the Nicaraguan government on the matter...except insofar as the Department feels that it should negotiate an agreement with Nicaragua as a matter of principle.'[64]

Here, Warren had hit upon a fundamental truth of the agreement. The commercial accord with Nicaragua was ill-conceived and poorly executed because it was based on a curious combination of the practical demands of US self-interest and vague expressions of inter-American solidarity and world peace. Both of these premises were considered more important than their effects in Nicaragua, because the principle of the matter had taken primacy over the results. In view of the existing trade patterns and the structure of the Nicaraguan economy, coherent American arguments in favour of the agreement could not be advanced. The United States had to rely on the power it enjoyed by virtue of the nature of its relationship with Nicaragua—a special relationship that the department had been insisting, since the departure of the marines, no longer existed.

Warren had implied that forcing a treaty might bring down the government, because the Nicaraguan public was outraged at what it saw as an

---

[63] 611.1731/134, Lane to Hull, 3 Oct. 1935; 617.003/267b, Hull to Lane, 1 Oct. 1935.

[64] 611.1731/134, Lane to Hull, 3 Oct. 1935; 611.1731/140, Warren to Hull, 1 Nov. 1935.

unfair accord and its criticism of the Sacasa administration was becoming 'so vehement as to make the negotiation of such an agreement inadvisable'. The State Department paid no regard to the warnings from its Managua legation. Sayre instructed the legation to stress 'the considerations which would seem to make an agreement of advantage to Nicaragua'. There being no such considerations in immediate and practical terms, Lane and Warren could deal only in potential benefits over the long term. These were possibilities that did not inspire the Sacasa government's great interest at the end of 1935, as it faced an openly hostile Guardia convinced of American backing. For the United States, the idea of concluding the agreement—as Warren had realized—had become simply a matter of principle.[65]

By the beginning of 1936, no constructive progress had been made since the previous September because of what Lane termed 'local inertia'. With the negotiations at a standstill, Nicaragua began to look elsewhere. Over the preceding months frequent press articles had been pointing to the desirability of closer commercial links with Japan, which had begun to seem the most welcome market for Nicaraguan coffee and cotton.[66] Less than a week after Lane informed the State Department of this turn in events, rioting broke out in Managua. The department had consistently ignored its representatives' warnings that this might happen.[67] Lane made a last effort to indicate the precariousness of the government's position, and argued that if the treaty were signed as it stood it would immediately form the basis of further attacks on the part of the Chamber of Deputies and the press. There was no sugar concession, and only one duty reduction had been conceded by the United States; but nine reductions and fifteen bindings had been demanded of Nicaragua. He suggested revising American demands: to request a reduction only on lard, with bindings on all the other items. This would have secured for the United States over 75 per cent of the value of the total concessions and bindings sought, while serving to counteract the impression that the United States was imposing a treaty disadvantageous to Nicaragua. The State Department, however, was not prepared to modify the agreement simply because Nicaragua considered it unfair, and suggestions that it might be

65 611.1731/140, Warren to Hull, 1 Nov. 1935; US Department of State, *Foreign Relations of the United States* (Washington DC: US Government Printing Office), 1935, iv, 84; 611.1731/142, Sayre to Warren, 15 Nov. 1935.

66 611.1731/145, Lane to Hull, 6 Jan. 1936; 717.94/2, Lane to Hull, 6 Feb. 1936.

67 These events, which owed much to Sayre's opposition to an Exim loan, are described in the following chapter.

unfair were considered irrelevant. 'The Department', Hull bluntly informed Lane, 'cannot consider seriously your suggestion.'[68]

The reason for this was simple. Washington had to assert economic domination in Central America while convincing the countries of the isthmus that reciprocity embodied an altruistic ideal of benefit to all. In order to do that the entire, hemisphere-wide programme had at least to begin to operate. Honduras had agreed to seventeen reductions and twenty bindings; Guatemala was about to agree to fifteen reductions and fifty-eight bindings; Costa Rica had consented to thirty reductions and seven bindings thus far. The department therefore insisted on all the reductions and bindings proposed in the Nicaraguan accord because US ability to impose such terms was essential to the entire programme. The republics were competing with each other as well as with the United States, and concessions to Washington could therefore undermine the relative economic position of each in the isthmus. Hence, for the programme to work to US advantage, the negotiations had to be conducted simultaneously. A refusal by Nicaragua to cooperate at this stage would arouse resentment in the rest of Central America and might jeopardize all the negotiations.[69]

In the end it was the practical demands of politics rather than any idealistic theories of economic internationalism that won the day. With the domestic scene increasingly ominous in the wake of the anti-government riots, the trade agreement came to represent for Sacasa his last leverage in an attempt to gain the favour of Washington, which until now had refused to save him from Somoza. Sacasa went to Congress and lobbied for a proposed accord in which Nicaragua would cut duties on nine US exports and bind the rates on another fifteen, in return for which Nicaragua was granted one tariff cut (on Peru balsam) and the nine items that constituted 90 per cent of its exports to the United States were allowed to remain on the free list. The treaty was signed on 11 March 1936.[70] The Sacasa administration now had three months left to it.

[68] 717.94/2, Lane to Hull, 6 Feb. 1936; 611.1731/173, Lane to Hull, 4 Mar. 1936; 611.1731/176, Hull to Lane, 6 Mar. 1936.

[69] Steward, *Trade and Hemisphere*, 220.

[70] US Department of State, *Foreign Relations*, 1936, v, 812–15; Steward, *Trade and Hemisphere*, 218; 'Reciprocal Trade Agreement between Nicaragua and the United States Promulgated', *Bulletin of the Pan American Union*, 70 (Oct. 1936), 809.

4

A New Neighbour Takes Charge, 1935–1936

> Precisamente por ésto, porque el General Somoza introdujo la escuela de la indisciplina y de la traición en el Ejército nicaragüense, su obra indigna de hoy tendrá tremendas e incalculables repercusiones en el futuro.[1]
>
> Juan Bautista Sacasa
> 1936

By the beginning of 1935 the positions of the main factions within Nicaragua were explicit. Lane reported that Somoza was 'definitely determined to be the next president'. The universal impression that Somoza was in control of the political situation, coupled with the prevalent sense that Sacasa's prestige was destroyed, brought about a shift in political distinctions within the country. As early as 1935, civilian political competition between the traditional parties was becoming something of a sideshow to a political process developing in terms of Somocista-military dominance.

Formerly, the prime division had been between Liberals and Conservatives; by the beginning of 1935, the chief question about the make-up of Congress was whether a senator or a deputy were *gobernista* or Somocista. In the view of the US legation, nine of the twenty-four members of the Senate were *gobernistas*, three were Somocistas, seven were Conservatives (though five of these latter tended to back Somoza), and five were doubtful. The forty-three seats in the Chamber of Deputies were divided between fourteen *gobernistas*, fifteen Somocistas, and thirteen Conservatives. There was a lone floating voter. The National Guard

---

[1] Juan Bautista Sacasa, *Cómo y por qué caí del poder* (Leon, Nicaragua: *s.n.*, 1936), 24.

had become the most potent political force in Nicaragua, but the congressional balance was held by Emiliano Chamorro and his Conservative followers.[2]

Judging Somoza's eventual accession as a probability that the State Department would not attempt to forestall, Lane now aimed mainly to prevent violence. He asked again, unsuccessfully, for permission to explain official recognition policy, since recognition of the Martínez regime in El Salvador had given the impression that Washington had reversed its stance. He worried that each new move by the Somocista faction intensified the antagonism of the Sacasa circle, and that the latter would make it more difficult for the *jefe director* to realize his ambitions through constitutional means. The minister appealed repeatedly to Somoza not to use force and the general promised that there would be no violence.[3]

Somoza had problems of his own. On 20 April the second company of the Guardia mutinied under Lieutenant Abelardo Cuadra and an attempt on Somoza's life was thwarted. Cuadra and seven others were sentenced to death. Sacasa attempted to stand firm on the issue and insisted that the sentences be commuted, but he could not stand firm alone. He urged Lane to influence Somoza not to insist on the execution since it would be 'unconstitutional and an act of open rebellion'. In the interests of peace, Lane made a lengthy case to Somoza in favour of sparing Cuadra. Somoza, however, was anxious about his own hold over the Guardia and wanted to execute the lieutenant as an example. In the end, it was only by emphasizing that the action would be 'distasteful' to the State Department that Lane dissuaded him from his course and again delayed a crisis.[4]

Arthur Bliss Lane, back in Managua after a prolonged stay in the United States, initially returned to Nicaragua a changed man. It is evident from the tone of his dispatches that his time in Washington had given him a better 'understanding' of the department's position. He now seemed much less inclined to offer 'advice' or to challenge the conventional wisdom. His patent impression of Sacasa as an inevitable loser was probably an echo of attitudes within the State Department, where apparently he

[2] 817.00/8196, Lane to Hull, 15 Mar. 1935; 817.00/8200, Lane to Hull, 8 Mar. 1935.
[3] 817.00/8200, Lane to Hull, 8 Mar. 1935; 817.00/8208, Lane to Hull, 16 Apr. 1935.
[4] 817.00/8208, Lane to Hull, 21 Apr. 1935; 817.00/8210, Lane to Hull, 22 Apr. 1935; 817.00/8211, Lane to Hull, 25 Apr. 1935; 817.00/8212, Hull to Lane, 27 Apr. 1935; 817.1051/912, Lane to Hull, 21 Apr. 1935.

had been relearning the new diplomacy. It had become accepted in Nicaragua that the United States would choose Sacasa's successor, and that the choice would be Somoza. Sacasa himself was convinced of this. 'If the United States is going to leave me all alone,' he shouted in English at Lane, 'then I shall have to take appropriate measures.' After six months in the United States, Lane could only reply that 'I did not feel it proper for me to take action to dissuade Somoza from his political activities.' As to Sacasa, he told his chiefs in Washington what he thought they wanted to hear: 'I feel . . . that this legation should no longer be used to pull his chestnuts out of the fire.' He asked permission to go to San Salvador for four days, purely in order to make plain his refusal to become further involved in local politics, since Somoza's campaign for the presidency was intensifying. Groups of the younger Somocistas had developed into *camisas azules*, paramilitary activists akin to their German and Italian peers. In the provincial towns their actions were opening a wide breach in local party politics. In Matagalpa, the Liberal Party split over these activities, which were geared towards modifying the constitution in order to allow Somoza's legal accession.[5]

It is clear that Somoza had been resolved for some time to secure the presidency, though he was anxious to do so by constitutional means if at all possible. Constitutional amendments, in his view, would obviate the necessity for open rebellion by allowing his election. This might not have been correct. Indeed, altering the constitution at this stage might have made violence more likely. Somoza seemed to believe that he would be elected if allowed to stand because the Guardia, overseeing the polls, would ensure the result.[6] Federico Sacasa, however, appears to have been engineering irregular elections since the day his brother took office. The previous year's congressional polls, in the US legation's view, were blatantly rigged. In the most recent Liberal primaries, Lacayo Sacasa's candidacy had been successful because the votes had been counted in the house of one of his supporters, without any opposition candidate present or any independent verification of the count. Somoza, in short, might not have been able to guarantee the result of the presidential elections to the extent he believed. Moreover, one of his chief obstacles under the constitution was article 105, which prohibited the candidacy of any close relative of the incumbent. Were Somoza to be successful in altering this article, it

[5] 817.00/8240, Lane to Hull, 18 June 1935; 817.00/8211, Lane to Hull, 25 Apr. 1935; 817.00/8230, Lane to Hull, 21 May 1935.
[6] 817.00/8265, Lane to Hull, 31 Aug. 1935.

raised the prospect of a Sacasa dynasty by legalizing the candidacies of any of the prominent Sacasas who chose to stand. Somoza's restraint was already showing signs of strain. Another Sacasa victory in presidential elections might have made a coup attempt inevitable.

A patent coup raised again the prospect of regionalized conflict. The Mexican and Salvadorean authorities remained hopeful that the United States would somehow prevent Somoza from becoming president. During his visit to El Salvador, Lane learned from official sources that President Martínez had offered Sacasa $300,000 plus arms and ammunition to instigate a movement against Somoza. In Managua, the Sacasa circle was urging the president to demand the general's resignation. The entire cabinet—with the exception of the minister of public instruction—was said to favour this course. Doña María told Lane that the material aid of El Salvador and Honduras was to be used against Somoza in the event of the latter's refusal.[7]

Trying to think the situation through on his own, Lane arrived at a conclusion that was probably conditioned by his recent conversations in Washington. He articulated 'a problem of great difficulty': that if the State Department announced it would not recognize an unconstitutional presidency, the statement would be interpreted as a desire to kill Somoza's candidacy and therefore as an interference in Nicaraguan affairs; but if Washington intimated it would recognize an 'illegal' president, that would strengthen the common impression that the United States was still intervening in Nicaraguan affairs and choosing Sacasa's successor.[8] Lane made no mention here of the problem with which he had been wrestling for some time: specifically, the possibilities that arose if the State Department were to give no indications of policy at all. This was a problem highlighted by widespread press reports that Lane was immersed in domestic politics and that, for example, after the minister's half-hour meeting with Moncada, the Liberal leader Dr Antonio Barberena had been chosen as the party's presidential candidate.[9]

The US government, through Lane, was inextricably involved in the situation. It could not be otherwise. The minister, however, now agonized less about the good neighbour policy. Though he clearly would have preferred Somoza to be stopped, his main aim now was to ensure that violence was minimized. The prospect of regionalized conflict over the

[7] 817.00/8225, Lane to Hull, 14 May 1935; 817.00/8239, Lane to Hull, 14 June 1935; 817.00/8289, Hull to Lane, 27 Sept. 1935.
[8] 817.00/8196, Lane to Hull, 15 Mar. 1935.
[9] 817.00/8262, Lane to Hull, 17 Aug. 1935.

Nicaraguan succession therefore drew him in deeper. Somoza attempted to induce the support of Arguello in his efforts to modify the constitution. When the foreign minister refused, Somoza announced that there would be a fight. Arguello expected a military coup by the second week in October.[10] An emboldened Somoza admitted to Lane that he intended to seek Sacasa's support for his presidential candidacy. To do this, he was going to send a detachment of National Guard officers to the presidential mansion on 15 September and, in the event of a refusal of support, would order military action. Aware of Sacasa's somewhat passive approach to matters requiring moral courage, and of the State Department's own aversion to taking action, Lane once more shouldered the burden. He considered it advisable, he told the State Department, 'to have a frank talk with Somoza before the political situation is permitted to get further out of hand'.[11]

At their meeting, Lane once again explained to Somoza the nature of US recognition policy, and stressed that the general's plans to change the constitution would amount to a coup if the president disapproved. With a knowing smile, Somoza replied that the Guardia would guarantee the fairness of the subsequent elections. In the face of this smugness, Lane's patience snapped. He had already been backtracking on the official attitude with which he had returned to Managua, and now he simply told Somoza that it was 'highly important' for him to reach an accommodation with the president. Changing his tone, Somoza assured the minister that there would be no violence, 'certainly not until 1 January 1937'. He subsequently did indeed delay his planned action against Sacasa, although he balanced this quiescence with a published declaration that he would 'brush aside' anyone who impeded his presidential ambitions. An exasperated Lane again sought permission from the State Department to repeat US recognition policy but the department, his chiefs told him, 'prefers that no further statement be made'.[12]

Trying to find a way of circumventing this instruction without derailing his career, Lane came up with an idea that was almost poignant. He telephoned Wilson and informed him that he intended, in his role as dean of the diplomatic corps, to make a speech during Nicaragua's independence celebrations. In the speech, he would refer to early Nicaraguan

10 817.00/8265, Lane to Hull, 21 Aug. 1935; 817.00/8296, Lane to Hull, 4 Oct. 1935.
11 817.00/8272, Lane to Hull, 10 Sept. 1935; 817.00/8279, Lane to Hull, 9 Sept. 1935.
12 817.00/8281, Lane to Hull, 14 Sept. 1935; 817.00/8275, Lane to Hull, 12 Sept. 1935; 817.415/13, Hull to Lane, 14 Sept. 1935.

patriots 'who had placed love of country and desire for peace and order above personal ambitions'. Wilson was dubious about this plan and he instructed Lane to do nothing. The minister was to issue neither a public statement nor, now, even a private warning to Somoza.[13]

No longer expecting help from Washington, Doña María and Federico Sacasa had been busy with plans of their own. At the end of September, Doña María received a large consignment labelled 'medicines' by express freight from San Salvador. The Salvadorean customs authorities had opened it and forwarded it to Managua despite the fact that the medicines consisted of ammunition.[14] The Sacasas had apparently won assurances of air support from El Salvador and Honduras in the event of hostilities with their own army. Somoza was aware of the plot. He refused thereafter to venture from the Campo de Marte, convoked his senior officers, and put them on alert. He told Lane that he could count on the loyalty of 90 per cent of the Guardia. Lane took the opportunity of recounting this to Sacasa when he arrived at the president's residence with a carefully worded telegram from Washington in which the State Department expressed the earnest hope that the Sacasa administration would not permit the aerial bombardment of Managua. Taking this as a prohibition, Doña María was outraged. 'In other words we are to do nothing,' she told Lane. 'We are to allow the present fine situation to continue. Somoza will be president and then the United States will be satisfied.'[15]

The first lady's irony matched Lane's own mood. When he had advised the State Department of María Sacasa's plan he had been careful to add, with what seems to have been every intention of sarcasm, that he assumed the Nicaraguan government would be 'allowed to take such steps as it considers advisable to meet the situation'.[16] Doña María's irony also held a basic truth. Sacasa could not hold his government together without support from beyond his borders. The situation to which intervention had given rise was inherently unstable and would continue to be so as long as a Sacasa, or indeed any weak civilian president, were incumbent. Outright US support for the constitutional government might have saved Sacasa, but for only as long as his presidential term—which had a little over a year to run. The next president was due to take office in January 1937. If the presidential circle had again tried to rig the elections, there

[13] 817.00/8283, memorandum, Wilson, 14 Sept. 1935.
[14] 817.24/306, Lane to Hull, 26 Sept. 1935.
[15] 817.00/8289, Hull to Lane, 27 Sept. 1935; 817.00/8292, Lane to Hull, 28 Sept. 1935; 817.00/8291, Lane to Hull, 28 Sept. 1935; 817.00/8293, Lane to Hull, 29 Sept. 1935.   [16] 817.00/8287, Lane to Hull, 26 Sept. 1935.

can be little doubt that the Guardia would have baulked at the return of another Sacasa to the presidential mansion, or of any of the more probable Liberal candidates then in the cabinet. Sacasa's ministers had, after all, been urging the president to drop bombs on Guardia headquarters.

Short of an abrupt change of heart on Somoza's part, therefore, or his sudden death, only outright US opposition would have prevented him from either seizing the presidency or installing his own candidate. In principle, US opposition could have been effected by public insistence on the 1923 treaty, but in the circumstances that prevailed in Nicaragua by this point such involvement would have been true interference, in the sense that intention and result would have coincided. Inaction on the part of the State Department, of course, gave rise to enduring accusations that Washington had chosen Somoza as the next president. For the Latin American division in Washington, and for Lane in Managua, these circumstances presented a political minefield, giving rise to scarcely credible diplomatic discussions between the representatives of sovereign states.

At the end of September, Federico Sacasa and Nicaragua's minister to Washington, Henri Debayle, did the rounds of the State Department in an effort to drum up support for the failing government of Juan Bautista Sacasa. The two Nicaraguans held what appears to have been a bizarre meeting with Willard Beaulac in which they attempted, for two hours, to elicit some statement of support from the diplomat. Reiterating the standard line that the intervention was happily over and that US relations with Nicaragua were now on the same footing as those with other states, Beaulac attempted, for two hours, not to make one. This left him with very little that he could actually say.

It was precisely because Washington's relations with Nicaragua were very different from those with other countries that Beaulac's task was so difficult. When the Nicaraguans raised the question of US recognition policy, Beaulac refused 'to make a commitment regarding [the US] attitude in a hypothetical situation'. Apparently testing every sentence before he uttered it, Beaulac finally told Sacasa that he was quite simply 'determined not to give him advice'. The Nicaraguans next tried Welles and Wilson, both of whom evidently remained impassive when confronted with Federico Sacasa's desperate plea for 'friendly moral assistance'.[17] Such was the principle of non-interference in practice. State Department personnel felt able to take this course now that the possibility of

[17] 817.00/8298, memorandum, Beaulac, 1 Oct. 1935; 817.00/8310, memorandum, Wilson, 16 Oct. 1935.

generalized conflict in Central America seemed to have disappeared. The waning of Doña María's plan did in fact represent a departure from the principle, the hypothetical situation in that case being judged worthy of State Department comment. The first lady's plan, however, highlights an important aspect of intervention that had not occurred even to Lane, who had done most of the thinking on the matter.

The Latin Americans who had urged outlawing intervention throughout the 1920s had done so more out of fear of, and resentment towards, the United States than out of any unyielding commitment to the principle. They were politically divided over the matter, and it was never addressed objectively. The prevailing 'them and us' mentality reflected an implicit perception that Pan Americanism was basically a contest. The issue of intervention was viewed as a Latin American struggle for the means of self-defence against US expansionism, and the impression given was that this amounted to the sum total of the matter.[18]

Intervention, however, was hardly absent within Latin America. Both El Salvador and Honduras had supported the Montevideo Resolution on the Rights and Duties of States, yet both had at least intimated that they were prepared to undertake the bombardment of the Nicaraguan army at the instigation of the Nicaraguan government. The Sacasas, of course, felt obliged to invite Central American intervention because of US non-intervention. The matter was therefore much more complicated than Latin American jurists had tended to suggest. US non-intervention was in any case seen as interventionist, and it simply gave rise to the possibility of intervention from elsewhere. No absolute rule of law could make provision for this, though both the jurists and Hull believed that it could.

Hull seemed to believe that the kind of law that governed the conduct of individuals within a state could somehow be expanded to govern the conduct of individual states. This was somewhat simplistic of Hull, but the Latin Americans who had fought for the issue were no less accountable. Seeing intervention entirely as a US–Latin American divide, with Washington's power apparently absolute, they argued that non-intervention would have to be absolute. In the diplomatic sphere, US non-intervention in Nicaragua was now probably as absolute as it could be in view of the historical record. It was the very austerity of good neighbourism that gave rise to more problems than it solved. The lack of

---

[18] See Enrique Aguirre y Fierro Harris, *La no intervención y la quiebra de la soberanía nacional* (Mexico City: Universidad Nacional de México, 1946); C. Neale Ronning (ed.), *Intervention in Latin America* (New York: Random House, 1938), 64–5.

pragmatism on both sides, the inability to be flexible on the absoluteness of non-intervention in Nicaragua, imperilled the principle itself. When the prospect of generalized conflict arose, the threat to the principle could be eliminated only by clear US interference. In the end, attempting to outlaw intervention was as useless as trying to outlaw war.

The good neighbour policy, an attempt to evade entanglements, burdened the Roosevelt administration with that most onerous of commitments: not to a party, or a country, but to a doctrine. Only Lane, stuck in the middle, dared to suggest that the new diplomatic idol might have feet of clay. Even Lane, however, constrained by his chiefs in Washington, found himself mouthing inanities. Trying to define sovereignty for Sacasa in October 1935, he asked the president: 'We do not "advise" Great Britain as to how its elections or political matters should be held. Why should we so "advise" Nicaragua?'[19] This argument, the standard line to which Lane had been trying to adhere since his return from Washington, must have been hard for Sacasa to absorb by late 1935. Viewing non-intervention as an absolute good, the State Department focused on the question of *whether* to become involved when it might perhaps have better served the interests of the United States, Nicaragua, Latin America, and inter-American law to consider how.

*

In Nicaragua, reports of an imminent coup continued to be received by the American legation throughout the final quarter of 1935. Jockeying for position on the part of Moncada and Chamorro, both now backing Somoza, appeared to be the main factor delaying a crisis. Somoza fuelled the tension by publishing reports in his *Nueva Prensa* that Sacasa intended to remain in power for two years after his term was meant to end.[20] In the first week of December there was a sudden rush of unusual military activity, and Sacasa and his family left Managua for León. Lane still wanted to be seen to be doing something. He continued trying to mediate between the main figures in the crisis, moving between Somoza, the Sacasas, Moncada, and Chamorro, and making constant references to US recognition policy.[21]

His chiefs' patience finally snapped. 'The Department desires you', Lane was told, 'to make no further statement which might appear to

[19] 817.00/8362, Lane to Hull, 4 Oct. 1935.
[20] Sacasa, *Cómo y por qué*, 114–15.
[21] 817.00/8339, Warren to Hull, 5 Dec. 1935; 817.00/8342, Warren to Hull, 6 Dec. 1935.

commit this government to any action in accord with any of the provisions of the Central American Treaty of Peace and Amity of 1923 or which might be intended to imply the possibility of such action.'[22] In other words, the department was hedging its bets. It would not say in advance that it would not recognize Somoza, because Somoza seemed likely to be the next president; and Hull, amid his programme of trade treaties, wanted to be able to deal with the next Nicaraguan government.

A career in the US foreign service does not seem to have been Arthur Bliss Lane's vocation. Subordination to the State Department, at least, was not one of his strong points. Despite this instruction he felt obliged to continue putting Sacasa's case not only to the department but to factions within Nicaragua. The Nicaraguan president simply lacked the stature and presence to do it. In mid December, Lane attended a conference at the presidential mansion between Federico Sacasa, Somoza, Chamorro, and the leading Conservative Cuadra Pasos. Chamorro announced that he would support Somoza's candidacy in the presidential elections. He probably wanted to open a definitive breach between Sacasa and Somoza so that the Conservatives, who held the congressional balance of power, could capitalize on their position. It must also have seemed clear to Chamorro that he was backing a winner in that most parties were increasingly, if not absolutely, certain that Somoza was Washington's favoured choice. Despite Lane's activities, this attitude continued to inform political thinking. Moncada's newspaper *El Liberal*, in its review of possible presidential candidates, referred to Arguello and Aguado as critics of US intervention and concluded that, since this meant that they would be looked on with disfavour by the United States, 'their election would therefore be impossible'.[23]

The beginning of 1936 found Somoza in confident mood. On 12 January a pro-Somoza demonstration was organized in the capital, formally to launch his still-illegal candidacy. About ten thousand people took part. The current rumour held that Lane had told the general that Washington would acquiesce if he now decided to make his move. The demonstration made the crisis more acute, a situation worsened by an anti-government meeting of Somocistas two days later at which immediate violence was suggested. Sacasa was still unable to bring himself to

[22] 814.[*sic*]00/1255, Hull to Lane, 30 Oct. 1935; 817.00/8317, Warren to Hull, 22 Oct. 1935; 817.00/8339, Warren to Hull, 5 Dec. 1935; 817.00/8342, Warren to Hull, 6 Dec. 1935.

[23] 817.00/8350, Lane to Hull, 16 Dec. 1935; 817.00/8354, Lane to Hull, 28 Dec. 1935.

discuss the situation with Somoza directly. Instead, a siege mentality prevailed on Tiscapa Hill. The presidential mansion was protected with extraordinary precautions and filled nightly with armed Sacasistas. Communication of even the most banal military information ceased between Somoza, on the one hand, and the president and his Chief of Staff, Antioco Sacasa, on the other. Unbridled criticism of President Sacasa by the Guardia persisted with impunity.[24]

The situation remained extremely tense throughout January 1936. Somoza repeatedly assured Lane that he would not fire the first shot, but it seemed plain that he could provoke the government into some action that he could claim was unconstitutional and then argue that he had been forced to act. There was, Lane informed the department with an admirable sense of understatement, 'less probability than was formerly the case for a satisfactory and peaceful solution to the electoral question'.[25] Just two days later, however, the situation took a surprising turn for the better. An agreement was worked out between Somoza and Sacasa. The general assured the president that his political activities would cease, that he would withdraw his presidential candidacy in return for assurances that he could remain *jefe director* in the next administration, and that the next president would fully meet the Guardia appropriation.[26] Oddly, Lane's own reports to Washington made no mention of where this initiative had originated. The president had seemed committed to making his last stand; he and his brother Federico had ceased all communication with the opposition; both Chamorro and Moncada, identifying their own interests with a coup, had been confident of Somoza's ascendancy; and Somoza's own resolve had seemed unshakable.

Lane, of course, had been warned repeatedly by the State Department to keep clear of the intricacies of Nicaraguan politics. But for two years Lane had been ignoring such instructions, or had argued with them, or had carried them out with obvious reluctance. It is reasonable to assume that it was Lane, unable to tell the State Department what he was doing in a last burst of activity before the crisis broke, who engineered the sudden rapprochement. Lane had nothing left to lose in Managua. He was being removed not only from Nicaragua but from the entire Latin American division. A month earlier he had received notice of his imminent transfer as minister to Lithuania, Latvia, and Estonia. Sacasa,

---

[24] 817.00/8357, Lane to Hull, 14 Jan. 1936; 817.00/8358, Lane to Hull, 21 Jan. 1936; *New York Times*, 13 Jan. 1936.   [25] 817.00/8365, Lane to Hull, 28 Jan. 1936.
[26] 817.00/8364, Lane to Hull, 1 Feb. 1936.

who was entirely dependent on him, actually tried to have this transfer revoked. By now, however, Lane was a liability in Managua. His alleged involvement in Sandino's murder, his prolonged interference in favour of the Sacasa government, and his apparently irrepressible tendency to challenge good neighbourism reflected badly on Latin American policy as conceived in Washington. Lane was to get his European posting, as he had requested before his arrival in Managua two years earlier, but he was to get it in disheartening circumstances.[27]

The assertions of many Latin American historians to the contrary, it seems to be true that Arthur Bliss Lane, working alone, nearly saved the Sacasa administration and forestalled Somoza's accession.[28] The Sacasa–Somoza rapprochement lasted almost two weeks before it dissolved. As the previous chapter described, Willard Beaulac had argued against a credit to Nicaragua from the Export-Import Bank to cover remittances to American companies. The Sacasa administration was therefore unable to furnish foreign exchange to the West India Oil Company. Cordoba collections awaiting remittance amounted to C$230,000, and the company refused to make any further shipments of fuel until the matter was settled. The National District began rationing petrol in small quantities. On 11 February, taxi drivers in Managua went on strike in protest at the rationing. The demonstrations turned into widespread riots involving as many as five thousand people.[29]

As the Guardia took over the rationing the situation assumed political significance, and by mid afternoon on 11 February the mob was still growing. Somoza saw a chance to make more political capital. Guardia officers occasionally led and encouraged the protesters, and by the evening the situation was almost out of control. A rumour took hold that Sacasa had ordered Somoza to fire on the crowd. When this report spread in the streets, the rioters began demanding that Somoza take over the government at once. Addressing the crowd, Somoza unsurprisingly encouraged this trend. Lane hurried to see the *jefe director* and secured his 'word of honour' that he would make no move against the government.[30]

---

[27] Vladimir Petrov, *A Study in Diplomacy: The Story of Arthur Bliss Lane* (Chicago: H. Regneny Co., 1971), 66–7, 74.

[28] Such assertions are rife. Guillermo Suárez Zambrana, for example, in *Los yanquis en Nicaragua* (San José, Costa Rica: Editorial Texto Ltda., 1978), maintains at some length (pp. 91–105) that Lane had in fact been working for two years *for* Somoza and *against* Sacasa because he 'no lo perdonaría [a Sacasa] el haberse entendido con Sandino'.

[29] 817.00/8368, Lane to Hull, 11 Feb. 1936.

[30] 817.00/8379, Lane to Hull, 14 Feb. 1936; 817.00/8379, Lane to Hull, 11 Feb. 1936; 817.00/8370, Lane to Hull, 12 Feb. 1936.

By the early hours of 12 February the situation was critical. Lane telephoned a report to Wilson and then went to see Sacasa 'with a view to averting bloodshed and civil war'. The situation remained tense but stable until 14 February, when further rioting erupted. The schools were closed and government employees were summoned to Tiscapa Hill. Reports of an imminent coup were rife. Somoza again promised Lane that he would take no action against Sacasa, but the president was right to argue that the agitation was being fostered by Somocistas.[31] In the event, the immediate threat dissipated in a matter of days but Somoza was no longer committed to his agreement with Sacasa. Arthur Bliss Lane left Managua on 14 March 1936 and never returned, and thereafter it became clear that Somoza's candidacy was on again.

On 16 March, Boaz Long replaced Lane in Managua. Conditions remained quiet during Long's first month as attempts were made to hammer out the details of another series of pre-election pacts between the parties. The talks included a proposal that the Liberals and Conservatives should support a joint presidential candidate for the 1936 polls. The parties had as yet failed to agree on a compromise figure, but both purported to remain committed to the proposal in principle. Discussion on the matter continued throughout the month in daily meetings between the parties' representatives and Sacasa. Both Arguello and Espinosa were in any case actively campaigning for the presidency during March. Somoza stated publicly that he would go as far as a civil war rather than have Espinosa become president, whereupon he reneged on the agreement he had reached with Sacasa and asserted that he would never accept a bipartisan accord if it were concluded. He told Sacasa directly that he would take Tiscapa Hill if such a pact were signed.[32]

Somoza had been planning for such an eventuality. In the outlying areas he began removing pro-Sacasa officers from the military posts and replacing them with his own men, leaving only two Sacasa strongholds: the Acosasco fort at León, commanded by Ramón Sacasa, and the presidential guard on Tiscapa Hill in Managua. He continued to give the impression that he enjoyed US support: *La Noticia* quoted the general as saying that he was 'en el corazón del ministro americano'. During the first week in May reports began reaching the US legation that an agreement had been concluded between the parties. In view of what Somoza had

---

[31] 817.00/8371, Lane to Hull, 12 Feb. 1936; 817.00/8378, transcript of telephone conversation, Lane and Wilson, 12 Feb. 1936.

[32] 817.00/8395, Long to Hull, 14 Apr. 1936; 817.00/8393, Long to Hull, 20 Mar. 1936; 817.00/8394, Long to Hull, 3 Apr. 1936.

previously said to him, Sacasa now considered the country to be in a state of civil war. Somoza's only hurdle was US recognition policy.[33]

*

Throughout early 1936, both Lane in Nicaragua and Frank Corrigan in El Salvador had been sending to Washington dispatches that amounted to a restrained critique of good neighbourism in general and of the difficulties surrounding non-interference in particular. These reports provoked some thought in the State Department. Welles in particular was struck by his ministers' dispatches. He felt that the personal influence of American ministers in Central America 'should be of the utmost value', and that 'non-interference should not be construed as a negation of the helpful and friendly advice on matters in which the Central American republics and ourselves, as well as, in a broad sense, all the American republics, have a legitimate interest.' Beaulac and Wilson, in their discussions with Federico Sacasa and Henri Debayle six months earlier, had construed non-interference in precisely such a way. Welles therefore outlined his views in a memorandum that, he suggested, should inform further consideration in the Latin American division with a view to formulating a definitive set of instructions for the Central American legations.[34]

Welles urged that the instruction be worded in such a way so as 'not to create by it the impression that this government is assuming a sterile policy of aloofness, but rather that it wishes to carry out in all sincerity a policy of effective friendship'.[35] The department's thinking on this issue centred on US recognition policy and was prompted in particular by Somoza's activities in Nicaragua and by developments in Honduras, where President Carías had convoked a constituent convention in an effort to prolong his term of office. By April, the department had decided that the United States should no longer be guided by the 1923 treaty. US officials were anxious about publicizing this policy shift, however, because of the situation in Nicaragua. They feared that an announcement of the change would be taken by Somoza as an invitation to overthrow Sacasa. Beaulac wrote to Duggan and Welles:

It is known that General Somoza's fear that we would not recognize him if he carried out a successful coup d'etat or revolution has been a strong deterrent to him

[33] 817.00/8386, Long to Hull, 20 Mar. 1936; 817.00/8394, Long to Hull, 3 Apr. 1936; 817.00/8395, Long to Hull, 14 Apr. 1936; 817.00/8400, Long to Hull, 5 May 1936; 817.00/8401, Long to Hull, 1 May 1936; 817.00/8402 Long to Hull, 7 May 1936.
[34] 710.11/2026, memorandum, Welles to Duggan, 17 Mar. 1936.
[35] 710.11/2026 [*sic*], memorandum, Welles to Duggan, 26 Mar. 1933.

in the past. It would be particularly unfortunate from our point of view if the impression were created that we were encouraging General Somoza, since he is, of course, already considered by many to be 'our man'.

As the department was aware, a problem arose if Somoza were to depose Sacasa anyway, and if the United States then recognized his government without having previously announced the change in policy that allowed such recognition. It could then be alleged that the policy was changed simply in order to allow Washington to recognize Somoza.[36]

Hull made a decision. An instruction over his signature was sent to US ministers in Central America on 30 April. It stated that US recognition policy would no longer be guided by the 1923 treaty, and forbade American ministers in the isthmus from making any comment whatever on the internal affairs of the countries to which they were accredited.[37] Somoza could now do what he wanted.

*

In Managua, the two parties were close to reaching an agreement on the procedure for the 1936 elections and after. In essence, it amounted to an accord to create a government of national unity. There would be a joint presidential candidate; a pre-agreed distribution of congressional seats; a constitutional reform satisfactory to both parties; the inclusion of Conservative ministers in the cabinet of what was expected to be a Liberal president; and an equal distribution of diplomatic posts between the parties.[38] While rumours circulated in the first week of May that the Liberals and Conservatives had reached an agreement, the *camisas azules* were back on the streets of towns throughout the country. In Managua they began military drilling in the main streets, marching six abreast. In mid month it was publicly announced that a pact had been reached between Chamorro and Cuadra Pasos for the Conservatives, and Crisanto Sacasa and Carlos Morales for the Liberals; as yet there was no agreement on a candidate.[39]

On 12 May, Somoza submitted an extraordinary document to Sacasa and to the executive committees of the two parties 'como contribución al mantenamiento de la Paz Nacional'. Among other things, this document proposed that the next president should be chosen by Somoza from among the Somocista Liberals, in return for his abandoning his own

[36] 710.11/2060, memorandum, Beaulac to Duggan and Welles, 21 Apr. 1936.

[37] US Department of State, *Foreign Relations of the United States* (Washington DC: US Government Printing Office), 1936, v, 134–6.

[38] Knut Walter, *The Regime of Anastasio Somoza, 1936–1956* (Chapel Hill: University of North Carolina Press, 1993), 48–9.

[39] 817.00/8408, Long to Hull, 8 May 1936; 817.00/8413, Long to Hull, 13 May 1936.

candidacy; that he should have immediate and absolute control of the Guardia and its arms 'para acabar de una vez con la zozobra en que ha vivido el país, reyendo que hay dos fuerzas enfrentadas una a la otra'; that the León fort should immediately come under the command of officers designated by him; that he should have complete control of military transfers and promotions; and that the government should at once provide the Guardia with 5,000 pairs of shoes. This proposal would have made Somoza the absolute power in Nicaragua, shielded by a figurehead president. The general nominated the Guardia's second in command, Rigoberto Reyes, as his candidate. Sacasa refused to accept the legality of Reyes's nomination, or that of any other member of the Guardia.[40]

The Guardia posts in the interior were put on full alert, with extra sentries night and day. Troops began intimidating government office-holders appointed via the Liberal Party organization, forcing them out of office and replacing them with Somocistas.[41] The US minister, Boaz Long, remained aloof from the intrigues that followed the confrontation between Sacasa and Somoza over Rigoberto Reyes, as the entire machinery of government was geared towards settling this single question. Personal resentments between those involved deepened during a rash of meetings between the government, the political opposition and the military. Proposals and counter-proposals were traded to no effect for a week, and the negotiations bogged down.[42]

In the meantime, *camisas azules* and Guardia personnel were staging riots in towns throughout the country. These provided a pretext for the Guardia to move in and place the local government under military control. On 27 May the National Guard took over Bluefields, Puerto Cabezas, and El Bluff. All civilian officials were replaced by Somocistas. The pattern was repeated on the following day in Granada, Matagalpa, Chinandega, and Masaya. Estelí and Ocotal were expected to follow within a matter of days. In this manner most of the country came under Somoza's direct authority by the end of the month. Only Corinto, León, Rivas, and Managua would then be held by government officials loyal to Sacasa. Long reported that the troops in Matagalpa admitted openly that they were simply waiting for the word from Somoza.[43]

[40] Ibid.; Sacasa, *Cómo y por qué*, 24–5, 98–103.   [41] Ibid. 23.
[42] 817.00/8420, Long to Hull, 23 May 1936.
[43] 817.00/8401, Long to Hull, 1 May 1936; 817.00/8423, Long to Hull, 27 May 1936; 817.00/8424, Long to Hull, 27 May 1936; 817.00/8426, Long to Hull, 28 May 1936; Eduardo Crawley, *Dictators Never Die: A Portrait of Nicaragua and the Somoza Dynasty* (London: C. Hurst, 1979), 92.

The women in Managua's markets, often reliable political barometers, began amassing substantial supplies of food. After more than three years of uncertainty about when the general would make his move it was evident to everybody watching, in Washington as well as Managua, that Somoza's hour had finally come. At the end of May it was announced that the negotiators of the two parties had chosen Leonardo Arguello as the coalition candidate for president; Rodolfo Espinosa was the vice-presidential candidate. From this point, events moved with remarkable speed. On 28 May, Sacasa asked for a US naval vessel to be sent to the east coast of Nicaragua. Hull refused. On 29 May, Chamorro made a similar request. There is no record of Hull's reply. Sacasa and Somoza both spent 29 May with their advisers, each refusing to accept the other's proposals for resolving the crisis. Somoza, with 1,500 troops and a large contingent of *camisas azules*, departed for Sacasa's stronghold of León, leaving Rigoberto Reyes to keep the peace in Managua.[44]

The capital remained quiet, but the population expected their political authorities to be changed. In the afternoon of 30 May, from León, Somoza radioed to Long his rejection of Arguello and Espinosa. His message required no political interpretation: 'We will die to the last man in the *Guardia Nacional* before we will accept that such men take over the presidency of Nicaragua.' Somoza decided to take the León fort. He telegraphed the president to order Major Crisanto Sacasa to surrender. The president ordered Major Sacasa to resist. In the evening, the members of the diplomatic corps convened to decide how to furnish their good offices for mediation. Sacasa ordered Somoza to return to Managua. Somoza ordered his men to attack the fort.[45]

In Managua, the first shots were fired on the morning of 31 May. Somocista loyalists soon took possession of most strategic buildings, the electricity plant, and the brewery. Sacasa still held Tiscapa Hill. A Somocista picket blockaded the city as heavy fire was exchanged between the presidential mansion and Reyes's Guardia positions for four hours. Long telephoned Duggan at the State Department in the midst of the fighting. He told his chief that Somoza intended to maintain Sacasa in the presidency under his, Somoza's, tutelage. Sacasa wanted no part of

[44] 817.00/8431, Long to Hull, 29 May 1936; 817.00/8427, Long to Hull, 28 May 1936; 817.00/8427, Hull to Long, 29 May 1936; 817.00/8429, Long to Hull, 29 May 1936; 817.00/8433, Long to Hull, 29 May 1936.

[45] 817.00/8435, Long to Hull, 30 May 1936; 817.00/8437, Long to Hull, 30 May 1936; 817.00/8436, Long to Hull, 30 May 1936; 817.00/8438, Long to Hull, 30 May 1936; 817.00/8439, Long to Hull, 30 May 1936; 817.00/8442, Long to Hull, 31 May 1936; Sacasa, *Cómo y por qué*, 107–9.

such a plan: he wanted the United States to send an aircraft to remove him safely from the country. With the Guardia under Colonel Reyes advancing on the residence, Sacasa was so terrified that he could not talk coherently. He was insisting only that he should be allowed to leave the country alive. Long wanted to meet Somoza at the station on his return from León, and to urge him not to attack the presidential mansion. Duggan refused permission. He also indicated that Sacasa must make his own arrangements for leaving Nicaragua.[46]

In Washington, State Department personnel were maintaining an equally blithe attitude towards Debayle in his frequent visits to the Latin American division. Non-intervention was taken to extreme lengths when the division refused Long permission to sign a communiqué to Somoza—already signed by the ministers of Great Britain, France, El Salvador, Honduras, and Mexico—exhorting him 'in the name of humanity' to end the violence. Several Latin American governments petitioned the State Department to avert US intervention but their efforts were unnecessary.[47]

While the Sacasa government disintegrated the State Department finally broke a long silence and issued a statement of its position. Asserting the hope that a peaceful solution would be found to the Nicaraguan crisis, the statement declared that 'the consideration by this government of its participation in any tender of good offices must depend in the first place on the willingness of all political factions, including General Somoza, to invite the good offices of other friendly American nations'. Unless the invitation were unanimous, the Roosevelt administration 'would under no circumstances even consider whether or not it would offer its good offices'.[48] This was meaningless. Somoza had no intention of seeking anybody's good offices.

On 4 June, Boaz Long and Fletcher Warren accompanied the Mexican minister (who was then the dean of the diplomatic corps) and the chargé of the Italian legation on a visit to Somoza. They were seeking a guarantee of protection for Sacasa and his family. Somoza agreed, and expressed the hope that the president would finish his term. Sacasa was disinclined to do this. He resigned as president on 6 June and left for El Salvador. The National Guard took effective control of Nicaragua.[49]

*

[46] 817.00/8440, Long to Hull, 31 May 1936: 817.00/83531/2, transcript of telephone conversation, Long and Duggan, 3 June 1936; Sacasa, *Cómo y por qué*, 26.

[47] 817.00/8439, Hull to Long, 31 May 1936; Petrov, *A study in Diplomacy*, 78.

[48] 817.00/8439, Hull to Long, 31 May 1936.

[49] 817.00/8459, Long to Hull, 4 June 1936; 817.00/8460, Long to Hull, 5 June 1936; *Newsweek*, 13 June 1936.

The day after Sacasa's resignation, the presidency was assumed by the *ministro de gobernación*, Julián Irías. He served for three days before Somoza's choice, Carlos Brenes Jarquín, was named head of a caretaker government. The Sacasa–Somoza divide within the Liberals remained entrenched, however, and the party split. In mid June a convention of Somocista Liberals under the banner 'Nationalist Liberal Party' nominated Somoza as the party's candidate for the December elections. The executive committee of the 'Constitutionalist' Liberals proclaimed Arguello and Espinosa as their candidates. The Conservatives bided their time.[50]

The government was gradually militarized as ever more departments were placed under Guardia control. As the military became increasingly high-handed and intimidating, Chamorro turned against Somoza. He instructed his party to support the Arguello–Espinosa ticket even though, according to Long, Espinosa was 'frankly hated by most of the Conservatives' and they viewed Arguello as 'weak and colourless'. A faction within the Conservatives, convinced that their choice lay between Somoza and civil war, rejected Chamorro's decision. Hence the Conservatives also split, into Traditionalist and Somocista Nationalist factions.[51]

Chamorro, Sacasa, and Adolfo Díaz, three of the four signatories to the agreement of 5 November 1932 fixing the nature of the National Guard's officer corps, all of them former presidents, lobbied the State Department in an effort to secure a guarantee of US supervision of the elections. Chamorro predicted a reign of terror if the polls were unsupervised and indicated that the Conservatives would probably abstain if free elections were not assured. Arguello, still in El Salvador, declared that his return to Nicaragua was contingent on the assurance of such supervision.[52]

Both the Traditionalist Conservatives and the Constitutionalist Liberals indicated that they would abstain if the United States refused to be involved, leaving Somoza as the only candidate. In conversations with Welles, Sacasa tried to argue that Washington retained a 'responsibility' in Nicaragua. Welles dismissed this line of reasoning and stated bluntly that 'political cooperation is out of the question'. Hull was

[50] 817.00/8537, Long to Hull, 18 June 1936; 817.00/8586, Long to Hull, 18 Sept. 1936; 817.00/8544, Long to Hull, 8 July 1936; Patricia Taylor Edmisten, *Nicaragua Divided* (Pensacola: University of West Florida Press, 1990), 19.

[51] 817.00/8586, Long to Hull, 18 Sept. 1936.

[52] 817.00/8582, Summerlin (Panama) to Hull, 11 Sept. 1936; 817.00/8593, Long to Hull, 25 Sept. 1936; 817.00/8594, Warren to Hull, 3 Oct. 1936.

similarly dismissive. His rejection of Sacasa was given much prominence in the Nicaraguan press.[53] The public saw it as confirmation that Somoza was the State Department's choice. Most Nicaraguans had felt this for years and were now resigned to it. Chamorro, having failed in Washington, was reported to have departed for Mexico in an effort to secure support for an armed revolt. This course was seen as pointless in Nicaragua, given Washington's apparent attitude towards Somoza. 'Most Nicaraguans', according to the American legation, 'think that the only sensible course is to let him go ahead.'[54]

Somoza resigned his military command. At the end of November the committees representing the Conservative and Liberal supporters of the bipartisan agreement decided to abstain from the presidential elections. The Arguello–Espinosa ticket was withdrawn, although the ballots reserved a space for it. Somoza, with Francisco Navarro as his running mate, was now the sole presidential candidate.[55]

*

In the same week, Cordell Hull and the US delegation arrived at Buenos Aires for an extraordinary conference of American states. The initiative had originated with Roosevelt. While Somoza had overrun the Sacasa government and prepared for the elections, the Roosevelt administration had focused much of its attention on deteriorating conditions in Europe and Asia. So too had the US Congress, which severely constrained any temptation Roosevelt might feel for foreign policy activism by the neutrality legislation of the mid 1930s. This stance reflected an intense US desire to keep foreign aggression away from the Americas. On 25 November, the day on which the American delegation arrived in Buenos Aires, Germany and Japan concluded the Anti-Comintern Pact.[56]

By the time that Somoza was ready to make his move in Nicaragua, the Roosevelt administration was promoting inter-American solidarity as a protective measure. The administration wanted a stable, secure western hemisphere. The Buenos Aires conference, in fact, was called the 'Inter-American Conference for the Maintenance of Peace'. A worried Roosevelt had told his cabinet that a German and Italian policy of

[53] 817.00/8604, memorandum, Duggan, 22 Oct. 1936; 817.00/8605, Ray to Hull, 27 Oct. 1936.   [54] 817.00/8605, Ray to Hull, 27 Oct. 1936.
[55] 817.00/8612, Ray to Hull, 24 Nov. 1936; 817.00/8619, Long to Hull, 7 Dec. 1936.
[56] Martin Gilbert, *Second World War* (London: Weidenfeld and Nicolson, 1989), 262; Irwin Gellman, *Good Neighbor Diplomacy: United States Policies in Latin America, 1933–1945* (Baltimore, Md.: Johns Hopkins University Press, 1979), 62.

dividing colonial areas might lead them to attack Latin America. A future president, he argued, might have to repulse an invasion of the sister republics by European dictators.[57]

By 1936 the good neighbour policy had developed into an instrument that would seek to forestall such a scenario. Roosevelt himself went to Buenos Aires to make the opening address. Before he left Washington, the president wrote to the US ambassador in Berlin, William Dodd, acknowledging that '[the] visit will have little practical or immediate effect in Europe but at least the forces of example will help if the knowledge of it can be spread down to the masses of the people in Germany and Italy.' Adolf Berle, an outstanding thinker among the Brains Trusters and one of the men who had worked on Roosevelt's speech for the conference, was even more direct. The speech, he said, was 'addressed to Europe more than the Americas for this conference is plainly a threshold to the possibility of dealing with Europe in a conference looking towards peace, but we are working against horrible odds in point of time.'[58] In these circumstances, US intervention in Nicaragua was not an option. It would have prompted an outcry from Congress; it would have provoked Latin America protests that might imperil the desired inter-American solidarity; and it would hardly have been a 'force of example' to the expansionist powers of Europe and Asia. For some time, moreover, there had been more mundane reasons for US acquiescence in Somoza's ascent.

Hull had consistently refused to let Lane issue any statement prejudicial to Somoza, or to permit official opinions to emanate from Washington. In early 1934 this owed something to Hull's desire to avoid charges of interference before the March conference of Central American states that was going to consider the future of the 1923 recognition treaty. The avowed ideals of good neighbourism were endlessly mooted by Hull as the reason for his stand, but a less exalted motivation is evident in Hull's enthusiasm for commercial reciprocity. There are several considerations to be noted here: that the figures involved in the US–Nicaraguan trade agreement were, from the American viewpoint, almost negligible; that the treaty proposals were plainly damaging to Nicaragua's economy; that the agreement was concluded over insistent objections from Lane; and that, almost from the day of the US marine evacuation, US diplomatic reports were indicating that a coup might be imminent.

[57] Gilbert, *Second World War*, 262; Gellman, *Good Neighbor Diplomacy*, 64.
[58] Quotations from ibid. 64.

For two and a half years, during which the commercial negotiations were continuing, these reports all proved to be premature. To Hull, however, it must constantly have seemed that the Sacasa government was in danger of collapse. He was therefore unable to assert in advance that the United States would not recognize a Somoza government, because if diplomatic relations were suspended the trade talks would have to be aborted. The accord with Nicaragua was unimportant in itself and the antithesis of good neighbour idealism, but the failure of negotiations in Nicaragua might jeopardize the programme throughout Central America, since equally reluctant countries of the isthmus might be motivated to suggest suspension of the talks. Such a development, in turn, would endanger the scheme for the bigger economies of the south, which imperilled Hull's vision of global commercial reciprocity. The correspondence from Washington to the Managua legation frequently instructed Lane to accelerate the negotiations. They had to be completed before something drastic happened.

Worth noting is that Welles's memorandum inspiring the 'definitive' instructions to the Central American legations, in which US recognition policy changed, was written less than a week after Sacasa signed the reciprocal trade agreement. Thereafter, he was no longer necessary. The United States reverted to a de facto recognition policy, and at Buenos Aires Hull was able to sign another protocol of non-intervention, this time without reservation. It was while he was discussing the protocol with the sister republics in Argentina that the voters in Nicaragua were casting their ballots.

Nicaragua's presidential elections were held without incident on 8 December 1936, one week after the Buenos Aires conference convened. The earliest returns gave the Arguello–Espinosa ticket 900 votes to Somoza's 48,000. As the counting continued and Somoza's tally grew, votes for his opponents were revised downwards. The Arguello–Espinosa ticket later polled 885 votes to Somoza's 48,282. By the time final results were given ten days after the elections, the total official vote for Arguello and Espinosa was less than their partial returns announced earlier: the bipartisan ticket won an official total of 169 votes in the presidential elections; Somoza polled 107,201. He resumed his post as *jefe director* of the National Guard on 18 December and took office as president on 1 January 1937. Shortly after his inauguration, his former boss Moncada commented: 'That young man on the hill will not last past next July.'[59]

[59] 817.00/8619, Long to Hull, 7 Dec. 1936; 817.00/8620, Long to Hull, 9 Dec. 1936; 817.00/8624, Long to Hull, 9 Dec. 1936; 817.00/8625, Long to Hull, 14 Dec. 1936; 817.00/8629, Long to Hull, 18 Dec. 1936; 817.00/8644, Long to Hull, 7 Apr. 1937.

5

Good Neighbour Diplomacy and Somoza's Retention of Power, 1937–1939

> General Somoza is a man of pleasing personality, unfailingly affable, ingratiating and persuasive, but is without stability of opinion as to anything foreign to his selfish aims . . . Culturally, he is a cipher, but clever enough to conceal his deficiencies . . . He seems to know nothing of the science of government or of political history and sees democracy only as a device for the easy domination of his country . . . Loyalty is not among his virtues . . . His anecdotal range is limited to smutty stories which he relates with keen enjoyment . . . He is a most acceptable dinner guest.[1]
>
> Meredith Nicholson
> US minister to Nicaragua

Such was one American minister's assessment of the man with whom the United States had to deal in Nicaragua upon the collapse of the Sacasa administration. As with Sacasa, Washington's attitude towards him, and Nicaraguan perceptions of that attitude, could not be but important factors in the durability of his government. His accession to the presidency and consolidation of power in the late 1930s coincided with a deteriorating world outlook. It cannot rightly be said that the Roosevelt administration actively installed him, but against a background of military aggression in Europe and Asia, as well as fears for the security of the Panama Canal, the sort of government he seemed likely to provide came briefly to represent for American diplomats and strategists the option most likely to serve Washington's interests in changing circumstances.

---

[1] 817.001 Somoza, Anastasio/50, Nicholson to Hull, 3 Apr. 1939.

There seems to have been little that was personal in such thinking: another, politically astute leader of forceful personality who could command the support of a dominant sector of the National Guard might (unless demonstrably anti-American) have served Washington's interests equally well. Sacasa, who had displayed none of those traits, had been manifestly unable to provide stability for Nicaragua over a long period. During that time the individual most likely to replace him not only was proclaiming a strident pro-Americanism but also seemed likely to offer a greater likelihood of long-term stability.

When Somoza took the oath of office there was little reason to believe that American thinking had changed simply because this particular individual would henceforth be in control. Other individuals, politically influential and with some base of support in the Guardia, would soon become apparent. If Somoza had been unable to provide stability in these circumstances there was no certainty, indeed no suggestion, that Washington would necessarily do anything to keep him in office.

As the early, economically disastrous period of Somoza's first term went by, however, the State Department came to believe that it could no longer be so sanguine about the outbreak of a disturbance in Nicaragua. That such strife would be directed at Somoza was secondary to the fact that it would be happening at all. The condition of isolated security that had informed an apparent departure from Washington's traditional Central America policy, as well as a commitment to the principle of non-interference, was to alter in nature during Roosevelt's second term. That change posed an insurmountable threat to the tenets of good neighbourism in the isthmus.

*

In Washington, nineteen days after Anastasio Somoza assumed the presidency of Nicaragua, Franklin Roosevelt was inaugurated for the second time as president of the United States. From the day of the marine evacuation to the election of Somoza and Roosevelt, world events had simply reinforced American isolationism: Hitler's rise to power in January 1933; the first German anti-Semitic measures; the assassination of the Austrian chancellor, Engelbert Dolfuss, in July 1934; the announcement of German rearmament in March 1935; the outbreak of the Ethiopian war in October of the same year; the remilitarization of the Rhineland in March 1936; and the outbreak of the Spanish Civil War four months later.[2]

---

[2] J. B. Duroselle, *From Wilson to Roosevelt: Foreign Policy of the United States* (London: Chatto & Windus, 1964), 237.

The conclusions of the Nye Committee in 1936, which found that the country's entry into World War I had been engineered by the manoeuvres of American bankers and arms manufacturers, nourished this isolationism and gave rise to the neutrality legislation of the mid 1930s. Congress, which renewed the Neutrality Act of 1935 for another year in February 1936, was profoundly isolationist, as was the public. In an election year it would not serve Roosevelt's interests to challenge these sentiments directly. In May 1937 he signed a new and indefinite Neutrality Act. As Europe drifted towards a crisis, the depth of US isolationism was perhaps best exemplified by the Ludlow Amendment, which seemed close to congressional approval in January 1938. The amendment proposed that, except in the case of an armed violation of American territory, a declaration of war would first have to be approved by popular referendum. It fell just twenty-one votes short of the two-thirds necessary for adoption. As Everett Kane has commented, Washington's first reaction to the appearance of European war clouds was to buy an umbrella.[3]

The effectiveness of that umbrella depended to some extent on the stand adopted by the sister republics of Latin America. US strategic doctrine dictated that national security was dependent on hemispheric security, especially in the strategically vital region of Central America and the Canal Zone. It was in an attempt to multilateralize neutrality that Roosevelt had initiated the extraordinary Inter-American Conference for the Maintenance of Peace at Buenos Aires in December 1936. Proposals aimed at securing a pledge of reciprocal assistance in the event of an attack on any one country by a non-American power proved unpopular with the sister republics, especially Argentina, which enjoyed good relations with Germany and had strong commercial ties to Europe. The United States eventually secured a promise of consultation at Buenos Aires, but at a price. The original American project was abandoned in the face of resolute Argentine opposition, and in accepting a Brazilian compromise the conference split it into two halves: a Treaty for the Maintenance, Preservation and Re-establishment of Peace, and an Additional Protocol Relative to Intervention. To pan-Americanize its own neutrality, the Roosevelt administration was obliged to renew the pledge of non-intervention it had made at Montevideo, but this time without reservation.[4]

[3] J. B. Duroselle, *From Wilson to Roosevelt: Foreign Policy of the United States* (London: Chatto & Windus, 1964), 245; Charles C. Alexander, *Nationalism in American Thought, 1930–1945* (Chicago: Rard McNally, 1969), 169; William Everett Kane, *Civil Strife in Latin America* (Baltimore, Md.: Johns Hopkins University Press, 1972), 133.

[4] Samuel Flagg Bemis, *The Latin American Policy of the United States* (New York: Harcourt, Brace and Company, 1943), 286; Kane, *Civil Strife*, 134.

In theory, this renewal might have led to a yet more rigorous application of the policy of apparent diplomatic indifference that had so concerned Corrigan in El Salvador and Lane in Nicaragua. In January of the
same year, Corrigan had posed fundamental questions about the value of
good neighbourism in a dispatch from which it is worth quoting at
length. He asked for a clarification of 'the positive aspects of the good
neighbour policy' because of his concern that 'powerful dictatorially
inclined leaders' were taking advantage of it:

The powerful influence of our missions is an established fact which leads political
elements in these countries, and the public as well, to expect either opposition or
co-operation. A completely negative policy is unlikely of acceptance and subject
to misinterpretation... Liberal elements, some of which have been formerly
active critics of the United States and bitter opponents of intervention, have indicated to me that the co-operation of the United States is more than welcome
when it seeks to retain progress and prevent bloodshed, and the establishment of
autocratic regimes and actual setting up of dictatorships... They feel that a liberal government, like that of the United States with its immense power and moral
influence, should lend its aid to co-operate in every peaceful way to retain
progress and ideals, and to aid the evolution of these countries towards real democratic republican government.[5]

As the previous chapter indicated, it was partly in response to this dispatch and to Lane's constant challenges that the department had issued
its representatives in Central America with definitive instructions as to
their conduct with respect to domestic politics in the isthmus. Those
instructions insisted on complete abstention from any comment on local
situations. Since the Roosevelt administration would henceforth recognize any force that appeared to be in control of a country in Central
America, this posture gave rise to the prospect that 'dictatorially inclined'
leaders might well choose to avail themselves of the benefits of good
neighbourism.

*

In Nicaragua, Somoza made his inaugural speech on 1 January 1937. He
referred at length to the good neighbour policy: 'the policy tending to
break down the restrictions imposed on international commerce and to
return to the principle of equality of treatment; the progressive march of
Pan Americanism which eagerly seeks a unity, and the affirmation and

---

[5] US Department of State, *Foreign Relations of the United States* (Washington DC:
US Government Printing Office), 1936, v, 126.

evolution of democratic forms'.[6] For the period of the inauguration, the US minister, Boaz Long, was assigned the title of Ambassador and designated Envoy Extraordinary and Minister Plenipotentiary. Long himself informed Somoza that this was a mark of respect for Nicaragua, though in the prevailing circumstances it could be interpreted as a personal mark of American backing for the new Nicaraguan president.[7]

Indeed, apart from the fact of Somoza's presidency, the most important event that the Nicaraguan press had to report was American recognition of it.[8] This matter had remained an open question right up to the inauguration. Even within the State Department it was not entirely clear. Sacasa and Chamorro had retained the services of a Washington law firm to present a legal case to the State Department concerning Washington's obligation to withhold recognition. Laurence Duggan told the visiting lawyers that the United States had 'no responsibility either legal or moral for whatever might happen to the *Guardia* or for whatever the *Guardia* might do'. Duggan acknowledged that Washington's instructions to its diplomats on US recognition policy in Central America meant that the question of recognition should not arise, but he was still unsure as to whether Long should attend the ceremony.[9]

Long himself believed that the general would ensure a protracted period of peace for Nicaragua and was 'convinced that he is only too willing to extend the hand of friendship to the political opposition'.[10] Public attitudes in Nicaragua were less certain. Sacasa had not seen out his mandate, and his term had to be completed by an interim president. It therefore took several months for the new government to become an accepted fact, but in time it gained some measure of substance and permanence. In its first six months the administration grew in strength and Somoza's personal position was reinforced. Order was maintained and the projects that the president contemplated seemed popular. A road-building programme was under way, and even larger projects had been mooted, including canalization of the San Juan River and the development of hydroelectric power. Such plans, in Long's words, 'appeal to the

    6 817.001 Somoza, Anastasio/15, Long to Hull, 8 Jan. 1937.
    7 817.001 Somoza, Anastasio/7a, Walton Moore to Ramírez Brown, 19 Dec. 1936; 817.001 Somoza, Anastasio/8, Ramírez Brown to Walton Moore, 21 Dec. 1936; 817.001 Somoza, Anastasio/12, Long to Hull, 26 Dec. 1936.
    8 817.001 Somoza, Anastasio/10, Long to Hull, 22 Dec. 1936.
    9 817.001 Somoza, Anastasio/65, memorandum, Duggan, 19 Dec. 1936; 817.001 Somoza, Anastasio/5, memorandum, Duggan to acting Secretary of State (R. Walton Moore), 18 Dec. 1936.
    10 817.001 Somoza, Anastasio/15, Long to Hull, 1 Jan. 1937.

hopes of grandeur which are characteristic of the Nicaraguan temperament'. Despite their impracticability, therefore, they were proving welcome.[11]

Substantial political threats were barely evident. The urban poor had been severely hit by the soaring cost of living but there was no attempt to organize urban workers. It was generally accepted that any move in that direction would be met by immediate Guardia repression. The National Guard as a fully national force had been less than three years old when its first major act was to remove the elected government. It had now acquired such a reputation that no worker was likely to risk arrest and a beating on suspicion of subversive activity. Long felt that if the offence were particularly objectionable, or if the guardsmen became especially vexed, 'the labourer would run a substantial risk of never being heard of again'.[12]

It was clear that the Guardia was the basis and motor of the Somoza government. Without it he could not have hoped to sustain himself. The influence of the Conservative sector in the National Guard had been partially eliminated as a result of transfers, and Somoza's men seemed firmly in control. There were occasional rumours of discontent over pay, and that the Chief of Staff (and minister of war), Rigoberto Reyes, harboured political ambitions, but as yet there were no indications that the Guardia was likely to be disloyal. By the end of the first half of 1937 the National Guard had taken over the administration of all state functions necessary for Somocista dominance: the tax service, the intelligence apparatus, the Pacific Railway, the postal service, the telegraph, government radio, the water system, and Managua's municipal administration. Under these conditions, in Long's opinion, opposition was 'hopeless'.[13]

The evident capacity of the regime to be repressive lessened the necessity for it actually to be so. The congressional opposition was theoretically free to act as it chose, but for the moment it was desisting from even gestures of political competition. The press was technically free, but an informal self-censorship prevailed and no objectionable material was being published. Somoza had also consolidated his hold over the civilian bases of power. His sector of the Liberal Party had always been somewhat unstable, including a large number of opportunists whose support was dependent on the financial advantage they could secure in return. The members of the Liberal old guard, however, although they tended to view Somoza as an arriviste, were getting used to him. Moncada, his former

[11] 817.00/8657, Long to Hull, 19 July 1937.   [12] Ibid.
[13] Ibid.; 817.00/8644, Long to Hull, 7 Apr. 1937.

boss and an influential Liberal, seemed prepared to offer support. Arguello returned to Nicaragua in April and arrived at a rapprochement with Somoza.[14]

The Conservatives were resentful, especially in their Chontales stronghold, but they were cowed by the regime's evident capacity to eradicate any threat they might pose. Somoza told a member of the US legation that he had proof of a Chamorrista plan to assassinate him, and that he had been urged by his ministers to shoot all those involved in the plot. Notwithstanding Long's assurance that Somoza would be willing to offer the hand of friendship to the opposition, some persecution of the Conservatives was apparent. The government itself organized a gathering of Conservatives in honour of the exiled General Emiliano Chamorro. As soon as the celebrations began, the Guardia arrested fifty-six of the invited guests.[15]

In the early months of his administration, therefore, Somoza faced no immediate political threat. His greatest problems were economic, and particularly financial. The merchants were discontented because they felt that they were not receiving equitable treatment from the Exchange Control Commission. The coffee producers were frustrated as a result of the National Bank's control of their exports. These sectors were largely inarticulate, however, while the mass of the people who suffered the most were impotent. Nevertheless, Long thought it probable that, unalleviated, the country's economic malaise could eventually have serious political repercussions.[16]

The economic recovery apparent in Guatemala, El Salvador, and Costa Rica by the mid 1930s was not evident in Nicaragua during Somoza's first year. Effective economic policy-making was hampered by a drastic fall in foreign exchange earnings as a result of export decline. Export values had been fluctuating since the start of the Depression, and by 1936 were equivalent to less than half of their 1929 value. There was some recovery in 1937 before a further decline in 1938. In 1937, moreover, the agricultural mainstay was severely affected by Brazil's abandonment of its coffee restriction and destruction programme. The price of Nicaraguan coffee fell by over a third and the crop itself was damaged by unseasonal rains. Falling export values obliged the government to limit imports. Export

---

[14] 817.00/8657, Long to Hull, 19 July 1937; 715.1715/781, Castleman to Hull, 21 Oct. 1937.
[15] 817.008634, Drew to Hull, 1 Feb. 1937; 817.00/8653, Long to Hull, 14 May 1937.
[16] 817.00/8657, Long to Hull, 19 July 1937.

decline and import suppression reduced revenues from taxes on foreign trade, the main source of government income.[17]

Nicaragua did not default on its external debt, merely suspending amortization payments, and imports therefore recovered less rapidly than elsewhere in Central America. An additional problem on the import side was that, at the time of Somoza's coup, Nicaragua had a large blocked balance of $2.9 million—that is, funds for imported goods deposited with the National Bank at a rate of C$1.1 to the dollar, or over C$3 million.[18] In August 1936, sales of Nicaraguan gold holdings abroad allowed payment of about $1 million of the blocked trade balance (60 per cent of which went to American companies), but increasing dissatisfaction with the National Bank's inability to provide foreign exchange led to the 'Vita Plan' of October 1936.[19] According to the plan, 30 per cent of the foreign exchange proceeds of Nicaraguan exports were to be negotiated with the National Bank at a rate of C$1.1 to the dollar, in order to provide the exchange necessary to reimburse the blocked balances. The remaining 70 per cent could be negotiated at a rate decided between the buyer and the exporter. In December 1936, all the French blocked balances were eliminated.[20]

In the first three months of Somoza's presidency the street exchange rate fluctuated between 200 per cent and 300 per cent and the Vita Plan was abandoned. On 15 March Somoza announced the appointment of James Edwards, an American financial expert, to formulate a new programme. Edwards initially proposed parity between the cordoba and the dollar, but in an effort to boost export values Somoza allowed the currency to depreciate, which naturally favoured oligarchic export interests and foreign companies. The 'Edwards Plan', announced on 21 July, contemplated stricter import control and reaffirmed the law of October 1935 requiring the Exchange Control Commission's prior approval for imports. All foreign exchange transactions were to be handled by the National Bank at a rate of C$2 to the dollar, and a 7.5 per cent tax was imposed on such transactions. On 3 August, Congress passed the new exchange control law.[21]

---

[17] *Commercial Pan America*, 70–2 (Apr.–May 1938), 65–6; Victor Bulmer-Thomas, *The Political Economy of Central America since 1920* (Cambridge: Cambridge University Press, 1987), 69, 326.

[18] 817.5151/354, memorandum, Carrigan to Long, 31 Dec. 1937.

[19] Vicente Vita was general manager of the National Bank.

[20] 817.5151/354, memorandum, Carrigan to Long, 31 Dec. 1937; *Commercial Pan America*, 58–60 (Mar.–May 1937), 38.

[21] 817.5151/354, memorandum, Carrigan to Long, 31 Dec. 1937; Bulmer-Thomas, *The Political Economy*, 22–3; 817.5151/280, vice-consul's report, Carrigan, 21 July 1937; 817.5151/283, Long to Hull, 3 Aug. 1937.

The stability to which the plan looked forward was hindered by some significant problems. The emergence of a border dispute with Honduras increased the need for foreign exchange to buy military equipment. The arms purchases were small, but they further eroded foreign exchange reserves. Sharp anxieties about the 1937 coffee crop pushed down the street value of the cordoba. The Exchange Control Commission, moreover, authorized imports for 1937 to a value greater than the exchange available to pay for them. A new series of blocked balances therefore arose, and by the end of the year collections were pending on about $1.5 million of goods imported since June.[22]

The black market exchange rate fluctuated wildly throughout the year and the National Bank ran short of exchange. Even on the black market the supply was small; foreign exchange holders were retaining their funds in expectation of better prices. The Exchange Control Commission was obliged to tell applicants for exchange to try the illegal market. Increased demand pushed up the street value of the dollar and the exchange rate occasionally reached 4 to 1.[23] By December the cordoba was so unstable that foreign exchange operations virtually ended. In March the street rate had been 1.5 to 1; at the end of the year it was 4.5 to 1, and business activity declined sharply as a result of uncertainty about future fluctuations.[24] Long felt that Nicaragua needed a loan, since exports were otherwise the only substantial source of exchange, and export revenues seemed likely to fall. Rains were affecting the coffee harvest, and the pickers were refusing to work for cordoba wages because of the collapse in the currency's purchasing power.[25] Somoza decided to abandon the Edwards Plan in December and to abolish most exchange controls. A new exchange control law, establishing a free exchange rate, was passed on 22 December. This included a 10 per cent tax in foreign exchange on the net value of all exports, and on all sales of exchange by the National Bank.[26]

These circumstances caused concern in the State Department, for a number of reasons. First, several American companies had restricted or entirely stopped exports to Nicaragua because of the delay in receiving payment, and of fears that payment might never be forthcoming. The department had already ruled out helping Nicaragua, or American firms,

[22] RG 38 C-10-d 6473-I, naval attaché's report, 21 Dec. 1938; 817.5151/354, memorandum, Carrigan to Long, 31 Dec. 1937.

[23] 817.5151/322, Long to Hull, 7 Dec. 1937.

[24] 817.5151/340, Long to Hull, 31 Dec. 1937.   [25] Ibid.

[26] 817.5151/327, memorandum, Gantenbein to Duggan, 21 Dec. 1937; 817.5151/332, memorandum, Drew to Duggan and Briggs, 30 Dec. 1937.

in this matter. In November 1936 the American Locomotive Company had argued for an Exim loan to Nicaragua to enable the government to buy two locomotives for the Pacific Railway. In the State Department, Willard Beaulac argued against any cooperation that would increase Nicaragua's external obligations at a time when the blocked balances indicated that the country was already overextended. Exim therefore declined to cooperate. Debayle called at the department in mid 1937 to seek a loan, but was told by Duggan that such a move was impossible.[27]

This posture raised other difficulties. Managua's barter arrangements with Berlin had given rise to a substantial increase in Germany's share of Nicaraguan imports in recent years, from 8.2 per cent in 1934 to 17 per cent in 1935 and 24 per cent in 1936.[28] The State Department was concerned that Japanese exports to Nicaragua might soon climb significantly. According to the US trade attaché in Nicaragua, Japanese commercial agents called frequently in Managua to 'offer merchandise at ridiculously low prices'.[29] The State Department had already asked Long to verify a *New York Times* story that the Japanese were trying to buy the entire 1936 cotton crop, paying 2¢ more than the market price; reportedly, the planters had agreed to accept Japanese merchandise in payment. The *Times* had also claimed that Germany paid a premium of 2¢ per pound for the Nicaraguan coffee crop in 1936, in return for Nicaraguan purchases of German goods. From Managua, Long stressed that Japanese agents were making strenuous efforts to increase bilateral trade with Nicaragua.[30]

Second, the State Department was concerned that Nicaragua's latest financial plan would violate the terms of the US–Nicaraguan reciprocal trade agreement. These concerns had prompted the department, despite Nicaragua's financial difficulties, to pressure Somoza not to increase the taxes on trade. Nicaragua had already withheld several proposed taxes following US protests that their imposition would breach the agreement. Edwards had to go to Washington to persuade the State Department of the need for such measures, but Harry Hawkins—his interlocutor in the trade agreements division and one of the architects of the reciprocal trade programme—was not in a mood to be convinced. Arguing that an official

[27] 817.77/326, memorandum, Beaulac, 16 Nov. 1936; 817.51/2535, memorandum, Duggan to Welles, 17 Aug. 1937.
[28] Victor Bulmer-Thomas, *The Political Economy*, 79.
[29] 817.5151/161, Ray to Hull, 19 Feb. 1936.
[30] 817.61321/8A, Hull to Long, 17 July 1936; 817.61321/10, Long to Hull, 22 July 1936.

exchange rate of 2 to 1 would nullify the concessions granted to American products in the commercial accord, Hawkins planned to tell Edwards that the US government would, regretfully, be unable to acquiesce in any action that eroded the concessions.[31]

Leroy Stinebower, the State Department's adviser on international economic affairs, disagreed with Hawkins. He argued that if Nicaragua believed the department would block trade-related measures designed to increase revenue, Somoza might feel obliged to call for the termination of the agreement. Stinebower did not think that the United States should put Nicaragua in such a position.[32] In any case, as Long argued from Managua, the effects of the agreement on the competitive position of American exporters in the Nicaraguan market had been slight. The best the minister could say about its effects on Nicaraguan trade and industry was that it had 'done no harm'. Among Nicaraguan officials the agreement had simply prompted resentment by frustrating the government's desire to tax trade. Government officials felt that Nicaragua had derived no benefit from the accord. Nicaraguan violations of the agreement, a reflection of the desperate need to increase revenue, were several— including an increase in consular invoice fees, a packaging tax, and an exchange surcharge on duty collections.[33]

Officials of the State Department's trade agreements division came to acknowledge that the accord provided little, if any, advantage to American trade. Anxious that Nicaragua should not formally call for the termination of the agreement (in case it sparked similar claims from other countries), the department was prepared to modify it at the beginning of 1938. An agreement of 8 February revised the accord, chiefly by suppressing the article that impeded changes in the methods used to determine dutiable value and convert currencies. This was something of a defeat for Hull, and he warned the Latin American division against 'giving undue emphasis' to the procedure. Even following modification, however, Nicaragua continued to violate the accord.[34]

---

[31] 817.5151/336, memorandum, Drew to Duggan and Briggs, 12 Jan. 1938; 611.1731/378, memorandum, Hawkins, 11 Nov. 1937.

[32] 611.1731, memorandum, Stinebower, 17 Nov. 1937.

[33] 611.1731/325, Long to Hull, 18 Jan. 1938.

[34] 611.1731/346, memorandum, Sappington, Division of Trade Agreements, 29 Jan. 1938; US Department of State, *Terminating Certain Provisions of the Reciprocal Trade Agreement of March 11, 1936 between Nicaragua and the United States*, Executive Agreement Series, 20 (Washington DC: US Government Printing Office, 1938); Dick Steward, *Trade and Hemisphere: The Good Neighbor Policy and Reciprocal Trade* (Columbia: University of Missouri Press, 1975), 219.

Third, the State Department noted the potential for political unrest that might be prompted by the cost of living. According to the US consulate, the cost of imported goods had risen by over 300 per cent between the departure of Sacasa and the end of Somoza's first year as president. Rents in Managua had climbed by 200 per cent while wages had been stagnant.[35] The situation had spurred widespread dissatisfaction among rural labourers and Managua's urban poor. The former began agitating for higher wages. Several small strikes were staged as agricultural labourers refused to work for the wages on offer. Business confidence was evaporating. The failure of the Edwards Plan and the perceived indecision of other government actions triggered a steady decline of public confidence in Somoza's ability to administer the country.[36] He did not seem to be aided in this by his cabinet, characterized by Long as 'men of mediocre talent'. As an example, Long referred to José Benito Ramírez, the minister of finance, 'whose only qualification for that position was the rather successful operation of a small shop'.[37] Vice-Consul John Carrigan pointed out that in these circumstances 'it may be possible for labour demagogues to bring about a measure of organization among the laboring classes. From such organization trouble might ensue.'[38]

The Guardia seemed to have retained institutional loyalty, but individual cases of restlessness among the guardsmen were increasingly apparent and there were sporadic incidents of insubordination. Despite pre-election promises, Somoza had done nothing to reorganize the Guardia. Posters had begun to appear in Managua demanding immediate help from the president and claiming that the troops' families were literally starving.[39] Since Somoza had campaigned on a platform of improving the living conditions of members of the military, and since the lower ranks were receiving subsistence wages, it was not certain that Guardia loyalty would prove enduring.[40]

*

In Washington, State Department officials appeared not to be alarmed by such reports. To the extent that they showed concern at all, none of it was

[35] 817.5151/341, memorandum, Carrigan to Long, 31 Dec. 1937.
[36] 817.00/8669, memorandum, Drew to Duggan and Briggs, 19 Jan. 1938; 817.00/8669, Long to Hull, 7 Jan. 1938; 817.00/8644, Long to Hull, 7 Apr. 1937.
[37] 817.00/8644, Long to Hull, 7 Apr. 1937.
[38] 817.5151/341, memorandum, Carrigan to Long, 31 Dec. 1937.
[39] 817.00/8644, Long to Hull, 7 Apr. 1937.
[40] 817.5151/341, memorandum, Carrigan to Long, 31 Dec. 1937.

for Somoza. They worried that Nicaragua's economic problems might be detrimental to American export interests. Hull was anxious that Somoza's financial difficulties might oblige the State Department to modify the trade agreement—not to help Somoza, but to obviate the unravelling of the programme in the event that Somoza called for the accord's termination.

The diplomatic traffic, both to and from Managua, was calmer than it had been for years. The department seldom instructed Long actually to do anything. He was not being asked to make investigations into feelings against the government, nor into the likelihood that such feelings might become militant. In his turn, the minister seldom asked his chiefs what they wanted him to do. It was understood. He monitored events, tried to assess their probable outcome, refrained from interference to the extent that he could while still performing his job as head of a diplomatic mission, and reported his judgement to Washington. The department noted his reports and, as in the case of the trade agreement's revision, reacted when necessary.

The conditions that the United States had claimed to be striving for at the beginning of 1933—to establish relations with Nicaragua on the same basis as relations with other countries—seemed to have been achieved. In 1937, in fact, the first year of what was to be an exceptionally long regime, US non-interference in Nicaragua came as close to being reality as it had ever been in the history of US–Nicaraguan relations. That circumstance gives pause for thought. It raises, in particular, the question of what made it possible. What conditions prevailed?

First, the political opposition in Nicaragua was not simply mute; it seemed to be completely deactivated. The traditional opposition was paralysed. The president dominated the machinery of the ruling party. The party was not monolithic, but the sector that did not support him was not at present overtly opposing him. There was little to be gained by doing so and potentially much to lose. Among the rural workers there had been a few, small, spontaneous work stoppages but they did not respond to any particular political agenda. The traditional opposition could not hope to capitalize on them. Second, the government apparently enjoyed for the moment the backing of a military force that dominated public administration and that had acquired a reputation for unwarranted violence. Troops occasionally complained about living conditions, and observers could occasionally speculate that the armed forces might be a threat to the government at some indeterminate future point, but there was no sense that such a danger was truly imminent.

Third, there was no external political threat to the Nicaraguan government and every indication that the administration would resist anything it perceived as an external ideological threat. The main non-American ideological competitor, although powerful, did not appear to have the capacity to make any great inroads in Nicaragua. The president had made plain in his inaugural address that he was determined to 'defend the people of Nicaragua from any attempt to violate its traditional spirit, avoiding the diffusion of exotic political theories'.[41] At the time, he was referring to Mexico. Later, at various stages, he would espouse the same attitude towards Italy, Germany, and the Soviet Union. The president tirelessly expressed his support, admiration, and affection for the United States. Fourth, there was a widespread perception in Nicaragua that the incumbent government was looked on with favour in Washington and, consequently, that any attempt to change it forcibly would be unlikely to flourish.

Fifth, the United States was determined not to engage with the competing forces of Europe and Asia. On the contrary, the US Congress was enacting legislation to prevent the American president from indulging any temptation he might feel to become involved in such strife. That very isolationism, underpinned by economic malaise in the United States and by the absence of any perceived threat to American interests in the western hemisphere, had encouraged the US government to renounce intervention and to launch a policy of solidarity in the Americas.

Finally, having renounced intervention and then been confronted by a potential external threat, Washington responded not with unilateral action but with a form of multilateral isolationism embodied in instruments of international law to which it and all Latin American countries subscribed. In short, under these strange conditions the head of the US diplomatic mission in Managua simply did not have very much to do in 1937. Good neighbourism as conceived in 1933 was a reality. It was an interlude, and it ended soon.

*

The first substantial rumours of a possible collapse of the Somoza regime began in early 1938. Throughout the previous year the public, while suffering economically, had remained largely ignorant of the true extent of Nicaragua's financial crisis, chiefly because of the self-censorship of

---

[41] 817.001 Somoza, Anastasio/15, Long to Hull, 8 Jan. 1937.

news that was against Somoza's interests. Censorship was now formal and imposed. On 22 January, Somoza announced at a press conference that he would not tolerate political discussion in the newspapers, nor 'in the pulpits'. He stated that any paper that was engaged in such discussions would be suppressed. 'I believe in liberty of the press and in free speech,' the president announced, 'but not when liberty does not promote the welfare of the people.'[42] To some extent public attention to domestic politics had waned during the Nicaragua–Honduras boundary dispute. Despite general dissatisfaction with the economic situation, political conditions had been relatively calm throughout the year and the administration, by means of editorials and carefully placed press releases, had kept public attention on matters outside Nicaragua.[43]

With the end of the border dispute, however, the focus of attention shifted back home. By the start of 1938 the exchange rate was 5 to 1 and there was little prospect of short-term improvement. In the previous three months, requests for permits to export had dropped to the point where foreign sales could be considered at a virtual standstill by the end of 1937. In mid January 1938, Long felt that the economy had reached a nadir. Rumours of unrest, and even of revolution, started to reach the US legation.[44] Emerging against a background of economic crisis, the rumours were fed by popular indignation at the clear evidence of Somoza's self-enrichment. He had begun buying land and property on a large scale, apparently with funds diverted from the treasury. Government employees and the business sector were being obliged to make contributions to a 'National Defence Fund', ostensibly for the purpose of buying arms in the event of hostilities with Honduras. That danger had now passed, and it was apparent that little of the money had gone towards national defence.[45]

In February and March, public speculation about the government's future was complemented by several incidents of outspoken threats against Somoza from the Moncada faction of the Liberal Party. In March, Moncada presided over a meeting of the more prominent old-line Liberals and made a critical speech in which he labelled Somoza a dictator.[46] The US legation believed that both Moncada and Rigoberto

[42] *New York Times*, 23 Jan. 1938.

[43] RG 38 C-10-d 6473-G, naval intelligence report, Captain J. J. Tavern, 17 Jan. 1938.

[44] Ibid.; 817.50/17, Long to Hull, 7 Jan. 1938; 817.50/15, Castleman to Hull, 16 Nov. 1937; 611.1731/325, Long to Hull, 18 Jan. 1938.

[45] RG 38 C-10-d 6433-G, naval attaché's report, 26 Jan. 1938.

[46] 817.00/8677, Long to Hull, 23 Mar. 1938.

Reyes were planning trouble, and that they would be able to realize their plans if the economy failed to improve.[47]

The opposition of both Reyes and Moncada had little to do with economic conditions. Reyes, it should be recalled, had been Somoza's candidate for president in the negotiations that preceded the collapse of the Sacasa administration. His popularity had been growing throughout 1937, and there was common talk of his succeeding Somoza for the new term beginning in 1941. US naval intelligence averred that Reyes had become the most popular man in the country by the beginning of 1938, and it was generally believed that he was viewed favourably in Washington. When Reyes's wife died in December 1937 a group of friends published a booklet about her. The publication was widely circulated in Nicaragua and seems to have been designed, apart from its purposes of condolence, to make a popular leader better known throughout the country.[48]

As to Moncada, throughout much of the period of the Sacasa government's slow disintegration he had been trying to put himself in a position to assume the presidency in the event that his erstwhile protégé, Somoza, staged a coup. The sudden emergence of articulate and influential opposition, significantly from within Somoza's own Liberal Party and the Guardia, was prompted not by economic decline but by the mounting evidence of the president's interest in amending the constitution so as to ensure his continuance in office after 1940. Constitutional revision would frustrate the ambitions of the National Guard's second-in-command and one of the Liberal Party's most influential leaders.

In the March meeting of prominent Liberals, Moncada warned his audience that if a constituent assembly were to be called, the party must be prepared to defend Liberalism 'against all comers' and to shed blood in a struggle against absolutism.[49] That the failure to improve the economy had prompted public dissatisfaction was a consideration that Somoza could largely discount. That his political ambitions had aroused resentment among the few individuals capable of leading militant opposition was a different matter. It widened, for example, the latent breaches in Guardia ranks, a development encouraged by Somoza's failure to improve

[47] 817.00/8676, memorandum, Drew to Duggan and Briggs, 17 Mar. 1936; 817.00/8676, Long to Hull, 9 Mar. 1936.

[48] RG 38 C-9-b 18361, naval intelligence report, Captain J. J. Tavern, 30 Dec. 1936; RG 38 C-10-d 6473-G, naval intelligence report, Captain J. J. Tavern, 17 Jan. 1938.

[49] 817.00/8677, Long to Hull, 23 Mar. 1938.

conditions in the military and the dissipation of the external threat with the resolution of the border dispute.

In the view of the Managua legation, the inherent instability of the Guardia was being exacerbated by economic conditions; rumours of Guardia discontent over pay were now arising daily.[50] The State Department expected political disturbances soon, as the dissatisfaction of the academy-trained officers drove them together. Captain Tavern, the US naval intelligence officer covering Nicaragua, believed that they were now the strongest faction in the country. Major Manuel Gómez, leader of the academy group, had been appointed as secretary to Reyes. Gómez told Tavern that 'the best thing that could happen to Nicaragua would be for the Guardia to take over the country and run it'.[51]

Tavern had confirmed reports of an officers' plot against the president; they had planned to assassinate him on 31 December. Somoza ordered the imprisonment of those most directly involved (Reyes apparently refused to arrest fellow officers) and shuffled the Guardia commands. He told Tavern that some officers had become 'ambitious'; he had transferred them to difficult posts in the expectation that they would resign.[52] Ominously, there were suggestions that Moncada was aware of the conspiracy. Drunk (or, as the naval attaché put it, 'drunker than usual') on the night in question and apparently unaware of the discovery of the plot, the general was reported to have remarked that he was going to the presidential mansion in order to be there when the news of Somoza's death arrived, so that he might take charge.[53] By March, the Guardia was displaying four separate allegiances: to Somoza, Reyes, Chamorro, and Moncada. The general belief in Managua was that a combined Moncada–Reyes faction could overpower the Somoza loyalists.[54]

Against this background, worker discontent could not be so easily disregarded. Rural labour had traditionally provided most of the manpower in Nicaragua's outbursts of civil strife, and if the National Guard split openly under its various influential leaders the economic conditions of the lower sectors might prompt greater militancy. US naval intelligence was concerned. The naval attaché pointed out that the three thousand communists (his evidence-free estimate) in Nicaragua had little power as

[50] 817.00/8669, memorandum, Drew to Duggan and Briggs, 19 Jan. 1938.
[51] RG 38 C-10-d 6473-G, naval intelligence report, Captain J. J. Tavern, 17 Jan. 1938.
[52] RG 38 C-10-d 6473-G, naval intelligence report, Captain J. J. Tavern, 1 Mar. 1938; RG 38 C-8-b 18733, naval attaché's intelligence report, Lamson-Scribner, 25 Jan. 1938.
[53] RG 38 C-10-d 6473-G, naval attaché's report, 26 Jan. 1938.
[54] 817.00/8676, Long to Hull, 9 Mar. 1938.

yet but that they were active in the dissemination of printed propaganda and might gain much greater influence if the economy did not stabilize. From Guatemala, the US legation reported that $2 million had been remitted from Moscow to the Spanish consul general in Mexico to be used for the dissemination of communist propaganda throughout the isthmus.[55] The lower sector's initial support for the regime seemed to be waning, and Somoza was beginning to see labour as a potential threat.[56]

*

In Washington, most of Roosevelt's attention to foreign affairs was focused elsewhere. In January 1938 he planned to convene the members of the diplomatic corps at the White House and advocate world peace, arms reduction, and equal access to raw materials. Chamberlain, about to recognize Mussolini's takeover of Ethiopia in return for a commitment to peaceful relations, rejected the plan. In March, German troops advanced into Austria. Roosevelt himself was concerned at this but at the State Department nobody was arguing for a robust response. The isolationist case, by contrast, was being made relentlessly, and with particular force by Joseph Kennedy, the ambassador in London. Some senior figures in the department, much more worried about Soviet Bolshevism than about German Nazism and innately anti-Semitic, saw no reason for the United States to make a stand on Western Europe.[57]

In these circumstances, however, isolationism itself increasingly demanded security. By the spring of 1938, State Department concerns about the possible penetration of Latin America by European countries was heightened by anxieties that those same countries might come to dominate Europe. The press took up the theme. In April, *Newsweek* reported that the sister republics were exchanging raw materials for 'fascist-made' armaments. According to the newspaper, Peru's police and pilots were being trained by Italian experts, Venezuela had received two Italian cruisers in return for oil, and Chile had just acquired sixty-five German and Italian military aircraft. 'Fascist propaganda', *Newsweek* declared in typical style, 'pours over the southern continent like tropical rain.'[58]

It seemed to be time to address German and Italian military influence in Latin America. A sudden series of meetings between State Department personnel, the armed forces, and military intelligence reached discomfiting

---

55 813.00B/11, DesPortes (Guatemala) to Hull, 19 Mar. 1938.
56 RG 38 C-10-d 6473-G, naval attaché's report, 15 June 1938.
57 Ted Morgan, *FDR: A Biography* (New York: Simon and Schuster, 1985), 488, 497–8.
58 *Newsweek*, 25 Apr. 1938.

conclusions. Naval intelligence reported the 'strenuous efforts' being made by Italy to spread fascism in Central America. The Italian minister in Managua had organized a programme for young Nicaraguans to travel to Italy, at Rome's expense, 'to study fascism'. In January, 400 tons of military material (listed on arrival as railway equipment) arrived from Italy. Long, instructed to monitor propaganda carried out by the German government or German nationals in Nicaragua, reported the 'clannishness' of the German colony and the extensive propaganda activities undertaken by the local German school.[59]

Major Kendall of the navy's Special Service Squadron proved particularly alarmist, asserting that Nicaragua's economic situation would push the Somoza government to accept assistance from elsewhere if the United States did not provide aid. He felt that 'the governments of Japan, Italy and Germany would be glad to have the opportunity of furnishing munitions to Nicaragua in return for certain concessions' on trade, and that Somoza would ask European governments for armaments while negotiating with the Japanese to build a canal.[60] The National Guard, moreover, was abruptly being viewed as a potential strategic liability rather than as simply a possible danger to Somoza. Kendall reported that the air corps was so disorganized that it was a menace to the peace of the whole isthmus, so inefficient as to constitute no deterrent to a revolution, and so unreliable that the pilots might be led into action against the government. He recommended that a US military mission be sent immediately to train the Guardia.[61]

As recently as October 1936, Duggan had told Debayle in Washington that the United States could not comply with Nicaragua's request for the re-establishment of a military academy under US marines. The stated reason was 'the current policy of scrupulous non-interference'.[62] Throughout 1937 and early 1938, legation and naval intelligence reports began to affect the scrupulousness of the policy, but the emergence of the border dispute with Honduras forced the State Department to put any new arrangements in abeyance. By mid 1938, however, the US War Department was prepared to designate an officer to establish an academy,

[59] 810.20/62, memorandum, unsigned, 21 Mar. 1938; RG 38 C-8-b 18773, naval intelligence report, Lamson-Scribner, 2 Jan. 1938; 817.24/356, Long to Hull, 27 Dec. 1937; 817.24/362, Long to Hull, 8 Jan. 1938; RG 38 C-10-g 20498, Long to Hull, 18 Mar. 1938.

[60] RG 38 C-10-d 6473-H, intelligence report, Special Service Squadron, Maj. D. J. Kendall, 25 Aug. 1938.   [61] Ibid.

[62] 817.20/26, memorandum, Duggan, 10 Oct. 1936.

and the State Department was simply waiting for a formal request from Managua.[63] Good neighbourism in Nicaragua was about to shift again in response to the world beyond the hemisphere.

*

In Nicaragua, the cost of living was still rising by mid year. On 8 June exchange control was reimposed in response to violent fluctuations and the official rate was set at 5 to 1. All of the government's economic panaceas had failed. For the first time, the country as a whole began seriously to feel real want. Lack of food, clothing, and medicines, and of the means to buy them, fostered mounting popular criticism of Somoza. 'Hungry stomachs', the American minister told his chiefs, 'are the best incentive to public disorder and hunger is indubitably the lot of a considerable number of Nicaraguans.'[64]

Diplomatic and military attention to Nicaragua had been stepped up but the State Department still failed to evince much anxiety about such reports. The trade agreement had been revised but modification had little effect on American interests. Financial assistance had been refused. Long was not being instructed to discourage opposition. The possibility that the country might pose a security problem, under whatever president, was more of a worry; hence the joint agreement of the War Department and State Department to help train the Nicaraguan armed forces. A more efficient Guardia might make it less necessary to worry about opposition to Somoza, but the fact that Somoza himself was the target of the opposition does not seem to have been the main motivation for the re-establishment of the military academy under an American officer. Long had been watching Reyes's ascendancy and Moncada's growing hostility with a certain detachment. There was no alarm in his dispatches and they prompted no alarm in the State Department. There was the traditional concern about 'disturbances' but no clear plan of how to respond if one were to break out, and certainly no suggestion that, in the event of such an outbreak, Washington would necessarily react differently than it had to the disturbance that ended Sacasa's mandate.

It was from this point, however, the second half of 1938, that unrelated but simultaneous developments conspired to undermine the apparent

[63] 817.20/30, Senator Townsend to Messersmith, 10 June 1938; 817.20/37, memorandum, Drew to Welles, 30 Jan. 1939.
[64] US Department of Commerce, Bureau of Foreign and Domestic Commerce, *Economic Review of Foreign Countries, 1938* (Washington DC: US Government Printing Office, 1939), 178; 817.00/8687, Nicholson to Hull, 6 Aug. 1938.

detachment of good neighbour diplomacy in Nicaragua. In August, the Sudeten Germans began provoking incidents to serve as a pretext for German military intervention in Czechoslovakia. In Nicaragua, during the same month, the Senate voted by 20 to 4 to approve a proposal for the election of a constituent assembly to rewrite Nicaragua's constitution.[65] The matter had been discussed in Congress since soon after Sacasa's departure, and the congressional committees were now ready to present the broad outlines of a new charter. The Conservatives on the committee of the Chamber of Deputies voted against the outline in the belief that the main aim of constitutional reform was to allow Somoza to continue in office after the end of his term. The Conservatives on the Senate committee voiced similar objections. Both chambers eventually gave their approval, however, and a legislative decree called for constituent assembly elections to be held in November; the assembly was to convene in December.[66]

This initiative seems very quickly to have pushed economic and other matters into the background. According to the US naval attaché, 'everything in Nicaragua at the present time evolves [*sic*] around the constitutional assembly'.[67] Congress dissolved itself on 22 August after convoking the elections. Until the constituent assembly was convened, therefore, Somoza was able to govern by executive fiat, a circumstance that gave him broad scope to repress any opposition. Nevertheless, for the sake of apparent legitimacy, he had to induce the participation in the assembly of the 'traditional' Conservatives under the (still exiled) Emiliano Chamorro, in addition to the Nationalist Conservatives who had supported his election in 1936. Three Conservatives, a minority, were therefore appointed to the technical committee that was to draft the new charter. The Conservative Party, moreover, automatically regained the legal status as a party that it had lost by abstaining in 1936. The peculiar form of 'proportional representation' used for the polls, however, heavily favoured the Liberals.[68]

In early October the two sectors of the Conservatives reached agreement, and the Nationalists allowed seven 'traditionals' to be placed on the Nationalist Conservative ticket for the elections.[69] The polls were held

[65] RG 38 C-10-d 6473-H, naval intelligence report, Lamson-Scribner, 26 Aug. 1938.
[66] Knut Walter, *The Regime of Anastasio Somoza, 1936–1956* (Chapel Hill: University of North Carolina Press, 1993), 91.
[67] RG 38 C-10-d 6473-H, naval intelligence report, Lamson-Scribner, 10 Oct. 1938.
[68] 817.00/8693, Nicholson to Hull, 14 Sept. 1938; 817.00/8688, Nicholson to Hull, 23 Aug. 1938; Walter, *The Regime*, 92.
[69] RG 38 C-10-d 6473-I, naval intelligence report, Lamson-Scribner, 10 Oct. 1938.

on 6 November without disturbances. The Conservatives eventually abstained in several departments, and the whole organization of the election favoured the Somocista Liberals. The ballots and ballot boxes were distributed by the quartermaster general of the National Guard and the results were available suspiciously soon.[70] The constituent assembly would be dominated by Liberals, and it seemed plain at the time that it would do whatever Somoza wanted. It was equally plain that what he wanted was to extend his term of office.[71]

Five weeks before the elections to Nicaragua's constituent assembly, German troops occupied the Sudetenland. Three days after the polls, on 9 November 1938, came Kristallnacht. An outpouring of indignation in Western Europe and the United States at this barbarism undermined most of the faith still prevailing that German aggression might end soon. At his 500th press conference on 15 November, Roosevelt told his audience: 'I myself could scarcely believe that such things could occur in a twentieth-century civilization.' From the start of the new year, rumours abounded about the next German step. Reports of a possible invasion of the Netherlands were being taken seriously by the British cabinet. In the three months that Nicaragua's constituent assembly took to produce the country's new constitution, Roosevelt began the laborious process of weaning Americans off isolationism. It was a monumental task. Among some senior figures in the Senate, particularly, isolationism was less a political position than a value system; intervention was seen not simply as a political error, but as a moral failing.[72]

Roosevelt invited the members of the Senate Military Affairs Committee to the White House on 31 January 1939 in an attempt to shake their faith. Outlining what he called 'a policy of world domination between Germany, Italy and Japan', the president, at considerable length, offered his own reading of current events:

There are two ways of looking at it. The first is the hope that somebody will assassinate Hitler and that Germany will blow up from within; that someone will kill Mussolini or that he will get a bad cold in the morning and die... The other attitude is that we must try to prevent the domination of the world... Now, it may come to you as a shock... but what is the first line of defense of the United States?... On the Atlantic our first line of defense is the continued independent

70 Walter, *The Regime*, 92.
71 RG 38 C-10-d 6473-H, naval intelligence report, Lamson-Scribner, 10 Oct. 1938; RG 38 C-10-d 6473-I, naval intelligence report, Lamson-Scribner, 14 Nov. 1938.
72 Alan Bullock, *Hitler and Stalin: Parallel Lives* (London: Fontana, 1993), 638, 646; Morgan, *FDR*, 501.

existence of a very large group of nations . . . Now if [Hitler] insists on going ahead to the westward, it is a fifty-fifty bet that [Britain and France] will be put out of business. Then the next step, which Brother Hitler suggested in the speech yesterday, would be Central and South America . . . Do not say it is chimerical; do not say it is just a pipe dream . . . This is the gradual encirclement of the United States by the removal of our first lines of defence.[73]

Roosevelt had no more illusions about Hitler. Between 16 and 18 March the Germans overran the whole of Czechoslovakia. The case for appeasement evaporated.[74] Five days later, Nicaragua was presented with its new charter.

The Nicaraguan constitution of 1939 made a direct appeal to the urban and rural workers with whom Somoza had been having some difficulties. It stated that unused *latifundia* would be divided into small and medium properties; it granted workers a weekly day of rest, a minimum salary, maximum working hours, compensation for work-related accidents, and free medical care; and it committed the state to establish a social security agency. The charter provided for a six-year presidential term with no re-election, although article 350 exempted the incumbent from this provision.[75]

The constituent assembly then did what the dissenting Conservatives had predicted: having transformed itself into the National Congress for the period until 15 April 1947, in an apathetic session marked by a clear lack of enthusiasm, it voted Somoza into the presidency until 1 July 1947. The Senate would now hold eleven Liberals, three Nationalist Conservatives, and one Traditional Conservative. The Chamber of Deputies would have thirty Liberals, eight Nationalist Conservatives, and six Traditional Conservatives. The new charter would not be submitted to the Supreme Court until after the court had been reorganized by the Somocista-dominated assembly on 1 May 1939. The US naval attaché took care to stress to his chiefs that the Nicaraguan people had been disenfranchised and that for the next eight years they would have no voice in the election of their executive, legislative, and judicial authorities.[76]

A new American minister, Meredith Nicholson, had arrived in June 1938 to replace Long. He was making the same point to the State Department, stressing that Somoza's retention of the presidency until

---

[73] Morgan, *FDR*, 503–4.   [74] Ibid. 506; Bullock, *Hitler and Stalin*, 649, 652.

[75] Walter, *The Regime*, 93; Richard Millet, *Guardians of the Dynasty* (Maryknoll, NY: Orbis Books, 1977), 193.

[76] 817.011/157, Nicholson to Hull, 23 Mar. 1939; RG 38 C-10-d 19539, naval attaché's report, 27 Mar. 1939.

1947 was 'not to be interpreted as evidence of public confidence or even admiration on the part of the great body of the people'. There was no public enthusiasm at the prospect, and there were no celebrations on re-election day. The attitude of the public at large was one of resignation although, in Nicholson's opinion, if left without hope of change the people might become violent. Nicholson, in fact, had urged the Conservatives not to boycott the polls. Whenever he spoke to members of the party he 'took the liberty of suggesting . . . that even when two or three are gathered together under proper auspices a situation is not hopeless'.[77]

The Conservatives were not impressed. They genuinely wanted to know if the US marines would return, a consideration that seemed to feature prominently in their political speculations, and believed that Somoza's actions provided cause for intervention.[78] These actions referred mostly to the president's remarkable penchant for self-enrichment. The US naval attaché did not believe that this warranted intervention, but he did feel that there was 'so much evidence of the complete decay of the moral fiber' of the Somoza administration that it merited particular US attention. He was so struck by the scale of the corruption that he sent to the director of naval intelligence a lengthy and detailed report entitled 'Moral Disintegration of the Present Nicaraguan Government'.[79]

In the bluntest terms, the naval attaché described a chief executive who had realized there was virtually no limit to the profit he could make if he applied himself diligently to 'graft and all forms of crookedness'. According to the intelligence report, Somoza had acquired a great deal of property at very low cost in Managua by intimidating the owners. He acquired a sugar mill and cornered the sugar market. He forced the owner of the Mercedes Dairy to sell the business to him at half its value and monopolized Managua's milk supply; he then increased the price. The mining companies were paying him a 5 per cent 'voluntary contribution' on the value of all exports. Cheques were issued personally to the president and deposited in a Canadian bank. In the expectation that a canal would soon be built in Nicaragua, Somoza acquired control of all the boats operating on Lake Nicaragua and, by means of various restrictions, forced the only competing company out of business. He secured properties along the most probable canal route at a fraction of their value.[80]

[77] 817.001 Somoza, Anastasio/50, Nicholson to Hull, 3 Apr. 1939.   [78] Ibid.

[79] RG 38 C-10-d 6473-I, naval attaché's report, 21 Dec. 1938.

[80] Ibid.; 817.001 Somoza, Anastasio/211, Baldwin to Hull, 2 Dec. 1939.

By now he had amassed a personal fortune estimated at between three and four million dollars. He treated Liberal Party funds as a personal bank account and exacted a payment of 1.5¢ per pound on all exported cattle. The pace he set was being taken up by much of the public administration. The naval attaché was aware that a certain degree of corruption had always been a feature of Nicaraguan public life, but he was staggered by the new levels to which Somoza was taking it. 'The whole core of the present administration is rotten,' he declared, 'and the decay has almost reached the outer skin'. The State Department was receiving similar reports from Nicholson, who described Somoza's methods of acquiring property as 'hitleresque' and who told his chiefs that 'what limit may be imposed on the man's rapaciousness by other means than a complete political turnover does not at this time appear'.[81]

State Department officials, then, had a fairly clear picture of Somoza. They knew that his re-election did not reflect regained popularity; that in fact he was unpopular and that there was a possibility that feelings against him might turn militant; and that he was setting standards of corruption at which American representatives in Managua could only marvel. Two months after Somoza was re-elected, Roosevelt received him in Washington with full military honours.

*

In the decades since 1939, the coincidence of these developments has been imbued by some observers with a particular significance for US–Nicaraguan relations. That Somoza engineered his own re-election through constitutional revision, and thereafter was promptly invited to Washington, has been interpreted as a highly public display of the Roosevelt administration's support for *somocismo*. At the time, the main significance of Nicaragua's 1939 constitution for bilateral relations was somewhat different. In the draft version it was located in article 4, and for weeks the State Department had been trying to avoid having to deal with it.

In August 1914, Washington and Managua had concluded the Bryan–Chamorro Treaty, whereby the United States was accorded the right to build a Nicaraguan canal and was leased the necessary territory for ninety-nine years in return for $3 million. The existing Nicaraguan constitution was incompatible with the treaty, since article 2 stated that

81 817.001 Somoza, Anastasio/74, Nicholson to Hull, 26 Apr. 1939; 817.001 Somoza, Anastasio/50, Nicholson to Hull, 3 Apr. 1939; 817.001 Somoza, Anastasio/53, Nicholson to Hull, 14 Apr. 1939; 817.00/6341, Nicholson to Hull, 24 June 1939; 817.001 Somoza, Anastasio/211, Baldwin to Hull, 2 Dec. 1939.

sovereignty was inalienable and that the government had no authority to make pacts affecting the sovereignty of the nation.[82]

At the start of November 1938, desperate for some form of economic assistance, Somoza told Nicholson that he intended to include in the new constitution a provision making the Bryan–Chamorro Treaty a matter of organic law, with the lease extended to perpetuity. He wanted to visit the United States in order to discuss the matter.[83] Hull did not welcome this initiative. He felt that the treaty was sufficient basis for US canal rights and was concerned that if the issue were to be raised now it would prompt disputes with Costa Rica and El Salvador, which had always challenged the agreement.[84]

Somoza pushed the issue. The Nicaraguan foreign ministry prepared a lengthy memorandum for submission to the State Department. While not questioning the validity of the Bryan–Chamorro Treaty, the document argued that the Nicaraguan case warranted reconsideration in view of the fact that the canal had not actually been built. The proposal was to modify the constitution in order to empower the government to alienate territory for the purposes of canal construction. Nicholson, like Hull, was fearful that renewed discussion of this issue would prompt resentment elsewhere in the isthmus, a case he made at length to Somoza and the foreign minister, Manuel Cordero Reyes. The Nicaraguans eventually agreed not to submit the memorandum to the State Department.[85]

Somoza nonetheless persisted. Leon Debayle, Nicaraguan minister in Washington, wrote to Hull at the end of November proposing a visit by Somoza to discuss the position established in the foreign ministry memorandum.[86] On the following day Debayle called on Welles and made a lengthy argument. Essentially, he contended that Nicaragua was in dire economic straits but that its greatest potential natural resource was paralysed by the failure of the United States to act on its treaty rights. Debayle asked that the United States pay for the canalization of the San Juan River.[87]

---

[82] US Department of State, *Foreign Relations*, 1938, v, 798–9.

[83] 817.812/736, Nicholson to Hull, 3 Nov. 1938.

[84] 817.812/736, Hull to Nicholson, 7 Nov. 1938. A contemporary account of Costa Rican claims is given in Ricardo Jinesta, *Confirmación de los derechos de Costa Rica en el Canal de Nicaragua* (San José, Costa Rica: Falco Hnos., 1937). The book's publication appears to have been prompted by a feeling that canal construction might be imminent.

[85] 817.812/739, Nicholson to Hull, 10 Nov. 1938.

[86] 817.812/748, Debayle to Hull, 30 Nov. 1938.

[87] 817.812/748, memorandum, Welles, 1 Dec. 1938.

Welles differed with Debayle's view and presented the American case. But a formal request had been made for a Nicaraguan president to visit the United States in order to discuss a bilateral treaty that might affect Nicaragua's constitution. The request had at least to be considered. Welles therefore wrote to Roosevelt summarizing the above developments and mentioning Somoza's desire to visit Washington in order to discuss the issues raised. Roosevelt's reply was brief. He simply returned Welles's letter to him with a handwritten note at the top saying 'Visit OK. FDR'.[88]

Roosevelt's cursory approval of a meeting with a foreign head of state, for what seemed a concrete and quite limited agenda, coincided with particular international and inter-American events. The Munich Agreement of September 1938, whereby Chamberlain agreed to Hitler's demands that the Sudetenland be ceded to Germany, had affected the agenda for the Eighth International Conference of American States scheduled for Lima in December, at precisely the time when Somoza was lobbying to go to Washington. The conference had been planned for some time, and the United States had not been giving it undue emphasis. On 6 November, however, the same day as the Nicaraguans elected their constituent assembly, Welles appealed for a united hemispheric front at Lima following the partition of Czechoslovakia. 'We will assure ourselves', he declared, 'that we are in a position . . . to be prepared to join with our fellow democracies of the New World in preserving the Western Hemisphere safe from any threat of external attack.'[89]

At the Lima conference the following month, the United States introduced a draft proposal for joint action against any subversion of western-hemisphere countries by 'fascist-oriented systems'. The eventual compromise proposal was announced by the delegates as the Declaration of Lima. This affirmed the intention of the American republics to help each other in case of a 'direct or indirect' foreign (that is, non-American) attack on any one of them. This was a virtual multilateralization of the Monroe Doctrine. In the Declaration of American Principles the conference again reinforced non-intervention. The sister republics resolved that 'the intervention of any state in the internal or external affairs of another is inadmissable'.[90]

[88]   817.812/748, Welles to Roosevelt, 12 Dec. 1938.
[89]   710.H-Continental Solidarity/1, press release, 5 Nov. 1938; Irwin Gellman, *Good Neighbor Diplomacy: United States Policies in Latin America, 1933–1945* (Baltimore, Md.: Johns Hopkins University Press, 1979), 74.
[90]   Doris A. Graber, *Crisis Diplomacy: A History of US Intervention Policies and Practices* (Washington: Public Affairs Press, 1959) 232; G. Pope Atkins, *Latin America in the*

The international context, then, was of increasingly probable war. The inter-American context was of growing solidarity to meet the security conditions that a probable war seemed to demand. And the bilateral context was established by Somoza's desire to induce US construction of a canal in Nicaragua. Washington had not initiated the invitation, and when Somoza went he was refused most of the aid he sought. For Somoza, however, US approval of his proposed visit had immediately positive repercussions. It directly bolstered his position in Nicaragua since it enabled the press to engage in an active propaganda campaign, one designed to stress the progress that the country had made under Somoza and the immense economic benefits that would soon be forthcoming as a result of his statesmanship.[91] It was naturally interpreted as a sign of US approval of his government. For the US diplomatic establishment the repercussions were more negative. From the sudden and enormous increase in traffic in the Latin American division in this period, it is clear that the plans for the visit were creating some real problems for the State Department.

The greatest difficulty was caused by the level of expectations that Somoza was raising in Nicaragua. The president made as much political capital as possible from the forthcoming visit, deliberately inciting public speculation as to its possible outcome and implying that it would solve all of the country's problems at a stroke. He made known that he was to seek American aid in four major areas: canalization of the San Juan River and construction of a parallel railway; American assistance in strengthening the reserves of the National Bank; further revision of the trade agreement for the purpose of granting tariff concessions; and the establishment of a government monopoly for the sale of oil products. These aims were being widely publicized throughout Latin America just as the United States— for the first time contemplating the possibility of an external attack—had intensified its campaign for inter-American solidarity. Hull was apprehensive at the coincidence. He instructed Nicholson to avoid giving any impression that favourable action on any of Somoza's proposals would be forthcoming, and to emphasize that the president should not publicize any expectations.[92]

International Political System (Boulder, Colorado: Westview Press, 1995); Edgar O. Guerrant, *Roosevelt's Good Neighbour Policy* (Albuquerque: University of New Mexico Press, 1950).

[91] 817.001 Somoza, Anastasio/66, Nicholson to Hull, 25 Apr. 1939.
[92] 817.001 Somoza, Anastasio/47a, Hull to Nicholson, 1 Apr. 1939.

Nicholson did so. Somoza launched a series of press conferences. The propaganda opportunity was too good to miss. The trip was soon the main subject of public debate; as it grew nearer, expectations were heightened. Nicholson reported 'an outpouring of personal opinion by political and businessmen for the success of Somoza's trip ... Certain it is that a bounteous Uncle Sam will take care of his nephew with grateful millions, in return for which Nicaragua expects to provide nothing.'[93] The rhetoric of fraternal good neighbourism, stepped up further as a means of fostering western-hemisphere solidarity, presumably encouraged such convictions.

The press began demanding 'justice' for the canal treaty and assistance in economic development, in return for a bilateral political agreement in the spirit of the Lima conference, as well as a military plan of defence. The media attention led most Nicaraguans to believe that Somoza would return from Washington with proposals for substantial American aid.[94] 'The general is advertising his visit to Washington to such an extent', Duggan warned his colleagues in the State Department, 'that it will *literally become impossible* for him to return to Nicaragua empty-handed.'[95] In short, expectations had been raised so high, and been so widely publicized in the region, that failure to meet at least some of them could undermine much of the effort that the State Department had been putting into its campaign of inter-American unity.

Duggan outlined in seven points how it was theoretically possible to help Nicaragua and to obviate charges of US indifference to a sister republic at a time of crisis: (i) canalization of the San Juan River; (ii) highway construction; (iii) a credit to the National Bank to help flatten out exchange fluctuations; (iv) an agricultural survey to determine the possibility of stimulating the production of non-competitive products; (v) the establishment of an agricultural experimental station in Nicaragua; (vi) Exim credits for a public works programme of harbour improvements at Corinto, hydroelectric projects, and the purchase of new rolling stock for the Pacific Railway; and (vii) encouraging American firms to undertake new developments in Nicaragua ('without of course in any way committing this government'). Duggan thought there was a possibility that the United Fruit Company (UFCO) might be persuaded to undertake rubber and abaca growing in Nicaragua.[96]

[93] 817.001 Somoza, Anastasio/76, Nicholson to Hull, 19 Apr. 1939.
[94] 817.001 Somoza, Anastasio/71, Nicholson to Hull, 25 Apr. 1939.
[95] 817.001 Somoza, Anastasio/48, memorandum, Duggan to Briggs and Drew, 1 Apr. 1939. Emphasis in the original.
[96] 817.001 Somoza, Anastasio/151, memorandum by Duggan, 27 Apr. 1939.

Nicholson constantly expressed his concern for what Somoza might *not* obtain on the trip, and warned that if the president returned empty-handed the current phase of pro-Americanism would immediately vanish and 'many of the possibilities which are now only fears on the part of American mining interests and others might quickly become sources of continued friction as well as of burdensome "milking"'. The US-owned power company and mining interests were already concerned about possible action under the new constitution's article 271 (establishing that the wealth of the subsoil belonged to the state) and article 263, which made no provision for legal guarantees in the event of a declaration of a state of economic emergency. Nicholson insisted on the need to find 'a suitable means of satisfying the avarice of the government and of quieting any possible repercussions', and suggested the radical step of purchasing the Corn Islands; he justified this in strategic terms because of their position relative to the Panama Canal.[97] This suggestion was not feasible, however, since the islands were already under long-term lease to the United States under the terms of the Bryan–Chamorro Treaty and Congress would not approve their purchase.[98]

Granting Somoza's request to visit the United States must have seemed like a good idea at the time. It was now transformed into a situation that appeared to pose a threat to American private business in Nicaragua and to inter-American solidarity. The department made hasty plans. The Office of the Chief of Engineers was asked to carry out a feasibility study of the canalization project. According to Welles the idea was 'not practicable' because of the cost. Neither the War Department nor the Navy Department considered the canal a worthwhile expenditure, and by mid April the department knew that the House Committee on Merchant Marine and Fisheries was going to vote for a third set of locks at Panama rather than for the Nicaraguan project.[99]

The Latin American division studied the possibility of an Exim loan to improve navigation on the San Juan River but was interested only 'if it can be determined that this can be done at a reasonable cost'. It could not be so determined. As to the possibility of a stabilization fund for the National Bank, Welles was unwilling to make any recommendations with regard to any financial assistance to the Nicaraguan government.[100] From

[97] 817.001 Somoza, Anastasio/81, Nicholson to Hull, 4 Apr. 1939; 817.001 Somoza, Anastasio/53, Nicholson to Hull, 14 Apr. 1939.
[98] 817.001 Somoza, Anastasio/90, Welles to Nicholson, 16 Apr. 1939.
[99] 817.001 Somoza, Anastasio/119, memorandum, Welles to Hull, 14 Apr. 1939.
[100] Ibid.

Managua, Nicholson also urged that no credit be offered, and that if a loan were extended it should be done only with the conditions of a mortgage on the bank and the right to name the bank's officials.[101] The State Department also refused to countenance reducing the duty on imports of Nicaraguan sugar.[102] The department having declined at the outset to provide the assistance Somoza sought, Duggan believed that 'in order to satisfy Nicaraguan public opinion, and General Somoza, *and to preclude the possibility of agitation throughout the Americas*, rather substantial proposals of a different character must be made'.[103] The most immediate option was highway construction.

A week after he had assumed office, Somoza had asked the Roosevelt administration for help in building fifteen miles of road running north from Tipitapa as a link in the Pan American Highway, and to this end C$165,000 was set aside with Irving Lindberg, the collector general of customs. From the United States, Nicaragua wanted direct financial aid, road-building equipment, and engineers. The State Department initially agreed to send engineers from the Bureau of Public Roads to conduct surveys for three bridges and for the road's final location. In addition, the United States was willing to provide construction equipment and an engineer to supervise the work. A direct financial contribution, however, raised problems.[104]

In June 1937 Thomas H. MacDonald, chief of the Bureau of Public Roads, had spoken to Willard Beaulac in the State Department about the possibility of an appropriation of $1 million to assist bridge and highway construction in Central America. Beaulac implied to MacDonald that this request would have State Department support. Sumner Welles disagreed. 'I do not believe', he wrote, 'that public opinion in this country, nor the Congress, would sanction any recommendation by the Department of State for an appropriation of $1 million...I think any such recommendation would be bad policy...I would strongly oppose any further appropriation by this government.' Welles insisted that the Central American republics could afford to use their own resources, and they were duly informed that the major part of the costs would have to be met by their respective governments.[105]

101 817.001 Somoza, Anastasio/53, Nicholson to Hull, 14 Apr. 1939.

102 817.001 Somoza, Anastasio/119, Welles to Hull, 14 Apr. 1939.

103 817.001 Somoza, Anastasio/151, memorandum by Duggan, 27 Apr. 1939. Emphasis added.

104 810.154/1117, Long to Hull, 9 Jan. 1937; 810.154/1118, Long to Hull, 19 Feb. 1937.

105 810.154/1178, memorandum, Beaulac to Welles, 8 June 1937; 810.154/1178, memorandum, Welles to Heath, 10 June 1937.

By April 1939, with Somoza's arrival imminent and few other proposals that the State Department was willing to consider, the road programme was the Latin American division's most viable option. In itself, however, this posed a further problem. Having indicated to the Central American governments that they must each pay for their own section of the highway, the department decided, as Duggan indicated, that it would 'probably be politically undesirable' to offer aid to Nicaragua and ignore the other republics. Hence it decided it would have to offer 'proportional assistance' to the rest of Central America.[106] In short, the State Department was willing to reverse US policy and substantially aid construction of the entire Central American section of the Pan American Highway in order to obviate Nicaraguan criticism of Somoza and anti-Americanism throughout the region. It was prepared to do this even though it had not yet decided whether the highway was a desirable objective. 'The time has come', wrote Duggan, 'for the Department to come to some considered opinion as to the utility of the Pan American Highway from every point of view.'[107]

By May, the State Department had decided to recommend an Exim credit of $2 million for 'a modest programme of road-building' and $500,000 to help stabilize the cordoba. The road-building programme was to be based on the Haitian and Paraguayan models: the United States would finance external expenditures, imported materials and equipment, foreign engineers, and the services of a US engineering firm; Nicaragua would provide domestic materials and labour. The half-million dollar credit to the National Bank, according to Welles's special assistant Emilio Collado, was partly to help eliminate exchange rate fluctuations and 'partly psychological'. The division's position on this matter had shifted markedly in less than a month. 'It is considered advisable', Collado now averred, 'to lend reasonable cooperation to Nicaragua in certain respects where there will be fairly definite benefit to the United States as well as to Nicaragua.'[108]

The two Exim credits were the sum of what Somoza secured in Washington. This level of assistance, and the attitudes that informed it, contrasted sharply with the reports being published in the Nicaraguan press, which were claiming that funds had been agreed to canalize the San Juan River, construct a parallel road, and develop the entire economy. The US legation's first secretary reported that there was no hint of any restrictions on the amount immediately available nor on its allocation. There prevailed a general feeling that further funds would follow.[109]

---

[106] 817.001 Somoza, Anastasio/151, memorandum by Duggan, 27 Apr. 1939.
[107] Ibid.   [108] 817.51/2601, memorandum, Collado, 1 May 1939.
[109] 817.51/2597, Castleman to Hull, 23 May 1939.

In Washington it had been clear from the outset that funds would not be made available for the bigger projects, precisely those that Somoza was aiming to secure and that had captured the imagination of the Latin American media. Public display, however, was relatively cheap, and might serve to distract attention from the visit's lack of concrete results. The US government, therefore, duly mounted a display. The ceremony attendant on Somoza's travel in the United States spurred very appreciative reactions in Nicaragua. Roosevelt personally met the general at the railway station, where he was received with military honours. He stayed overnight in the White House. Nicholson pointed out that because Somoza was now a symbol of hope for Nicaragua, there was 'no indication of any attempt to overthrow the government in his absence'. He reported a newspaper headline: 'Taken as Accomplished—the Canalization of the San Juan River and Electrification of the Country's Railways. Many Millions for Nicaragua.' The article continued: 'all [Latin] America is now in Washington with President Somoza... Nicaragua is in this moment the touchstone of international justice, the living testimony of an elevated policy.'[110]

Not even Nicholson knew what Somoza had actually managed to get. Before the general's return to Nicaragua, Nicholson cabled the department: 'It will be as well for us to have here, against Somoza's return, a pretty clear idea of what he carries in his game bag... He may be expected to encourage the idea on his arrival that he has enjoyed good hunting.'[111] Since he had substantially less in his game bag than he had suggested he could bring home, Somoza was uncharacteristically quiet. By July he still had not informed the Nicaraguan public of the concrete results of his trip, though he had vaguely implied that he had secured almost all of his aims: that a canal would be built, that there would be a parallel road, that other roads would be constructed, that the cordoba would be stabilized, and that a range of other public works would be undertaken, all with American money.[112]

Somoza's visit to Washington in 1939 has given rise to a legend of personal regard between him and Roosevelt. The legend has found its most popular expression in one wearyingly reiterated (and almost certainly apocryphal) vulgarity that Roosevelt is supposed to have uttered,

[110] 817.001 Somoza, Anastasio/115, Nicholson to Hull, 19 May 1939; *New York Times*, 14 May 1939; Bryce Wood, *The Making of the Good Neighbor Policy* (New York: Columbia University Press, 1961), 155.

[111] 817.001 Somoza, Anastasio/155, Nicholson to Duggan, 19 May 1939.

[112] RG 38 C-10-d 6473-I, naval attaché's report, 23 July 1939.

and which for some commentators appears fully to embody Washington's attitude to Anastasio Somoza.[113] It was a myth, one that Somoza astutely encouraged. He referred frequently to his 'friend' Roosevelt in speeches, declared a two-day national holiday on Roosevelt's re-election in 1940, and, on the occasion of FDR's birthday in 1942, renamed one of Managua's main thoroughfares 'Avenida Franklin Roosevelt'.[114]

To the extent that this notion acquired widespread veracity in Nicaragua it probably deterred opposition to Somoza, especially in the war years when the mobilization of the US military establishment in Central America appeared to support it. In reality, the State Department was trying to salvage what it could from what had become a public relations disaster, offering a relatively low level of assistance not chiefly to safeguard Somoza but to obviate anti-Americanism in Nicaragua and the danger of what Duggan had termed 'agitation throughout the Americas'. For his own part, Roosevelt does not seem to have given much further thought to Somoza once the general went home. The frequent messages that Somoza sent to him were routinely handled by a presidential aide. To one such message, which Somoza signed 'Su Afmo. Amigo A. Somoza G.', the White House's routine reply was addressed to 'President Afmo Amigo Somoza'.[115]

There were, then, strategic considerations behind US actions, but Somoza's personal position in Nicaragua does not seem to have loomed large in such thinking. Basic stability was more at issue. It was while Somoza was in Washington that Germany and Italy concluded their formal military alliance, the 'Pact of Steel'.[116] Political support for the United States throughout Latin America now seemed to be not simply

---

[113] Since the vulgarity in question so monotonously persists in historical studies of US–Central American affairs, it is worth noting that it clearly predated Somoza's presidency, and that what was possibly its first appearance in print was a reference to FDR himself. A book published in 1934 says this: 'After the 1932 Chicago Convention [at which Roosevelt was first nominated for the presidency], General Hugh Johnson . . . was asked what he thought of his nomination. Johnson replied by recalling a story of a county convention of Democrats in which the wrong man had been chosen. Driving home from the meeting, two politicians were comparing notes. Both had opposed the successful candidate. One said to the other, "Damn it all! . . . he's a son of a bitch!" The other man sighed and said nothing for a long time. Then he cheered up. "After all," he observed, " . . . he's *our* son of a bitch".' See John F. Carter, *The New Dealers: By the Unofficial Observer* (New York: Simon and Schuster, 1934). Emphasis in the original. In the context of US–Nicaraguan relations, it seems quite plausible that one of the most recurrent quotations of inter-American historiography originated with Somoza rather than with Roosevelt. The language, certainly, was much more Somoza's style, and the notion conveyed would have served him well.   [114] Millet, *Guardians*, 197.

[115] Ibid. 197, 217 n. 41.   [116] Bullock, *Hitler and Stalin*, 656.

a vague inter-American ideal but a strategic necessity. In the new circumstances, good neighbourly non-interference might be a strategic liability without pro-American solidarity on the country's southern flank.

Diplomatic thinking was slowly coming in line with military thinking. Dictatorship could simultaneously be viewed as distasteful while serving the best interests of the United States and also of the sister republics. Lieutenant Colonel Joseph Pate, US military attaché for Central America, wrote of Somoza:

I do not question the desirability of an executive of these small countries remaining in office for a period longer than the four years which has heretofore been the case. The principle of 'continuismo' is a bad one, owing to its being so diametrically opposed to our own ideas of what constitutes a democratic form of government...But as long as the present dictators of Central America do not swing in their aims and ambitions and policies in the direction of European totalitarianism, they undoubtedly represent the best, most secure, and most efficient system of government these small republics can have at their present state of political infancy.[117]

This kind of sentiment can be held to have undermined the highly moral tone that had informed good neighbour rhetoric for the previous six years; a corrupt authoritarian was a guest at the White House. Indeed, such thinking has been held to invalidate all the claims of good neighbourism as a new way of conducting US policy towards Latin America. But the context had changed, and the moral abstractions behind Hull's thinking of half a decade earlier no longer seemed sufficient to sustain a policy towards the region.

The State Department had no illusions about Somoza. In January, one of the Latin American division's most prominent spokesmen, Ellis Briggs, had made a speech in which he asserted that in all Latin American countries except Brazil there was an allegiance to democratic government 'in form'. In some countries (Chile, Colombia, Costa Rica, and Venezuela) there was a practice of democratic principles 'in substance'. In Central America, Briggs observed 'personalized government, dictatorships if you will, very strongly centralized but not at present to any appreciable degree "totalitarian" in the European sense'. What is interesting about this speech is that Briggs was addressing an audience at the Army War College and spent much of his time lauding the new level of cooperation between the War, Navy, and State departments in the conduct of US foreign

---

[117] 817.001 Somoza, Anastasio/92, intelligence report, 18 April 1939.

policy. 'Never', he declared, 'has cooperation been so close, so effective and so efficient.'[118]

Briggs was evidently not exaggerating. In Managua, the diplomat Nicholson now worried about the combat-readiness of the Guardia. The US naval attaché worried about anti-Americanism and matters of presidential succession in Central America. Following Somoza's return to Nicaragua, the attaché reported to the director of naval intelligence that the Germans and Japanese had a special interest in the economic penetration of the isthmus. He characterized the incumbent Costa Rican government as 'decidedly pro-German' but pointed out that Rafael Calderón, sole candidate for the term beginning in 1940, was pro-American: 'with his election, which is practically assured, the opportunity will be offered for the United States to replace the strong German influence in the country.'[119] Somoza's election had also been assured, and he was evidently pro-American. If the cooperation between the State Department and the US military establishment was as close as Briggs claimed, that circumstance must have been welcome in Washington. Within two months, it was much more than welcome.

[118] RG 38 C-9-b 18685-A, transcript of an address by Ellis Briggs at the Army War College, 12 Jan. 1939.
[119] RG 38 B-10-t 17816, Lamson-Scribner to the director of naval intelligence, 25 July 1939.

6

The United States, Nicaragua, and World War II, 1939–1941

And then came Adolf Hitler, creator of the first authentic Pan Americanism to flourish in this western world.[1]

On 1 September 1939, German troops invaded Poland. Britain and France declared war on the Reich two days later. In the first week of hostilities the Germans destroyed the Polish air force, overcame infantry resistance, and besieged Warsaw. Within two weeks the Russians were moving into eastern Poland. On 3 September Joseph Kennedy, the US ambassador in London, told Roosevelt: 'It's the end of the world, the end of everything.'[2] Roosevelt announced his determination to keep the United States out of the war, although strict neutrality was not an issue for him. Self-interest and the survival of American values, he felt, demanded Germany's defeat. In this he was supported by the public: at the outbreak of war a Gallup poll indicated that 84 per cent of respondents favoured victory for the Allies. Despite this preference, congressional and public isolationism remained powerful. In his efforts to secure changes to the neutrality legislation, therefore, Roosevelt had to be attentive to widespread concern that he might force the country into war.[3]

From Latin America the declarations of neutrality were swift. The sister republics understood that the war posed collective problems

---

[1] Hubert Herring, *Good Neighbors: Argentina, Brazil, Chile and 17 other Countries* (New Haven: Yale University Press, 1941), 4.

[2] Robert Dallek, *Franklin D. Roosevelt and American Foreign Policy, 1933–1945* (New York: Oxford University Press, 1979), 198.

[3] *Public Opinion Quarterly*, 4 (1940), 102, quoted in William E. Leuchtenburg, 79–95; 'Franklin D. Roosevelt and the New Deal, 1933–1940', in Arnold A. Offner (ed.), *America and the Origins of World War II, 1933–1941* (Boston: Houghton Mifflin, 1971), Dallek, *Franklin D. Roosevelt*, 199–202.

attendant on the disruption of trade and transport. The United States, for its part, appreciated that the region was now the world's leading source of raw materials independent of the direct control of any major power. US military planners, moreover, argued that the defence of the Panama Canal must extend from Cuba to the Galapagos Islands and include Mexico, Colombia, Venezuela, the Brazilian bulge, and all of Central America.[4]

The immediate inter-American reaction to the war was therefore the General Declaration of Neutrality agreed at the Panama Meeting of Foreign Ministers, wherein the American republics stated their unanimous intention not to become involved in the conflict. Meeting for eleven days from 23 September 1939, the conference aimed to discuss means of coping with the economic problems raised by the war and of attenuating the economic instability that might expose Latin America to German penetration. The Roosevelt administration further wanted to establish a neutrality zone in the Atlantic, closed to belligerent ships.[5]

The conference established an Inter-American Neutrality Committee at Rio to study infringements of neutrality and to recommend inter-American responses; and an Inter-American Financial and Economic Advisory Committee to deal with monetary instability and the loss of European commerce. The gathering also endorsed a 300–1,000-mile neutrality zone. Significantly for good neighbourism's later development, in the General Declaration of Neutrality the American republics resolved that they would 'take the necessary measures to eradicate from the Americas the spread of doctrines that tend to place in jeopardy the common inter-American democratic ideal'.[6]

*

Despite the good neighbour policy, Washington's position in Latin America at the outbreak of hostilities was hardly imperturbable. The reciprocity that the United States had tried to induce through seven years of non-interference in Central America was now a specific and immediate need rather than an ill-defined goal. The wartime significance of the

[4] Robin R. Humphreys, *Latin America and the Second World War*, i (London: Athlone Press, 1981), 1, 7, 43.   [5] Ibid. 47; Dallek, *Franklin D. Roosevelt*, 205.
[6] US Department of State, Report of the Delegation of the United States of America to the Meeting of the Foreign Ministers of the American Republics, Panama, September 23–October 9, 1939, Conference Series, 44 (Washington DC: US Government Printing Office, 1940), 63–4; Dallek, *Franklin D. Roosevelt*, 205; Gordon Connell-Smith, *The Inter-American System* (London: Oxford University Press, 1966), 111–12; Philip Leonard Green, *Pan American Progress* (New York: Hastings House, 1942), 93–4; Leuchtenburg, '*Franklin D. Roosevelt*', 82.

isthmus and the Canal Zone therefore prompted a reorientation of good neighbourism as a policy of absolute non-interference began to look like a potential strategic liability. The new conditions demanded that economic, military, and political patterns at the region-wide level be viewed in another light.

Economically, the United States had been losing ground to Germany in Latin America's trade relations. Berlin's aggressive commercial strategy, based on compensation trade and using government subsidies for manufactured exports, was undercutting American and British goods. In the late 1930s, as US–German rivalry began to swing from economic competition to direct confrontation, Germany's economic position in Latin America began assuming geopolitical significance. By 1938, Germany was providing 16 per cent of Latin America's imports (up from 9.5 per cent in 1932) and was taking 10.5 per cent of the continent's exports (up from 7.4 per cent in 1932). The country was thereby a more important supplier than Britain, and was expanding as a market while sales to Britain were declining.[7]

Militarily, South America was a virtual European monopoly until the late 1930s. The US military mission system exerted limited influence, while German and Italian missions had a long tradition of providing arms and training. In 1937 Nicaragua's total imports from Italy, valued at $291,690, consisted almost entirely of military supplies that arrived in 1938.[8] In that year the US army had just six military attachés in Latin America. In Panama, Lieutenant Colonel Joseph Pate was responsible for representing the US army in Venezuela, Colombia, and all of Central America. There were then just two American military missions, in Brazil and Guatemala. These circumstances had worried the State Department throughout 1938, leading to the series of meetings described in the previous chapter between representatives of the departments of State, Defense, War, Navy, Army, and Military Intelligence.[9]

Politically, Washington had less cause for concern in Central America than in the Southern Cone, but strategic planning was being approached in

[7] US Tariff Commission, *Foreign Trade of Latin America*, report 146 (Washington DC: US Government Printing Office, 1942), 24.

[8] 617.00/6, H. Bartlett Wells to Hull, 24 March 1939; William Everett Kane, *Civil Strife in Latin America* (Baltimore, Md.: Johns Hopkins University Press, 1972), 123; Stetson Conn and Byron Fairchild, *The Framework of Hemisphere Defense* (Washington: Department of the Army, Office of the Chief of Military History, 1960), 173.

[9] Conn and Fairchild, *The Framework*, 173; 810.20/62, 'Cooperation between the United States and Latin America in Military and Naval Matters', unsigned State Department memorandum, 21 Mar. 1938.

hemisphere-wide terms and the Latin American division's perceptions of German diplomacy in South America came to influence the administration's thinking on the isthmus. In an attempt to increase its direct control over German communities in Latin America, Berlin was organizing local Nazi movements in each colony, often by means of teachers sent from Germany to work in the immigrants' school systems. Propaganda abounded, disseminated by a German-language press subsidized by the Reich's diplomatic missions. Washington's concern was reflected in Roosevelt's use of a spurious 'secret map' that purported to show Germany's intention to divide South America into five 'vassal states'. Central America at least appeared politically secure on the surface. There was a danger, however, that non-interference might come under threat in Nicaragua in the face of underlying unrest. Adolfo Fernández, Emiliano Chamorro's chief agent in Nicaragua, had approached about a hundred Liberal and Conservative lawyers and had 'got them to swear themselves to the destruction of Somoza'.[10]

Such, then, were the immediate North American, Latin American and inter-American reactions to the outbreak of war; and such was the relative position of the United States in Latin America at the onset of hostilities. For Washington, short-term planning to confront potential dangers on the military, economic, and diplomatic fronts faced significant obstacles that had been raised by the good neighbour policy itself. From the outbreak of hostilities, Central America and the Canal Zone—crucial to the two-ocean naval strategy of the United States—were deemed very sensitive. It was not easy, however, for the Roosevelt administration suddenly to realize its desire for isthmian security in terms of the general orientation of Depression diplomacy, which had insisted—in Hull's striking phrase—on 'religious adherence' to an austere policy of non-interference. Simultaneously, the strength of isolationist sentiment in the United States impeded any moves that seemed to err from absolute neutrality. Roosevelt sought to warn Americans of the dangers he perceived, but his efforts to urge consideration of the consequences of inaction had to be tempered by forthright declarations that the United States would not become involved in the war, which tended to detract from the force of such efforts.[11]

The administration had to reconcile similarly conflicting motives in Latin America: to alert the sister republics to the potential risks, to counteract any positive impressions of European authoritarianism, and

---

[10] Michael Grow, *The Good Neighbor Policy and Authoritarinism in Paraguay: United States Economic Expansion and Great-Power Rivalry in Latin America during World War II* (Lawrence: Regents Press of Kansas, 1981), 34–6; 817.00/8748, Nicholson to Hull, 27 Feb. 1940.   [11] Kane *Civil Strife*,128 ; Dallek, *Franklin D. Roosevelt*, 205–6, 211.

to promote a united, continental front without seeming to impair Latin American neutrality or sovereignty.[12] The latter consideration was particularly significant in Central America, where the dangers of internal security threats were crucial for hemisphere planning. In Nicaragua specifically, the conflicting challenges were to avoid blatant interference while convincing the opposition of the dangers of instability in the prevailing circumstances.

With its energy focused on the war in Europe, the Roosevelt administration had to plan for the worst case. As the succession of German victories in Europe appeared to make that case increasingly bad, it seemed correspondingly important in Washington at least to contain those situations, such as that in Central America, that were controllable by virtue of US power. Since the administration could not predict with any certainty the outcome of particular upheavals, it was important, where possible, to forestall them. This suggested a potentially radical revision of the good neighbour policy. Non-interference, the basis of good neighbour diplomacy in Nicaragua for the past seven years, was under threat.

*

In Nicaragua, political speculation at the outbreak of war continued to centre on Somoza's durability. This was dependent on the state of his two major props—his diplomatic relations with the United States and control of the National Guard—and on the volatility of the internal opposition. Throughout the first half of 1939, a month had seldom passed without some rumour to the effect that a revolution was scheduled. The US legation in Managua had duly reported these to Washington, but as each failed to materialize into any significant movement the Latin American division had come to accord them ever less consideration.

Events in Europe during the early months of the war altered this thinking only slightly. Six months after the outbreak of hostilities, Nicholson remained sanguine about the prospects of continued tranquillity in Nicaragua. In February 1940, while noting that political unrest was 'vociferous', the minister felt that the manoeuvrings of the Chamorrista Conservatives and the growing disaffection among prominent Liberals reflected 'the mutterings of unarmed and timid men' who, at best, had 'the organizing ability of a good office boy'.[13] Nicholson's view of the prospects for political stability was to change markedly within two months.

---

[12] Dallek, *Franklin D. Roosevelt*, 211.
[13] 817.00/8748, Nicholson to Hull, 27 Feb. 1940.

Politically, good neighbourism in Nicaragua until 1939 had pursued a largely rigid policy of non-interference to the extent that such a policy seemed feasible. There had been exceptions, the consequences of which were significant for Nicaragua, but in terms of the conduct of diplomatic relations those exceptions were, in themselves, relatively minor. Maintenance of Somoza's presidency had come to seem desirable, but it had not been pursued as a policy objective with any great degree of positive action. The changing world situation demanded some shift in this approach as the diplomats and military strategists in Washington abruptly had to address a series of concerns in Nicaragua that previously would have received little or no consideration.

First, US policy-makers had at least to consider the possibility of some form of Nazi-inspired putsch. Central America's German communities tended to live apart from the local populations, and for Washington it was important that in many Latin American countries there were more Germans or individuals of German descent than there were Americans.[14] Berlin assumed their allegiance to the fatherland, and it was argued in the State Department that, given the means and opportunity, these expatriate colonies could stage a Nazi-inspired protest against an incumbent government in the model of the Sudetenland. Those Nicaraguans involved in the export trade to Germany and Italy were naturally disposed towards cordial relations with authoritarian governments in Europe. Germany had begun special radio propaganda for Central America as early as 1935, and by 1939 was broadcasting sixteen hours a day to the American republics.[15]

The FBI noted that Nicaragua had the smallest number of German and Italian nationals of any country in the isthmus: 212, compared with 2,720 in Guatemala and (even more worrying for US defence planners) 2,334 in Panama.[16] Nicaragua's German colony, however, does seem to have been largely sympathetic to the Nazis, and while not numerous it was exclusive. There had been very little marriage outside the community, and the German school in Managua was active in the production of Nazi propaganda. During Somoza's visit to Washington, US officials had urged him to keep the activities of Germans and Italians under 'very careful

---

[14] Joseph S. Roucek, 'Minorities: A Basis of the Refugee Problem', in American Academy of Political and Social Science, *Annals*, 203 (1939), 10.

[15] Mark S. Watson, *Chief of Staff: Prewar Plans and Preparations* (Washington DC: Department of the Army, Historical Division, 1950), 86–7; Alton Frye, *Nazi Germany and the American Hemisphere, 1933–1941* (New Haven: Yale University Press, 1967), 72.

[16] RG 38, FBI report, 'Axis Penetration in Nicaragua', Mar. 1942.

consideration'. *La Prensa* was carrying a substantial amount of pro-German material, including articles favouring a trade agreement with Berlin. On 11 March the first press denunciation of the US–Nicaraguan trade agreement appeared. On 7 June *La Prensa* declared: 'We flatly deny that the precepts of Catholic doctrine are opposed to all forms of totalitarianism... We cannot but admire Mussolini and his Roman genius.' The German consulate in Managua had circulated among German nationals a questionnaire demanding the names of any anti-Nazi Germans, as well as of 'anti-Nazi individuals of other than German nationality'.[17]

Second, Washington had to view more seriously the possibility of a 'traditional', non-Nazi revolt. In late 1939 the US legation in Costa Rica reported that the indefatigable Emiliano Chamorro was massing arms on the coasts of Mexico and Panama. He planned to charter a ship and open a two-pronged attack on Nicaragua. President Carías of Honduras was said to be encouraging the movement and had promised aid. Both the US minister in Costa Rica and the US military attaché for Central America had received the same information from different sources. Hornibrook in San José considered his information very reliable. The revolution, he claimed, was due to begin in November.[18]

Previously, such reports would have raised few eyebrows in Washington. The information would have been registered, the risks weighed, some minimal action on the part of diplomatic personnel in Nicaragua considered, and some vague instruction—often an instruction to do nothing—would have been dispatched. Such a course now seemed less possible. The assistant secretary of state, George Messersmith, ordered an FBI investigation into reports of an armed movement against the Somoza government. Hornibrook at the San José legation—approached by the movement's leaders in the ubiquitous effort to discern Washington's attitude to any attempt to oust Somoza—was instructed to give a response which, though apparently trite, was significant. Hornibrook told Chamorro's lieutenants

[17] 817.001 Somoza, Anastasio/130, memorandum, Duggan to Welles, 4 May 1939; ibid.; RG 38 C-10-g 20498, Boaz Long to Hull, 18 Mar. 1938; 817.001 Somoza, Anastasio/130, memorandum, Duggan to Welles, 4 May 1939; 817.911/41, Nicholson to Hull, 12 May 1939; 817.00 Spanish/1, Castleman to Hull, 9 June 1939. As late as 1945, Harold Finley, chargé at the Managua embassy pending the arrival of a new ambassador, warned that the German colony in Nicaragua was 'large and well-organized', with an 'active chapter of the Nazi party comprising individuals of wealth and influence'. Many of the children of Nicaraguan Germans, he claimed, were 'ardent and active Nazis'. See RG 226 XL 6434, report by Finley, 24 Jan. 1945.
[18] 711.17/280, Hornibrook (Costa Rica) to Hull, 6 Nov. 1939; 817.00 Revolutions/22, Hornibrook to Hull, 6 Nov. 1939.

that the Roosevelt administration would not look kindly on any attempt to disrupt the peace in Nicaragua. By that point, the American military attaché in Mexico had reported that arms had been found on a ship of the Ward Line. It was a large shipment—425 cases of rifles, machine guns, handbombs, and ammunition—weighing 160 tons.[19] The year ended without Chamorro's insurrection but the situation appeared increasingly tense against a background of economic decline.

Third, therefore, US policy-makers had to re-examine what seemed to be a high level of popular discontent that cut across all social divisions. The conditions of the *peones* and day labourers, always miserable, had become particularly pitiful. Their existence now, according to the military attaché Hardy, was 'slow death by degrees'. Daily wages had fallen to 60 *centavos* (about 9¢ at the street exchange rate). In the interior, the peasants had been forbidden to carry machetes, from which previously they had been inseparable. The sector was unorganized, but traditionally it had formed the bulk of Nicaragua's revolutionary movements and its members now seemed ripe for any violent initiative that would distract them from their miserable existence.[20]

Members of the moneyed class, normally hostile to any disturbance, were alienated by Somoza's greed. Forced to make contributions to his private fortune and often obliged to sell their properties to him at a fraction of their real value, they were showing some indications of desperation. Hardy's assessment of this sector was more tentative, but it was nonetheless telling. They might, he felt, 'be willing to join in any sort of movement, whether a coup or an out and out revolution', or they might give financial backing to 'any desperate scheme as a gamble to keep from losing their fortunes without even that desperate chance'. Nicholson agreed with this. His contacts in the upper sector led him to believe that they would rather lose their funds in a revolution than have two-thirds of their wealth taken by Somoza.[21] This tendency extended into the salaried employee and small business sector. Here, a general mood of desperation had set in. Hardy noted that this group did not yet favour violence, but it was evident that it might be persuaded to join a popular coup within Somoza's Liberal Party.[22] This possibility was not completely remote.

[19] 817.00 Revolutions/21, Messersmith to J. Edgar Hoover, 1 Dec. 1939; 711.17/280, Hornibrook to Hull, 6 Nov. 1939; 817.00 Revolutions/25, military attaché in Mexico to State Department, 6 Oct. 1939.

[20] 817.00/8753, military attaché's report, 14 Mar. 1940.

[21] Ibid.; 817.00/8754, Nicholson to Hull, 20 Mar. 1940.

[22] 817.00/8753, military attaché's report, 14 Mar. 1940.

Fourth, therefore, the state of the political parties seemed to be a further source of potential instability. Most Nicaraguans were Liberals, but the party was divided. Though the Somocistas retained control of the party machinery, Somoza's modification of the constitution to ensure his continuance in office had intensified bitterness within his own faction, which he did nothing to placate. Absorbed with his own private business rather than with affairs of state, Somoza seemed to have lost the confidence of many Somocista Liberals and of those Conservatives whom he had co-opted.[23]

The Conservative Party had virtually disintegrated by the late 1930s. Chamorro, in exile in Mexico, had been replaced by no leader of comparable standing or charisma. To protect their fortunes, many of the wealthier members of the party had turned to the Liberals, or simply become politically inactive. Conservative activity, however, had recently revived. It staked its hopes on the possibility that Somoza might voluntarily relinquish power once he was as wealthy as he wanted to be, on a desire for pressure from the United States, and on the chance of a Liberal Party coup.[24] Some attempt at such a coup did not seem out of the question in view of the state of the National Guard.

Fifth, the condition of Nicaragua's armed forces was a source of renewed concern for Washington. The Guardia, as previous chapters have indicated, was created with innate instabilities throughout the ranks. The military, as the primary prop of a personalist political system that was remarkably corrupt, suffered extreme demoralization. Officers profited blatantly by their positions. The enlisted men made money simply by making illegal arrests unless they were paid not to do so. Criminals were enlisted into the Guardia and then employed in Somoza's businesses.[25]

Efficiency, morale, and discipline deteriorated. By 1939 the Guardia had had no field training or target practice for years. Many weapons were unserviceable.[26] Real wages had fallen: a captain was earning about $40 a month. The concerns of US intelligence coincided with those of the diplomats. 'There is no doubt', Nicholson asserted, 'as to the demoralization not only of the privates but also of the officers . . . There is serious doubt as to the military efficiency of any unit of the National Guard in Managua.' The US naval attaché argued that there was a possibility of

---

[23] 817.00/8753, military attaché's report, 14 Mar. 1940.   [24] Ibid.
[25] 817.105/18, Nicholson to Hull, 13 Feb. 1940; Manuel Cordero Reyes, Carlos Castro Wassmer, and Carlos Pasos, *Nicaragua bajo el régimen de Somoza* (San Salvador: Imprenta Funes, 1944), 25.
[26] RG 38, C-10-f 9341-B, naval attaché's report, 6 Sept. 1940.

mutiny in the Guardia, a danger of which Somoza himself was aware. He was placing ever less confidence in his army for support and had set about building up within the military academy a group fanatically loyal to him. He had also been eliminating Guardia officers trained in the academy and replacing them with dependable individuals who had no military training. He was hoping that a good aviation corps, equally loyal, would keep the Guardia in the Campo de Marte under control.[27]

Colonel Charles Mullins of the US marines had been appointed head of the military academy in April 1939. This appointment had allowed Somoza to remove control of the academy from Guardia commanders who might pose a threat. Somoza had even intimated that he wanted Mullins to take over command of the Guardia itself from Rigoberto Reyes, the minister of war and Chief of Staff. The Guardia had been left largely in Reyes's hands during the previous year, as Somoza occupied himself with his business activities. Reyes, Somoza's nominee for the presidency in May 1936 (and by 1938 one of the most popular men in the country, according to US naval intelligence), seemed increasingly ambitious to succeed the president.[28]

Colonel Mullins's loyalties were somewhat divided in Nicaragua. Though his position represented an aspect of US foreign policy, he was directly involved in the creation of an armed force loyal to one man. As military and diplomatic thinking in Washington tended to converge in the face of war beyond the hemisphere, Mullins's role and his ill-defined relationship to the legation placed Nicholson in what should have been (given that US policy was still avowedly based on non-interference) an awkward position.

Nicholson, however, was in no doubt as to what Washington should want in Nicaragua. Meeting regularly with representatives of the emerging opposition and impressing upon them the Roosevelt administration's desire for political stability, he was proving an effective check to revolutionary enthusiasm. His activities on Somoza's behalf were in counterpoint to all other legation, military intelligence, and FBI reports outlining the mounting opposition to the president. In December 1939 Nicholson's deputy, LaVerne Baldwin, told the State Department that the Somoza administration was 'a government ridden from top to bottom with graft, wasting the substance of a state which needs every *centavo* in the face of existing world conditions, and the ever-present extreme

---

[27] 817.00/8753, Nicholson to Hull, 15 Mar. 1940; 817.105/18, Nicholson to Hull, 13 Feb. 1940; 817.1051/998 military attaché's report, 14 Mar. 1940; RG 38 C-10-d 6473-I, naval attaché's report for Dec. 1939; Cordero Reyes, Castro Wassmer, and Pasos, *Nicaragua*, 24.   [28] 817.1051/998, military attaché's report, 14 Mar. 1940.

poverty of its lower class, beyond the comprehension of any American who has not seen it'. By the beginning of 1940 Somoza had earned what Hardy termed 'the almost unanimous dislike of the Nicaraguan public'.[29]

A final source of concern for Washington was therefore Somoza himself. Quite apart from the bitterness prompted by his avarice during the first years of his presidency, he was now ill. Recurrent chronic malaria had left him physically weak, and he had suffered two heart attacks. By January 1940 the legation considered his condition grave. Surgery the previous September (allegedly for a hernia) was quietly reported to have revealed testicular cancer. In general, both army and naval intelligence judged the possibility of a change in the government to be 'excellent'. All that was lacking, according to the military attaché, was a leader, arms and funding. Lack of leadership, guns, and money being a serious setback to revolutionary intent, Hardy's alarm lacked force. His impression of the depth and scope of feeling against Somoza was striking, however, as were his anxieties that continuation of the prevailing circumstances could develop genuinely revolutionary conditions. By March 1940 the State Department was taking more seriously the constant reports of widespread plots against the Somoza regime.[30]

The Conservative opposition in exile was reportedly massing arms for an attempt against the government; the economy was deteriorating; mass discontent brought further potential for public disorder; Guardia discipline was uncertain; and Somoza himself was ill. In these conditions, the nature of Somoza's relationship with the American diplomatic establishment in Managua and Washington was crucial. By the spring of 1940, the Managua legation concurred with the assessment of military intelligence. Nicholson, sanguine about the dangers to Somoza at the start of the year, noted the 'prevailing discontent from the top to the bottom of Nicaraguan society', and by April he was convinced that there would be a revolution within nine months.[31] With non-interference still the official policy, this assessment raised the question of what he, and Cordell Hull, were going to do about it.

*

In Washington, the State Department's burst of activity following the outbreak of war had waned. Hull, 69 years old and in poor health, was absent

[29] 817.001 Somoza, Anastasio/211, Baldwin to Hull, 2 Dec. 1939; 817.00/8753, military attaché's report, 14 Mar. 1940.
[30] 817.00 Somoza, Anastasio/214, Nicholson to Hull, 12 Jan. 1940; 817.00/8753, military attaché's report, 14 Mar. 1940; 817.00/8748, memorandum, Drew to Duggan, 5 Mar. 1940.   [31] 817.00/8762, Nicholson to Hull, 19 Apr. 1940.

for long periods and subject to criticism for his apparent inability to devise coherent responses to international conditions.[32] The legation and military intelligence reports from Managua had some effect on his Latin American division in late 1939 and early 1940, though the response among the career diplomats was initially one of unease rather than alarm. For Hull, however, the suggested US responses did produce real alarm. The secretary remained hostile to any shift in the policy of non-interference, from which Nicholson's recommendations and activities were suggesting a substantial departure.

US responses to Nicaragua were therefore confusing in the early months of the European war. Since military planning had yet to be fully integrated into the policy-making process, it initially seemed that the doctrine of non-interference could remain firm. This owed as much to Hull's continuing commitment to the principle as to what good neighbourism had come to mean in Nicaragua through the application of that principle. Fear of American reprisals was a significant factor preventing Nicaragua's dissenting groups from acquiring the unity of purpose required for concerted action against the government. The opposition faced a dilemma: on the one hand the State Department's hands-off policy, by allowing Somoza's ascent, had fostered the general's image as 'Washington's man'; this image was encouraged by his visit to Washington the previous May. On the other hand, Washington's man was being startlingly corrupt in the midst of a severe crisis and seemed intent on staying in the presidential mansion for a long time. The question was how to bring down such a government, in such a context, without jeopardizing what meagre hopes of alleviation existed in the form of American assistance. The Conservatives, for example, were fearful to take action because they were anxious that any movement to overthrow the regime would result in the cancellation of plans to build a Nicaraguan canal.[33]

In identifying such fears, and in playing upon them to Somoza's advantage by direct interference, Nicholson pre-empted a later shift in US policy and was reprimanded by Hull. Chamorro, striving to fund arms purchases abroad, instructed his deputy in Nicaragua, Dr Pasos Montiel, to organize the Conservatives in order to place them on a better footing for armed and civic struggle. Nicholson, in response, went off on an unauthorized diplomatic tangent.[34]

[32] Gellman, *Good Neighbor Diplomacy*, 117–18.
[33] 817.00/8753, military attaché's report, 15 Mar. 1940.
[34] 817.00/8762, Nicholson to Hull, 19 Apr. 1940.

The minister arranged a meeting with Pasos and asked him 'to question whether in the case of a revolutionary upset Nicaragua would continue to profit by the Somoza–Roosevelt Agreement, namely the Export-Import Bank loan and stabilization fund, and the prospects for a San Juan Canal'. This question left little by way of interpretation; it was a threat. It was also somewhat cynical. The State Department had known for a year that there was no possibility of a canal being built, but since it had not been in the interests of the department or Somoza to publicize the fact, neither had given an indication of the plan's demise. Somoza, in fact, had implied that it was a real prospect. Pasos Montiel left his interview with Nicholson 'conscious that the United States would not support a move at the present time by the Conservatives to upset the existing government but was, as he would understand it, *supporting the Somoza government*'.[35] This was something of a policy shift, one initiated in Managua rather than in Washington.

Such activities sustained Somoza's confidence in the face of widespread popular resentment. Convinced that Washington wished him to retain power, both he and the minister had been thinking in military as well as diplomatic terms. They were aware that the general could not remain in office without the full support of the Guardia. If the military's sympathies switched, Somoza might fall and the United States would be confronted, in Nicholson's words, with 'the arrival at the top of the most ruthless individual who could obtain the support of the Guard by personal charm or extravagant promises'.[36] Nicholson therefore asserted the 'necessity' of offering the services of an American officer to reorganize the National Guard 'if it [the US government] *desires to maintain Somoza in power* or, a more basic consideration, to avoid the outbreak of a revolution shortly within Nicaragua'. This view was shared by US naval intelligence, which argued that a US mission to reorganize the Guardia at this point 'might eliminate the necessity of military intervention by a larger force at some future date'.[37]

Nicholson further appreciated that violence could not be forestalled indefinitely without some attempt to combat the ills of the economy, and he insisted on another 'immediate necessity': an American manager for the National Bank and a financial supervisor for as much of the country's

[35] 817.00/8750, Nicholson to Hull, 3 Mar. 1940. Emphasis added.
[36] 817.00/8753, Nicholson to Hull, 15 Mar. 1940.
[37] Ibid.; 817.5151/519, Hull to Nicholson, 16 Apr. 1940; RG 38 C-10-f 9341-B, naval attaché's report, 6 Sept. 1940. Emphasis added.

expenditures as possible. This line of reasoning must have been shocking enough to Hull. Nicholson, however, evidently ignorant of the secretary's sensibilities, went further. He felt it necessary to ask the department how he should respond if Somoza, confident that Washington wished him to retain control, should turn to the United States 'for even more forceful aid'. By this, Nicholson meant military intervention.[38]

Hull was outraged at the attitude implicit in Nicholson's assumptions about the good neighbour policy, the manner in which the minister had already acted upon them, and his disregard of the 'definitive' instructions on non-interference that Hull had issued to the Central American legations four years earlier. In a blistering cable to the Managua legation, the secretary quoted at length from the 1936 instructions. He stated that the United States was glad to comply with requests for advice, but claimed that such compliance would never be undertaken 'to enable a particular individual or faction to gain or maintain control of the government'. Hull insisted that there was not the 'slightest desire on the part of this government to intervene directly or indirectly in the internal affairs of Nicaragua', and told Nicholson to 'refrain from permitting any such impression to be conveyed to the Nicaraguan government'.[39]

The Managua legation, the career diplomats in Washington, and military intelligence already acknowledged that fundamental modifications of good neighbourism might be necessary in the face of rapidly deteriorating world conditions. Hull's anger, however, did not only reflect his own slowness to adjust. It also indicated his appreciation of what he rightly saw as a sensitive problem: specifically, the formidable task the United States faced in inducing Latin American security cooperation without resorting to methods which appeared too conspicuous, and which might therefore jeopardize the very solidarity—in hemisphere-wide terms—that the United States wished to cultivate.[40] Indifference to the fate of a pro-American head of state might ensure his fall and thereby imperil hemisphere security, but blatant intervention would endanger continental solidarity at a critical moment, which in turn threatened hemisphere security.

Hull's attitude was therefore not unreasonable, but by the time he reprimanded Nicholson it was already being overtaken by events. A week earlier the Germans had marched over the Danish border. Two months

---

[38] 817.00/8753, Nicholson to Hull, 15 Mar. 1940; 817.5151/519, Hull to Nicholson, 16 Apr. 1940.   [39] 817.5151/519, Hull to Nicholson, 16 Apr. 1940.
[40] William L. Langer and S. Everett Gleason, *Challenge to Isolation, 1937–1940* (New York: Harper, 1952), 147.

later Paris fell, the British fleet was endangered, and the German navy could operate beyond the eastern Atlantic. The management of good neighbourism was being taken from Hull's hands by events beyond the hemisphere. Hull's idea—that it was not Washington's concern who governed Nicaragua—was rapidly becoming obsolete as the political, economic, and strategic components of good neighbourism coalesced into a general policy of defence to prepare the United States to cope with war.

*

In Nicaragua by mid 1940, the elements of instability evident in the first six months of the year had caused what Hornibrook in Costa Rica termed 'a veritable sea of rumours' that a revolution against Somoza was imminent. At the beginning of June a large arms cache was discovered at El Golfito in Costa Rica for an incursion into Nicaragua. The Nicaraguan minister in San José, who had taken to wearing a Colt revolver at all times, believed that Nazis were strongly organized in Nicaragua and were prepared to strike at the opportune moment, especially if there were further German victories. When this assessment appeared to be proving correct the central tenet of good neighbourism in Nicaragua abruptly, and very publicly, disintegrated.[41]

The occasion for the breakdown was a bizarre episode in late 1940 when Somoza's desire to remove a man who might come to pose a threat to him coincided with Nicholson's severe anxieties about the Nazi menace. According to Nicholson, 'Conservatives and Nazis' had been influencing Rigoberto Reyes, the Chief of Staff, to consider rebellion. The minister believed that Reyes enjoyed an alarming degree of support within a factionalized Guardia and was convinced that he had been chosen by 'Nazi-Fascist elements' to replace Somoza. Reyista officers, he reported, had been tapping the president's telephones and were tampering with his mail.[42]

Reyes was dispatched on a trip to Washington in October 1940. During his absence a thorough search was made of all desks and records at the Campo de Marte Guardia base. All arms were transferred to the presidential mansion; the personnel at the Masaya fortress was reorganized. There was a complete turnover of all officers at Reyes's headquarters. Entire companies and units were shifted. Nicholson thought that

---

[41] 817.00/8763, Nicholson to Hull, 7 June 1940; 817.00 Revolutions/43, Hornibrook to Hull, 6 June 1940.   [42] 817.00/8884, Nicholson to Hull, 13 Nov. 1940.

Somoza's position was precarious.[43] He strongly recommended that a US destroyer be sent immediately to Corinto, 'informally, casually, and as part of routine patrol duties'. Sacasa, in vain, had made precisely the same request in May 1936, but in the second half of 1940 it was just such a movement that the United States felt obliged to curb. William Paley, the president of the Columbia Broadcasting System, would shortly be reporting to Roosevelt following a tour of Latin America that 'a well-planned revolt backed by not very many well-aimed guns and a few airplanes can succeed in some of the weaker Latin American countries, countries which unfortunately, from our standpoint, are near the Canal Zone.' Nicholson believed that the arrival of a US warship 'would forestall any immediate endeavour by Nazis and Conservatives to take advantage of disgruntled officers and sympathizers with Reyes'.[44]

The USS *Goff* was dispatched on 4 November and arrived at Corinto two days later. Significantly, Nicholson was clear that the threat was being held in abeyance by precisely two factors: 'the close co-operation existing between the legation and General Somoza, and the visit of an American destroyer'. The situation calmed; Reyes resigned six days later. Within less than a week, however, there were indications of renewed trouble on the east coast. The British chargé had been approached by 'representatives of the anti-Somoza groups there' about the propitiousness of the time for revolt. Nicholson urged that another warship be sent to Bluefields or Puerto Cabezas.[45]

In Washington, Welles was not anxious to revert to a policy of gunboat diplomacy but he nevertheless suggested compliance with Nicholson's recommendation as a means of averting internal disorder. He felt that action should be undertaken as soon as it could be done without arousing unnecessary comment. Senior naval officials had indicated that a ship could be dispatched immediately but Welles insisted this would 'make the action very conspicuous, which will defeat the purpose of the visit'.[46] If this meant anything it signified that the inter-American solidarity born of Washington's repudiation of interference, through the rigidly austere

---

[43] 817.00/8876, Nicholson to Hull, 10 Oct. 1940; 817.00/8877, Nicholson to Hull, 2 Nov. 1940; 817.00/8884, Nicholson to Hull, 13 Nov. 1940.

[44] 817.00/8877, Nicholson to Hull, 2 Nov. 1940; Paley is quoted in Conn and Fairchild, *The Framework*, 187.

[45] 817.00/8887, Hull to Nicholson, 4 Nov. 1940; 817.00/8881, Nicholson to Hull, 6 Nov. 1940; 817.00/8883, Nicholson to Hull, 12 Nov. 1940; 817.00/8885, Nicholson to Hull, 15 Nov. 1940.

[46] 817.00/8885, memorandum, Welles to Wilson, 30 Nov. 1940; 817.00/8885, Nicholson to Hull, 15 Nov. 1940; 817.00/8885, memorandum, unsigned, 5 Dec. 1940.

good neighbourism of the 1930s, now had to be protected by suspending that policy in favour of the more traditional forms of coercive diplomacy. If the symptoms of the departure were too blatant, however, the United States would endanger the very solidarity it was attempting to protect. The destroyer *Borie* arrived at Bluefields on 14 December.[47]

Though the event never materialized, rumours of rebellion continued to reach Nicholson. He believed that the plans of the violent opposition had been forestalled for now by the show of US naval force and by his own activities. 'Anti-Somoza elements', he asserted, 'realize that an appeal to arms would be welcomed by the Nazi and Fascist elements in the world'. Presumably, therefore, such elements also realized that an appeal to arms would be unwelcome in Washington. Nicholson's course was coincidentally aided by the progressive mobilization of the US military establishment. Visible evidence of American military power was now pervasive. The movement of bombers, pursuit planes, and destroyers was receiving close attention in the local press.[48]

Nicholson, disregarding Hull's vehement reaffirmation of good neighbour principles, unfailingly identified American interests with Somoza's continuance in office. He was also unfailing in identifying almost any threat to Somoza with Nazism. As the international context of Nicaraguan politics and US policy changed, so Washington's perceptions of threat in Nicaragua—at least as reflected in the views of its diplomats—shifted markedly. It was no longer a question of settling local 'disturbances' that hindered US interests, nor even of containing the regional threat of Mexican 'bolshevism'. It was a matter of global import. The disparate elements of opposition to Somoza, from ambitious generals to Chamorrista adventurers, were suddenly all 'Nazis'. So strong was this conviction that, occasionally, they were actual 'Germans', the race that was overrunning continental Europe, and Nicholson saw them everywhere.

By the end of 1940 Nicholson was heartened by Somoza's belated efforts to control German propaganda, by his removal of 'pro-Nazi' ministers from his cabinet, and by 'his knowledge that *Germans* are posted at strategic points such as fords, bridges, airfields and power plants'. This, the minister felt, 'will result in constant and close attention to this combined fifth column, Nazi and *perhaps in part* Conservative threat to his own position in office'.[49] In August 1939, Reyes would have been a politically ambitious military officer backed by what Nicholson himself had

---

[47] 817.00/8888, Nicholson to Hull, 16 Dec. 1940.   [48] Ibid.
[49] 817.00/8877, Nicholson to Hull, 2 Nov. 1940. Emphasis added.

characterized as timid men with the organizing ability of an office boy. By October 1940, when the Royal Air Force was committing much of its fighter command to the Battle of Britain, Reyes was a movement, furthering the global aims of Nazism, while Nicaragua's 212 Germans were somehow spread out over the national territory, watching bridges.

Nicholson's interpretation of the situation in Nicaragua reflected a particular view of that situation's broader context, and in Washington the context was being portrayed in dramatic terms. On 16 May 1940, six days after the German invasion of the Low Countries, Roosevelt had told Congress:

From the fjords of Greenland it is only six hours to New England... If Bermuda fell into hostile hands it would be a matter of less than three hours for modern bombers to reach our shores... From a base in the outer West Indies, the coast of Florida could be reached in 200 minutes... The islands off the west coast of Africa are only 1,500 miles from Brazil. Modern planes starting from the Cape Verde islands can be over Brazil in seven hours... And Pará, Brazil, near the mouth of the Amazon River, is but four hours to Caracas, Venezuela; and Venezuela is but two and a half flying hours to Cuba and the Canal Zone; and Cuba and the Canal Zone are two and a half hours to Tampico, Mexico; and Tampico is two and a half hours to St. Louis, Kansas City and Omaha.[50]

This vision, of the American Midwest less than twenty-four hours away from German oppression, proved compelling. The apparent acceptability of such notions in Washington seems to have helped Nicholson overcome any apprehension about further reprimands from Hull.

Concerned that there should be no doubts in Washington, Nicholson provided the department with a definitive statement of what he felt should form the basis of American policy in Nicaragua: 'There remains the possibility that any desperate attempts by Nazis to create disturbances would draw the attention of the United States more closely to this area... It is to the government of General Somoza, backed by his Guardia, that we must look for the maintenance of peace and order.'[51] Ten months earlier, Hull had chided Nicholson with reminders that good neighbourism precluded the provision of support that enabled any particular individual to retain power. In accepting Nicholson's recommendations this time, department officials were willing to admit, albeit tentatively, that it reflected a policy shift that would not have been

[50] Samuel Rosenman (ed.), *Public Papers and Addresses of Franklin D. Roosevelt* (New York: Random House, 1938), ix, 199–200, quoted in Edgar O. Guerrant, *Roosevelt's Good Neighbour Policy* (Albuquerque: University of New Mexico Press, 1950), 155–6.
[51] 817.00/8888, Nicholson to Hull, 16 Dec. 1940.

countenanced at the time of the Buenos Aires conference. 'In our support of any existing government in the other American republics,' Lawrence Duggan warned the Latin American division, 'we are always faced with the latent possibility that we are curbing natural political activity and maintaining a regime in power that does not have popular support. This possibility definitely exists in Nicaragua.'[52]

No mere possibility, such was in fact the reality. As the US minister Pierre Boal reported from Mexico, where State Department personnel and US intelligence agents were keeping a close watch on the activities of the Chamorro brothers, the exiled Conservative leader 'believes, as do most Nicaraguans, that the United States...has kept Somoza president of the country'. Recognizing the advantages therein, Somoza played the American card to its full advantage, taking every opportunity to identify US interests with the continuance of his government. Nicholson was reciprocating in ways that Arthur Bliss Lane, in an earlier context, would have found unthinkable. Lane had worked for peace; Nicholson, in at least one sense, was working for Somoza.

*

Why, then, in such a short period, did Hull let the principle of non-interference be so dramatically abandoned? Why was Nicholson allowed to lapse from religious adherence? There are three considerations to be noted here. First, and most obvious, is the rapid change in the circumstances within which US policy was formulated and applied. The changed context demanded that strategic planning be incorporated more fully into good neighbourism. Strategic thinking, which required as much stability as possible in Nicaragua, altered US political objectives. The new objectives would entail interference.

Second, and less plainly obvious, is that Roosevelt's determination to aid Britain would be served by fuelling American fears of Axis penetration in the western hemisphere. If American interests could be portrayed as imperilled close to home, Roosevelt's Atlantic activism could expect broader support. But if Roosevelt was going to dramatize the threats to Latin American governments, his administration also had to be seen to be doing something about those threats. Inherent in this ploy was the danger that any appreciation of the real scope of externally generated threats would be lost in the general air of drama. Third, and most abstrusely, is that the nature of the new, more interventionist diplomacy was not dictated solely

---

[52] 817.00/8925, memorandum, Duggan, 7 Feb. 1941.

by the changed circumstances. It was also determined to a large extent by the fact that good neighbourism in Nicaragua, indeed in all of Latin America, had to date been founded on the tenet of *non*-interference.

Changing policy, first, in changing circumstances. From the autumn of 1939 to the spring of 1940, US neutrality was based on apparently reasonable perceptions: that the Maginot Line would hold firm; that German defences would withstand Allied assaults; that Britain would preserve control of the seas; and that the Reich would fall in a war of attrition. It was apparently not, as Kennedy had announced, the end of the world. Hence the Latin American division's reversion to pre-war patterns. The alarm of September 1939, that the United States might be dragged into war, faded to calm.

The storm broke suddenly in the spring of 1940. On 9 April the Germans marched into Denmark and overran the country in hours. Norway held out for a few weeks longer. On 10 May German forces turned to the Low Countries: Holland held out for five days, Belgium for eighteen. Italy declared war on 10 June, and France capitulated twelve days later. Britain now stood alone in Europe and the American public mood changed almost overnight. Roosevelt moved towards a crisis government of national unity and at that point military planning became central to good neighbourism.[53]

What was the thinking in Washington? In June 1940 the European war seemed, in effect, to have ended. Impeded by the English Channel and the Royal Air Force, Germany was unable to invade Britain; but simultaneously it appeared inconceivable that Britain could invade continental Europe. Between 27 May and 2 June, the Dunkirk evacuation brought 340,000 men of the British expeditionary force out of the Channel ports. With Britain's prospects seeming poor, Washington's 'Hemisphere Defense' rearmament programme of June 1940 practically acknowledged that it would be fruitless to provide more arms to the Churchill government. In that month Harry Hopkins, special adviser to Roosevelt and effectively deputy president, wrote: 'The only assumption it is safe for us to make at this time is that Germany, having won the war within the next few weeks, will proceed immediately in Latin America along the lines indicated by her past and current activities. Her preponderance over us now is at its maximum.'[54]

[53] Leuchtenburg, *'Franklin D. Roosevelt'*, 83–5.

[54] Eric Hobsbawm, *Age of Extremes: The Short Twentieth Century 1914–1991* (London: Michael Joseph, 1994), 39; Roger Parkinson, *Encyclopaedia of Modern War* (London: Granada Publishing Limited, 1979), 117; Leuchtenburg, *'Franklin D. Roosevelt'*, 86.

Many US officials believed that Germany would soon win the European war and attack the western hemisphere. Following France's surrender, the Uruguayan Congress revealed plans for a German uprising in the country. As the German advance continued, Roosevelt was receiving reports of Nazi subversion throughout Latin America. Washington now had to consider the danger of an attack on the region if Germany were to gain control of the French fleet and West African bases.[55]

In these circumstances the possibility of Latin American appeasement prompted concern in Washington. Berlin was warning the region's governments that Britain would fall by the autumn, and that they would be dependent on German-occupied territory for markets. In a gesture of appeasement, nine Latin American governments declined to send their foreign ministers to the Havana Meeting of Foreign Ministers in July 1940. The meeting convened after the German invasion of France and Holland, amid fears that Berlin might seize French and Dutch territories in the western hemisphere. Hull worried that if Britain were defeated the subsequent upsurge of German power in Europe and the Atlantic would oblige Latin American countries to align themselves with Berlin for the sake of expediency.[56]

In response to such fears, Roosevelt approved secret US–Latin American military talks at the end of May 1940. When the State Department suggested that the navy mount a show of force off Brazil and Uruguay, the president dispatched a cruiser to Rio and Montevideo. Welles, a bitter opponent of Hull on many issues, came to agree with his chief's interpretation. Fearful that apparent US acquiescence in the face of subversion might lead most of Latin America to 'run helter skelter to Hitler', he argued for four cruisers and a destroyer group to be sent to the east coast of South America, and for a lending programme to allow Latin American governments to buy arms. Several destroyers were sent on 'shakedown cruises' to Latin America, and plans were made to transport 10,000 US troops to Brazil in the event of an emergency.[57]

Germany's political and military objectives in Latin America were largely unknown in Washington, but the trend of events dictated that the Roosevelt administration plan for the worst possible scenario. Hence the Havana conference had adopted the Convention on the Provisional

[55] Gellman, *Good Neighbor Diplomacy* 108; Dallek, *Franklin D. Roosevelt*, 233.
[56] Grow, *The Good Neighbor Policy*, 33–4; Dallek, *Franklin D. Roosevelt*, 235; Leuchtenburg, 'Franklin D. Roosevelt', 89–90.
[57] Grow, *The Good Neighbor Policy*, 33; Dallek, *Franklin D. Roosevelt*, 235.

Administration of European Colonies and Possessions, which established the principle of 'no transfer': at Hull's urging, the American republics agreed to establish a collective trusteeship over European possessions in the Caribbean.[58] On such a foundation, the purely political and the military aspects of US policy towards Latin America were linked. In effect, the good neighbour policy was partially militarized.

In the summer of 1940 the thinking about defence moved from the military planning boards to the cabinet meetings. In July the War Department's military intelligence division asked the offices of the Chief of Staff and Secretary of War for a decision on Washington's basic military objectives in Latin America. The good neighbour policy had emerged at a time when the US military establishment's links with its peers in Latin America were slight. The intelligence division wanted to know if the United States now wished to increase the military efficiency of the republics to the point at which they would be of material aid as allies in defence. The answer from the Chief of Staff and the Secretary of War was in the negative. The goal was to be 'better mutual understanding...In attaining our objective we should concentrate on those countries of most immediate military importance to us. Our objective does not comprise expectations on our part of being able to use Latin American forces as effective allies in war.'[59]

The United States, then, did not intend that Latin American forces should repel an invasion of their own territory. None of the Central American countries had the military resources to deter a German attack. That the American aim should be 'better mutual understanding' had far-reaching implications for Nicaragua. Declining to rearm the countries of Central America to become effective allies in defence, the Roosevelt administration was ultimately depending on its own military power to safeguard US security south of the Rio Grande. The military response to disturbances was thereby reincorporated into political thinking. This was particularly significant for the region that marked the outposts of the canal, the area where, formerly, such a response had been most emphatically rejected.

Important in this regard was that, while policy became a programme of defence, the conception of defence was correspondingly broadened. A corollary was that security superseded other individual political and economic considerations. While the Roosevelt administration would not

[58] Leuchtenburg, '*Franklin D. Roosevelt*', 90.
[59] Conn and Fairchild, *The Framework*, 173, 178–9.

depend on Latin American forces, it would in Central America have to depend in the first instance on specific governments: hence the need for 'mutual understanding'. The alternative, military intervention, would have to be a last resort. In view of the historical record, some governments in the region were unconvinced that Germany was a greater threat to their sovereignty than was the United States. In South America particularly, it might have been hard to induce support for Anglo-Saxon liberal democracy in Vargas's Brazil, Castillo's Argentina, or Morínigo's Paraguay—countries where Germans and Italians really were influential—if the United States were to invade Nicaragua. The strategic planning dictated by events in Europe was already undermining Hull's adamant declaration (at this point only three months old) that in Nicaragua the United States had no desire to help any particular government retain power.

Inter-American military staff conversations had already begun. In June 1940 US army and navy liaison officers, disguised as tourists, began arriving in Latin American capitals. Captain Maxwell Taylor of the army and Major Clayton Jerome of the marines were received in Managua on 12 June to prepare the staff talks with Somoza. He had recently bought 5,000 Enfield rifles from the United States and assured the American officers that he could contribute an army of 40,000 men. During the preparatory talks he was careful to stress that he still did not have enough rifles to arm such a number. The Guardia then consisted of 3,538 officers and men, with a trained reserve of 4,000.[60]

Somoza was more than willing to cooperate with the suggestions of the American officers. He wanted US troops on Nicaraguan territory since their presence might appear to provide tangible evidence of American support for his regime at a time when dangers to it were becoming apparent. He suggested the establishment of an arsenal on the Gulf of Fonseca, under the protection of American marines. Admitting that there were some Nazis sympathizers in his government and 'quite a few' active Nazis in the country, he expressed absolute confidence in his ability to control any fifth-column activity if he were provided with the necessary weaponry.[61]

The staff talks themselves were held on 26 August, when Major Mathewson of the US army, Major Jerome of the marines, and Captain

---

[60] Humphreys, *Latin America*, i 69; 810.20 Defense/114a, Hull to Nicholson, 5 June 1940; 810.20 Defense/30, Nicholson to Hull, 6 June 1940; 810.20 Defense/114 3/4, Muccio to Hull, 15 June 1940.

[61] 810.20 Defense/114 3/4, Muccio to Hull, 15 June 1940.

Riefkohl of the navy arrived in Managua. The discussions were meant to ensure that Nicaragua and the United States would cooperate to counter threats both external and internal. The entire point of the talks, according to the operations division of the War Department, was 'to facilitate the entry of American troops into countries threatened either by external aggression *or internal disorder*'.[62] At this point the line between good neighbour diplomacy and US security policy disappeared. The bilateral staff conversations apparently produced a sense of anticipation that the military establishments of Central America could 'receive modern type weapons to organize their units on a modern pattern, and to maintain law and order within their boundaries, and to maintain the integrity of their governments, as well as the defence of the western hemisphere'.[63] This last point read, unfortunately, as something of an afterthought.

The Roosevelt administration was going to help maintain the 'integrity' of the Somoza regime because of perceived threats both external and internal. The administration, however, overstated the external threat to Latin America in the second half of 1940, a time when Hitler had no plans to attack the western hemisphere. US apprehensions were not groundless, but there can be little doubt that some of the overstatement was deliberate. Carleton Beals and other journalists were certainly dramatizing the danger of Axis penetration.[64] When Paris fell, according to opinion polls, most Americans were convinced that the Germans would try to infiltrate Latin America.[65]

Roosevelt exploited such public anxieties, not because of the good neighbour policy but because of his war policy, since his deliberate incitement of public fears about German incursions in Latin America enabled him to aid the British war effort. The security zone announced at the Panama conference, for example, though portrayed as a means of safeguarding the Americas, also helped Britain by limiting the need for Royal Navy patrols in the western Atlantic.[66]

Though such ploys were not wholly to do with Latin America, they benefited Somoza in Nicaragua by inspiring concern about any sign of

---

[62] 810.20 Defense/114 3/12A, Hull to Nicholson, 4 Aug. 1940; 810.20 Defense/114 4/12, Flournoy to Hull, 7 Aug. 1940; RG 165 OPD 336 LA, 8 Aug. 1945, memorandum, Lt Gen. Brett, emphasis added; Humphreys, *Latin America*, *i*, 80.

[63] RG 165 OPD 336 LA, 8 Aug. 1945, memorandum, Lt Gen. Brett.

[64] Beals's 1939 book, *The Coming Struggle for Latin America* (London: Cape, 1939), is a particularly alarmist tract.

[65] Dallek, *Franklin D. Roosevelt*, 235; Gellman, *Good Neighbor Diplomacy*, 109–11.

[66] Ibid. 113, 115.

instability. Nicholson, for his part, seems to have overstated the threat to Somoza from within the country. If his alarmism is typical of the kind of information that the Latin American division was receiving from its diplomats, the Roosevelt administration's tendency to overestimate Berlin's designs on Latin America is understandable. Rumours reaching US diplomatic and intelligence personnel in the isthmus endlessly insisted that some movement was about to topple the Nicaraguan government. With the exception of a peculiar period in 1937, however, such reports had always abounded, at least since the marine withdrawal of 1933. In that period only Somoza, who controlled an army, had made such a rumour reality. With the exception of his coup, the capacity of any anti-government movement to take power does not appear to have changed since then. What changed, and radically so, was the context in which the rumours circulated.

Pro-Axis sentiment in Nicaragua was simply not strong enough to command sufficient popular support to bring down the Somoza government.[67] The way in which US policy was changing, however, was not shaped exclusively by abnormal circumstances in Nicaragua or Europe. It was also determined by the nature of good neighbourism in the previous several years. Non-interference enabled Somoza to claim, without fear of contradiction, that Roosevelt was his personal friend and that Washington had a keen interest in his retaining power. This was widely believed in Nicaragua. Such a conviction allowed the general to disregard the scope and depth of resentment he had provoked by his own greed. In fact, his much-vaunted American patronage enabled him to indulge his avarice further. By the end of 1939 it was clear to the US legation that the president had 'shamelessly exploited the prestige accruing from his reception [in the United States] as representing assurances of direct support from the American government, and *for that reason* has been able to increase greatly the amount of his holdings with a minimum of protest'.[68]

Additionally, his insistent encouragement of the belief that he enjoyed American backing, in the absence of any official indication to the contrary from Washington, gave rise to the consideration that any government that replaced his might be less than cordial to the United States. Any unfriendly regime near to the canal, of course, would have

---

[67] Feelings, however, did initially run high. Before German breakthroughs in Belgium, Holland, and France, the Nicaraguan cities of Corinto, Grenada, and Managua were pro-German, and there prevailed a vigorous anti-British feeling which the US chargé was 'at a loss to account for'. 817.00 Nazis/21, Muccio to Hull, 10 July 1940.

[68] 817.001 Somoza, Anastasio/211, Baldwin to Hull, 2 Dec. 1939. Emphasis added.

to be treated as potentially pro-Axis. Such thinking was explicit in the Managua legation. LaVerne Baldwin, who had been astounded at the scale of Somoza's corruption and appalled at the poverty of the population, intimated to the State Department that it might be necessary for the United States to help Somoza retain power for the simple reason that, in view of his strident pro-Americanism, 'any overthrow of his government would be followed by . . . one which will certainly attack any American interests which received privileges through the efforts of Somoza'.[69]

Such considerations prompted a reorientation of good neighbourism in Nicaragua. The disposition of the country's government being consistent with the traditional objectives of US policy for the region, policy reverted to that of maintaining the status quo. Militarily, such a goal had always been easy to achieve: a month after the Nicaraguan staff conversations, Lieutenant General Van Voorhis, commander general of the Canal Zone, drew attention to the fact that it would be far simpler to keep a friendly government in power than to try to change a pro-Axis regime once it was established. If a serious political breakdown did occur, the possibility of actual armed intervention was not inconceivable. According to Van Voorhis, a few hundred ground troops airlifted from the Canal Zone would contain such disturbances pending the arrival of a larger force from the United States.[70]

US intervention, however, might be counter-productive in light of the previous seven years of good neighbour rhetoric, and allowing a pro-American dictatorship to flourish was a better substitute. In July 1940 Roosevelt approved a memorandum from the war plans division concerning the proposed national policy on supplying arms to Latin America. This outlined the strategy to be adopted for arming each republic to the extent determined necessary by a War Department estimate. Nicaragua was to be provided with sufficient munitions 'to insure internal stability'.[71] This decision, a milestone in US-Nicaraguan relations, seemed wholly rational in Washington during the second half of 1940. Military planning had produced a political objective: the maintenance in power of Anastasio Somoza. That Somoza was remarkably corrupt, that he was not exactly a vigorous defender of the cause of democracy in Nicaragua, seemed at the time to be secondary considerations.

[69] 817.001 Somoza, Anastasio/211, Baldwin to Hull, 2 Dec. 1939.
[70] Conn and Fairchild, *The Framework*, 187–8.
[71] 810.24/123,4/21, memorandum, War Plans Division, 27 July 1940.

That he might establish a regime that would hold sway for the next forty years, of course, was a possibility given no consideration at all.

Before the end of 1940, therefore, the political and strategic aspects of good neighbourism were coalescing. Through diplomatic pressure Nicholson had been impressing on the internal opposition that Somoza enjoyed Washington's political support; it was implied that economic assistance would be forthcoming only if Somoza remained president; and the US military establishment was recommending arming the general in his own interests and, in extreme cases, was willing to consider armed intervention to maintain him in power. Notwithstanding all of Hull's memoranda and diplomatic dispatches to the contrary, internal stability in Nicaragua was to be achieved by strengthening the hold of the National Guard to allow Anastasio Somoza to retain the reins of government.

This remained US policy for the rest of 1940 and 1941. As far as the political aspects of good neighbourism in this period are concerned, the Managua legation had to do little except report potential dangers to the State Department and then help to eliminate them. Elimination took little effort, consisting mostly of Nicholson's informing representatives of the opposition that Washington would be displeased at any attempt to subvert public order. Implicit in such thinking was that the situation was temporary, that it was demanded by emergency conditions which would eventually subside. The non-interference principle, once sacrosanct, was suspended. Nicholson interfered blatantly on Somoza's behalf. His constant and vocal presence at pro-Somoza public functions must have boosted the president's personal standing and morale substantially. As the tendency of both parties to engage in this practice intensified during 1941, the modification of good neighbourism became a self-generating process. Somoza's strident pro-Americanism was now publicly reciprocated by Nicholson's overt *somocismo*, which seemed further to heighten the prospect that any movement to oust him would be liable to backing from the totalitarian powers, or at least that the posture of any government that replaced his could not be assured to be pro-American. Hence the desirability of his retaining power.[72]

It is important to keep in mind, however, that Nicaragua was not simply a listless object of US decision-making. Changing conditions prompted a new American policy in Nicaragua from mid 1940 onwards, but the same changes also altered Somoza's strategy. The general himself remained a source of concern for US diplomats and intelligence officers

[72] See e.g. 817.001 Somoza, Anastasio/232, Nicholson to Hull, 6 Feb. 1941.

throughout this period. While his continued residence in the presidency came to be perceived as expedient, naval intelligence could claim with some justice that 'the one source of worry in Nicaragua is President Somoza and his government'.[73]

The US naval attaché believed that Somoza's pro-Americanism was insincere, that the president's attitude was dependent on the financial, military, and political support he expected from the United States, and that his only true loyalty was to himself: 'President Somoza and his government would be one of the first to switch his support from the United States to any other nation offering him opportunities to secure personal gain...I suspect he might be having dealings in private with those opposed to our policies.'[74]

In other words, if the United States could forestall—through diplomatic pressure, the threat of economic sanctions, and the offer of military assistance—what it saw as the potential for a revolt in Nicaragua, the Roosevelt administration still perceived a latent danger that the government itself might deal with the Axis. Washington was aware that Somoza's loyalties were dependent on what he could get in return. As late as October, Nicholson—reporting Somoza's frequent assertions of friendship with the United States—noted that this indicated 'that we are still the highest bidder therefor'.[75]

The general's pro-Americanism was certainly less a matter of love for the United States than an appreciation of the fundamental nature of Nicaragua's power relations during the period of Depression diplomacy and then of global war. Essentially, he was an astute political opportunist; as late as the spring of 1940, Nicholson was reporting that both Somoza and the manager of the National Bank favoured increased trade with Germany, and that relations between the regime and the Geerz firm—the main agent for German sales in Nicaragua—were 'exceptionally close'.[76] The opportunism was well reflected in a dispatch from John Muccio, the legation's first secretary, who reported that until the fall of France, whereupon the US military establishment began to mobilize, Somoza had on his desk a portrait of Hitler. After Paris surrendered the picture of Hitler was replaced by one of Roosevelt.[77]

[73] 813.00 Nazis/12, naval attaché's intelligence report, 6 June 1940.   [74] Ibid.
[75] 810.20 Defense/285, Nicholson to Hull, 13 Oct. 1940.
[76] 817.00 Nazis/15, Nicholson to Hull, 9 Apr. 1940.
[77] 817.00 Nazis/15, Nicholson to Hull, 9 Apr. 1940; 817.00 Nazis/22, Muccio to Hull, 26 July 1940.

The rationale for such behaviour was straightforward. Until the summer of 1940 measures for hemisphere defence were only cautionary, and Somoza wished to maintain cordial relations with Germany. This was practical politics. Latin American countries rightly saw the need to preserve good trading relations with each of the competing powers. The onset of naval warfare in the Atlantic in 1939 inevitably heightened their commercial dependence on the United States as shipping was disrupted, but the governments of the region acknowledged that Germany might come to dominate the European economy in its entirety. As the US legation in Asunción reported, the main question in the minds of Latin American leaders was 'whether greater prosperity and comfort for each nation will result from a German world order or an Anglo-Franco-American system... From their standpoint it is common prudence to favour and conciliate those powers which will hold a predominant place in the future.'[78]

Somoza was displaying the same prudence. The main German legation for Central America (located in Guatemala) had been endeavouring to influence the Nicaraguan delegation to the Panama conference in an effort to muster support for a condemnation of the British blockade of foodstuffs en route to Germany. Of the Nicaraguan delegates—the foreign minister, Manuel Cordero Reyes, and the treasury minister, José Jesus Sánchez—it was considered significant by US intelligence that Sánchez was named at the last moment. He was seen as a strong advocate of closer trade relations with Germany and was perceived in Washington as having substantial influence over Somoza. 'While Somoza talks a good American line,' the naval attaché insisted, 'his government would not hesitate to enter into relations with those in the opposite camp to the detriment of the United States if personal gain could be realized.'[79]

When the United States began to mobilize, however, the general became abruptly anti-Axis, since in the new situation he could anticipate American arms, financial aid, and positive political support. Until then he had done nothing to stem the distribution of Nazi propaganda in Nicaragua, while propaganda in favour of Poland and Finland had been severely repressed.[80] By the end of 1940, however, most Nicaraguans were thoroughly scared of the Nazi threat and Somoza was claiming a desire to control Axis propaganda 'to the point of crushing

[78] Grow, *The Good Neighbor Policy*, 38–9.
[79] RG 38 C-10-h 22745, naval attaché's report, 22 Sept. 1939.
[80] 817.00 Nazis/21, Muccio to Hull, 10 July 1940.

it out'. He had given orders that all propaganda packages sent by German sources should be seized.[81] Nicholson reported with patent admiration that the president wished to help the fight against racist totalitarianism by putting every German in Nicaragua into a concentration camp. Such an attitude, the minister felt, 'should be complemented and reinforced in every way by anything the United States feels it may do in the circumstances'.[82]

*

Economic reinforcements were forthcoming. Pro-Axis sentiment was not widespread in Nicaragua, but the country's economic conditions confronted American planners with a simple equation: unalleviated economic difficulties might produce political unrest, and political instability would be a strategic liability. Such thinking was explicit in the State Department. As Laurence Duggan, chief of the Latin American division, wrote of US policy on Latin American economic development: 'at the beginning of the thirties the US government was doing even less than private organizations; it was doing nothing at all. By the end of the thirties it was white hot with enthusiasm, born of fear of the Nazis.'[83]

Three days after Britain and France declared war on Germany, Somoza declared a state of national economic emergency. Congressional legislation provided for control of imports, exports, and prices, prevention of exchange speculation, and a check on the placing of large orders based on a fear of world shortages and currency depreciation. Economic conditions remained bleak. Inflation was running high: the combined cost-of-living index, taking 1937 as a base year 100, climbed to 224 in 1939 and to 269 by 1941.[84]

In 1938 there had been a heavy decline in the value of both exports and imports over the previous year. The coffee crop suffered from severe rains, and world prices were at unusually low levels. There was also a serious decline in banana shipments, largely as a result of sigatoka disease. Cotton

[81] 817.00 Nazis/35, Nicholson to Hull, 28 Oct. 1940.

[82] 817.00 Nazis/33, Nicholson to Hull, 26 Oct. 1940.

[83] Laurence Duggan, *The Americas: The Search for Hemisphere Security* (New York: Holt, 1949), 160.

[84] 817.5151/478, Nicholson to Hull, 6 Sept. 1939; 817.50/21, Nicholson to Hull, 13 Sept. 1939; Chase National Bank of the City of New York, *The Countries of Central America: A Financial and Economic Review* (New York: Chase National Bank, 1943), 11; Knut Walter, *The Regime of Anastasio Somoza, 1936–1956* (Chapel Hill: University of North Carolina Press, 1993), 80; Victor Bulmer-Thomas, *The Political Economy of Central America since 1920* (Cambridge: Cambridge University Press, 1987), 99–100.

exports were down by 50 per cent.[85] By 1938 the dollar value of Nicaragua's exports was half that of any Central American country and constituted the lowest in Latin America with the exception of Panama.[86]

Underlining the concerns prompted by lower trade values were the problems of trade patterns. The share of Nicaragua's total exports going to Germany grew from less than 10 per cent in 1932 to 21 per cent in 1937, during which period the American share fell from 65 per cent to 55 per cent. The US position in Nicaraguan imports also showed a downward trend, from 63 per cent in 1932 to 54 per cent in 1937. This again favoured Germany, whose percentage share had almost doubled in the same period. By 1938, Nicaragua had reached fourth place on the list of Latin American countries that sent more than 10 per cent of their exports to Germany.[87] At the outbreak of war, Britain and Germany accounted for about 12 per cent of the country's exports and some 17 per cent of imports.[88]

In 1939, Nicaraguan coffee accounted for a third of total exports, and Germany was taking 20 per cent of the shipments. Similar problems faced the cotton industry. There had been no cotton exports from Nicaragua at the start of the Depression, and in 1932 shipments were valued at less than $500. By 1937, when cotton accounted for nearly 10 per cent of all exports, the entire industry depended on Germany and Japan.[89] The war threatened severe disruption to the Nicaraguan economy.

It was appreciated in Washington that the outbreak of hostilities entailed grave possibilities of strategic vulnerability in the isthmus. Commercial trends throughout Latin America, in fact, prompted fears that Berlin might absorb US markets in the region. A US government analysis cautioned that if the Latin American trade of Britain, France, and other European nations were to be added to Germany's existing share by virtue of conquest, 'German-controlled European trade would far exceed

[85] US Department of Commerce, Bureau of Foreign and Domestic Commerce, *Economic Review of Foreign Countries, 1938* (Washington DC: US Government Printing Office, 1939), 177.   [86] US Tariff Commission, *Foreign Trade*, 121.

[87] Horace B. Davis, 'The Influences of the Second World War', in Latin American Economic Institute, *The Economic Defense of the Western Hemisphere* (Freeport, NY: Books for Libraries Press, 1942), 6.

[88] *Commercial Pan America*, 4–6 (Apr.–June 1940), 175.

[89] US Tariff Commission, *Foreign Trade*, 124–5; Jaime A. Zuloaga Z., 'The International Economic Relations of Latin America', *Commercial Pan America*, 10/1 (Jan. 1941), 6.

that of the United States', seriously imperilling 'the economic position of the United States in the other American republics'.[90]

Roosevelt appreciated that the disruption of European markets would entail an accumulation of surpluses in Latin America and the emergence of problems similar to those at the start of the decade. New buyers had to be found for some $525 million worth of commodities that had previously gone to Europe. In June 1940, therefore, the White House announced a $2 billion hemisphere plan to market the production of Latin American staples. This proposal met opposition from agricultural and business leaders at home as well as in Latin America, where some governments objected to US control of their economies. Hull, in addition, feared that the plan would jeopardize his reciprocity programme.[91]

International hostilities, however (which the reciprocal trade agreement programme was supposed to inhibit), were abruptly rendering reciprocity obsolete. Reciprocity now had to be bought. In July 1940, following the demise of his original plan for surpluses, Roosevelt asked Congress to boost the credit available for Export-Import Bank operations by half a billion dollars to aid Latin America through the financing and marketing of part of the region's surpluses. In September, Congress authorized Exim to increase its capital from $200 million to $700 million and to lend up to $500 million to Latin American countries to strengthen their finances and establish new industries that might contribute to defence.[92]

The loss of the European market for Nicaraguan coffee was potentially disastrous. Ordinarily, more than 90 per cent of the country's production had been exported, and the year before the outbreak of war the main European markets (Germany, France, and the Netherlands) had together taken 43 per cent of the shipments. By 1940, moreover, the average price for coffee exports had dropped to the lowest point for any year since 1924.[93]

In November 1940, Latin America's coffee-producing countries and the United States concluded the Inter-American Coffee Agreement.

[90] 'Totalitarian Activity in the Other American Republics', January 10, 1941, quoted in Grow, *The Good Neighbor Policy*, 34.

[91] Dallek, *Franklin D. Roosevelt*, 234; Lew B. Clark, 'One Year of War, and United States Trade with Latin America', *Foreign Commerce Weekly*, 1/2 (12 Oct. 1940), 48.

[92] Dallek, *Franklin D. Roosevelt*, 234; 'Will Loans by the US Export-Import Bank be a Real Aid to Latin-American Economy', *Congressional Digest*, 19/12 (Dec. 1940), 315; Green, *Pan American Progress*, 102.

[93] 817.51/2701, memorandum, Ray to Collado, Bursley, and Bonsal, 23 May 1941; 817.51/2708, memorandum, Cabot, 25 Feb. 1942; *Commercial Pan America*, 10/4–6 (Apr.–June 1941), 260; US Tariff Commission, *Foreign Trade*, 127.

The accord aimed to foster the orderly marketing of coffee on terms equitable to producers and consumers on the basis of four annual quotas: an export quota for each producing nation, regulating shipments to the United States; an additional quota governing exports elsewhere; an import quota on the volume to be received into the United States from each producer; and an aggregate quota for US imports from sources other than the American republics. The quotas were administered by the Inter-American Coffee Board, in which the United States controlled twelve of the thirty-six votes. Nicaragua had one vote.[94]

Nicaragua's annual allotment for coffee exports to the United States was set at 195,000 bags of 60 kilograms each. This amounted to a maximum export quota to the United States of 25,740,000 pounds. The country's allotment for exports to the rest of the world was set at 15,048,000 pounds. These limits compared favourably with sales in 1939, when exports of Nicaraguan coffee to the United States stood at 24,609,684 pounds.[95] The quotas were periodically increased. Despite the loss of European markets, therefore, Nicaragua's coffee exports remained fairly buoyant. Average annual shipments for 1941–5 were equivalent to about 85 per cent of average shipments in the years immediately preceding the war. In 1941, Nicaragua shipped to the United States 24,000,000 pounds of coffee valued at $2,085,000. This was seven million pounds less than that shipped in the previous year, but the value was greater than 1940's $1,926,000. After the coffee agreement, spot prices for Nicaraguan coffee in New York rose from an average 6.6¢ a pound in the first ten months of 1940 to 7.6¢ in December. The price continued to climb in 1941 and 1942. By 1943 it stood at 13¢ a pound. Thus, while export volumes of Nicaraguan coffee during the war years were nearly 15 per cent below those immediately before the war, export values averaged about 25 per cent higher.[96]

The United States also increased financial and technical aid, although only following a struggle between the State Department and Exim. As a result of Somoza's visit to Washington, Nicaragua had been extended an Exim credit of $500,000 to stabilize the cordoba and $2 million for

[94] US Tariff Commission, *Economic Controls and Commercial Policy in Nicaragua* (Washington DC: US Government Printing Office, 1947), 18.   [95] Ibid. 19.

[96] US Tariff Commission, *Foreign Trade*, 52; US Department of Commerce, Bureau of Foreign and Domestic Commerce, *Foodstuffs Trade with Latin America, Trade Promotion Series*, 214 (Washington DC: US Government Printing Office, 1941), 10; *Commercial Pan America*, 10/4–6 (Apr.–June 1941), 260; US Tariff Commission, *Economic Controls*, 20; 817.51/2699, Baldwin to Hull, 27 Mar. 1941.

road-building. At the end of 1940 the Nicaraguan minister in Washington asked the State Department for another Exim credit to refund Nicaragua's sterling debt, the republic's only foreign debt, which had fallen by the year's end to £401,180 ($1,604,720) and which on current sterling rates could have been retired on a favourable basis. Exim refused to comply with this request on the grounds that it set 'an undesirable precedent'.[97]

At the beginning of 1941, Somoza asked Nicholson about a further loan to complete the Nicaraguan section of the Pan American Highway and to build a trans-isthmian road. He also wanted the $500,000 stabilization fund increased to $1 million.[98] LaVerne Baldwin, the chargé in Managua pending the arrival of a new minister, made a lengthy case for further credits, undermining, in the process, pessimistic reports from Irving Lindberg, the collector general of customs. By the beginning of 1941 the government surplus stood at C$3 million and, though much of this was in fixed assets, Baldwin felt that the republic was well able to pay the C$120,000 per month under the existing road-building arrangement; in fact it could afford to increase this to C$200,000 a month to take care of any further highway projects. Baldwin argued, moreover, that the dollar exchange available from a stabilization fund and a new Exim loan would enable Nicaragua to eliminate its existing blocked balance of $1 million, and he clearly hoped that there would be favourable discussions between the bank and the Nicaraguan minister in Washington.[99]

Exim, however, saw 'no need' to double the stabilization fund. This stance partly reflected a tendency to see the Exim issue almost exclusively in hemispheric terms. Congressional debate focused very largely on outstanding amounts already owed by 'Latin America' to US investors.[100] The State Department lobbied for a credit on the grounds that Nicaragua's strategic significance obliged the United States to prevent the country's economic difficulties from making it a strategic liability. Exim eventually succumbed, and on 8 March 1941 decided to loan Nicaragua a further $2 million for highway construction. By the end of the year the State Department was recommending that the existing credits be refunded and amplified into a single credit of $5 million.[101]

[97] 817.51/2696, memorandum, Collado to Bonsal and Duggan, 15 Nov. 1940.

[98] 817.51/2693, Nicholson to Hull, 21 Jan. 1941.

[99] 817.154/27, Baldwin to Hull, 18 Feb. 1941.

[100] 'Will Loans by the US Export-Import Bank', 317; 817.51/2699, Baldwin to Hull, 27 Mar. 1941.

[101] US Tariff Commission, *Economic Controls*, 10–11; 611.1731/376, H. Bartlett Wells to Hull, 3 Jan. 1940.

Overall, during the period of the European war Nicaragua enjoyed more favourable economic conditions than any other Central American country. By mid 1940, earlier fears that the country's total foreign trade would fall sharply relative to 1939 seemed unfounded. On the contrary, contemporary Nicaraguan figures show the total value of the country's foreign commerce for the six months ending in June 1940 to have been C$8.9 million, a figure 3 per cent higher than that for the corresponding six months of 1939. This owed much to steady advances in the production and export of gold, from $3.5 million in 1939 to almost $6 million in 1940 (when Nicaragua became the sixth largest producer in Latin America), and to $8 million in 1941, when gold accounted for 61 per cent of total exports.[102]

For the whole period 1938–41, the value of Nicaraguan exports more than doubled from C$5.8 million to C$12 million. Imports also doubled.[103] The United States successfully absorbed Nicaraguan exports whose normal markets were lost, and enhanced its own position as a source of Nicaraguan imports. In 1938, the United States had taken 67 per cent of Nicaragua's exports and provided 60 per cent of imports; by 1941, the United States was buying 96 per cent of the country's exports and supplying 88 per cent of imports.[104]

*

In Washington, Roosevelt declared an unlimited national emergency in May 1941 and warned that the western hemisphere was imperilled by German plans for world domination. 'It would be suicide', he announced, 'to wait until they are in our front yard … It is stupid to wait until a probable enemy has gained a foothold from which to attack.'[105]

---

[102] US Tariff Commission, *Foreign Trade*, 52; US Tariff Commission, *Economic Controls*, 5, 19–20; US Department of Commerce, Bureau of Foreign and Domestic Commerce, *US Trade with the Central American Republics in 1942* (Washington DC: US Government Printing Office, 1944), 22; *Commercial Pan America*, 10/11–12 (Nov.–Dec. 1941), 392. A substantial part of the gold exported was owned by US and Canadian companies, and only a portion of the total proceeds (estimated by the US chargé at 25 per cent) was returned to Nicaragua. 611.1731/380, H. Bartlett Wells to Hull, 7 Aug. 1940.

[103] Chase National Bank, *The Countries of Central America*, 10.

[104] Brownlee, *Cooperación económica de los Estados Unidos con Nicaragua* (Managua: Imprenta Democrática, 1945), 16. Jaime Wheelock and Luis Carrión view this in a negative light: 'Durante la II Guerra Imperialista … los Estados Unidos pasaron a absorber el 90 por ciento del valor de las exportaciones totales del país, quedando éste convertido en un simple apéndice de la economía norteamericana. Nicaragua funcionó durante los años de la guerra como simple abastecedora de las materias primas que la industria bélica norteamericana necesitaba.' Jaime Wheelock and Luis Carrión, *Apuntes sobre el desarrollo económico y social de Nicaragua* (Managua: Secretaría Nacional de Propaganda y Educación del FSLN, 1980), 27.   [105] Dallek, *Franklin D. Roosevelt*, 236.

US policy in Nicaragua proceeded according to such thinking in 1941, the key word being 'probable'. Evidently, any threat to the status quo was probably directed by the enemy.

Throughout the year, therefore, Washington explicitly acknowledged the undesirability of any disturbances in Nicaragua, and by extension the desirability of Somoza's retaining power. Any move to oust Somoza, of course, would have been unconstitutional. But since no such move could be allowed to amount to a 'disturbance', it was not plain how Washington's objectives could be reconciled with a policy of non-interference. Consequently, the very notion of non-interference simply disappeared from the diplomatic traffic. It was not a policy option to be applied, much less a diplomatic abstraction to be contemplated. Without that constraint, meeting the objectives required little actual diplomatic effort.

The United States was supporting the Nicaraguan economy. In the area of diplomacy, Nicholson continued to impress upon the internal opposition that the Roosevelt administration would not look kindly on any disturbance in Nicaragua—with the implicit threat that such an action might cause the United States to stop supporting the Nicaraguan economy. The American legation was also kept busy throughout 1941 with what by now must have been permanent 'discreet investigations' into the feelings among the lower sectors and the Guardia.

Additionally, throughout the year Nicholson publicly associated the Somoza government with the Roosevelt administration and the war effort. At the end of January 1941, Colonel Mullins held a banquet for Somoza. At that event, Nicholson made a speech in which he pointed out 'the success of President Somoza in working in the interests of all classes of the Nicaraguan people', and he paid tribute to the general's 'vigorous support of the cause of democracy'.[106] Though the former suggestion was somewhat arguable and the latter, in domestic terms, faintly comic, 'the cause of democracy' was a phrase whose meaning had shifted in the previous six months. The new perception would eventually make it less necessary that Somoza (or his sons) should work in the interests of all classes of the Nicaraguan people.

Economic policy and diplomatic activity to sustain the Somoza government were reinforced by US intelligence activities throughout 1941. The US naval attaché had warned that 'if we are to expect strict

---

[106] 817.001 Somoza, Anastasio/232, Nicholson to Hull, 6 Feb. 1941.

control of German and other non-American activities by the governments of these countries we must not hesitate in lending our support to
their efforts in this control'.[107] Hence the surveillance of the external
opposition, chiefly the Chamorro brothers. It is evident from the sheer
volume of intelligence traffic in this period that American agents were
kept busy monitoring the activities of the Chamorros. They were certain
that Segundo Chamorro was in the pay of German agents. In Mexico, the
FBI infiltrated his Committee for Free Nicaragua and turned up evidence
that the movement was being financed and armed from Berlin.
Chamorro was also in regular contact with members of the German
propaganda office in Mexico City. The US legation in Honduras was
instructed to be alert for any Nicaraguan refugees, particularly the
Chamorros, preparing to use Honduras as a base from which to attack
Nicaragua.[108]

The need for such activity on the part of American officials increased
in direct proportion to the decline in Somoza's standing within
Nicaragua. The consequent security helped compensate for some crass
political mistakes on his part. The coronation of his daughter Lilian as
queen of the Guardia in late 1941, a ceremony of absurdly extravagant
display and vast expense, gave rise to widespread discontent, especially
among the more devout Catholics and the guardsmen. The Guardia met
the full cost—each private was assessed at C$7 out of a monthly salary of
C$30—and in many cases the burden produced real hardships.[109]

Against such a background, US intelligence activities on Somoza's
behalf were not crucial to his survival, but they were important for his
own sense of security. In the autumn of 1941 he suggested that the FBI
help him to set up a domestic security service. The US War Department
recommended that a Spanish-speaking FBI agent be sent to Managua.
The bureau was disposed to assist, and by February 1942 Jack Shaw had
been assigned to train a secret security agency in Nicaragua.[110]

[107] 813.00 Nazis/12, naval attaché's intelligence report, 12 June 1940; *New York Times*,
21 Aug. 1940.
[108] 813.00 Revolutions/3, FBI report, 21 Oct. 1940; 817.00 Revolutions/52, Erwin
(Honduras) to Hull, 21 Aug. 1941.
[109] 817.00/8905, Boal to Hull, 19 Nov. 1941. A diamond-studded crown was placed
on her head by the archbishop, while part of the National Guard paraded in Roman clothing, complete with sandals: see William Krehm, *Democracies and Tyrannies of the Caribbean*
(Westport, Conn.: Lawrence Hill & Co., 1984), 117.
[110] 817.105/23, Hoover to Berle, 8 Aug. 1941; 817.105/23, Berle to Boal, 5 Sept.
1941; 817.105/26, Boal to Berle, 13 Sept. 1941; 817.105/26, Welles to Boal, 21 Feb.
1942; 817.201/2 Chief of Staff to Welles, unspecified date, 1940.

Throughout the year, as US concern over the defence of the western hemisphere continued to increase, potential threats to Somoza were being addressed by the American diplomatic establishment in terms that were very similar to those of the intelligence agencies.

Welles informed the Managua legation that he was in possession of 'unquestionably authentic information that the Japanese legation in Mexico city is engaged in fomenting revolutionary disturbances in Nicaragua'. The Managua mission was to pass on this information to Somoza and to suggest that he 'redoubles his precautions'.[111] In the meantime General Roberto Hurtado, a Nicaraguan refugee who had been identified as the main Japanese agent in these operations, was deported to the United States, where Berle was trying 'to cook up some procedure by which he is kept in the country, because he is a lot less dangerous in the United States than he is in Mexico or Central America'.[112]

American diplomats were convinced, apparently sincerely and perhaps correctly, that Chamorro and Hurtado were being funded by the German diplomatic mission in Tegucigalpa. Christian Zinsser, the German minister to Honduras, was declared *persona non grata* and expelled in March 1941 for activities incompatible with his diplomatic status. Hull alerted the legations in Honduras and Costa Rica to monitor any Nicaraguan refugees preparing to use those countries as bases for an attack on Nicaragua.[113] In August, the British minister in Guatemala told the American legation there that he had 'absolute proof' that Nicaragua's under-secretary of foreign affairs was in the pay of the German minister to Central America.[114]

This kind of thinking made things easier for Somoza. It was largely unnecessary for him even to demonstrate that activities directed against him were, in the naval attaché's phrase, 'non-American'. On the contrary, they had to be assumed to be anti-American because of the effect of seven years of non-interference in Nicaragua. The policy had allowed Somoza to gain power and was therefore seen in Nicaragua as interference. Non-interference had therefore led to anti-Americanism. In a war, the potential consequences of anti-Americanism had to be forestalled by interference that enabled Somoza to retain power. Somoza, however,

---

[111] 817.00 Revolutions/253, Welles to Flournoy, 9 July 1941.

[112] 817.00 Revolutions/257, memorandum by Berle, 25 July 1941.

[113] 817.00/52 Erwin to Hull, 21 Aug. 1941; Lawrence Martin and Sylvia Martin, 'Nazi Intrigues in Central America', *American Mercury*, 53 (July 1941), 66.

[114] 817.00 Revolutions/253, Welles to Flournoy, 9 July 1941; 817.00 Revolutions/152, Erwin to Hull, 21 Aug. 1941.

could not be fully trusted; and because he could not be trusted he had to be kept sweet by evidence of Washington's wish that he retain power. With regard to arms supplies, this was a hemisphere-wide policy. In a memorandum written at the end of June 1940, Roosevelt asserted that, in an effort to keep Latin American governments 'sweet', he had decided to 'let them have a few tiny driblets of arms'.[115]

Finally, therefore, economic, diplomatic, and intelligence activities were being complemented by the operations of the US War Department. The latter had already initiated action through the southern command at Panama to survey Nicaraguan airfields; it had urged the FBI to train a Nicaraguan secret police; and its missions policy envisaged 'a more liberal attitude than heretofore'. Members of the House Military Affairs Committee visited Managua in August 1941 to check on the progress of military collaboration.[116] The Managua legation continued its discreet investigations into any rumour of a plot to oust Somoza, but by October the War Department's operations were making the diplomats' activities superfluous. A Lend Lease agreement of that month promised Nicaragua $1.3 million in military equipment at a cost of $900,000. Payment was deferred until July 1947, whereupon all obligations of the republic to the United States were to be considered discharged. This, according to the chief of naval operations, Admiral Stark, was 'just common sense'. The Nicaraguan National Guard never used any of this hardware against the Axis, nor was it meant to. The arms were to help ensure internal political stability, and as a consequence they guaranteed the continued dominance of Anastasio Somoza.[117] Within two months, Somocista ascendancy seemed even more necessary.

---

[115] Memorandum, Franklin D. Roosevelt to Marshall, 'National Latin American Arms Policy', 24 June 1940, quoted in Donald Dozer, *Are We Good Neighbours?* (Gainesville: University of Florida Press, 1959), 78.

[116] 817.00/8900, Boal to Hull, 29 Aug. 1941.

[117] 817.00 Nazis/25, Cabot to Hull, 12 Aug. 1941; 817.00/8905, Boal to Hull, 19 Nov. 1941; 817.24/10–1641, 'Lend Lease Agreement between the United States and Nicaragua, 16 October 1941'; Humphreys, *Latin America*, ii, 11; Richard Millet, *Guardians of the Dynasty* (Maryknoll, NY: Orbis Books, 1977), 199; Connell-Smith, *The Inter-American System*, 117.

7

The Good Neighbours at War, 1942–1944

On 7 December 1941, Japanese aircraft attacked Pearl Harbor. Congress issued a declaration of war on 8 December, and three days later Hitler and Mussolini declared war on the United States. In the first three months of global war the Japanese captured Singapore, Rangoon, Guam, and Manila. American airpower in the Philippines and Allied naval forces in the Java Sea were destroyed. By early March 1942 Burma, the Malay peninsula, and the Dutch East Indies were overrun. Australia and India were endangered. News from the Pacific in the early months was all bad but the Pearl Harbor attack, abruptly resolving Roosevelt's problems with regard to US involvement, had in one sense been a relief for both the president and Churchill. As the prime minister told Roosevelt by telephone on the day of the attack, 'this certainly simplifies things'.[1]

The news from elsewhere was also disheartening. By the start of 1942 Germany controlled the greater part of the European continent. The invasion of the Soviet Union in June 1941 had brought German troops to the outskirts of Moscow by October, and the Soviet government began evacuating to Kubyshev. After the winter of 1941–2, the Germans advanced into the Caucasus and the lower Volga valley. In the Atlantic, the Germans were sinking British ships faster than replacements could be built. In North Africa, Rommel's forces had driven back the British almost as far as Tobruk by the end of January 1942. In the same month the Rio conference of American foreign ministers set up an Inter-American Defense Board of military advisers from all countries to

---

[1] 740.0011 Pacific War/848c, Hull to the diplomatic representatives in the other American republics, 7 Dec. 1941; 740.0011/786, Boal to Hull, 8 Dec. 1941; Eric Hobsbawm, *Age of Extremes: The Short Twentieth Century 1914–1991* (London: Michael Joseph, 1994), 40; Robert Dallek, *Franklin D. Roosevelt and American Foreign Policy, 1933–1945* (New York: Oxford University Press, 1979), 312, 325, 331–5.

recommend responses to any challenges to hemisphere defence, and an Emergency Advisory Committee for the Political Defense of the Continent to coordinate measures against Axis subversion.[2]

Of the eleven western-hemisphere countries that signed the Declaration of the United Nations in January 1942, nine were in the Caribbean and Central America. That same month, German submarines began what Berlin's U-boat command termed 'the happy time' in the Caribbean Sea. Sinkings rose from 13 in January to 142 in May and June. A total of 336 ships were destroyed in 1942 and the burden of Caribbean defence fell naturally to Washington. The United States, according to Somoza, provided Central America's only chance of survival.[3]

*

Nicaragua, with its armed force of 3,500 men, issued a declaration of war on 16 December against Germany, Japan, Italy, Hungary, Rumania, and Bulgaria. Two days after Pearl Harbor, Somoza effected the *ley marcial,* a rider to the 1939 constitution, which empowered him to detain anyone indefinitely without a warrant; military authorities could eliminate, 'at whatever cost', any perceived threat to public order under abnormal circumstances; military courts would try all cases of treason or rebellion.[4]

Domestic political conditions seemed calm in the months immediately following the good neighbours' entry into the war, although the elements of instability evident in 1940 and 1941 had not waned. At the end of the first full month of the Pacific War, a US intelligence report evaluated Somoza's position with optimism and some relief. The assessment was spurred by an assumption that domestic conditions in Nicaragua

[2] Alan Bullock, *Hitler and Stalin: Parallel Lives* (London: Fontana, 1993), 792, 832; Hobsbawm, *Age of Extremes,* 39–40; Roger Parkinson, *Encyclopaedia of Modern War* (London: Granada Publishing Limited, 1979), 112; Hugh Brogan, *The Pelican History of the United States of America* (Harmondsworth: Penguin, 1987), 589–90; G. Pope Atkins, *Latin America in the International Political System* (Boulder, Colo.: Westview Press, 1995), 214.

[3] Correlli Barnett, *Engage the Enemy More Closely: The Royal Navy in the Second World War* (London: Hodder & Stoughton, 1991), 442–3; Robin R. Humphreys, *Latin America and the Second World War* (London: Athlone press, 1981), i, 1; Samuel E. Morison, *History of United States Naval Operations in World War II,* 1: *The Battle of the Atlantic, September 1939–May 1943* (London: Oxford University Press, 1948), 198; William L. Langer and S. Everett Gleason, *Challenge to Isolation, 1937–1940* (New york: Harpes 1952), 101; *New York Times,* 13 Dec. 1941.

[4] Knut Walter, *The Regime of Anastasio Somoza, 1936–1956* (Chapter Hill: University of North Carolina Press, 1993), 112–13; Martin C. Needler (ed.), *Political Systems of Latin America* (Princeton, N J: Van Nostrand, 1964), 102.

would determine the extent to which Axis agents might impede hemisphere unity and cause Washington to divert military forces away from
the main objectives of the war. In that light, US intelligence lauded
Somoza as 'thoroughly co-operative' and averred with relief that 'under
the present constitution the Somoza administration will continue until
1947 and opposition to it is negligible'.[5] This assessment remained
unchanged two months later. A March 1942 intelligence report on Axis
penetration in Nicaragua asserted that the only opposition to Somoza was
'the Conservative Party, consisting mainly of large landowners and the
pro-Franco group centred at Granada'.[6]

The American minister disagreed with this appraisal. Aware that
Somoza had been losing ground politically over the past year, he felt that
trouble was brewing and that 'the political situation might soon become
acute'.[7] The Conservatives, in fact, seemed to present little danger.
Disorganized and without effective leadership, they were unable even to
improve their standing with the legation. Three Conservative leaders—
Guillermo Pasos Montiel, Alfonso Estrada, and Adolfo Cardenas—
approached the new US minister, Pierre Boal (transferred from Mexico to
replace Nicholson in July 1941), and told him of their desire to establish
'a very intimate relationship with the legation'. To this end Managua's
Conservative club intended to give a dinner dance in honour of Boal's
daughter Mimi, an act of ingratiation that Somoza prevented by simply
closing down the club.[8]

Other developments were more worrying. First, the mounting hostility of the dissidents in the Liberal Party seemed to pose a much graver
danger than the Conservatives. Nicaragua's entry into the war, by providing a pretext for Somoza to suspend constitutional guarantees and ban
meetings of more than four people, hindered the dissidents' capacity for
organization, but their resentment was patent. The US legation reported
that Luis Debayle, the director of public health and Somoza's brother-
in-law, was spending at least C$15,000 a month cultivating the
Guardia and warned that he might soon win sufficient backing to arrange
a coup.[9] Second, public dissatisfaction with Somoza continued to run
high as living standards declined sharply in the face of mounting price

[5] RG 226, Research and Analysis Report 168, 'A Survey of Elements of Instability in the
Latin American Sector', 30 Jan. 1942.

[6] RG 226 14427, 'Axis Penetration in Nicaragua', Mar. 1942.

[7] 817.00/4–2142, Stewart to Bonsal, 21 Apr. 1942.

[8] 817.00/8906, Boal to Hull, 1 Jan. 1942.

[9] 817.00/4–2142, Stewart to Bonsal, 21 Apr. 1942.

rises while the government held public sector wages below the level of inflation.[10]

Third, and particularly worrying for the State Department with the United States at war, dissatisfaction with Somoza was linked to anti-Americanism. Most Nicaraguans held Washington responsible for the failings of the regime. J. Edgar Hoover's informants advised him that the United States was 'held guilty in internal matters to a much greater degree than was done under similar circumstances some time ago'. The FBI attributed this to German propaganda. In fact, US diplomats and intelligence agents could not agree on the extent of German propaganda or the influence of the Axis powers in Nicaragua. *La Prensa*, the most significant newspaper, did evince a somewhat tepid support of the democracies. Its publisher, Pedro Joaquín Chamorro—a religious fanatic in the FBI's opinion and a strong supporter of the Franco movement—also owned *El Diario Nicaragüense*. American intelligence believed that the latter was 'strictly falangist' and that it was on the Nazi payroll, receiving monthly funds from the German legation. The FBI reported that the Chamorros, in exile in Mexico, were closely allied with 'Axis and fifth column movements' in Nicaragua.[11]

Naval intelligence, on the other hand, claimed that Axis influence was simply not apparent, while the FBI and the legation separately reported that German propaganda was not particularly extensive and was generally received unfavourably. It seems unlikely that German propaganda was solely responsible for Nicaraguan anti-Americanism. Anti-Americanism had never receded. Only a decade had passed since the military evacuation, and in that time the perception persisted that the United States had promoted Somoza, installed him in the presidency, and kept him there.[12]

The opportunities for the Axis to wield influence in Nicaragua were limited. The country's German and Italian communities were the smallest in Central America. There was one Japanese resident. Sixty individuals from among the German community were listed as Nazi sympathizers by US intelligence. These, with some Italians, were interned at the estate of one Ulrico Eitzen. Pro-Axis individuals were also detained at the Guardia

---

[10] Jeffrey Gould, *Dangerous Friends: Somoza and the Labour Movement* (mimeographed document, Managua, 1985), 10; Victor Bulmer-Thomas, *The Political Economy of Central America since 1920* (Cambridge: Cambridge University Press, 1987), 87.

[11] 817.00/8913, Hoover to Berle, 5 May 1942; 817.00/8906 Boal to Hull, 1 Jan. 1942; RG 226 14427, 'Axis Penetration in Nicaragua', Mar. 1942.

[12] RG 226 20633, naval attachés report, 7 Sept. 1942; 817.20/91, memorandum by Bonsal, 3 Mar. 1942; 817.00/8959, Stewart to Hull, 19 Feb. 1943.

hospital and the Hormiguero prison. The lone Japanese was similarly interned. The Americans even placed a spy, one Renner, among the detainees to inform upon their activities and conversations during their incarceration.[13]

Some threats did receive Axis backing, but for the most part they predated the war. Chamorrista conspiracy, for example, a perennial feature of Nicaragua's political life, persisted. Segundo Chamorro, according to US intelligence, 'hates the American form of government and has intimated that he would work for the Germans in any way he could'. He and Emiliano, ever hopeful, had formed the Central American Revolutionists with the aim of overthrowing all of the isthmus's dictators. Since the dictators were pro-American, the Revolutionists were *ipso facto* anti-American, anti-democratic, and pro-Axis.[14]

Fourth, there were the endless anxieties about the loyalty of the military. Apart from the worrying prospect of Liberal dissidents buying the Guardia's affections, Washington's problems were exacerbated by such matters as a personal clash between Somoza and Colonel Charles Mullins, the American head of the military academy. The row was activated by Conservative militants, who spread the claim that Mullins had been ordered by the State Department to inform Somoza of the need for an election soon.[15] This dispute aroused widespread publicity and spurred an assumption that political activity within the National Guard could now be undertaken. Cochran at the US legation expected 'a scramble for power within the Guardia'.[16]

Incensed, Somoza had asked that Mullins be transferred. This was no minor matter, since Mullins was perceived in Nicaragua as much more than the head of a military school. It was generally assumed that, in the event of any emergency, Mullins—with the weight of US power behind him—would assume command of the Guardia in support of Somoza.[17] It was further accepted that Rigoberto Reyes, despite the loss of his position as Chief of Staff, retained a strong following among the junior officers. This posed the danger that if anything were to happen to Somoza, Reyes (identified by the FBI and the legation as a Nazi) might be the strongest man in the country.[18]

[13] RG 226 10944, J. Edgar Hoover to Colonel William J. Donovan, 2 Feb. 1942; RG 226 12776, Hoover to Donovan, undated.
[14] RG 226 14427, 'Axis Penetration in Nicaragua', Mar. 1942.
[15] 817.00/8914, Cochran to Hull, 13 May 1942.
[16] 817.00/8914, Cochran to Hull, 26 June 1942.
[17] 817.00/8914, Cochran to Hull, 13 May 1942.
[18] 817.00/8923, Stewart to Hull, 26 June 1942.

These conditions prevailed during early 1942, although American intelligence continued to give assurances that Somoza was in no immediate danger. By the spring, however, the internal and external opposition were more active and the situation again showed signs of deteriorating. At the end of April a plot was discovered against the president's life. The attack was to take place during his visit to Bluefields on 25 April and was foiled when Guardia troops stopped the attackers' car. One would-be assassin was killed in the subsequent chase; others were found to be members of the Conservative Party. A large number of Conservatives in government service were immediately dismissed. Somoza's informants now advised him of the possibility of a Conservative disturbance timed for the start of May. He ordered a general detention of party leaders, as well as members of the rank and file. By the middle of the month Cochran was advising that the political pot was seething. Somoza's difficulties had extended to his own cabinet. The FBI believed that he was having 'a great deal of trouble' with his ministers and was considering a complete cabinet reshuffle to substitute controllable men.[19]

Debayle's plans to cause trouble within the Liberal Party, moreover, now seemed close to fruition. Legation dispatches had been relating Debayle's activities for some time, but such reports now assumed greater urgency. Much of the concern was sparked by Debayle's evident confidence. He baldly told the legation's commercial attaché that 'if conditions become critical and it is necessary I will throw [Somoza] out and take over. This I can do without much difficulty.'[20] Such confidence is notable for its expression in such forthright terms to a member of the American legation. It may have been simply a trial balloon on Debayle's part to gauge Washington's reaction to the possibility of his ousting Somoza, but it seems unlikely that he would have made such a claim if objective conditions indicated that it was absurd.

This raised a problem. Among the general public, the popular perception of Somoza as a creature of Washington had generated anti-Americanism. In the circumstances there was little that the United States could do to counteract such thinking. American efforts to sustain the Nicaraguan economy, for example, which might reasonably have been expected to help dissipate anti-Americanism, in fact reaffirmed it since

[19] 817.00/8910, Cochran to Hull, 4 Apr. 1942; 817.008914, Cochran to Hull, 13 May 1942; 817.001 Somoza/237, Cochran to Hull, 4 May 1942; 835.00/1209 Hoover to Berle, 25 May 1942; 817.00/8914 Cochran to Hull, 13 May 1942.

[20] 817.001 Somoza/266, Stewart to Hull, 24 Aug. 1942; 817.001 Somoza/247, Stewart to Hull, 19 Sept. 1942; 817.00/8955, Stewart to Hull, 12 Dec. 1942.

those efforts were seen as a means of sustaining Somoza. These sentiments being impossible to eradicate in the circumstances, they had to be disregarded somewhat by US policy-makers. More worrying for the State Department, however, was a perception among the political elite of a Somoza with ambivalent US support. It had become apparent that, under Boal, the legation distrusted Somoza, a fact of which the president and his ministers were aware. Hence the 'trouble' he had with them, an attitude reinforced by the publicity surrounding the Mullins dispute.[21] By the summer of 1942, Somoza's position seemed less secure than US intelligence had claimed at the beginning of the year.

*

Hope was at hand in the shape of James Bolton Stewart. In the midst of these unsettled conditions the State Department decided to replace Boal in Managua. Stewart, according to *Time*'s Central America correspondent William Krehm, was 'a pleasant, mild-mannered person'. Krehm's claim that the minister lacked the strength of character to resist Somoza's charm appears to be borne out by the evidence.[22] Stewart's subsequent conduct was certainly remarkable given the avowed principles of US diplomacy in Nicaragua. On the bases of customarily vague instructions from Washington and his own judgement, Stewart noted the steady emergence of an emboldened opposition and then tied the American legation to the Somoza regime.

Stewart saw little alternative in the circumstances, given the nature of his instructions. Despite the intervening upheavals and vastly changed global outlook, these had altered little since Sacasa's term. 'We attach the very greatest importance', Philip Bonsal the assistant chief informed his minister, 'to the maintenance of political and economic stability there.'[23] This objective and its implications, Somoza's retention of power, were clear enough. As to the manner in which diplomacy was to be conducted, however, such instructions raised many questions. Stewart's penultimate predecessor, Meredith Nicholson, had perforce acted on the basis of his own assumptions regarding American policy and had been taken to task by Hull. Stewart's thinking proceeded along similar lines to Nicholson's, but his conduct took him far beyond the limits that even Nicholson had observed.

[21] 817.001 Somoza/238, J. Edgar Hoover to Berle, 14 May 1942.
[22] William Krehm, *Democracies and Tyrannies of the Caribbean* (Westport Conn.: Lawrence Hill & Co., 1984), 120.
[23] 817.00/7–2142, Bonsal to Stewart, 4 Sept. 1942.

Arthur Bliss Lane had consistently refused invitations from Somoza to participate in any event that had a clear political intent, and he had forbidden all legation personnel from so doing. In July 1942, however, when Somoza made a trip to León, a crowd of 20,000 people saw him inaugurate a workers' club while flanked by Stewart, Cochran, and Colonel Fred Cruse, Mullins's replacement as head of the military academy. Somoza also visited the university and factories, and attended several meetings with representatives of different social groups. Stewart accompanied him on virtually every occasion.[24]

Stewart's presence on such trips, and at Somoza's public rallies, thereafter became habitual. According to Krehm, the relationship between the two men was such that Somoza, demonstrating a fondness for puns, would refer to Stewart as 'my steward', while the minister, to visiting journalists including Krehm himself, 'would recount the doings of Tacho like a doting aunt'.[25] Krehm is not a dispassionate observer, but his assessment is supported by the evidence of Stewart's own dispatches from Managua, which are replete with indications of his affection for Somoza, admiration for the president's 'achievements' (a recurrent theme), and sympathy for his difficulties as opposition mounted.[26]

Politically, such a relationship must have been useful to Somoza in the second half of 1942. By then, according to FBI intelligence, his greed had 'gone a bit too far' and his own mistakes had afforded the opposition substantial ammunition. The absurd coronation of the queen of the Guardia and the Mullins episode added force to dissatisfaction promoted by Somoza's business activities, which had become a leading topic of conversation in political and upper social circles. He was so engrossed in these that he simply neglected government affairs. There were few profitable business enterprises from which he did not derive an income. Stewart worried that Somoza was 'blind to the waning of his popularity', which Hoover translated for Berle at the State Department as 'losing his grip'. Hoover, whose informants throughout 1942 were reporting a widespread belief in Nicaragua that there would be at least an attempt to oust Somoza, warned the State Department that 'if the president continues to amass such a private fortune in the midst of misery and hunger, he will sooner or later provoke the mass to action.'[27]

[24] 817.00/7–2142, Bonsal to Stewart, 4 Sept. 1942; 817.001 Somoza/241, Stewart to Hull, 23 July 1942.   [25] Krehm, *Democracies and Tyrannies*, 120.
[26] 817.001 Somoza, Anastasio/246, Stewart to Hull, 24 Aug. 1942.
[27] 817.00/8944, Hoover to Berle, 7 Oct. 1942; 817.001 Somoza/246, Stewart to Hull, 24 Aug. 1942; 817.001 Somoza/247 Stewart to Hull, 19 Sept. 1942; 817.00/8955, Stewart to Hull, 26 Dec. 1942.

This unsettled atmosphere produced a scare in September, when the British chargé in Managua and the Nicaraguan Chief of Staff received telegrams from their respective counterparts in Costa Rica asking if there had been a coup in Nicaragua. Somoza immediately declared a state of emergency and began rounding up Conservative leaders. Few were found in their beds when the sweep began at 1.00 a.m., and the remainder were arrested on their return hours later. Since they all refused to explain their whereabouts, Somoza was convinced that some movement was indeed planned.[28] The State Department demanded that Stewart provide more detail. His reply did not entirely calm fears in Washington. He felt that the arrests did not indicate an attempt against the regime, but they did reflect the insecurity of the government. Such concern was underlined by intelligence reports that Somoza was considering retirement and that Debayle was still plotting against him. 'I do not consider the situation critical,' Stewart advised, 'but I do think it is deteriorating.'[29]

In these circumstances Stewart's constant presence at pro-Somoza functions was, by any objective judgement, an interference at a time when the president's position seemed to be weakening. Even if Stewart had been less accommodating, however, it was now inescapable that non-interference was not a practical aim. At times of tension and sudden upsurges of vocal opposition, political rumours invariably included references to the United States as if a fictional source in Washington or in the American legation gave them greater veracity. By 1942 the good neighbour policy could not have been the same as that announced by Roosevelt in 1933. The ideal he expressed in his inaugural speech had always been more a matter of natural political development than of design. It evolved as a compromise from the isolationist-internationalist struggle of the Depression, in response to conditions that no longer prevailed, and its tenets were impracticable policy objectives with which to engage in global war. As implemented it seems unlikely that it could have worked in a manner that could be judged beneficial to Nicaragua, and by 1942 it was no longer viable for the United States.

US policy was now geared simply to the preservation of the status quo. This was entirely for reasons of security. Politically, Somoza was largely viewed with distaste in Washington. Even J. Edgar Hoover, whose job it was to worry about US security, found the Somoza regime objectionable.

[28] 817.00/8929, Stewart to Hull, 5 Sept. 1942.

[29] 817.00/8929, Hull to Stewart, 8 Sept. 1942; 817.00/8930, Stewart to Hull, 9 Sept. 1942; 817.001 Somoza/245, Hoover to Berle, 26 Aug. 1942; RG 38 20633, naval attaché's report, 7 Sept. 1942.

Economically, US interest was largely limited to ensuring that Nicaragua's problems did not become so acute as to provoke instability that would be detrimental to American security interests. US business lobbying appears to have been minimal. Investment, in relative terms, was very low. As of 1 January 1941, US direct investment stood at $8.6 million, compared with $25 million in Costa Rica, $38 million in Honduras, and $68 million in Guatemala.[30] At issue was the security of the canal. While such a policy seemed legitimate in the circumstances—in March 1942, Welles voiced fear that the Japanese might be in a position to attack the canal by the summer—the need for it was at least partly a consequence of the good neighbour policy itself.[31]

For months, intelligence reports had been indicating the possibility of an attempt to overthrow Somoza. A problem inherent in good neighbourism was that the president's unpopularity, coupled with a popular belief that he had attained and retained the presidency through the manoeuvrings of the State Department, gave rise to the possibility that, in the context of a war, any replacement government would not be amicably disposed towards the United States. In short, because the good neighbour policy had hereto failed to convince Nicaraguans that the United States wished them nothing but good, and had no interest in promoting the ambitions of any one of them, it had to be discontinued.

Stewart asserted that 'the United States wields a tremendous influence on the course of political events in Nicaragua. This is not to say that it does so intentionally or even willingly; nor does it imply any departure from the principle of non-intervention now so strongly entrenched in our foreign policy.'[32] Apart from his comment on 'influence', Stewart's statement is manifestly untrue. Adoption of a de facto recognition policy in 1936 had undoubtedly encouraged Somoza's military plans against Sacasa, but had been championed by the State Department as evidence of the termination of US intervention in Central America. In this period that policy reverted to the position before good neighbourism, whereby regimes assuming power by virtue of a revolution or coup would not be recognized as legitimate. In the new circumstances this policy reversal could be, and was, similarly championed as a strengthening of non-interference.

[30] Dexter Perkins, *The United States and the Caribbean* (Cambridge, Massa.: Harvard University Press, 1947), 198. Perkins's figures are from the Division of Economic Information of the Pan American Union.

[31] 817.20/92, memorandum by Welles, 3 Mar. 1942.

[32] 817.00/8959, Stewart to Hull, 20 Jan. 1943.

According to Hull, it was now a 'travesty of the doctrine of non-intervention' to recognize such governments.[33]

Non-interference, even non-intervention on a military level, had long ago disappeared as policy. In fact, that military intervention was not realized in practice owed something to political interference. Implicit in such thinking was that the situation would be temporary. Diplomatic doctrine was therefore not so much abandoned as suspended. Hence Stewart did not have to wrestle with the principles of good neighbourism as Lane had done. He was not, until very late in the day, taken to task by the State Department as Lane and Nicholson had been for blatantly contravening those principles. Indeed, the notion of non-interference rarely arose in his correspondence with Washington.

By 1942, non-interference was an irrelevance. If dissatisfaction with the Somoza regime reached the point of violence it could be met, as Van Voorhis had made plain, by the dispatch of US ground forces. Such an endeavour, however, would have entailed a reallocation of much-needed resources and was in any case avoidable. The United States therefore continued to attempt to attenuate the economic problems that might provoke a revolt, and to assist Somoza politically and militarily in order to create conditions in which a revolt would seem inadvisable.

*

Economic diplomacy was tailored to such objectives throughout this period, when shortages of supply and accompanying high prices created problems throughout Latin America. In response to high inflation, in December 1941 Somoza established a Board for the Control of Prices and Commerce (Junta de Control de Precios y Comercio), which acted as the price control authority until July 1944 (when it was replaced by another body). In 1942 price controls were introduced for necessities such as flour, milk, corn, butter, lard, and beef. The ceilings, established at retail level, were periodically fixed for indeterminate periods. The board was accorded broad powers to impose penalties for violations of its orders but the sanctions were generally light or were not enforced. Hence there was little deterrent to offenders. Indeed, greater price increases occurred in the period immediately following the introduction of price control than before.[34]

[33] US Department of State, *Bulletin*, 10, (1 Jan. 1944), 20–1; Cordell Hull, *Memoirs* (New York: Macmillan, 1948), ii, 1396; Bryce Wood, *The Dismantling of the Good Neighbour Policy* (Austin: University of Texas Press, 1985), 9–10.

[34] US Tariff Commission, *Economic Controls and Commercial Policy in Nicaragua* (Washington DC: US Government Printing Office, 1947), 21–3.

This situation was worrying for both the US legation and the FBI, since it was clear to both that Somoza and his advisers were speculating in precisely those goods whose prices were climbing most rapidly. In mid 1941 beans and rice, the country's basic foodstuffs, stood at C$0.12 per pound and C$0.17 per pound respectively. By the autumn of 1942 both cost C$0.24. The retail price of corn had almost doubled over the same period. Lard had been selling for C$0.81 per bottle in 1942. By the autumn of the following year the price had reached C$3.80. Hoover's agents informed him that economic conditions among the lower sector were completely desperate by September 1942, when people could not even buy corn for tortillas. He believed that these circumstances posed a danger because they provided scope for anti-American propaganda and because 'an individual who knew how could stir up a revolt within a few days if given the opportunity to do so'.[35]

The US legation thus responded with its own propaganda. The commercial attaché conferred frequently with Sr Mendieta, the president of the Price Control Board, as to how the Nicaraguan public could be informed of the sacrifices being made by its American counterpart. Mendieta was busy producing press articles that stressed American hardship while the legation fed him a constant supply of suitable material for publication, thereby making the board the legation's public relations department.[36]

Other measures were being adopted in Washington. The Nicaraguan ministers of finance and foreign affairs arrived at the State Department in the first week of March to discuss progress in carrying out the arrangements discussed at the Rio conference, particularly the completion of work on the Inter-American Highway, a possible increase in credit to the National Bank, and help with Nicaragua's agricultural production.[37] Nicaragua had amassed 1,840,000 kilograms of low-grade, short-fibre cotton whose usual export markets were Germany and Japan. The Nicaraguan delegation in Washington wanted to sell it to the United States, and the US government proved accommodating. By the summer an agreement had been reached whereby the Commodity Credit Corporation of the United States bought, at a price of C$5 per kilogram, the excess production of the 1942 cotton crop, all previous crops, and all crops to be produced until the end of the war.[38]

[35]   817.00/8935, Stewart to Hull, 19 Sept. 1942; 817.00/8938, Hoover to Berle, 24 Sept. 1942.   [36]   817.24/480, Stewart to Hull, 10 July 1942.
[37]   710 Consultation/693, Collado to Welles, 28 Feb. 1942.
[38]   817.61321/16, memorandum, Bonsal to Collado, 13 Apr. 1942; 817.61321/18, Messersmith to Hull, 17 July 1942.

Having lost its Asian sources of some vital raw materials, the United States was looking to Latin America as an alternative supplier. Following the Havana conference, the Office of the Coordinator of Inter-American Affairs (OCIAA) had been set up under Nelson Rockefeller to implement projects fostering Latin American exports to the United States. Procurement agencies such as the Rubber Reserve Company were instituted to buy the products.[39] In general these projects had little effect on Central America, although Nicaragua undoubtedly benefited from US aid in the promotion of rubber production.

The OCIAA sent a rubber expert, George Seeley, to assess conditions in the country. Seeley and the legation recommended an agreement between Washington and Managua providing for the sale of all rubber stocks and future production to the United States. On 22 April 1942 the Rubber Reserve Company and the National Bank of Nicaragua reached an agreement whereby the former was to buy all of Nicaragua's excess production. The price was fixed at 33 ¢ per pound, with a premium of 2.5 ¢ per pound for any purchases between 200 and 700 tons, and of 5 ¢ per pound for purchases over 700 tons during any one year.[40]

On 15 July 1942 a US–Nicaraguan memorandum of understanding outlined another plan for the production of raw materials. An experimental agricultural station was set up in Nicaragua to concentrate on the production of rubber, manila hemp, and plants used in the manufacture of medicines. Over the following year Washington spent $90,000 promoting the production of rubber, which the Rubber Reserve Company then bought. By 1943 rubber was the country's second most important agricultural export commodity and Nicaragua was the second biggest Latin American producer after Brazil. The number of Nicaraguans tapping and collecting crude rubber grew from 300 in August 1942 to about 7,000 by the end of 1943. Moreover, these earned more than they had when working on the banana plantations. The increase in rubber production therefore partly offset the effects of the rapid decline in banana shipments.[41] All US initiatives to sustain Nicaragua's economy during 1942 and 1943 were in this way related to the war effort, an attempt to

[39] Bulmer-Thomas, *The Political Economy*, 90; Perkins, *The United States and the Caribbean*, 198.

[40] 810.6176/265, Cochran to Hull, 23 Apr. 1942; 810.6176/265, Hull to Stewart, 8 May 1942.

[41] Roland Brownlee, *Cooperación económica de los Estados Unidos con Nicaragua* (Managua: Imprenta Democrática, 1945), 28, 30–4; 817.50/37A, Smith to Hull, 'Annual Economic Report for 1943', 16 Mar. 1944.

ensure continuing stability by forestalling economic decline. The most obviously political programme of good neighbour economics in this period was Washington's policy on Nicaraguan gold-mining.

In the early 1940s, Nicaraguan export earnings were highly dependent on gold. In 1942 the republic sent $8.7 million of gold to the United States, about two-thirds of the latter's total gold purchases from Central America. Nicaraguan merchandise exports to the United States in 1942, by contrast, amounted to only $4.6 million. By April, shipping problems had caused a shortage of mining equipment. Unalleviated, this would entail the cessation of production and the closure of the mines. The repercussions were likely to be substantial. Thousands would immediately be made redundant and the government stood to lose the significant tax revenue derived from gold exports. Closure would entail the removal of foreign drafts brought into the country in 1941 through the National Bank amounting to $1.65 million. The entire eastern half of the republic might be paralysed because, with no requirements for freight, shipping would be suspended. This problem worried the FBI; Hoover wrote to Berle at the State Department pointing out the 'grave internal disorders' that would arise if the situation were not remedied. The State Department was swift to recommend the export of mining equipment to Nicaragua as soon as possible.[42] This plan, however, as will be seen below, was beset by problems inherent in wartime good neighbourism.

A similar difficulty arose towards the end of the year. The requisitioning of banana boats by the US navy entailed a severe reduction in shipping facilities for bananas. Rationing made it hard for the companies to buy insecticide, thereby increasing the danger of banana blight. Exports declined drastically. By October the food shortage difficulties in the east-coast banana regions were severe, particularly in Bluefields and Puerto Cabezas. There was now no shipping from the United States and none was expected. The FBI recommended immediate action on Washington's part since the discontent featured a high degree of anti-Americanism, and 'it is axiomatic in Nicaragua that an element which becomes anti-United States will at some time become anti-Somoza'. This was an interesting indication of American thinking. Arthur Bliss Lane had worried that feelings against Somoza, which were acceptable, might

---

[42] US Department of Commerce, Bureau of Foreign and Domestic Commerce, *US Trade with the Central American Republics in 1942* (Washington DC: US Government Printing Office, 1944), 2; 817.50/25, Hoover to Berle, 15 May 1942; 817.50/34, Berle to Hoover, 27 May 1942.

prompt anti-Americanism, which was not. The FBI worried that anti-Americanism might intensify anti-Somoza feeling, which was now unacceptable. With no apparent evidence and unmindful of the possibility that his thinking was no less axiomatic, Hoover blamed the criticism on 'pro-Axis elements'.[43]

Conditions deteriorated further when Standard Fruit closed its commissaries and refused to sell wholesale to the Chinese shopkeepers serving the local population. While the price of rice was at 18 centavos per pound in Managua, it had risen to 50 centavos in the east, and the fruit company, which serviced the entire community in Puerto Cabezas, was rationing flour and milk. The company's preparations for the liquidation of its holdings around Puerto Cabezas included dismantling its every machine in the town for shipment to La Caba in Honduras, ripping up the water system, and razing all company houses and buildings. In Bluefields nearly 30 per cent of the working population had already been made redundant since banana shipments ceased at the beginning of 1942, and the new moves fuelled the resentment of an already anti-American population. Pro-Axis elements would have been largely superfluous, but again the State Department was swift to respond, recommending the dispatch of a project team from the OCIAA to undertake a relief programme with funds of $30,000.[44]

*

Economic assistance, complemented by overt diplomatic pressure on the part of the US legation, was underpinned by two other elements of US policy: intelligence activities and military aid. The FBI had had agents working in Nicaragua on Somoza's behalf for some time. In the summer of 1942, when the bureau was worried about a possible move against the government, it sent an Agent Clegg to Managua to interrogate two Germans, a Spaniard, and an individual referred to as 'Case L', all of whom were thought to be German agents. Clegg's interrogation produced 200 pages of transcript and information about German espionage networks, including individuals resident in the United States and the Canal Zone. The interrogation also uncovered a plot to assassinate Somoza.[45]

[43] Bulmer-Thomas, *The Political Economy*, 93; 817.00/8938, Hoover to Berle, FBI report, 24 Sept. 1942; 817.5018/2, Hoover to Berle, FBI report, 8 Oct. 1942.

[44] 817.50/28, memorandum, Wood to Collado, 3 Dec. 1942.

[45] 817.00/8925, memorandum, Division of American Republics, 7 July 1942.

On 16 March 1942 Somoza created the Department of National Defence to oversee the establishment of a security apparatus answerable only to him. The FBI agent Jack Shaw, sent from Washington the previous year to train local personnel, was now head of the service. Shaw had become a close friend of Somoza, who told him that he relied on the bureau to a great extent in his attempts to control subversion against the regime.[46] Subversion seemed unlikely to flourish in any case when the military aspects of US policy became apparent. Stewart, observing a military parade to honour Somoza's birthday, recognized the political implications:

Thanks to Lend Lease the group this year appeared with steel helmets, bore machine guns, automatic rifles, rifle mortars and trench mortars ... No simple rising *en masse*, organized with shotguns and hunting rifles, could hope to prevail against the Guardia so armed ... Consequently, it does not appear to be too much to say that the United States has contributed to make the military not only more powerful but almost absolute. In the future, political campaigns will probably begin and end within the Guardia—with the populace voting, if permitted, simply a pro forma approval and authentification of the decisions already taken.[47]

Therein lay a fundamental consideration in what was to become the Somoza 'dynasty': that its roots lay much less in what is often erroneously seen as Washington's installation of the general as head of the National Guard, or as president, than in the relatively small and, in Admiral Stark's words, 'common sense' measures that the United States took to safeguard the canal by promoting internal stability for a brief period in the early 1940s. As Stewart pointed out, the tendency to view the Guardia as a significant political actor was not fully emphasized until late 1942 and early 1943, which was when Lend Lease began to take effect. Lend Lease gave the Guardia more military might than it could have hoped for and an image of invincibility. Henceforth, the manoeuvres of the internal opposition would always have to include overtures to the National Guard.

This, however, had relatively little to do with good neighbour diplomacy, since the defence planners were largely bypassing the diplomatic establishment. Indeed, Stewart had to ask the State Department to ascertain for him in Washington what exactly the War Department had been giving to the National Guard. The Latin American division was alarmed at these developments. As a department memorandum made plain, the

[46] RG 226 15146, FBI report, 8 Apr. 1942; 817.00/8959, Stewart to Hull, 19 Feb. 1943; 817.00/8974, FBI report, Hoover to Berle, 20 Apr. 1943.
[47] 817.00/8959, Stewart to Hull, 19 Feb. 1942.

fact that the embassy made the request indicated 'all too clearly how little we [in the State Department] know about Lend Lease transactions'. The State Department wanted an opportunity at least to examine requests for military equipment before the transfers were authorized. 'In the case of weapons which might be used for political purposes', a division memorandum argued, 'the Department would have an opportunity to express its views.'[48] Within eighteen months, the department's views on Nicaragua would be wholly at odds with those of the War Department.

Another consideration in this respect was the presence of US troops on defence bases in Nicaragua after 1942. There was a US naval post on the Gulf of Fonseca, and by mid year arrangements were being made for American forces to use Puerto Cabezas as a ferry route for pursuit planes, and for the construction of a base at Corinto for aircraft and motor torpedo boats. The presence of American troops led many Nicaraguans to assume that such forces would be used to support Somoza in the event of a revolution.[49] Just a decade had passed since the US marine corps had last evacuated Nicaragua, and their return at a time when Somoza appeared to be under threat must have had a significant psychological effect.

Indeed, if FBI intelligence is to be believed, most Nicaraguans must have felt that keeping Somoza in power was the whole point of American troops being in the country. In the autumn of 1942 Hoover sent the State Department a bureau analysis which claimed that 'the great majority' of Nicaraguans were ignorant of the fact that there was a war on.[50] Washington could do little to correct such ignorance or to counteract the perceptions to which it gave rise. In March 1942, John Cabot in the Latin American division was not inventing some complicated rationale for keeping Somoza in power when he worried that

there is to all intents and purposes a military vacuum in Central America which might lead the Japs [*sic*] to believe that an attack there would pay dividends. If the army at Panama cannot even garrison the Central American countries it certainly could not retake them if they were seized by surprise attack. It would therefore be well, I think, to do all that can prudently be done to strengthen the existing defenses there.[51]

[48] 817.24/869, memorandum, Tomlinson to Cabot and Bonsal, 19 Oct. 1942.

[49] RG 165 OPD 600.12 CDC, memorandum, Orme Wilson to Colonel K. F. Herford, 27 Aug. 1942; OPD 100.12 CDC, memorandum by Brigadier General Crawford, 28 Aug. 1942; 817.20/90, memorandum by Cabot, 3 Mar. 1942; 817.00/9007, Stewart to Hull, 13 Oct. 1943.   [50] 817.00/8938, FBI report, Hoover to Berle, 24 Sept. 1942.

[51] 817.20/92, memorandum, Cabot to Bonsal, 3 Mar. 1942.

Despite American efforts, however, by early 1943 Somoza's future seemed in some doubt. Stewart was disheartened by this, characteristically arguing that Somoza had given the country peace and prosperity such as it had never known, that he had done this without undue harshness, and that, despite his arbitrariness, 'none of his enemies has been shot since he became president'.[52] Somoza's worst enemy was himself. By the spring of 1943 his popularity had plummeted. He had by now lost the backing of much of the Liberal Party, many cabinet ministers and higher government officials, and, in the FBI's view, the overwhelming majority of the population. Such scope does not seem to have sprung from political repression, curtailment of civil liberties, or human rights abuses. For most Nicaraguans, grievances appear to have been barely political at all. By mid 1943 Somoza owned—at least to the knowledge of the US embassy—forty-eight houses, fifty-one cattle ranches, forty-six coffee plantations, eighteen cattle-fattening farms, eight sugar cane farms, seventy-six city lots, sixteen uncultivated rural properties, thirteen industrial concerns, three Miami apartments, and a large amount of money in American banks.[53] Even Hoover, no innocent, marvelled at his 'uncontrollable' greed.[54]

All government employees had to give 5 per cent of their salaries to the Liberal Party, whose bank account Somoza used as his own. Following Nicaragua's declaration of war he was able to expropriate some of the country's best coffee estates from German landowners. Cattle exporters were paying a levy of 1.5¢ per pound directly to him; mining and textile firms were making similar 'donations'. Government funds were used to build access roads to his estates while government employees were sent to work on his farms. The national railway gave priority to servicing his private businesses. Its maintenance shops were used mostly for servicing the industrial and rural machinery used in those businesses, and its rolling stock was preferentially used for transporting his cattle. Securing import permits and export licenses required substantial bribes, and they were often denied to Somoza's political opponents. The Price Control Board gave preference to certain imports in favour of those businesses in which Somoza and his loyalists had financial participation. It became impossible to establish or run any kind of business without Somoza's permission or participation.[55]

[52] 817.00/8959, Stewart to Hull, 19 Feb. 1943.
[53] 817.001 Somoza, Anastasio/262, Stewart to Hull, 30 Aug. 1943.
[54] 817.00/8967, Hoover to Berle, FBI report, 6 Mar. 1943.
[55] Ibid.; Tony Jenkins, *Nicaragua and the United States: Years of Conflict* (New York: F. Watts, 1989), 51; Manuel Cordero Reyes, Carlos Castro Wassmer, and Carlos Pasos, *Nicaragua bajo el régimen de somoza* (San Salvador: Imprenta Funes, 1944), 25–31.

Even Stewart, an admirer, was surprised by the extent to which Somoza indulged his own avarice. It was to this factor that the minister ascribed the collapse in the president's popularity in the past year. His own Liberal collaborators were now fiercely critical of his business practices and he had alienated intellectual groups through the establishment of the University of Nicaragua in Managua, raising fears in León and Granada that their campuses were being supplanted.[56] Among the lower sectors he was despised. One-cordoba notes, issued at the time of his daughter Lilian's wedding and bearing her portrait, were being returned to the National Bank in large numbers with a skull and crossbones drawn across her face and words such as 'robo' and 'hambre' written on them. The lower class, however, had limited political influence. Although the ground seemed fertile for left-wing agitation, potential activists were discouraged by the regime's evident capacity to eradicate them.[57]

The greatest danger posed by Somoza's avarice was not the resentment it prompted among the general population but the way in which it interfered with the normal conduct of business among the elite, thereby raising again the prospect of a Liberal Party coup. Somoza's greed simply made it too difficult for Liberal businessmen to operate, and by March 1943 it was apparent that the dissidents' desperation had finally pushed them to make a determined attempt to remove him. Under the leadership of the textile businessman Carlos Pasos, a long-standing member of the party, they had been cultivating sectors of the Guardia (the FBI claimed that they were backed by 'a large number of officers') and had allies among the Conservatives. The US legation concurred with the FBI that Pasos could count on some measure of Guardia support. The group approached the Guatemalan minister in Managua in an effort to secure arms to start a revolt. Guatemala refused and the minister informed Cochran at the American legation, who had already received the information from other sources and had informed Washington. Pasos persisted; by mid March the situation seemed delicate. A coup was reportedly planned for the next time Somoza left Managua.[58]

Pasos intended to overcome US disapproval by holding what the FBI termed 'a so-called free election' within two months after his coup, with the vice-president of the Liberal Party, Manuel Cordero Reyes, as his

---

[56] 817.00/8959, Stewart to Hull, 19 Feb. 1943.   [57] Ibid.
[58] 817.00/8961, Cochran to Hull, 3 Mar. 1943; 817.00/8966, Cochran to Hull, 15 Mar. 1943; 817.00/8967, FBI report, Hoover to Berle, 6 Mar. 1943; 817.00/8972, FBI report, Hoover to Berle, 6 Apr. 1943.

candidate. The alleged plan was to take advantage of one of Somoza's visits to his Montelimar estate to seize control of the garrisons at León, Granada, Chinandega, Masaya, and Managua, and block Somoza's only exit from Montelimar. The FBI believed that if such an action proved successful at the start it might successfully place Cordero Reyes in the presidential mansion.[59] Somoza himself took the threat seriously. General Abaunza, the minister of war, was dismissed; all Nicaraguan ministers in Central America were reassigned; Somoza ordered a shake-up of the Guardia commands. Octavio Sacasa, commander of the Managua and presidential battalions, was sent as military attaché to Washington and replaced by Major Julio Somoza.[60]

In a personal letter to Philip Bonsal, acting chief in the Latin American division, Cochran advised that the plan had been disrupted as a result of the Guardia transfers and that it would be some time before the group could reorganize itself. Washington's position, moreover, was made clear to Pasos: on the next occasion on which Somoza did leave Managua—a five-day trip to Chinandega—the acting legation chief, Cochran, accompanied him.[61] The military shake-up and legation activities seemed to neutralize the immediate threat, but US intelligence believed that there was still a possibility of revolution headed by Carlos Pasos with what Guardia support he could secure.[62]

Somoza now galvanized this coalescing opposition by making evident his determination to amend the constitution to allow him to remain in office beyond 1947. Such was the aim of his visit to Chinandega, where government-organized demonstrations called on him to revise the constitution accordingly. Cochran felt constrained to point out to the State Department that these demonstrations 'were not in any sense a spontaneous expression of the popular will'. Cochran was able to observe this directly, since he was part of Somoza's entourage. He attended, along with Somoza and the entire cabinet, a meeting of municipal authorities and, like them, he signed the minutes.[63]

Cochran, and presumably Stewart, appeared unmindful of the possibility that any true expression of the popular will might have been nullified by the acting legation chief's very presence. In this respect his presence was an interference, although perhaps less thoughtlessly so than

59 817.00/8972, FBI report, Hoover to Berle, 6 Apr. 1943.
60 817.00/8967, FBI report, Hoover to Berle, 6 Mar. 1943.
61 817.00/3–1743, Cochran to Bonsal, 17 Mar. 1943.
62 817.00/8967, FBI report, Hoover to Berle, 6 Mar. 1943.
63 817.00/8975, Stewart to Hull, 13 Apr. 1943.

Stewart's subsequent protestations suggested. Following the events in Chinandega, Stewart complained to the department about a widely publicized story that Cochran had signed a manifesto supporting a constitutional amendment and Somoza's continuance in office. The story was originated by *La Nueva Prensa*, Somoza's newspaper.[64]

Somoza was insisting that amendments were necessary in order to embody the principles of the Atlantic Charter in the constitution. In other words he was identifying his own ambitions with the war effort, and with the wishes of the United States. He tried to give an impression of a close relationship with Roosevelt and the benefits that he had, as a consequence, secured for Nicaragua; implicit was that another leader would be unable to obtain the same benefits from Washington. In this ruse he was helped by a mistake on the part of Leo Rowe, president of the Pan American Union. Unaware that the proposed inclusion of the Atlantic Charter in the Nicaraguan constitution was simply a pretext to secure amendments, Rowe sent Somoza a telegram congratulating him on the initiative. This gave the president a chance to 'prove' that 'Washington' approved of his plans; he arranged for the telegram to be reprinted prominently in all the newspapers.[65] He also hedged his bets. It was rumoured that if they approved constitutional revision, senators and deputies would receive C$15,000 each.[66]

Somoza's ambitions, however, seemed to be endangering his position; they provided impetus to the opposition and further isolated the president. The Liberals' bitterness was reinforced by a conviction that if Somoza engineered his re-election in 1947 he would be unlikely to step down in 1953. They were certain he wanted to be president for life.[67] The combination of boundless avarice and political ambition proved a potent spur to opposition activism. In June *La Noticia*, a leading daily, published a manifesto signed by forty-seven prominent professionals, all members of the Liberal Party, attacking the constitutional proposal. Somoza's immediate closure of the paper simply fanned the flames.[68] During the summer the opposition became increasingly bold; by mid June it was open, though it still lacked the means to effect real change. Following the closure of *La Noticia*, another group of prominent Liberals published a second manifesto against constitutional reform.[69]

[64] Ibid.   [65] 817.00/9008, FBI report, 25 Oct. 1943.
[66] 817.00/8975, Stewart to Hull, 13 Apr. 1943; 817.00/8977, Stewart to Hull, 25 May 1943.   [67] Cordero Reyes, Castro Wassmer, and Pasos, *Nicaragua*, 33.
[68] 817.00/8979, Stewart to Hull, 7 June 1943.
[69] 817.00/8982, Stewart to Hull, 9 June 1943.

The US embassy (the legation was raised to the status of embassy in April 1943, when Stewart was designated ambassador) grew anxious for Somoza's safety as events seemed once again to be drifting towards a crisis. By the middle of the year, according to US intelligence reports, the president's determination on the constitutional issue had aroused so much resentment that the possibility of his assassination was being discussed in political circles. The FBI was worried enough to speculate on the probable impact of his death: 'a wild scramble for power among Conservatives, Liberals, the *Guardia* and the Debayle family'.[70]

Somoza was now more isolated than at any point in his career. It was believed in the State Department that he had lost all meaningful support and that his only backing came from the immediate circle that shared in the spoils of office.[71] Stewart thought he would have to use repression. 'Nicaragua's genial, hard-working, benevolent dictator will have to use the mailed fist from now on if he is to prevent his enemies, now actively "on the hunt", from forcing him out of high office.'[72] Somoza, however, did not use the mailed fist. On the contrary, he began to appear hesitant. Carlos Pasos and Manuel Cordero Reyes were ordered to leave the country by 7 August. They appealed to the Supreme Court, which seemed about to rule in their favour and thereby embarrass Somoza. The president backed down and placed them under house arrest for a few weeks. The apparent indecision simply emboldened the opposition.[73]

The Guardia began once more to prompt concern; Somoza was alarmed as what Stewart termed 'ambitious elements' appeared openly. Though pay increases had been decreed in an attempt to forestall inroads by the Pasos group, these had not yet been effected and the economic distress of the guardsmen remained unalleviated. The Liberal dissidents, moreover, looked set to become a majority in the party during the second half of 1943. Former President Moncada, Somoza's ex-patron and now a senator, had become the most outspoken congressional critic of the regime. Moncada had real influence with the public and the Guardia, and was cooperating with the Conservatives, as well as with the Pasos–Cordero Reyes Liberal group in opposition to the government. Luis Debayle continued to engage in anti-Somoza activity. Another

[70] 817.00/8967, Hoover to Berle, 6 Mar. 1943.
[71] 817.00/8995, memorandum, Tomlinson to Cabot and Bonsal, 13 July 1943.
[72] 817.00/8991, Stewart to Hull, 22 June 1943.
[73] 817.00/8999, Hoover to Berle, FBI report, 11 Aug. 1943; 817.00/9003, Stewart to Hull, 4 Sept. 1943; 817.00/9007, Stewart to Hull, 13 Oct. 1943.

influential Liberal, Debayle also seemed to have secured military backing and had cultivated allies among the Conservatives.[74]

In this context of intense agitation, the situation of the lower sectors was no longer extraneous. 'The Masses—Background for Trouble' was the heading in one lengthy dispatch from the US embassy outlining Somoza's isolation. In September 1943 a new Central Executive Committee of Nicaraguan Workers issued a manifesto calling for union organization and a labour code. There was also Mexican interest in Nicaraguan labour: Vicente Lombardo Toledano visited during 1943. Somoza, who earlier had dismissed workers' organizations as 'communistic', had imprisoned or exiled labour leaders but he now began to make some overtures. Travelling throughout the country and inaugurating workers' clubs en route, ardently terming himself a labourer's son, the president repeatedly declared his interest in improving the lot of the workers. The conditions of the general population worried Stewart for two reasons. First, a hostile public was 'embarrassing' and provided an auspicious background for the work of the Conservatives and Liberals working against the president. Second, the National Guard recruited from the masses, and popular ill will raised the possibility of further Guardia disaffection.[75]

Stewart, like every good neighbour diplomat who had preceded him in Managua since 1936, saw his own period in Nicaragua as Somoza's darkest hour and judged the president's position to be 'more insecure than ever before'. He observed as 'notable' the likelihood of Guardia defection, the absence of reliable popular, business or landowning support, a new and strong opposition leadership emerging from within the Liberal Party, and the ground gained by the Conservatives. The only two areas in which Somoza might claim to have won rather than lost ground, in fact, were in his plausible appearance of being backed by the Roosevelt administration and the progress made with US assistance in finance and foreign exchange, as well as in road-building. 'World War Two', Stewart declared at the end of 1943, 'has convinced the opposition that the United States would oppose a revolution against Somoza. His strength may be undermined when the war is over.'[76] This proved temporarily to be the case; but when hostilities ended, Somoza's durability—irrespective of opposition or war—was going to have to be undermined by a US government still opposed to revolution.

[74] 817.00/8990, Stewart to Hull, 18 June 1943.   [75] Ibid.
[76] 817.00/8990, Stewart to Hull, 18 June 1943.

Faced with an unusual level of political dissent, distrustful of Guardia loyalty, and unable to unite the Liberals, Somoza made heavy use of his best ploy: the public assertion that his ambitions were backed by the United States and that he and Roosevelt were good friends. This gambit, which had not failed in the past, retained some of its persuasiveness. Emiliano Chamorro, still in exile, believed that popular discontent would not lead to a mass revolt 'principally because no-one believes that the State Department would not intervene in the case of an armed uprising, which means that with the good neighbour policy we are worse off than ever'.[77]

*

Was Chamorro's statement justified? His conviction, and the events that prompted its assertion, raise questions about the extent of Somoza's unpopularity, US attitudes towards him, and the nature of his dependence on the United States. A strong clue to the validity of Chamorro's complaint lies in the fact that the complaint itself was expressed in a personal letter he had sent to the former president Adolfo Díaz, which US intelligence agents had simply seized in Costa Rica as part of their routine mail intercepts to monitor opposition to the Somoza regime. US intelligence found Somoza easy to handle and wanted him to remain in the presidency. Jack Shaw, the FBI's man in Managua, had developed a very close relationship with him.[78]

The US defence establishment similarly endorsed Somoza, finding him the most viable option compatible with US security concerns. Stewart was unwavering in his support and unfailingly identified Somoza with American interests. The ambassador, displaying the paternalism that the *Time* correspondent William Krehm found so disheartening, considered the Somoza years 'a golden era...for this formerly turbulent little country', and noted with sadness the upsurge of opposition as 'a great pity from the standpoint of the peace and progress of the country'.[79]

Stewart's attitude, it bears repeating, went beyond geopolitical thinking. It was personal. Much as he wanted political stability, he favoured a particular individual. Arthur Bliss Lane, perhaps the only American minister of the good neighbour period to remain untouched by Somoza's evident charm, had also acted out of a sense of personal loyalty. Lane's conduct, however, derived from a sense of loyalty to the constitutional

---

[77] I817.00/8990, Stewart to Hull, 18 June 1943; 817.00/8980, Des Portes (Costa Rica) to Hull, 2 June 1943.   [78] 817.00/8974, Hoover to Berle, 20 Apr. 1943.
[79] 817.00/8991, Stewart to Hull, 22 June 1943.

government of Juan Sacasa; his personal feelings towards Sacasa bordered on contempt. In contrast, Stewart's personal regard for Somoza is patent in his dispatches.

By now, few Nicaraguans can have had much faith in the prospect of self-determination. Internal political attitudes were still based in large part on assumptions derived from the experiences of the pre-Roosevelt period. Most Nicaraguans seem never to have questioned those assumptions, even when they were invalid in the mid 1930s, and by now they were valid again. With evidence of US military power pervasive, the appointment of an American officer to run the military academy, and the rearmament of the Guardia with Lend Lease equipment, Washington's backing for Somoza was, within Nicaragua, an accepted fact of life. In this sense, the sincerity of Hull's idealism and his earlier, genuine efforts to cut a new path in diplomatic policy were lost on Nicaragua. The facts of the historical record and circumstances beyond the hemisphere inhibited their realization.

The Nicaraguan foreign ministry made no important decision without consulting the American embassy. Somoza took pains to be seen in the company of the US ambassador, as a means of assuring the public that he maintained close and friendly relations with the United States. He often consulted Stewart on matters of state, as if on a personal basis. As the ambassador reported to his chiefs, Somoza was 'most responsive to any suggestion as to how a particular situation should be handled'.[80] A report of such a relationship, which would have provoked blistering replies to Lane or Nicholson, drew no response from Washington.

There was no popular demand for a constitutional change or for Somoza's re-election. The public reaction was one of resignation.[81] Again, this owed much to the president's success in linking, at least in the public mind, his ambitions with the wishes of the United States. US policy objectives and Somoza's ambitions had momentarily coincided. They had not always done so, however, and would not do so for much longer. Perhaps that is why Stewart was suddenly to find himself behind the times of diplomatic thinking in Washington, his analysis neglecting consideration of the broader picture. In March 1943, when the FBI had claimed there was a definite possibility of open rebellion headed by Liberal dissidents with some Guardia support, the German army had surrendered at Stalingrad. The Axis powers never regained the military initiative and it was clear at the time that they would be unlikely to do so. The Allied

[80] Ibid.   [81] 817.00/8975, Stewart to Hull, 13 Apr. 1943.

'Torch' landings had almost cleared North Africa of Germans. By the summer, when Stewart was lamenting the waning of the Golden Era of Somoza, the Battle of the Atlantic was won, if not ended.[82] Good neighbourism, consequently, started to shift.

*

The US government, in all its multiplying branches, determined Somoza's durability not purely in reaction to the rise and fall of the Allies and the Axis, nor to fluctuating conditions in the western hemisphere, nor even to Nicaragua's national—and Somoza's personal—ups and downs. Such determinants were pivotal to foreign policy-making but other factors, much closer to home, were also important. Conflict, even simple rivalry between government agencies and the individuals in each of them, shaped Washington's response to Nicaragua in this period. It has been pointed out that until World War II, the management of Latin American affairs remained largely under the control of career men at the State Department whose authority was unchallenged as they conducted each of good neighbourism's relationships with the countries to the south. The war brought the military into the policy-making process, but it also brought in a range of other organizations and hundreds of bureaucrats who for the most part were unfamiliar with foreign relations.[83]

As the foreign policy establishment of the US government mushroomed, Latin American affairs fell under the influence of groups that had had little or no part in the construction of good neighbourism, that differed from those who had (as well as with each other) as to the policy's meaning, and that in turn were influenced by factors unconnected to the policy's original aims.[84] The creation of the OCIAA in July 1940[85] as an advisory body to the Council of National Defense was a case in point. Set up with $3.5 million, rising to $8 million by 1942, it caused friction with other agencies that had been working in the same areas for years with little funding. Its staff, as they readily admitted themselves, were little acquainted with Latin America.[86] John Cabot, chief of the State

[82] Hobsbawm, *Age of Extremes*, 41; Parkinson, *Encyclopaedia of Modern War*, 284–5; Brogan, *Pelican History*, 596.

[83] Randall Bennett Woods, *The Roosevelt Foreign Policy Establishment and the 'Good Neighbor': The United States and Argentina, 1941–1945* (Lawrence: Regents Press of Kansas, 1979), p. xi.   [84] Ibid.

[85] It was then known as the Office of the Coordinator of Commercial and Cultural Relations between the American Republics.

[86] Philip Leonard Green, *Pan American Progress* (New York: Hastings House, 1942), 108–10.

Department's Division of Caribbean and Central American Affairs, told Colonel Blake-Tyler of the British legation that the good neighbour policy had degenerated into a race between various government agencies, especially the OCIAA, to see which could secure the most goodwill in Latin America.[87]

Career diplomats like Cabot, losing exclusive jurisdiction to encroaching analysts and policy-makers from the treasury, the Caribbean Defense Command, the Board of Economic Warfare, the Foreign Economic Administration, the FBI, and army and navy intelligence, began to channel energy into protecting their rights as makers of policy, to the detriment of links forged by the policy itself.[88] Personal and bureaucratic antagonisms, giving rise to distinct perceptions of foreign policy objectives, had a substantial effect on the methods used to secure those objectives. In the State Department alone, two competitive camps were vying for control of good neighbourism; communication between them was minimal as each tried to expand its influence at the other's expense in making policy recommendations to Roosevelt.[89]

The Latin Americanists, led by Welles, Duggan, Bonsal, and Welles's special assistant Emilio Collado, had made their careers on Latin American relations. Experts on the region, they viewed global affairs from a western-hemisphere perspective. The internationalists, led by Hull and the assistant secretary of state Breckenbridge Long, took the broad Wilsonian view and felt that, since US interests were superior to all others, the United States should be the supreme moral factor in international development. Inter-American relations, for them, were simply part of a much wider network of international links. Their knowledge of Latin America was shallow, their perceptions of the region were occasionally simplistic, and their assessment of local situations in Latin America tended to be based on the attitudes to the war evinced by the latters' governments.[90]

Many of the problems inherent in managing Nicaragua as a good neighbour, and of the difficulties facing Washington's representatives in Managua, can be seen to stem in part from infighting unrelated to Nicaragua. The war, which saw the blooming of US government agencies reach full flower, exacerbated the attendant difficulties. The War Department's posture, for example, expanded beyond simple defence.

[87] Wood, *Dismantling*, 63.
[88] Woods, *Roosevelt Foreign Policy Establishment*, pp. xi–xii.   [89] Ibid. 22.
[90] Ibid. 23–6.

It was not merely training military forces; it was consolidating military governments. Those American military officers who did not start acting like diplomats (and some did) could still hold political sway. A gaffe on the part of Mullins, for example (or Lindberg, as will be evident below), could be as damaging as one on Stewart's. The War Department, for all practical purposes, had been bypassing Stewart in its dealings with Somoza.

The State Department was similarly at odds with other agencies, to the detriment of good neighbourism. With the onset of the mining crisis described earlier in this chapter, the department made a special request that the Board of Economic Warfare (BEW) send to Nicaragua a mining engineer, Mr Guy Bjorge, to investigate the problem. FBI and other intelligence reports, it should be recalled, were bleakly pessimistic about the prospects for political stability in the event of a mining breakdown.[91] What happened as a consequence is worth outlining at some length because of the way it sheds light on the institutional mechanisms of wartime good neighbourism in Nicaragua.

Bjorge arrived with instructions from the BEW to investigate the possibility of an alternative programme under which the mines would indeed be closed down but other work would be undertaken to soften the economic blow. The State Department was alarmed at this challenge to its own view, which was that the United States should provide the supplies necessary to keep the mines open. Cochran at the Managua embassy was therefore told to stress to Bjorge that Roosevelt had made a personal commitment to Somoza that Nicaragua's mines would continue to receive equipment and materials to operate at normal levels. Cochran, in effect, was being told to pressure Bjorge, the objective being that the engineer should produce a report 'primarily from the viewpoint of the fulfillment of [Roosevelt's] pledge'.[92]

Similar pressure was being applied in Washington, but the BEW was resisting. Its own dispatches to Bjorge continued to stress the need for alternative programmes. Coordinating the conflict at the State Department, John Cabot contemplated direct sabotage. He hesitated only because he felt it might be useful, at some later date, to have on file Bjorge's suggestions as supplemental recommendations for bolstering Nicaragua's economy. He then opted for sabotage in any case, demanding of the BEW that Roosevelt's commitment should be accepted as a directive to all government agencies.[93]

[91] 817.24/465, memorandum by Cabot, 26 May 1942.   [92] Ibid.
[93] 817.24/487, memorandum, Cabot to Bonsal and Wright, 4 June 1942.

Such infighting caused uncertainty as to the allocation of resources and raised serious problems in Nicaragua by the end of the year. Managua could not properly administer the necessary controls under the allocation system without knowing the BEW's attitude to the mines' application for supplies for 1943.[94] This situation was further complicated by the arrival in Managua of two officials of the OCIAA, sent to Nicaragua to investigate the need for a food supply programme or for some other scheme to mitigate the economic effect of closing the mines. Stewart in turn had to resort to sabotage. He was, he told the State Department, 'endeavouring to restrict the activities of these officials until a definite policy on gold mines is announced by the BEW'.[95]

The State Department engaged the BEW in bureaucratic battle through most of the year. At times, in Managua and Washington, the activity of the conflict was frenetic; at others it was more subtle. Forcefully polite memoranda passed back and forth between the two agencies, while each sent confidential instructions to its representatives on the spot. While the policy-making establishment in Washington bickered over policy, Nicaragua's mines languished and Somoza's stock—figuratively and literally—continued to plummet. Aware that a policy shift away from Roosevelt's pledge would prompt anti-American resentment from Somoza, government officials, and labour, the US embassy argued that if the BEW decided that the mines should close it would largely offset what goodwill already existed as a result of other American programmes in Nicaragua. Gold was the main export, the only industry of any size, and the government's main source of tax revenue. Somoza had already sent his foreign minister to Washington to induce action from the BEW. US diplomats in Managua and Washington had similarly tried in vain. The situation threatened deep-rooted animosity if it were not remedied.

By the start of 1943 the arena for this particular battle had shifted to another agency, the War Production Board (WPB). In a personal letter to Stewart, Bonsal made clear that he wanted to fight.[96] Hull, characteristically out of touch, told Stewart that the discussions with the WPB were proceeding satisfactorily and that an agreement would soon be reached to supply the mines on the basis of 1940 imports. Hull felt that this was a reasonable interpretation of Roosevelt's commitment to Somoza.[97] Emilio Collado, special assistant to Hull's rival Welles, demurred.

[94] 817.24/628, Stewart to Hull, 23 Dec. 1942.   [95] Ibid.
[96] 817.24/633B, Bonsal to Stewart, 30 Dec. 1942.
[97] 817.24/628, Hull to Stewart, 6 Jan. 1943.

Outlining a compromise proposal for the authorization of 2,000 tons of equipment for Nicaragua as against requests for 8,000 tons, he complained that this was 'at best a feeble execution of the President's commitment to President Somoza'.[98]

Hence the State Department, competing with the BEW and obliged to lobby the WPB, could not even present a united front. Welles began to tire of it. Lobbied by American agents of the Nicaraguan mining industry and lobbying in his turn, in December 1942 Welles had presented a lengthy argument to Don Nelson, chairman of the WPB. In essence, Welles agreed to the suspension of mining supplies to Latin America with the exceptions of Nicaragua and Colombia. He argued that the economic stability of both countries was so dependent on mining operations that the WPB should not be swayed by the BEW and should make every effort to maintain supplies.[99]

By the end of the following month, however, Welles was losing steam. Considering Collado's compromise proposal, he felt that the State Department should not fight the matter further. Collado glumly commented to Acheson that if his recommendations were accepted at the next BEW meeting 'the Department might well acquiesce, though not necessarily with great joy'.[100] Having retreated this far, the State Department had no spirit to fight the BEW's conclusion, which went further. The BEW decided to supply Nicaragua with just 2,000 tons of mining equipment up to July, and to make no further supplies thereafter. Beyond that date, the BEW would not approve export licence applications for the necessary materials. Between 3,000 and 7,000 workers were likely to be laid off by the year's end, and a production drop of 40 per cent over the 1942 level was expected. The political repercussions promised to be substantial, but by the time they became evident the United States would be looking somewhat askance at the Somoza regime.[101]

The State Department's inability to present a united front in the mining crisis was symptomatic of intra-departmental infighting that was now intense. The main antagonists were Hull and Welles. They had always clashed. Hull resented Welles's greater access to Roosevelt, the undersecretary's old friend, his clear loyalty to the president rather than to himself, and his lack of interest in his, Hull's, own advice. R. Walton Moore,

98   817.24/644, memorandum, Collado to Acheson, 26 Jan. 1943.
99   817.24/656A, Welles to Nelson, 29 Dec. 1942.
100 817.24/644, memorandum, Collado to Acheson, 26 Jan. 1943.
101 817.24/644, Collado to Acheson and Bonsal, 30 Jan. 1943.

Hull's candidate for under-secretary and the man whom Welles had beaten for the position, had long since begun a whispering campaign against him.[102]

Welles had often played Hull's role as the chief maker of foreign policy, a circumstance that damaged morale in the department. Rash incidents of public drunkenness and importuning could no longer be ignored, and by the autumn of 1943 Welles's position was untenable. He resigned in September and was replaced by Edward Stettinius. Hull claimed this as a victory, asserting that Welles had been undermining him and that, consequently, Roosevelt forced Welles to go. According to William Phillips, the former under-secretary, the personality clash between Hull and Welles 'adversely affected the conduct of our foreign relations for several years'.[103]

The institutionalization of external relations in the war years, exacerbating the rivalries inherent in the State Department, finally disintegrated good neighbourism's more abstruse claims to be foreign policy as philosophy. Policy could hardly be an ethos when its makers so wilfully nurtured petty jealousies and sabotaged each other's claims to be guardians of its guiding flame.

*

In Nicaragua, while good neighbourism continued to collapse, Stewart was busy throughout the rest of 1943 accompanying Somoza on what were unambiguously political trips throughout the country, part of the president's campaign to secure constitutional changes designed to allow him to remain in office, on which he was paying particular attention to the clergy, the Guardia, and labour. Stewart tended to spend several days with the presidential party on these trips, which invariably followed the same pattern.

Arriving in a village, Somoza would proceed directly to the church, where he would be met by the priest, who delivered a eulogy. Somoza would then address the public in the main square. The speech always mentioned himself and Roosevelt in terms that suggested they were good friends. Local political leaders, in their speeches, made similar mention of Roosevelt. The decorations for the presidential visit usually placed

---

[102] Irwin Gellman, *Good Neighbor Diplomacy: United States Policies in Latin America, 1933–1945* (Baltimore, Md.: Johns Hopkins University Press, 1979), 13, 69–70; Wood, *Dismantling*, 2.

[103] Hull, *Memoirs*, ii, 1227–30; Woods, *Roosevelt Foreign Policy Establishment*, 103; William Phillips, *Ventures in Diplomacy* (Boston: Beacon Press, 1952), 186; Wood, *Dismantling*, 2.

Roosevelt's portrait next to that of Somoza. The president concluded his speech to the public by ordering that something be built, or that the church, school, or hospital be repaired.[104] He would then proceed to the local Guardia barracks, where the speeches would attempt to portray him as a father to his *muchachos*. Somoza personally distributed blankets and clothing to the troops. During all such trips, Stewart reported with admiration, Somoza was 'informal, very human and full of fun'.[105] It is hard to credit that Stewart failed to appreciate that his constant presence on such trips, at a time when Somoza was trying to amend the constitution so as to retain office, and when the opposition was gathering momentum, might be interpreted as US interference in Nicaraguan politics. The State Department, certainly, would be viewing it in that light (and with some anger) within a month. Stewart's other dispatches plainly reflect his awareness that a prime underpinning of the regime's stability was its apparent closeness to the Roosevelt administration.[106]

It was in this context of political manoeuvring to promote or impede Somoza's re-election plans that Nicaragua entered the new year of 1944. His determination to perpetuate himself in the presidency caused the incipient split in Liberal ranks to become an open breach. The Liberal Party convention in León opened on 5 January with a twofold objective. First, it aimed to reform party doctrine in order to suspend or eliminate the principle of *alternabilidad*. A bill to modify the constitution was already before Congress, awaiting the start of the new session in April. Somoza, whose present term was to end in 1947, hoped to remain in office until at least 1953.[107]

Second, the convention aimed to unify the Liberals around Somoza by expelling from the party's governing board Manuel Cordero Reyes and Carlos Pasos, leaders of the Liberal dissidents. The convention, characterized by the FBI as a gathering of 'public employees and a number of rubber stamps', consisted of delegates dependent on Somoza for their livelihoods. The president arrived at León with a full complement from the military academy, plus the presidential guard and a large force of secret police. Machine guns were much in evidence. The attitude of the people of León to the presidential party was overtly hostile and sullen.[108]

104 817.001 Somoza, Anastasio/264, Stewart to Hull, 16 Dec. 1943.   105 Ibid.
106 Ibid.
107 817.00/9050, FBI report, Hoover to Berle, 1 Feb. 1944; 817.001 Somoza, Anastasio/268, memorandum by Cochran, 13 Jan. 1944.
108 817.00/9050, FBI report, Hoover to Berle, 1 Feb. 1944.

The convention failed to unify the party. On the contrary, the dissident faction was solidified. The US embassy's informants noted that an attempt to 'convert' dissidents was unsuccessful; strong-arm methods had to be used to prevent them from expressing their views and from attending the meetings. With the Guardia keeping dissenters under house arrest, Somoza pushed the amendment to party policy through the convention. The dissident faction under Carlos Pasos finally broke with the traditional party and by March 1944 had formed the Independent Liberal Party. It seemed possible that the Independents might join forces with the Conservatives.[109]

The text of what was to have been Carlos Pasos's speech to the convention received wide circulation in Managua. He condemned press censorship, denial of freedoms of speech and assembly, curtailment of the right to travel freely within the country, Somoza's usurpation of judicial functions for personal ends, the improper use of taxes, the denial of banking privileges to political opponents, political imprisonment, the president's personal exploitation of the cattle industry, and the wholesale dismissal of public employees who refused to sign petitions favouring Somoza's re-election or to attend rallies in his honour. In the event, Pasos never made this speech. After the first session he was prohibited from coming within one block of the González Theatre, in which the convention was being held. Manuel Cordero Reyes was placed under house arrest.[110]

Of the two men, Pasos represented the dissidents' militant wing. Cordero Reyes was the opposition's statesman and diplomat, its 'cleverest man' in the view of the FBI. On 12 January, while under house arrest, Cordero Reyes suddenly died, apparently of a cerebral haemorrhage. Many Nicaraguans were convinced that he had been poisoned. The FBI believed that his death, and the manner in which it was perceived to have occurred, removed a restraining element and made violence more likely than before.[111]

*

[109] 817.00/9026, memorandum, Cochran to Cabot and Bonsal, 28 Jan. 1944; Richard Millet, *Guardians of the Dynasty* (Maryknoll, NY: Orbis Books, 1977), 200; Gould, *Dangerous Friends*, 14; Hugo Cancino Troncoso, *Las raíces históricas e ideológicas del movimiento sandinista: Antecedentes de la Revolución Nacional y Popular Nicaragüense* (Odense: Odense University Press, 1984), 95.

[110] 817.00/9050, FBI report, Hoover to Berle, 1 Feb. 1944; 817.001 Somoza, Anastasio/268, memorandum by Cochran, 13 Jan. 1944.

[111] Ibid.; 817.00/9020, Stewart to Hull, 13 Jan. 1944; 817.00/9019, Stewart to Hull, 12 Jan. 1944; 817.00/9026, memorandum, Cochran to Cabot and Bonsal, 28 Jan. 1944; 817.00/9050, FBI report, Hoover to Berle, 1 Feb. 1944.

In Washington, the foregoing events placed the State Department in a difficult position. It is important to understand US attitudes to Somoza at the beginning of 1944 because those attitudes were to shift markedly in the course of the next eighteen months. In January 1944 it was still desirable in Washington that Somoza should remain in office until the war was over, or at least clearly seen to be won. That he should meanwhile inspire severe hostility among Nicaraguans, as well as some distaste in the State Department, was for the moment tolerable. Still implicit in this attitude was that the situation was temporary; hence the suspension, in practice, of non-interference. As theory, non-interference still somehow mattered. Mooted very occasionally in departmental memoranda, it retained its venerability as a notion that the Roosevelt administration had once effected, and to which it would again aspire in a saner world. At the start of 1944 it began to seem that the world might soon become more sane. Still unknown, however, was when.

For now, the United States wanted Somoza to remain in office. As he appeared increasingly besieged, more forceful use of US influence to help him stay in office might be necessary, because if he fell to a sudden and violent outburst Washington might be unable to manage the transition at a time when managed stability seemed vital. The State Department, however, did not want him to stay in office forever, and thus could not exert too much pressure on the opposition.

Hence such a simple matter as a telegram of condolence on Cordero Reyes's death became a diplomatic minefield, not only in terms of protocol but also in terms of national and international events. Manuel Cordero Reyes had been a distinguished Nicaraguan. A minister of foreign affairs for several years, he had met Hull at the inter-American conferences in Montevideo, Buenos Aires, and Lima, as well as during Somoza's visit to Washington. The telegram should have been simple, standard, diplomatic procedure. Instead, it had diplomatic thought in Washington careering between fears of sparking a revolution, the need to secure the president, and the desire to safeguard US interests beyond Somoza.

John Cabot, chief of the State Department's Division of Caribbean and Central American Affairs, discussed a draft with Bonsal and advised him that the telegram—not simply its substance but its existence—'is frankly dangerous. It may be the spark for which the powder magazine has been waiting and I would therefore not ordinarily suggest it. I nevertheless feel that it should go.' This display of cross-thought continued as

Cabot justified his advice. He favoured sending the telegram, he said, because he wanted

> to make it clear *to the opposition elements in Nicaragua* that our policy of non-intervention is not another way of backing up the existing regime *to the last ditch.* It will be an unmistakable indication that this is not the policy of this government, in spite of recent indications which might have lent color to such a belief. We must remember, however, that it would be grist in the mills of those who believe Cordero Reyes was assassinated.[112]

What did this mean? If the opposition was to assume that the State Department would not support Somoza to the last ditch, to what extent would it support him? Moreover, if such a signal to the opposition was acceptable, indeed desirable, why should Cabot worry that the signal might encourage opposition? Good neighbourism in Nicaragua was mutating. The State Department seemed to think that opposition to Somoza would finally become irresistible. That he should eventually leave the presidency was desirable, but his departure had to be in the department's time. The pace of events had to be decelerated without antagonizing the opposition; and members of the opposition had to be sent signals without, as yet, encouraging them to oust Somoza. This confusion characterized a policy that was in the process of coalescing into something more concrete than the vague strategy that had been ignoring Stewart's strange activities.

Stewart had been present at the banquet in León the previous month when Somoza had formally announced his plans to continue in office. The ambassador's presence incited concern in the Latin American division. Cabot's response to the news suggests that the ire had been brewing for some time, and that Stewart's chiefs had been ever less happy with their ambassador's conduct. 'This seems to me the last straw,' Cabot declared. 'It is obvious that Mr. Stewart should not have attended an avowedly political banquet. It is bad enough for him to run around the countryside with Somoza on his junkets, but it is a rule in all parts of the world, I believe, that our diplomatic officers do not attend political functions.' Cabot wanted it made explicit that US prestige was not to be used as an instrument for the maintenance of the status quo in Nicaraguan politics, and he asked that immediate instructions be sent to Stewart.[113]

---

[112] 817.00/9020, memorandum, Cabot to Bonsal, 14 Jan. 1944. Emphasis added.

[113] 817.00/9016, memorandum, Cochran to Cabot and Bonsal, 12 Jan. 1944; 817.00/9016, memorandum, Cabot to Bonsal, undated.

Bonsal decided to outline US policy in a personal letter to his ambassador. He began by making it bluntly clear that Somoza, from the State Department's viewpoint, seemed doomed: 'there are lots of situations which, it seems to me, may eventually be due for a more or less violent liquidation.' He continued with his hope 'that this can be delayed until after the war, for it would obviously be most unfortunate from every point of view for there to be any trouble in this area while this is going on'. He concluded, however, that 'we do not wish to be placed in a position of doing *anything* which would appear to place our prestige behind any political regime'.[114]

This was not an instruction; it was not even advice. It was simply a restatement of a problem. Stewart was expected to decipher it and to devise some course of action that helped keep Somoza in office against widespread opposition until the war was over, without doing *anything* that suggested that the United States had any interest in Somoza's remaining in office. Such a monumental task would have been beyond even Lane, who was doubtless an abler diplomat than Stewart. Non-interference was somehow to be striven for in the certain knowledge that it was, for the moment, impossible in practice.

Precisely because of Stewart's political involvement in Nicaragua, Cabot and Bonsal planned to issue a general instruction to US missions in Central America on what form policy should take. In the event Cordell Hull, author of the impractical 'definitive' instructions sent to all legations in Central America in 1936, took charge. As the scope and intensity of political activity throughout the isthmus threatened general turmoil, Hull saw fit to reintroduce the notion of non-interference into diplomatic instructions as if it had never been absent. He reminded his diplomats in Central America that 'a basic tenet of this government's policy—that of non-interference in the internal politics of the other American republics—is undergoing a severe test at a delicate moment'.[115]

As far as Nicaragua was concerned, the secretary's anxiety was both late and disingenuous. The basic tenet of policy to which he referred had decayed through simple lack of use. It was Stewart's disregard of the tenet that required Hull's writing this instruction at all. Hull nonetheless declared that the State Department was gratified by US diplomats' tact in managing to avoid committing themselves. Warning American

---

[114] 817.00/9016, Bonsal to Stewart, 12 Jan. 1944. Emphasis added.
[115] 817.00/9016, Bonsal to Stewart, 12 Jan. 1944; 813.00/1340a, Hull to the diplomatic representatives in Central America, 2 Feb. 1944.

representatives against 'any act of omission or commission' that might reflect on internal political conditions in Central America, he asserted that 'in more than one situation, refusal to act would have been interpreted as far more significant from the viewpoint of internal politics than a positive non-committal gesture'.[116]

After eleven years of good neighbourism, this was the first official recognition that the fundamental flaw inherent in the policy even existed. It still remained to occur to Hull, however, that *any* act of omission or commission by the United States could reflect on political conditions in Nicaragua. His reference to acts of omission vaguely suggested some shift in policy (previously, diplomats' actions had been condemned in specific instances; now, inaction in other instances would also be discouraged), but in the end it was hard to discern what Hull was actually saying. He managed to make an observation that was manifestly correct, that 'the respective missions will doubtless find it difficult to define the line where friendliness towards the government of an allied sister republic ends and friendliness towards a particular regime begins'. Concluding with a request that his diplomats offer suggestions on how to make the policy of non-intervention clear in countries where doubts about it lingered in the public mind, Hull demanded discretion of his representatives and signed off.[117]

As a clarifying statement of policy, all of this was, in practical terms, of strictly limited use. Unmindful that there might be any contradiction in his declaration, Hull resorted, like Bonsal, to reiterating the problem rather than suggesting a solution. The problem might have been less thorny, and US diplomats' confusion about how they were meant to operate on a day-to-day basis less acute, if Hull could recognize that friendliness towards a particular regime began at the point at which US battleships arrived at Nicaragua's coasts to intimidate anti-regime elements, or when FBI agents were involved in covert operations on behalf of the regime's leader. It could also be argued, of course, that this was the point at which friendliness towards the government of an allied sister republic began—such government in Nicaragua being, by definition, a particular regime. Hull was splitting very fine hairs while affecting to believe that it all made perfect sense. His words, moreover, contained an implicit admission that good neighbourism's basic tenet, for eleven years, had failed. The public mind in Nicaragua clearly had, and would continue to have, strong reservations about Washington's commitment to good neighbourly non-interference.

[116] 813.00/1340a, Hull to the diplomatic representatives in Central America, 2 Feb. 1944.   [117] Ibid.

8

Becoming Bad Neighbours

Military dictatorships and unconstitutional regimes are to be
deplored, but it is no function of the government of the United
States to attempt to impose the practice of democracy upon other
governments or peoples...

But it is not incompatible with these policies [of non-intervention and non-interference] to state unequivocally the self-evident
truth that the people and government of the United States cannot
help but feel a greater affinity and a warmer friendship for those
governments which rest upon the periodically and freely expressed
consent of the governed.[1]

Cordell Hull
November 1944

The sense of affinity that the United States felt with rulers whose authority derived from popular consent helped bring Somoza's government to
an end. This was not simply an end result; it was the State Department's
specific intention. The changed global outlook, as the Allies continued
their successes against the Axis, coincided with shifting political conditions throughout Central America. Those circumstances were prompting
a gradual reorientation of good neighbourism towards pre-war patterns
just as the internal opposition in Nicaragua began to cohere, and as the
external opposition began to emerge as an armed resistance. As Somoza
became dubious about what had hereto been significant props—his
diplomatic relations with Washington and the loyalty of the National
Guard—he adopted two new and apparently contradictory stratagems:
playing up to the Nicaraguan labour movement and playing on fears of
communist expansionism.

---

[1] 710.11/11–144, Hull to Stewart, 1 Nov. 1944.

By the spring of 1944, middle-class agitation against the Martínez regime in El Salvador had found responsive echo among an officer corps already resentful over the privileges accorded to paramilitary groups. The antagonism was intensified by Martínez's amendment of the constitution in order to allow him to remain in office beyond March. The military rebellion that broke out on 2 April was crushed by loyalist troops and paramilitary forces, but the subsequent retribution against rebel officers prompted widespread popular indignation that led directly to a general strike. Amid scenes of public unrest a 17-year-old American, whose family had been resident in El Salvador for decades, was shot dead by a policeman while standing in front of his house. When pressure from Walter Thurston, the US ambassador, was added to the agitation in the streets, Martínez was forced to step down.[2]

In Guatemala, the students at San Carlos staged a demonstration on 24 June to press their demands for the restoration of the university's institutional autonomy. The protest became an anti-Ubico march for full political democracy in which the Charter of the United Nations was read to the crowd while a delegation of some three hundred professionals handed over a petition seeking the reintroduction of constitutional guarantees. The student strike, which expanded to lawyers and doctors, led to a general stoppage that brought the economy to a standstill. The movement had such momentum, and the United States so signally failed to back Ubico, that the president resigned on 1 July.[3]

In Honduras, public agitation did not reach an intensity sufficient to bring down the government, but the Carías regime was troubled by the precedent set in the neighbouring countries. The movement against Martínez in El Salvador inspired a demonstration by three hundred Honduran women on 29 May, demanding that political prisoners be released. More protests in early July were severely repressed but a trend seemed clear throughout the isthmus. Among Nicaraguans, the prevailing sense was of 'two down, two to go'.[4]

In Nicaragua, Somoza was trying to secure Senate passage of a bill to guarantee his re-election. He was playing up to the opposition and, in

---

[2] James Dunkerley, *Power in the Isthmus: A Political History of Modern Central America* (London: Verso, 1988), 119–120; Ralph Lee Woodward, *Central America: A Nation Divided* (New York: Oxford University Press, 1985), 230–1; William Krehm, *Democracies and Tyrannies of the Caribbean* (Westport, Conn.: Lawrence Hill & Co., 1984), 14–17, 23, 26.

[3] Dunkerley, *Power in the Isthmus*, 136; Krehm, Democracies and Tyrannies, 48.

[4] Dunkerley, *Power in the Isthmus*, 121–2; 817.00/7–544, Stewart to Hull, 5 July 1944.

what was to be a significant development, was making preparations to secure labour support in a similar manner to Picado in Costa Rica. New labour legislation was expected soon. Hedging his bets, Somoza bribed members of Congress who had originally opposed his re-election plans, with the exception of Carlos Pasos, who was arrested. The detention sparked several protests.[5]

In the summer of 1944, the anti-Somoza forces finally staged public protests like those of their counterparts in the countries to the north. The Liberal dissidents had reached an understanding with the Conservatives. The students allied with both parties in an upsurge of intense agitation. On 8 June, Somoza extended the suspension of constitutional guarantees until June 1945. 'The people of Nicaragua', a US intelligence officer noted, 'are practically 100 percent opposed to Somoza.'[6] As the events of the next two months were to show, this assessment was suspect. That Somoza survived the summer of 1944 owes much to the fact that Nicaraguan labour stood by him throughout. At the beginning of June, however, conditions seemed threatening.

As the Conservative and Independent Liberal parties joined forces, the leadership of the Nicaraguan Socialist Party (Partido Socialista Nicaragüense, PSN), exiled since the late 1930s, emerged to agitate for a labour code. From Mexico, Bursley reported that 'a revolution is brewing in Nicaragua . . . It will break out at an early date.' The opposition was eager to make plain to the State Department that no Nazis would be involved in the movement, and that in fact it would be anti-Nazi. To counteract precisely such claims, Somoza declared all opposition activity Nazi-fascist, though this was beginning to seem unlikely. The US embassy in San José, on the basis of intercepted mail between Nicaraguan exiles, informed the department that Chamorro had returned highly optimistic from his trip to the United States, where a Nicaragua Democratic Committee had been organized, and that he expected a change of government in Nicaragua at an early date.[7]

Towards the end of June, illegal demonstrations brought disturbances onto the streets in front of the US embassy. The opposition was protesting

[5] 817.00/9052, FBI report, Hoover to Berle, 26 Apr. 1944; 817.00/4–2444, military attaché's intelligence report, 24 Apr. 1944.

[6] RG 226 OSS 77773, Lieutenant Colonel GSC [*sic*], chief of the intelligence branch, Security and Intelligence Division, 5 June 1944.

[7] 817.00/9059, Bursley (Mexico) to McGurk, 13 May 1944; 817.00/9062, memorandum, unsigned, to Cabot, 15 June 1944; 817.00/9066, San José embassy to State Department, 15 June 1944; Jeffrey L. Gould, *Dangerous Friends: Somoza and the Labour Movement* (Mineographed document, Maragua, 1985), 10–11.

under banners that declared their sympathies with the movements in El Salvador, Honduras, and Guatemala. At one such gathering the crowd was addressed sympathetically by the Mexican chargé and the Salvadorean minister. The demonstrators then moved on to the presidential palace, where they were dispersed by Guardia troops who clubbed them with rifles. Stewart believed that some of those arrested were being summarily executed in prison. At night, Guardia patrols became pervasive on Managua's streets. As his enemies grew in number and bitterness, Somoza seemed to have insufficient patronage to go round. The Guardia appeared loyal but his hold on it was less firm than before and he was concerned about its future support. Ubico's fall had spurred anxieties among the Nicaraguan officer corps, which realized what might happen in Nicaragua. According to the US embassy, a secret counting of noses was under way in military circles.[8]

Moncada and other Liberal leaders, alarmed at the scale and intensity of the opposition and fearful of the precedent set in neighbouring countries, urged Somoza not to pursue his plans for re-election. Fernando Saballos, vice-president of the Supreme Court, was leaving for the United States, where he intended to urge the Nicaraguan ambassador, Guillermo Sevilla Sacasa, to use his influence with Somoza not to proceed.[9]

Sensitive to pressure exerted by the opposition, and to the general trend of events in the isthmus, Somoza felt it necessary to declare himself opposed to re-election. He was not, however, abandoning his plans entirely. Rather, he intended to give up the presidency within the next two years and then to enter the race as a private citizen. This ploy proved no check to the dissident Liberals, nor to the opposition of the public. Nicaraguans had become accustomed to regarding the four Central American dictators as a group, and as they began to fall it appeared unlikely that Somoza would be able to stand alone. The leaders of the Nicaraguan opposition were already thinking in terms of a post-war world, and believed that the new governments in El Salvador and Guatemala would aid their cause. On 28 June a procession of three thousand women, bejewelled society ladies and servants, all dressed in mourning, paraded the Managua streets to demonstrate their sympathy with the students. The crowd halted outside the US embassy, where the speeches were made.[10]

[8] 817.00/6–2744, Stewart to Hull, 27 June 1944; 817.00/6–2344, Stewart to Hull, 23 June 1944; Miguel Jesús Blandón, *Entre Sandino y Fonseca Amador* (Managua: *s.n.*, 1980), 20; 817.00/7–544, Stewart to Hull, 5 July 1944.

[9] 817.00/6–2344, Stewart to Hull, 23 June 1944.

[10] 817.00/9068, Stewart to Hull, 24 June 1944; 817.00/6–2644, Stewart to Hull, 26 June 1944; 817.00/6–2744, Stewart to Hull, 27 June 1944; 817.00/7–544, Stewart to Hull, 5 July 1944; Manuel Cordero Reyes, Carlos Castro Wassmer, and Carlos Pasos,

These precarious conditions continued into a tense July, when Managua was alive with rumours that the government was about to fall. Vehement attacks on Somoza circulated in the form of mimeographed sheets; flyers to lawyers and doctors urged a strike. Guardia night patrols were strengthened. A Liberal Party meeting on 3 July caused great excitement because the dissidents were expected to be in a large majority: anti-Somoza sentiment was so strong that it seemed likely that the president would be unable to attend.[11] In a deft tactic, opposition demonstrators began marching with American flags. The flag was used, effectively so in Managua and Matagalpa, as a shield against Guardia repression. Understating, Stewart informed the State Department that 'the prospects for stability are not (repeat not) improving'.[12]

As Sacasa had done a decade earlier, the besieged Nicaraguan president turned to the United States for salvation. Making strenuous efforts to identify his government with Washington, he wanted the State Department to ban the opposition's use of the American flag, or to give him the authority 'not to respect it'.[13] An item in *Flecha* falsely reported that he had received cordial congratulations from Hull for the gentlemanly way in which he was handling the disturbances. The president, according to Stewart, was 'seeking any straw in the wind which would seem to indicate our support in these troublous times'.[14] This included plans for an American Independence Day parade to the US embassy, where the schoolchildren of Managua were to be drawn up in formation carrying little Nicaraguan and American flags. Thereafter, Somoza planned to deliver a speech from the embassy balcony.[15]

It was at this point that American diplomatic correspondence began to display a noticeable shift in attitude towards the Somoza regime, and that US policy towards Nicaragua began to evince some of the characteristics of the 1930s. The general was refused permission to deliver the speech from the embassy balcony, and Hull's dispatches began to reveal his concern about visible American involvement in Nicaraguan politics.[16]

Nicaragua bajo el régimen de Somoza (San Salvador: Imprenta Funes, 1944), *passim*; 817.00/6–2844, Stewart to Hull, 28 June 1944; Krehm, *Democracies and Tyrannies*, 123.

[11] 817.00/7–344, Stewart to Hull, 3 July 1944.

[12] Ibid.; 817.00/7–344, Stewart to Hull, 3 July 1944.

[13] 817.00/7–644, State Department memorandum, unsigned, 6 July 1944.

[14] 817.00/7–744, Stewart to Hull, 7 July 1944; 817.00/7–944, Stewart to Hull, 9 July 1944.   [15] 817.415/6–2944, Stewart to Hull, 29 June 1944.

[16] 811.415/6–2944, Hull to Stewart, 30 June 1944. Stewart was, nevertheless, characteristically accommodating. Somoza made his speech from a platform erected across the street from the embassy, after which Stewart invited him in for a drink: 817.00/7–444, Stewart to Hull, 4 July 1944.

This anxiety was brought sharply into focus when a general strike appeared imminent. On 6 July doctors, dentists, and lawyers did not open their offices in Managua; hospital workers failed to report for duty; most shops were without employees; many schools and the university remained closed. The prospects seemed bright for a general stoppage over the following days. 'The great majority of the people', Stewart reported, 'seek General Somoza's resignation.'[17]

The disquiet was such that Somoza renounced his re-election plans, believing that this would enable him to regain the support of two-thirds of the dissident Liberals; Moncada was apparently willing to support him on such a basis. The American embassy, however, was not optimistic; Stewart informed his chiefs that 'almost anything could happen'.[18] US military intelligence concurred, believing that some orderly transfer of power was impossible. According to the military intelligence division, Somoza 'could never turn over the government as Martínez and Ubico did and get out of the country alive'.[19]

With hindsight, it can be seen that the people of Nicaragua reached a turning point in the summer of 1944 and, having reached it, failed to turn. The strike did not become general. The fact that the PSN leadership split over the issue was central to its collapse, but the conduct of the American collector general of customs in Managua is not to be gainsaid. Lindberg signed an order announcing that any establishment closing its doors would be seized, its goods confiscated, and its right to engage in any future business denied. Any foreigner joining the strike would be deported. Lindberg's actions were unauthorized, and Stewart was instructed to reprimand him. In Washington, Cabot was outraged about this because it amounted to undeniable US interference in Nicaraguan affairs. Lindberg was subsequently removed from his post and the customs collectorship was eventually terminated, but by then his intervention had had its effect.[20]

His interference, however, was overshadowed by the results of the strategy pursued by the Nicaraguan labour movement. Somoza had been promising a labour code since early in his administration but the legislation had never been enacted, probably because the potential gains in

[17] 817.00/7–644, Stewart to Hull, 6 July 1944.
[18] 817.00/7–444, Stewart to Hull, 7 July 1944.
[19] RG 226 84918 Military Intelligence Division, Fred T. Cruse, chief military attaché in Central America, 20 July 1944.
[20] 817.00/7–744, Stewart to Hull, 7 July 1944; 817.00/8–1244, Stettinius to Stewart, 12 Aug. 1944; 817.00/7–744, memorandum by Cabot, 7 July 1944.

labour support would not have countered the expected growth of business sector opposition. In the late 1930s and early 1940s some measures had been implemented, to limited effect: construction of some low-cost housing; Somoza's inauguration, in January 1940, of the first *casa del obrero* (in effect a social club, given the restrictive nature of its regulations); a law on industrial safety applying to the mining companies.[21]

The significant increase in the number of urban workers during the war made labour a more effective source of potential support. In September 1943 a new Central Executive Committee of Nicaraguan Workers issued a manifesto calling for union organization and a labour code. By 1944, therefore, as middle-class agitation increased, Somoza was courting Nicaraguan labour as a counterbalance. In May 1944 he opened a workers' congress, reviving his old promise of a labour code and social security measures. Although the congress did not endorse his re-election plans, Conservative and business opposition to any labour code virtually guaranteed labour support for the regime.[22]

Consequently, as calls for a general strike spread, several unions issued a pamphlet, *A Serious Appeal to All Workers*, which denounced plans for a stoppage. A handbill circulated by the organizing committee of the Nicaraguan Workers' Federation claimed that the students were tools of middle-class Liberals, Conservatives, and 'Nazi-fascists'. The PSN, for its part, called on Nicaraguans to oppose any action that might cause civil strife. Since the Conservatives were so resolutely anti-union, the PSN refused to support a strike that, it claimed, was being demanded by the Conservatives. Other labour organizations provided strong support for the regime on the grounds that Somoza had provided schools, offered low-interest loans to smallholders, and was promising a labour code.[23]

In this maze of contradictions the dissident Liberals and the Conservatives—mostly substantial industrialists and merchants to whom radicalism was inimical—were in a strange alliance with the Mexican government and the radicals of the Central American Democratic Union (Unión Democrática Centroamericana). At the same time, the Mexican labour leader, Vicente Lombardo Toledano, was enjoining his listeners to distinguish between dictators: Somoza, having

---

[21] Knut Walter, *The Regime of Anastasio Somoza, 1936–1956* (Chapel Hill: University of North Carolina Press, 1993), 101–3.

[22] 817.00/9007, Stewart to Hull, 13 Oct. 1943; Walter, *The Regime*, 101, 136–7; Dunkerley, *Power in the Isthmus*, 123; 817.00B/8–1744, J. Edgar Hoover to Berle, FBI report, 17 Aug. 1944; Gould, *Dangerous Friends*, 11.

[23] Walter, *The Regime*, 137–9; Dunkerley, *Power in the Isthmus*, 123.

given labour the freedom to organize and hold a congress, was not to be categorized with Central America's other autocrats.[24] In effect, Nicaraguan workers had no community of interest with those who, in the summer of 1944, might have brought down Somoza in the same manner as Ubico and Martínez had fallen. Nicaraguan labour would not support an opposition that in power might give it nothing, against a government that had given a little and had promised a lot more.

*

With the support of the Nicaraguan labour movement and an absence of support from the US government, Somoza was able to withstand the opposition during the tense days of June and July 1944, although there remained an undercurrent of bitter resentment towards him.[25] In mid July the ministers of education and the interior, the Nicaraguan minister to Costa Rica, and the presidential secretary all resigned over his plans for re-election. The demonstrations in Managua had receded by August, however, and there were only sporadic student protests in León. This owed much to the continuing loyalty of the Guardia and to Moncada's support at a critical time, but perhaps most to Somoza's continuing honeymoon with labour. A labour code was expected by the end of the year. In the wake of the summer's disturbances, one union after another sent the president statements of support, making the opposition's strategy of passive resistance somewhat futile.[26]

Labour allegiance, however, was balanced by the first clear evidence of a distinct clash of interests between Somoza and Washington. It became apparent to the president that the United States might not back him in critical circumstances, and he summoned Stewart to complain of the unsympathetic attitude displayed by the State Department and the embassy during the crisis. Affecting concern that the department was encouraging Mexican efforts to overthrow Central American governments, he expressed his sorrow that Stewart had recently received a number of Somoza's adversaries, among them Pedro Joaquín Chamorro, editor of *La Prensa*, and Carlos Cuadra Pasos and Julio Cardenal of the

---

[24] 817.00/3–2745, Finley to Stettinius, 27 Mar. 1945.
[25] Gregorio Selser, *Nicaragua de Walker a Sandino* (Mexico: Mex-Sur Editorial, 1984), 251–2; Marco Antonio Valle Martínez, *La dictadura somocista* (Leon: Comité Político Universitario UNAN, 1980), 29; Jaime Wheelock and Luis Carrión, *Apuntes sobre el desarrollo económico y social de Nicaragua* (Maragua: Secretaria Nacional de Propaganda y Educación del FSLN, 1980), 28; Blandón, *Entre Sardino*, 22.
[26] 817.00/8–1744, Stewart to Stettinius, 8 Aug. 1944.

Conservatives, as well as leading Liberal dissidents.[27] The State Department, for its part, was newly perturbed at efforts to involve the United States in domestic politics. Stewart was instructed to inform Somoza of the department's displeasure that Washington's position was being 'misunderstood... particularly in consequence of the Nicaraguan government's efforts to mislead public opinion'.[28]

For two years, of course, Stewart had been making efforts to ensure that the department's position was unequivocally understood, but that position was not the same as the one to which the department now referred. With victory in the war in sight, and with political conditions in Nicaragua so unsettled, US attempts to return to a pre-war policy towards the country aroused the old problems associated with that policy. Stewart, echoing Hull's views of a decade earlier, felt that any attempt to 'clarify' Washington's attitude now would be tantamount to intervention. He was convinced that silent neutrality was the best course, and he advised the State Department that this was the approach he intended to take.[29] In this he was aided by the remarkable degree of calm that characterized the domestic political scene in the autumn and winter of 1944. Mass deportations of opposition leaders (on 14 July alone, forty-four were exiled to Costa Rica, El Salvador, and the Corn Islands) helped take the momentum out of the civic opposition, as did the closing of *La Prensa*.[30]

Externally, however, the exile community was achieving some success in securing finance and arms. Reports from US embassies in the isthmus suggested that the activities of the exiles, reinvigorated with the arrival of their deported leadership, were intensifying. US intelligence was routinely monitoring their plans by intercepting their mail, which tended towards somewhat easily decoded allusions to the right time and place for 'planting the sesame seed'. By the beginning of August, sectors of the exile community constituted an armed opposition in Costa Rica and Honduras. John Erwin, the ambassador in Tegucigalpa, sent to Washington an intercepted exile communication authorizing Hector Medina Planes, head of the Liberal Party's supreme council, to purchase portable arms and to establish relations with Guardia officers in order to secure their support in a revolt. Funds were apparently available for both

[27] 817.00/7–1044, Stewart to Hull, 10 July 1944.
[28] 817.00/7–1544, Hull to Stewart, 15 July 1944.
[29] 817.00/7–1944, Stewart to Hull, 19 July 1944.
[30] 817.00/7–1444, Stewart to Hull, 14 July 1944; 817.00/9–2744, Stewart to Secretary of State, 27 Sept. 1944.

purposes.[31] At the end of August, Cabot was voicing concern in Washington as a result of repeated FBI reports that a revolution was definitely planned, and that a large quantity of arms had already been transferred from Costa Rica to Nicaragua.[32]

The apparent danger was made concrete at the end of September, when a band of Nicaraguan refugees under General Roberto Hurtado attacked a detachment of Costa Rican troops and disarmed them. It was expected that the Pasos group would return to Nicaragua in the north via the Gulf of Fonseca to attack Chinandega and León. It also seemed likely that the rebels to the south might attempt to invade in Chontales; Guardia reinforcements were deployed along the border. On 30 September two Nicaraguan government planes were machine-gunned in the frontier region of Los Chiles, Costa Rica. President Picado closed the border, and the Costa Rican authorities arrested thirty-six Nicaraguans armed with guns and grenades. A week later the Guardia took on an invading force under Noguero Gómez and Hurtado at San Jorge in Costa Rica. Gómez and four of his men were killed in the engagement.[33]

Internal conditions remained calm throughout the rest of the year but US diplomats and intelligence officers believed that the current of public opinion, especially among the Managua business sector, was clearly against Somoza. Continued labour support, however, lessened the likelihood of success for any new movement of passive resistance. Certainly emboldened by this circumstance, apparently affected by the calm, and possibly under the illusion that it reflected regained popularity, in December Somoza called for plebiscites of the Liberal Party to choose delegates to a convention that would nominate the next presidential candidate. The delegates represented Liberal voters in each department, with one delegate for each 1,000 voters or fraction thereof over 500. They were 'chosen' at plebiscites that, in practice, were managed by local party leaders on instructions from Managua. Amid the prevailing political calm,

[31] 817.00/7–2044, embassy in Costa Rica to Hull, 20 July 1944; 817.00/7–2844, embassy in Costa Rica to Hull, 28 July 1944; 817.00/8–244, Erwin to Hull, 2 Aug. 1944.

[32] 817.00/8–344, FBI report, J. Edgar Hoover to Berle, 3 Aug. 1944; 817.00/8–2344, memorandum, Cabot to Stettinius, 23 Aug. 1944.

[33] 817.00/8–2344, memorandum, Cabot to Stettinius, 23 Aug. 1944; 817.00/9–2744, Stewart to Secretary of State, 27 Sept. 1944; 817.00/9–2944, Stewart to Secretary of State, 29 Sept. 1944; 817.00/10–244, Stewart to Secretary of State, 2 Oct. 1944; 817.00/10–344, Military Intelligence Division report, 3 Oct. 1944; 817.00/10–344, Military Intelligence Division report, 3 Oct. 1944; 817.00/10–1044, Stewart to Secretary of State, 10 Oct. 1944; 817.00/10–1244, Washington (at the US legation in San José) to Secretary of State, 12 Oct. 1944.

the call for plebiscites came like a bombshell.[34] The elections were more than two years away; the Liberal Party was divided; and as yet there were no official Somocista, Liberal dissident, or Conservative candidates. What seemed clear, however, was that Somoza's candidacy was on again.

*

In Washington, good neighbourism continued to mutate. Three weeks before Stewart reported his suspicions that those arrested in the Managua protests were being executed by the Guardia, the Allies had put 150,000 men onto the beaches of Normandy. In the Pacific, the strategy of advancing island by island had brought US marines to Saipan in June. By August, the Soviet army was on the outskirts of Warsaw. In mid September, at the Quebec conference, the Allies were seriously discussing whether to turn post-war Germany into an entirely agricultural economy. The European war was not finished, but it clearly seemed to be won.[35]

It was against this background that the State Department's faith in Somoza's durability was being undermined. Routinely tapping his telephone, US intelligence had made the department aware of Somoza's own anxieties about his chances of survival. Armed, external opposition had engaged Guardia detachments in actual combat. Organized, internal opposition had emerged en masse for the first time. The president's hold had been shown to be much less than absolute. The State Department, moreover, was uncertain how long his honeymoon with labour would last. In the department's Central American affairs division, Cochran was convinced that labour would turn against Somoza as soon as it had secured as much as it felt possible, or as soon as the president began to repent his concessions. If the relationship ended abruptly the prospects seemed bright that he would be forced violently out of office. The opposition, moreover, was home-grown. It had been making strenuous efforts to emphasize that it was anti-Nazi. Stewart's incipient apprehensions that it might be pro-Soviet, receiving support from the Russian embassy in Mexico, were dismissed by the US ambassador in Mexico City.[36]

If Somoza could be obliged to renounce his plans for another term, the transition to a new government might be relatively smooth. If he persisted, a violent breakdown in public order seemed probable.

[34] 817.00/12–1444, Stewart to Hull, 14 Dec. 1944.
[35] Ted Morgan, *FDR: A Biography* (New York: Simon and Schuster, 1985), 721, 730.
[36] 817.00/7–644, unsigned State Department memorandum, 6 July 1944; 817.00/2–645, memorandum, Cochran to Cabot, 23 Feb. 1945; 817.00/7–1944, Messersmith to Duggan, 19 July 1944.

Moreover, while it was unlikely that the Soviets had had much to do with the disturbances of June and July, there was no assurance that they might not become involved in future outbursts. George Messersmith, the ambassador in Mexico, had 'no illusions with regard to Oumansky [the Soviet ambassador to Mexico]...I know his tendency towards over-activity...That Oumansky wants to interfere [in Nicaragua] and that all his inclinations are in that direction we have no doubt whatever for that is the character of the man.'[37] In these circumstances Stewart's decision to return to the 1930s policy of silent neutrality raised problems for Washington.

In the nineteenth century and the early twentieth, the United States had positively indicated its attitude to a government in Nicaragua, or to an opposition movement, by its actions. Prolonged, active involvement by the United States came to inform political thinking in Nicaragua as the anticipated support or opposition of Washington was incorporated into political planning and activity. Since such thinking continued to persist in the mid 1930s, American inaction—good neighbour rhetoric notwithstanding—was subject to interpretation, incurring for the Roosevelt administration enduring accusations of responsibility in the ascendancy of Somoza.

In the late 1930s and during the war the question of interpretation did not arise, as Nicholson and Stewart defused plans for opposition to the regime and as Lend Lease provided the Guardia with the necessary hardware to ensure internal stability. By the mid 1940s, US activities in Nicaragua during the previous ten years again began to inform political thinking at a time when the need for interpretation recurred with a return to the inaction of silent neutrality. This time, in contrast to the turbulent years of the Sacasa administration, Washington's hands-off policy was taken to evidence support for the incumbent government. In the summer of 1944, as student and middle-class agitation mounted to prompt the emergence of an Independent Liberal Party, and as even Guardia officers began to voice concern about Somoza's re-election plans, opposition unrest was characterized by an intense criticism of the United States for supporting the president. Somoza himself, simultaneously, began to appreciate that the State Department was withdrawing from him.

By September 1944 the Germans had been driven from France and Belgium, and Allied troops were on German soil. American troops

---

[37] 817.00/7–1944, Messersmith to Duggan, 19 July 1944.

returned to the Philippines in October, and by the following month Japan was within bombing range of Allied air strikes. The United States had sacrificed more than a quarter of a million Americans in a battle for democracy against dictatorship.[38] In that light, continued American backing for Somoza was an embarrassment, and accusations that US support was persisting caused Hull further anxiety. With a deeper knowledge of European totalitarianism than he could have wished for, and a greater appreciation of *somocismo* than he could have been expected to enjoy in the mid 1930s, Hull rejected Stewart's 'silent neutrality' and with it the policy of absolute non-interference that he had championed for over a decade. In a dispatch to the Managua embassy that he wrote shortly before his retirement, Hull evinced an attitude that Arthur Bliss Lane had vainly attempted to have him adopt in 1934. Stewart was instructed to use this statement in his private conversations with Somoza whenever he deemed it appropriate:

The Department has been much concerned at reports which have been reaching it indicating a widespread misunderstanding by many of the peoples of this hemisphere of this government's policy of non-intervention. Charges have been made with increasing frequency that by furnishing arms and ammunition to certain governments under Lend Lease the United States has been supporting dictatorships and has enabled them to remain in power by force . . .

Military dictatorships and unconstitutional regimes are to be deplored, but it is no function of the government of the United States to attempt to impose the practice of democracy upon other governments or peoples . . .

But it is not incompatible with these policies [of non-intervention and non-interference] to state unequivocally the self-evident truth that the people and government of the United States cannot help but feel a greater affinity and a warmer friendship for those governments which rest upon the periodically and freely expressed consent of the governed.[39]

Eight weeks later, his health deteriorating, Hull resigned. His departure occasioned substantial personnel changes in the State Department. Latin American policy moved to the jurisdiction of individuals whose aims were different from those of the internationalists. Nelson Rockefeller was appointed to the post of assistant secretary of state for Latin American affairs. New individuals took charge of the Latin American desk. Dudley Bonsal, brother of Philip and a veteran Latin Americanist, was brought

[38] Roger Parkinson, *Encyclopaedia of Modern War* (London: Granada Publishing Limited, 1979), 285.   [39] 710.11/11–144, Hull to Stewart, 1 Nov. 1944.

in. Avra Warren, a career foreign service man and a supporter of Welles, was named chief of the desk.[40]

*

In Nicaragua, aware that the American diplomatic establishment was turning against him, Somoza began to concentrate on the US military establishment. Towards the end of 1944 he started lobbying for the sale of more military equipment from the US War Department. The State Department intervened to block the sale and the War Department temporized. Frustrated at the delay, Somoza wrote personally to Roosevelt. He linked American interests to Nicaraguan stability and assured FDR that 'the armaments in the hands of the National Guard ... are in friendly hands which will do honour to the cause of democracy'.[41]

With the fall of Ubico and Martínez, the State Department was dubious about Somoza's prospects should he pursue re-election. By the beginning of 1945 he seemed to be less than the natural winner he had appeared in 1936, and the department was dissociating itself from the regime. US prestige was at stake: if Somoza were supplied with American arms and remained in office beyond 1947, Latin American critics would hold Washington guilty of promoting military dictatorship. In concluding his letter to Roosevelt, however, Somoza played what he thought was his ace:

Nicaragua is a stronghold and a breakwater against the communism which diligently seeks to infiltrate Central America as an aspect of Mexican policy and as a disquieting problem for the future. It does not escape my thoughts that sooner or later our continent will have to face the influence of Russia, and that the United States will take the leadership, as today, with the same courage and vision devoted to the defence of our future.[42]

The State Department had already contemplated this. Concerned simultaneously with a future Russian attempt to establish military missions in Latin America, and with the blow that American prestige would suffer should a re-armed Somoza engineer his own re-election, the State Department was uncertain which strategy to adopt. It decided to

---

[40] Randall Bennett Woods, *The Roosevelt Foreign Policy Establishment and the 'Good Neighbor': The United States and Argentina, 1941–1945* (Lawrence: Regents Press of Kansas, 1979), 168–9; *Newsweek*, 3 Sept. 1945, 50.

[41] 817.23/4–745, Somoza to Roosevelt, 23 Dec. 1944; Eduardo Crawley, *Dictators Never Die: A Portrait of Nicaragua and the Somoza Dynasty* (London: C. Husst, 1979), 103; Richard Millet, *Guardians of the Dynasty* (Maryknoll, NY: Orbis Books, 1977), 201–2.

[42] 817.23/4–745, Somoza to Roosevelt, 23 Dec. 1944.

postpone a decision pending the outcome of military staff conversations that were shortly to consider future security collaboration between Managua and Washington.[43]

The temporizing was helped by a continuation of the lull in internal political activity in Nicaragua. Harold Finley, the chargé d'affaires at the Managua legation and head of mission until a new ambassador arrived, reported that he had nothing to report, 'literally nothing of any consequence'.[44] The current against Somoza seemed to be growing in Managua and other towns, but not so much as to raise concerns about stability. An air of resignation had descended as the opposition reconciled itself to Somoza seeing out his term. It was not, however, reconciled to his starting a new mandate.[45]

A lot of the politicking was happening behind closed doors, and much of it consisted of Somoza's byzantine plans to keep himself in power. The US embassy was informed of a Somoza–Sacasa–Debayle family conference at the start of February, which reached a series of decisions on the question of the succession. According to the embassy's informants, Somoza would reorganize the Supreme Court to ensure that it was pliable before the next elections. He would then resign the presidency and turn over the office to his designate, Benjamín Lacayo Sacasa. Lacayo would immediately confirm Somoza's appointment as *jefe director* of the National Guard, and would call elections with Luis Debayle as the official candidate. Debayle would win the elections and Somoza, as head of the Guardia, would run the country through him. A further possibility, in the opinion of the American embassy, was that Debayle would 'make a mess of being president' and that the National Guard, in order to restore order, would put Somoza back into office.[46]

That Somoza might remain in control but not in office was not a comforting thought in the State Department, where officials believed that the artifice would fail to check an upsurge of armed and civic opposition, thereby making a transition unmanageable.[47] As the policy of silent neutrality began hardening into something resembling outright opposition, the word 'dictator' began to appear for the first time in confidential State

[43] 810.20 Defense/2–2645, Finley to Stettinius, 26 Feb. 1945; 817.20 Missions/11–1744, Stettinius to Finley, 29 Jan. 1945.

[44] 817.00/2–645, Finley to Cabot, 6 Feb. 1945; 817.00/3–345, Finley to Cochran, 3 Mar. 1945; 817.00/3–2745, Finley to Stettinius, 27 Mar. 1945.

[45] 817.00/3–2745, Finley to Stettinius, 27 Mar. 1945.

[46] 817.00/2–645, Finley to Cabot, 6 Feb. 1945.

[47] 817.00/2–645, memorandum, Cochran to Cabot, 23 Feb. 1945.

Department memoranda about Somoza. Much depended on how far he took his plans for re-election. From Washington, Cochran cabled to Finley in Managua that 'the Department has been leaning over backwards for many months to avoid giving the impression of lending support to the so-called dictators or to *continuismo* as such, while at the same time maintaining its position on non-interference in internal affairs'.[48]

That the US State Department should have to lean over backwards in order to demonstrate that it was *not* doing something reflects the contortions that diplomatic policy had to perform in a situation where the department favoured a particular outcome (the departure of Somoza) but where, in the name of non-interference, it had perforce to reject invitations from the main political actors that it interfere in order to ensure Somoza's departure. Even as a principle, however, non-interference in Nicaragua had very little time left to it. Two weeks after Cochran called Somoza a dictator, Franklin Roosevelt died.

*

In Nicaragua, a month after Harry Truman took the oath of office and two weeks after Adolf Hitler committed suicide, Somoza's candidacy was confirmed. In May he sought advice from the new, amenable Supreme Court on whether the constitution barred him from running for the presidency. His private secretary made a speech in his presence declaring that the Nicaraguan people wanted him to stay in office; handbills were being distributed averring that a continuation of his mandate was the best course for Nicaragua. By July it was official, and Somoza embarked on another tortuous manoeuvre around the constitution.[49] He wanted the Supreme Court to declare that his present mandate was not the result of an election according to the terms of the constitution, because he had been appointed by a constituent assembly in 1939. Since he had not been 'elected' he was not prohibited from *re*-election and could run for the presidency in 1947.[50]

Difficulties were at hand, however, in the form of the new US ambassador, Fletcher Warren, who took up his post in Managua on 10 May 1945, three days after Germany surrendered. Long acquainted with Nicaragua, Warren had worked at the Managua legation with Arthur

[48] 817.00/3–1445, Cochran to Finley, 29 Mar. 1945.

[49] 817.00/5–2945, Fletcher Warren to Stettinius, 29 May 1945; 817.00/7–1245, Fletcher Warren to Stettinius, 12 July 1945.

[50] 817.00/7–1245, Fletcher Warren to Stettinius, 12 July 1945; 817.00/7–2045, memorandum, Cochran to Avra Warren, 2 May 1945.

Bliss Lane in the fraught period when Lane was trying to prevent Somoza from overthrowing the Sacasa government. Warren decided, and soon convinced the State Department, that a revolution was inevitable if Somoza pursued his plans for re-election. The stratagem in the Supreme Court, made public in a favourable editorial in *Novedades* (which Somoza owned), 'came like a bombshell with a delayed fuse that has not yet exploded'. Conditions seemed ripe for a repeat of the summer of 1944. Warren told his chiefs that the dissident Liberals would be able to secure arms in Mexico for this purpose, and would be supported by the Mexican government.[51]

It was at this point, the summer of 1945, that the State Department stopped leaning over backwards. Informed by a renewed sense of democratic idealism in the wake of victory over Nazism, the Central American affairs division prepared a lengthy memorandum for Nelson Rockefeller on the policy that the United States should adopt towards Somoza. To Cochran, chief of the division (and another an old Nicaragua hand), Somoza's plans to run for a new term seemed 'ill-timed historically as well as locally. A clean democratic wind is sweeping the world. The peoples of the hemisphere have had the Four Freedoms preached at them for years— and want them.' Cochran, agreeing with his ambassador in Managua, warned that the public reaction to Somoza's plans would reach 'fever heat' and that the Liberal dissidents would stage a revolution.[52]

This was the turning point in US policy towards Somoza, the point when American attitudes towards non-interference coincided in both theory and practice, and when US interference began to coincide in both intention and consequence. It found expression in a policy recommendation that seemed clear-headed in comparison to the contortions that US diplomacy had until recently had to perform, and that could have been written by Arthur Bliss Lane a decade earlier:

Recommendation: In the interests of democracy as a prime tenet of our political faith, in the interest of President Somoza himself, in the interest of our relations with Nicaragua and in the ultimate best interests of the United States, it is recommended you [Rockefeller] address a letter to Ambassador Warren requesting him orally and informally to tell President Somoza that the Department views with concern and regret his apparent decision to seek re-election in direct violation of the clear intention of the Nicaraguan constitution; that it feels this

[51] 817.00/7–2245, Fletcher Warren to Stettinius, 2 July 1945; 817.00/7–2445, Fletcher Warren to Stettinius, 24 July 1945.
[52] 817.00/7–2545, memorandum, Cochran to Rockefeller, 25 July 1945.

decision is contrary to the spirit of democracy and that it can only react disastrously upon his administration and upon his interests...

It will be held that this is intervention in the internal affairs of Nicaragua. Perhaps it is, but the United States cannot avoid such a charge in any case. Its failure to act (when Somoza has made so much of his close ties with the United States and the fact that he can 'get more' from us than another president) would be negative intervention—especially if we choose this time to implement the staff conversations by giving the Guard arms, ammunition and airplanes, as is contemplated. We cannot avoid the *charge* of intervention; and if we are to play a part (and we cannot avoid doing so) let it be on behalf of democratic processes.

Possibly the leftists—and it is highly fashionable in certain countries to term any opposition 'Communist'—will exercise much influence. But we can neither look on with disinterest while the people of Central America are kept in a state of economic and political peonage, nor fight real Communism with a passive attitude. On the contrary, the United States wears the mantle of greatness, willingly or not, and I should like to see it stand forth in the world proudly and positively for the principles which made it great.[53]

Conditioned by democratic idealism, this was the beginning of a new realism in which non-interference no longer counted among the principles that made America great. The Truman administration, via Fletcher Warren, now began putting this recommendation into effect amid Nicaragua's premature election campaign. The opposition established a more unified front. In mid August the PSN, fulfilling Cochran's prediction of six months earlier, announced it would not support re-election and joined forces with the Independent Liberals, the Traditional Conservatives, the Unionist Party, and the students of Managua University to denounce Somoza. Fifty members of the PSN were abruptly taken by truck to the Honduran border and expelled.[54]

In the view of the Managua embassy, disorders were now inevitable. In Costa Rica, President Picado was telling Hallett Johnson, the US ambassador, that of the thirty to forty thousand Nicaraguans in the country, most were violently opposed to Somoza. He believed that they would either buy more arms on the black market or smuggle them into Costa Rica from Mexico and Guatemala. The governments of these two countries, he maintained, would approve arms exports for the purpose of ousting Somoza. The embassy in Managua believed that Nicaraguan exiles in Costa Rica were in possession of a thousand rifles and a

---

[53] Ibid. Emphasis in the original.
[54] 817.00/8–2045, Fletcher Warren to Stettinius, 20 Aug. 1945.

million rounds of ammunition, with a further thousand pistols already cached in Nicaragua. The revolutionaries had reportedly amassed $100,000 in cash.⁵⁵

Exile activity was advancing in parallel with urban discontent inside Nicaragua. Francisco Navarro, vice-president in Somoza's first cabinet and the leader of the mainstream Liberals in Matagalpa, declared himself unwilling to oversee Somoza's re-election campaign in the town. Francisco Fiallos, another ostensible Somocista Liberal, resigned as *jefe político* of Matagalpa. His brother Mariano, the education minister, had just resigned over Somoza's plans to extend his term. Managua was orderly but the students were restless, and the occasional cry of 'death to Somoza' was heard in the streets.⁵⁶

Somoza's campaign continued through August, although he indicated that he would step down if he received 'so much as a whisper' to that effect from the United States. Warren suggested to Edward Stettinius, Welles's successor as under-secretary, that 'perhaps something louder than a whisper from the United States would now be required to make him step down from his office'.⁵⁷ In Washington, Nelson Rockefeller started whispering a little louder at Somoza. He called in the Nicaraguan ambassador, Guillermo Sevilla Sacasa, and informed him that if Somoza ran for re-election it 'might create certain difficulties for him [and] would seriously affect relations between the two countries'.⁵⁸

Somoza decided to play for time. Informed of Rockefeller's sentiments, he relayed to the State Department that he would not go through with the election when the time came, and that Rockefeller should know that the whole business of re-election was 'a big game'. On the following day he confirmed this to Warren.⁵⁹ He was, nevertheless, resentful of the department's attitude, and for the first time he started to speak in less than glowing terms about the United States. In public speeches he began making unflattering references to 'Yankees' and told the Guatemalan minister to inform President Arévalo that he, Somoza, was tired of Yankee favours; he preferred a Central American union to be created with the cooperation of

⁵⁵ 817.00/7–2645, memorandum, Cochran to Avra Warren, 17 Aug. 1945; 817.00/8–345, Johnson to Stettinius, 3 Aug. 1945; 817.00/8–1845, Fletcher Warren to Stettinius, 18 Aug. 1945.
⁵⁶ 817.00/8–345, Fletcher Warren to Stettinius, 3 Aug. 1945; 817.00/8–1845, Fletcher Warren to Stettinius, 18 Aug. 1945.
⁵⁷ 817.00/8–645, Fletcher Warren to Stettinius, 6 Aug. 1945.
⁵⁸ 817.00/8–745, Rockefeller to Fletcher Warren, 7 Aug. 1945.
⁵⁹ 817.00/8–845, Fletcher Warren to Rockefeller, 8 Aug. 1945; 817.00/8–945, Fletcher Warren to Rockefeller, 9 Aug. 1945.

Mexico. The FBI saw this as further proof of growing Mexican influence in Central America.[60]

Such conduct can hardly have helped Somoza's case in Washington. American opposition hardened as his campaign continued in defiance of Rockefeller's diplomatic but unequivocal warning. He now eliminated the Traditional Conservatives from the National Electoral Board that was to supervise the 1947 presidential polls. The Nationalist Conservative Party, which had helped elect Somoza in 1936, had practically disappeared during his long incumbency. Somoza now sent an executive bill to Congress stating that the two main Nicaraguan parties were the Traditional Liberals and the Nationalist Conservatives. This would ensure that the electoral board was in sympathetic hands. The board's president was to be designated by the Supreme Court, which was amenable to Somoza.[61] Neither this nor further mass expulsions seemed like 'a big game' to the State Department, even though the strategy collapsed within a week when former members of the Nationalist Conservatives met to dissolve the party.[62] In mid September the leading Liberals Enoc Aguado, Roberto González Dubón, and Altamirano Brown publicly announced their defection to the Independent Liberals.[63]

Warren was meanwhile hosting representatives of the various opposition groups, all of whom sought to induce US pressure on Somoza and US supervision of the polls, and many of whom expected a revolution if Somoza were to run. Warren, for his part, was doing what he could to keep the situation calm without committing the United States to any particular course of action. He told Aguado of his anxieties about a possible revolution, and suggested that such a development would not be in Nicaragua's best interest. To this point, Warren seems to have retained faith in Somoza's promise to Rockefeller that he would not seek re-election—a belief evident in his assertion to the State Department that the Independent Liberals would return to the Liberal fold once it became clear that Somoza was going to stand down. The ambassador could only point out to Aguado, therefore, that the Somoza administration had twenty months left to run, and that 'many things can transpire in that length of time'.[64]

[60] 817.00/8–1545, FBI report, J. Edgar Hoover to Lyon, 15 Aug. 1945.
[61] 817.00/8–1845, Fletcher Warren to Stettinius, 18 Aug. 1945.
[62] 817.00/8–2445, Fletcher Warren to Stettinius, 24 Aug. 1945.
[63] 817.00/9–1245, Fletcher Warren to Stettinius, 12 Sept. 1945.
[64] 817.00/9–2545, Fletcher Warren to Stettinius, 25 Sept. 1945; 817.00/9–1345, Fletcher Warren to Stettinius, 13 Sept. 1945.

Irrespective of what the United States might do, several considerations suggested that Somoza would be able to install his own designate in the presidency. First, the opposition was really united only in its opposition to him. The Independent Liberals and the Traditional Conservatives were not entirely happy in the same camp, a fact of which Somoza was aware. He knew that it would be difficult for his opponents to unite behind a single candidate, and his manoeuvring was designed in part to prevent public opinion from settling on a given individual. Second, that Somoza was confident of ensuring an amenable successor was evidenced by the fact that he was still expanding his property interests and was not consolidating his assets for export abroad, as might be expected if he anticipated problems with the new government. Third, he knew he could control the selection of the Liberal candidate and the elections themselves. The delayed plebiscites for the Liberal convention to select the party's presidential candidate, now scheduled for 21 October, would plainly consist of Somocistas ready to do the president's bidding. He would also control the National Electoral Board. The Guardia would supervise the actual voting.[65]

The constant worry for the State Department was that the opposition's restraint might not last until Somoza made public his promise to Rockefeller. If he did not fulfil the promise, civil strife seemed inevitable. 'There can be little doubt', Warren told the department, 'that General Somoza's continuation in the presidency after 1947 would result in revolution. He has been in office too long to escape it. He has built up a backlog of hatred and dissatisfaction which is imposing.' In the meantime, Warren worried that what he termed 'the crescendo of hate' against Somoza might prompt the president to be repressive, which would then galvanize the opposition into immediate violence. In his view, all the elements for local disturbances were already present, and they would intensify as the election neared.[66]

By the end of September 1945, the presidential campaign (for polls that were still more than a year and a half away) was heated. The alliance between the Independent Liberals and the Conservatives seemed to be working satisfactorily; they had agreed on a campaign plan. Both sides' strategies were straightforward. Already certain of controlling the electoral machinery, Somoza wanted to force the opposition to announce candidates early, so that he could systematically discredit them. He would then

---

[65] 817.00/9–2545, Fletcher Warren to Stettinius, 25 Sept. 1945; 817.00/9–1345, Fletcher Warren to Stettinius, 13 Sept. 1945.   [66] Ibid.

appear as the outstanding statesman running against an inexperienced mediocrity. The opposition aimed to thwart Somoza's plans by fighting a negative campaign that focused on his own shortcomings, and then going to the polls behind a single candidate selected as late as possible.[67]

The campaign promised to be tense, 'one of the bitterest in recent Nicaraguan history', according to Warren, who was certain that a revolution was unavoidable unless Somoza were removed completely from the picture. The opposition, he felt, might deliberately antagonize the president in order to invite repression, thus securing a pretext for action. On the other hand the opposition might go through with the election and then, if Somoza or his designate were the victor, revolt. 'It seems to me', Warren told his chiefs in Washington, 'that such developments should be avoided.'[68]

How Washington was to avoid such developments became clearer as the autumn progressed. It was Warren who came up with the original idea. He wanted the State Department to initiate efforts to find a single presidential candidate on which all the main actors, including Somoza, could agree. Such an accord was to be based on guarantees of protection for Somoza, his family, and his properties once the single candidate had assumed the presidency.[69] By now, the good neighbour policy had come so far that Warren had no qualms about suggesting direct US interference in Nicaraguan politics. This was not simply a reversion to pre-war thinking; it was a return to the attitudes of the period before good neighbourism. The ambassador thought that circumstances would make such a course acceptable to Somoza. The president's faith in the Guardia had been shaken; the military was assuming a political role of its own, separate from its *jefe director*. According to Warren, 'he can hardly believe now that it is entirely a Somoza institution. He must realize that it is a factor like the Independent Liberals or the old line Conservatives which he must constantly keep in mind.'[70]

It is important to note in this respect that the United States did not expect an opposition victory to bring any greater degree of democracy to Nicaragua. Warren, at least, was clear and insistent on this point in his dispatches to Washington. While his desire to have Somoza removed from the scene is plain, he did not fudge the issue (in fact he laboured the point) of what was likely to follow Somoza. He did not believe, for example, 'that democratic forces in or outside Nicaragua will receive any

[67] 817.00/2645, Fletcher Warren to Stettinius, 26 Sept. 1945.   [68] Ibid.
[69] Ibid.   [70] Ibid.

better support from the opposition than they are receiving from President Somoza'. Most particularly, he doubted that the United States would receive 'as effective and wholehearted support after May 1, 1947' as it had been getting from Somoza.[71]

This was no longer the point. From Washington's perspective the issue was simply to get Somoza out of the presidency. Not to do so appeared likely to invite a revolution, which would work directly against US interests. Hence the State Department's anxiety that Somoza might not make public his promise to Rockefeller until shortly before the elections: in the meantime, the bitterness among the opposition and the public at large seemed likely, at best, to plague US–Nicaraguan relations in a post-Somoza era and, at worst, to spark a revolution before it was made public knowledge that an uprising was unnecessary. Warren therefore wanted the electoral problems solved as soon as possible, and asked the State Department for permission to try to secure a multi-party agreement on a single candidate.[72] Within a week, his request was academic. In the first week of October it became apparent that Somoza had no intention of fulfilling his promises on re-election. The opposition was about to force the State Department's hand, and Washington was going to have to force Somoza out.

*

Five weeks earlier, Spruille Braden, the US ambassador in Argentina, had made a public address in Buenos Aires:

One by one there appears [in Argentina] almost every element with which fascism has been served in its infamous stratagem since the days of the so-called 'March upon Rome': subversion and organized disorder by the government itself; . . . the calculated use of violent methods; . . . the use of intimidation . . . We would not be loyal to our country or to the principles which we profess to defend if, once we discover activities of this nature, we do not report them openly and hasten to pull them out by the roots . . . Otherwise we should have to declare as morally lost this very war which we won with so much sacrifice.

This was one of Braden's last official acts in Buenos Aires. The following month he was transferred to Washington to replace Nelson Rockefeller as assistant secretary of state for Latin American affairs.[73]

In his final year as Secretary of State, Cordell Hull had waged a campaign against the Argentine government of General Edelmiro Farrell and his minister of war, Juan Domingo Perón, which became a personal vendetta. By September 1944 he was referring publicly to the Argentine government as 'fascist'. The American press having joined him in this campaign, the State Department was under steady media pressure not to 'appease' the Argentines. By 1945 a large body of American public opinion was under the impression that Argentina was governed by Nazis who had consistently supported the Axis. Unilateral threats and non-recognition brought Washington's strategy to an impasse by the spring of 1945. Although the year-old Argentine government was finally recognized by Washington in April of that year in return for some concessions, the United States still tried to block Argentina's entry to the United Nations at the San Francisco conference in the same month. Those efforts were undermined by the other countries of South America, which refused to support Washington's position. Braden therefore decided to increase the pressure on his return to Washington, in a policy that received further attention in the American press.[74]

The press in Nicaragua was also paying much attention to events in Argentina. The opposition campaign began to stress perceived similarities between Somoza and the Argentine dictators, and the perceived gulf between US policy towards Nicaragua and policy in the Southern Cone.[75] By the first week of October it was clear that the nominating convention of the Liberal Party was going to announce Somoza's presidential candidacy on 21 October. Meeting in Managua and León, the Independent Liberals and the Conservatives agreed to send a high-profile delegation to the United States to pursue an anti-Somoza campaign in the US media, and to make public appeals that the Truman administration prevent bloodshed in Nicaragua. The delegation, which planned to leave for Washington immediately after the announcement of Somoza's candidacy, would include Juan Bautista Sacasa, General Carlos Pasos, Carlos Cuadra Pasos, and Enoc Aguado.[76]

This development prompted concern in Washington. The State Department did not want a 'Nicaragua situation' fed to the American press while the Argentina situation remained unresolved. The department

---

[74] Dexter Perkins, *The United States and the Caribbean* (Cambridge, Mass.: Harvard University Press, 1947), 169, 171; Bryce Wood, *The Dismantling of the Good Neighbor Policy* (Austin: University of Texas Press, 1985), 43, 50, 56–61, 70–98, *passim*.
[75] 817.00/10–845, Fletcher Warren to Stettinius, 8 Oct. 1945.   [76] Ibid.

instructed Warren to discourage the trip, an instruction that he promptly carried out. Aguado promised him that the delegation would not travel before 1 November, and that the opposition would make no preparations for the journey without consulting Warren first.[77] The State Department had a little more than two weeks to devise a plan.

Apprehensive at the prospect of the Nicaraguan opposition trying its case in the US media, Warren was of the opinion that 'the matter can be arranged with much less commotion and confusion *if we are willing to play a definite role*'. He asked to be recalled immediately to Washington for consultation on what form policy should take, and intended to be back in Managua before the plebiscites of 21 October.[78] While Warren travelled home, the State Department debated the issues. The opposition's tactics posed a dilemma. To prevent the delegation from coming would be seen as interference. To allow it to come and then refuse to see it would be viewed as endorsement of Somoza's plans for re-election, and therefore as interference. To meet the delegation would require asserting a US position, which the opposition could use in the press and thereby invite charges of US interference.[79] Since an accusation of interference was unavoidable the State Department decided to interfere, albeit as diplomatically as possible, in its own interests. Importantly, the department was at last willing to face the fact that what it was about to do amounted to interference.

Having accepted that, the department was able to produce an actual strategy that was proactive rather than reactive. The analysis and liaison section of the Division of American Republics began preparing an evaluation of political conditions in Nicaragua. The final version, a thirty-seven-page document entitled 'The Rule of President Anastacio [*sic*] Somoza in Nicaragua since 1936', was clearly designed to illuminate Somoza in a highly unfavourable light. It appears to have been part of a strategy on the part of the diplomats in the State Department's Latin America sections to ensure that they secured the approval of the Secretary of State for what they were going to do to Somoza. Ranging wide over what were now being perceived as the enormities of the Nicaraguan president, the report stressed that Somoza had remained in power through 'violence and unprincipled trickery'; that he had completely controlled

77 817.00/10–1245, Fletcher Warren to Stettinius, 12 Oct. 1945.
78 817.00/10–1045, Fletcher Warren to Stettinius, 10 Oct. 1945, emphasis added; 817.00/10–1045, Byrnes to Fletcher Warren, 10 Oct. 1945.
79 817.00/10–1145, memorandum, Cochran to Braden and Briggs, 11 Oct. 1945.

the country for the benefit of himself, his family, and his friends; that he had done nothing to improve the lot of ordinary Nicaraguans; and that he had been dictatorial in suppressing basic freedoms.[80]

On the basis of this strikingly new assessment of the Somoza government, Cochran made some blunt recommendations. First, the department would tell Somoza that his re-election would prompt an unfavourable US public reaction and that US foreign policy was responsive to public opinion. Second, it would suggest that he retire completely from public life, in order to obviate the danger that he might continue in power if not in office; the department was prepared to do this despite its awareness that, in Cochran's words, 'there is no assurance that the new regime would be as efficient or as friendly to us'. Third, the department would inform the opposition of what it was going to say to Somoza. Fourth, it would endeavour to secure some guarantee from the opposition that Somoza's assets would be left alone if he were to withdraw. Fifth, the United States would not suggest the election of a single candidate, 'taking the attitude that the Nicaraguans are adult and should work out their own problems'. Sixth, the State Department would urge on Somoza freedom of assembly and the press, the return of the exiles, and the holding of honest elections. Finally, the Truman administration would instruct American firms in Nicaragua to stop paying tribute to Somoza personally.[81]

It is worth noting that, having mapped out a pragmatic and realistic strategy for solving the Nicaragua problem, one of the State Department's options for addressing that problem should consist of telling the Nicaraguans to solve their own problems. The doctrine of non-interference retained some residual venerability. Cochran's final comments on this strategy, however, reveal that the central tenet of good neighbourism, or rather the effect of that tenet's application in Nicaragua, was finally being understood in Washington:

This may work. If so, we may avoid a revolution—and possibly, of course, fall into a period of political turmoil and unrest; a risk we must run. Or, it may not work, in which case we are no worse off than we are now and at least have the record clear. We shall, of course, be accused of intervention no matter what we do or do not do.[82]

[80] 817.001 Somoza, Anastasio/11–645, 'The Rule of Anastacio Somoza in Nicaragua since 1936'. Report prepared by the Division of American Republic Analysis and Liaison, Department of State, Nov. 1945. [81] Ibid.
[82] Ibid.

The State Department was much less inclined, or indeed able, to sit on the fence because its interests were running counter to the objectives of the US War Department in Nicaragua. Brigadier Luther Smith, chief of the military missions section of the Caribbean Defense Command, had visited Managua in late February 1945 to be made an honorary member of the Nicaraguan air force and to be decorated with the Presidential Order of Merit. Smith made plain that the War Department was keen to impede the establishment of non-US military missions in Latin America, especially Russian, British, and French missions. He announced that it was the War Department's purpose to train and arm the National Guard 'so that it might easily be integrated into the American Army in case of need'.[83]

The State Department, however, did not want to let the War Department give weapons to Somoza or modernize the Guardia. Avra Warren, director of the Office of Latin American Affairs, pointed out to his ambassadorial namesake in Managua that even a request for arms placed the State Department in a difficult position. If Somoza were to receive US arms following his declared intention to continue in office, then he, the Nicaraguan public, and all of Central America would assume that Washington supported his plans.[84]

The State Department's determination in this matter brought it into conflict with the War Department. Colonel Bartlett, chief of the US military mission in Nicaragua, wanted to secure additional American officers and enlisted men for the mission. In July, when Cochran in Washington was telling Fletcher Warren that the State Department wanted Somoza out, Bartlett was urging Somoza to write to Warren requesting the extra personnel. Sick with amoebic dysentery, in a foul humour, and plainly aware of the ambassador's attitude towards him, Somoza said that he would do no such thing, and that he was 'bored and tired' of writing such letters to Washington without effect.[85]

Bartlett persisted. He suggested that Somoza should write to General Brett, commanding general of the Caribbean Defense Command, requesting an invitation for Nicaraguan cadets to be trained for three-week periods in the Canal Zone. Bartlett assured Somoza that the State Department would approve. He was wrong; Somoza was much more perceptive. He did not doubt, he told Bartlett in the middle of a lengthy

83 810.20 Defense/2–2645, Finley to Secretary of State, 26 Feb. 1945.
84 817.20/7–1845, Avra Warren to Fletcher Warren, 20 Aug. 1945.
85 RG 165 OPD 336 Nicaragua, memorandum by Bartlett, 13 July 1945.

harangue, the goodwill of General Brett or the War Department, but he was convinced that the State Department was blocking every military request he made. 'I doubt that we will be given even a pocket knife,' Somoza complained, 'since we might cut ourselves with it.' The analogy was apposite, and the assessment correct.[86]

Fletcher Warren was doing all he could in Managua to block the Caribbean Defense Command from helping Somoza; in Washington, the State Department was playing the same game with the War Department. The consequent inter-institutional bitterness was well reflected in an angry dispatch to the War Department's operations division from Lieutenant Colonel Merrill, assistant adjutant general of the Caribbean Defense Command. Subtitled 'difficulties in furthering military relationships with the Nicaraguan government as a result of local State Department officials' attitudes', the report was a litany of complaints about blocking manoeuvres on the part of Warren and his staff at the Managua embassy.[87]

The manoeuvring continued throughout the autumn in both Managua and Washington. When Brett at the Caribbean Defense Command told Warren to invite Somoza to Panama for the graduation ceremonies of Nicaraguan cadets already in the zone, the State Department objected and the assistant chief of staff J. E. Hull instructed Brett to take no further action.[88] Somoza, his temper cooled, did eventually ask Warren about the possibility of establishing a jungle training centre run by US marines, with additional officers for the mission. Warren suggested to his chiefs that they tell the War Department to instruct the Caribbean Defense Command to find an excuse for refusing the request, specifically because of the political situation.[89]

The State Department won this particular bureaucratic tussle, sometimes taking it to detailed lengths. In October, when the War Department proposed ('as a gesture of good will and as a small token of his excellent cooperation with the US Army during World War Two') presenting Somoza with a single carbine of which he was fond, the State Department protested that such a presentation was undesirable 'for political reasons'.[90]

*

[86] Ibid.

[87] RG 165 OPD 336 Nicaragua, memorandum by Lt Col. E. D. Merrill, 17 Aug. 1945.

[88] RG 165 OPD 336 Nicaragua, J. E. Hull to Brett, 21 Sept. 1945.

[89] RG 165 OPD 336 Nicaragua, Fletcher Warren to Secretary of State, 27 Oct. 1945; RG 165 OPD 336 Nicaragua, Lyon (State Department) to Col. D. Divine, 30 Oct. 1945.

[90] RG 165 OPD 336 Nicaragua, Col. A. D. Reid to Avra Warren, 5 Oct. 1945; RG 165 OPD 336 Nicaragua, Avra Warren to Reid, 26 Oct. 1945.

Two weeks after the War Department asked the State Department about giving Somoza a single rifle, Fletcher Warren returned to Nicaragua with a clear policy in time for the Liberal plebiscites of 21 October. Voting was calm and there was no violence. Somoza was taking no chances: official cars transported government officials to the polling stations, where they were plied with alcohol and free meals. Warren was sure that groups were being transported from poll to poll for the purpose of multiple voting.[91]

On the following day he had to receive the press in order to account for his trip to Washington, and unashamedly lied that it had been for personal reasons. He told the reporters that Nicaragua was wholly capable of solving any problem arising from the election campaign and the question of the presidential succession without appealing to any outside force, an assertion that even Warren should have found embarrassing in view of the real purpose of his trip.[92]

Meeting Somoza on the same day, Warren realized that the president had devised a new tactic. He planned to go the United States in order to see his son graduate from West Point in June 1946. Before leaving, he intended to deposit executive power in one of the three designates to the presidency (the vice-presidents) and turn over the Guardia to a new chief. He would stay in the United States until the 1947 elections. During that time he would confer with the State Department and, on the basis of those discussions and events in Nicaragua, would decide whether to be a candidate for the presidency. It was evident to Warren that Somoza felt events in Nicaragua during his absence would be such that the State Department would want him to be a candidate. Firm in his conviction that he was the only man capable of running the country, Somoza had apparently persuaded himself that it was his duty to the Nicaraguan people to be re-elected for a new term.[93]

Somoza's new ploy prompted further debate in the State Department. Cochran argued that if the department could be sure that Somoza would remain in the United States for the whole period between his son's graduation and the elections, the department might consider encouraging the trip, provided that Somoza was not receiving the attentions of a head of state. Since he would probably rush back home if the situation deteriorated, however, Cochran urged that the department discourage the visit.[94] This instruction was sent to Fletcher Warren less than a week later,

91 817.00/11–145, Fletcher Warren to Stettinius, 1 Nov. 1945.
92 817.00/10–2245, Fletcher Warren to Stettinius, 22 Oct. 1945.   93 Ibid.
94 817.00/10–2245, memorandum, Cochran to Braden, 24 Oct. 1945.

on 25 October. The ambassador kept it for almost three weeks before using it to its full, dramatic effect.

In Nicaragua, political conditions remained tense. Now ill with both amoebic dysentery and malaria, Somoza withdrew to his estate at Montelimar.[95] According to the US embassy, most of the Conservative rank and file believed that the opposition could expect nothing from the United States, a view shared by many of the Independent Liberals. They concluded that they would have to rid themselves of Somoza as best they could, probably with the help of Mexico and Guatemala. In late October the Guardia raided a party given by the students of Managua and León for the Guatemalan minister to Nicaragua. Shots were fired, and forty students had to be conducted under the minister's diplomatic immunity to the sanctuary of his legation. During the festivities, the minister had reportedly made a speech in which he declared that liberty in Nicaragua could be achieved only by blood on the streets. On the following day the government closed the central university, whereupon a crowd of students charged the doors, prompting another Guardia intervention.[96]

Rumours of a general strike took hold in a matter of days. Aguado, Espinosa, and their allies were organizing a school strike that was intended to grow into a generalized stoppage. Labour leaders had pledged support. The schools did not open on 26 October. Somoza was making laborious efforts to win over Aguado, offering him any government position in return for his support, but to no avail.[97] On 4 November, leaders of the Independent Liberals and labour movement met to reach an understanding. It seemed likely to the US embassy that labour would probably issue some statement repudiating communism and pledging its support to the Independent Liberals.[98] Somoza, Warren reported, was weaker than at any time since July 1944. Reports from León, Matagalpa, and other towns indicated that the president was losing ground. He did not seem to realize how fast his position was deteriorating.[99]

Most ominously, the Guardia's institutional loyalty was suspect. Two camps were apparent, one under the Somocista Major Gaitán, and

[95] 817.00/10–3045, Fletcher Warren to Stettinius, 30 Oct. 1945; 817.00/11–545, Fletcher Warren to Stettinius, 5 Nov. 1945.

[96] 817.00/10–2545, Fletcher Warren to Stettinius, 25 Oct. 1945; 817.00/10–1745, Benson to Secretary of State, 17 Oct. 1945; 817.00/10–2245, Fletcher Warren to Stettinius, 22 Oct. 1945.

[97] 817.00/10–2545, Fletcher Warren to Stettinius, 25 Oct. 1945; 817.00/10–2645, Warren to Stettinius, 26 Oct. 1945.

[98] 817.00/11–545, Fletcher Warren to Stettinius, 5 Nov. 1945.

[99] 817.00/11–1245, Fletcher Warren to Stettinius, 12 Nov. 1945.

another under Colonel Hermógenes Prado, who was said to be working with the opposition.[100] Warren reported suggestions in some Guardia quarters that 'Somoza should be bumped off'. Colonel Camilo González, previously known in military circles as Somoza's 'trigger man', was said to be interested in taking some action against the president as soon as it became clear that Somoza was losing. (As is made plain below, González's plans were different. Warren did not yet know that the colonel was acting under Somoza's orders.)[101] Some of the younger officers, however, were speaking openly of what would be done as soon as Somoza had departed the scene. A list was apparently being compiled of all those to be assassinated as soon as the Guardia took over. 'All of this', Warren told Washington, 'adds up to the readiness of the Guardia to assist in the removal of Somoza or to take advantage of his removal to forward individual or group interest.'[102]

There seemed little hope that Somoza could withstand a revolution by deploying his army. He angrily demanded the immediate recall of the American military attaché, Colonel Frederick Judson. Judson had told the younger Guardia officers that the political appointees should be expelled. He had also been arguing that the Guardia should be non-political, remarks interpreted by the officers as meaning that they should be disloyal to Somoza. Judson had further assured the officer corps that they would receive no US arms or ammunition until the present crisis had passed.[103]

The State Department's whispering to Somoza, apparently, was having little positive effect. On the contrary, it was helping to prolong a situation conducive to a revolution or a coup. The department therefore decided, finally, to shout. Warren went to see Somoza on 10 November. The president, still sick, had lost 20 pounds. He remained as cocksure as always, however, displaying an utter contempt for the opposition. Warren, not without reluctance, burst his arrogance.

The State Department had sent Warren a telegram outlining its attitude to Somoza's proposed visit to the United States in order to see his son graduate from West Point. It was, superficially, an innocuous

---

[100] 817.00/11–545, Fletcher Warren to Stettinius, 5 Nov. 1945.

[101] The two men had been friends for decades. In 1921 they were arrested together for counterfeiting gold coins.

[102] 817.00/11–745, Fletcher Warren to Stettinius, 7 Nov. 1945.

[103] 817.00/11–1245, Fletcher Warren to Stettinius, 12 Nov. 1945; 817.00/10–3045, Fletcher Warren to Stettinius, 30 Oct. 1945.

communication. In context, however, its meaning was clear. It said, in its entirety: 'The Department understands President Somoza's natural desire to see his son graduate from West Point and assumes that his visit for that purpose would be unofficial since no invitation has been issued by this government. The Department would consider an extended visit inconvenient.'[104] Warren now showed this telegram to Somoza, to devastating effect. The ambassador related the scene in a personal letter to Cochran:

As you can imagine, it was one of the most unpleasant conversations I shall ever have. There is something terrifying in seeing disintegrate the confidence of an egotist in himself... It was a body blow. I doubt if in his entire career he has ever had anything hit him so hard. His first reaction was: 'well, that's that.' He waited a little bit in silence and then the physical reaction set in. I felt sorry for him. When I left, he was crying.[105]

Before he started to cry, Somoza claimed that he did not want to be president again, and declared his readiness to meet responsible Conservative and Liberal leaders to select a strong single candidate for 1947. Warren therefore felt free to tell opposition leaders that Somoza was prepared to meet them for that purpose.[106]

*

Having apparently engineered a successful resolution to the problem of Nicaragua's presidential succession, Warren had five days to savour what seemed like a diplomatic coup. On 15 November, Somoza presented the ambassador with his latest and simplest ploy. The president had decided simply to bluff it out: to disavow his pledge to the State Department, ignore Washington, and go through with his re-election in the expectation that the United States would not interfere to stop him. He was going to use non-interference against itself just as the policy was being abandoned. He told Warren that because Rockefeller was no longer an official of the department, he, Somoza, no longer considered himself bound by a promise he had made 'personally' to Rockefeller. Warren told his chiefs: 'as of this moment he is very much in the race for re-election. He told me specifically to transmit this info [*sic*] to the State Department... He stressed his belief that the United States had no intention of intervening in Nicaragua.'[107]

[104] 817.001 Somoza, Anastasio/10–2945, Byrnes to Fletcher Warren, 29 Oct. 1945.
[105] 817.00/11–1245, Fletcher Warren to Cochran, 12 Nov. 1945.
[106] 817.00/11–945, Fletcher Warren to Stettinius, 9 Nov. 1945.
[107] 817.00/11–1545, Fletcher Warren to Stettinius, 15 Nov. 1945; Jones, 'Good Neighbor, New Style', 317.

Yet again, Warren was sure that a revolution was imminent. In Mexico, Chamorro and Carlos Pasos had bought arms, antiquated but in large quantities, with the aid of the governor of Quintana Roo. They hoped to organize an expedition to Nicaragua's Atlantic coast. Guardia planes were ordered to Puerto Cabezas with extra ammunition for the garrison. The deterioration of Guardia loyalty continued to worry the State Department as the intra-military division became more evident. In Managua, Warren believed a story told him by Debayle, who had only recently resigned as the Guardia's medical director, that two National Guard companies were about to stage a mutiny over rumours that he, Debayle, had been arrested. The troops were not calmed until he was found to be free.[108]

The State Department decided to shout a little louder at Somoza. The new Secretary of State, James Byrnes, signed a dispatch to Warren that the ambassador was to show to Somoza. It reproduced part of a speech made by Ellis Briggs at the University of Pennsylvania. A response to Somoza's assurance that the United States would not intervene to block his ambitions, the dispatch informed the Nicaraguan president of the following sentiments:

This doctrine of non-intervention... does not preclude speaking our mind on issues we consider vitally important. It involves no sacrifice of integrity on our part, no surrender of principles, no turning a deaf ear to the voice of liberty raised by any people anywhere... We do not intend to intervene and impose democracy... But we obviously feel a warmer friendship for and a greater desire to cooperate with those governments that rest on the periodically and freely expressed endorsement of the governed. The policy of non-intervention does not imply the approval of local tyranny.[109]

Armed with this clear exposition of the attitude of the US government, Warren went to see the foreign minister, Leonardo Arguello. His pretext was a late November resolution by Panama's constituent assembly urging the president to sever diplomatic relations with Nicaragua, Honduras, and the Dominican Republic, and proposing inter-American consultation on political conditions in those countries. Warren pointed out to Arguello that Somoza's position was weakening abroad as well as in

---

[108] 817.00/11–2845, Fletcher Warren to Stettinius, 28 Nov. 1945; 817.00/11–1645, Fletcher Warren to Stettinius, 16 Nov. 1945; 817.00/11–1945, Fletcher Warren to Stettinius, 19 Nov. 1945; 817.00/11–2045, Fletcher Warren to Stettinius, 20 Nov. 1945; 817.00/11–2145, Fletcher Warren to Stettinius, 21 Nov. 1945.

[109] 817.00/11–1545, Byrnes to Fletcher Warren, 23 Nov. 1945.

Nicaragua. He told Arguello: 'The president is considered a dictator in the other American republics.' Arguello asked: 'inclusive all?' Warren said yes. 'Will you tell the president that,' Arguello enquired, 'or shall I?'[110]

Warren did it himself. He took to Somoza the dispatches relating to his re-election plans that had gone back and forth between the embassy and the State Department, many of them unflattering. He then passed him Byrnes's message. Somoza read it and asked what it meant. Warren said: 'Mr President, in my opinion they are telling you that this means you. Your government is considered to be that of a dictator, and the Department is trying to indicate to you its position.' Somoza, deliberately obtuse, complained that as a friend he deserved better treatment from the State Department: 'It should tell me exactly what it wants.' Warren replied that he was sure that the president now knew exactly what the department wanted in Nicaragua, and that it would be difficult for Washington to avoid the consultation proposed by the Panamanians.[111]

Once again, Somoza declared to Warren that he would eventually withdraw from the presidential race; this time he was prepared to put it in writing. He wrote a formal memorandum for him: 'I formally make the offer to the Department of State to renounce my candidacy in not more than thirty days.' This was a deft tactic. On the one hand, it seemed to indicate his sincere willingness not to seek re-election. On the other hand, it was an offer that the State Department could not even consider: it was not the department's job to accept or reject such offers from foreign heads of state. That Warren did not consider this is evident from the manner in which he transmitted Somoza's new promise to the department. That Somoza realized it should probably be assumed. He was too astute a politician not to have appreciated the implications of what he had written. The State Department's predictable reply came by return. 'This government', Warren was instructed to inform Somoza, 'would not entertain such an offer for one moment... The decision in the matter must be exclusively his.'[112]

Somoza had already made a decision, but it was useful to have obliged the State Department to put in writing that the choice was his own. He knew at the time, although the State Department did not, that he planned to forestall a potential coup or civilian uprising by staging a fake

[110] 817.00/12–645, Fletcher Warren to Secretary of State, 6 Dec. 1945.
[111] 817.00/11–2945, Fletcher Warren to Stettinius, 29 Nov. 1945.
[112] 817.00/11–2945, Fletcher Warren to Stettinius, 29 Nov. 1945; 817.001 Somoza, Anastasio/11–3045, Byrnes to Fletcher Warren, 30 Nov. 1945.

coup. To this end he had arranged for his old friend Colonel Camilo González, the presidential Chief of Staff, to simulate a military rebellion, depose him, and then, in the words of the intelligence report on the matter, 'shoot up the town and precipitate general turmoil'. During the disturbances all three designates to the presidency (the vice-presidents), Cole, Montenegro, and Sacasa, as well as the main Conservative and Independent Liberal leaders, were to be murdered. Somoza, who in the meantime would have announced his retirement and withdrawn to Montelimar, could then return to Managua, resume control of the Guardia, and command the troops to restore order. He could then govern provisionally until he could convoke another constituent assembly to draft a new charter granting him the presidency for a further six years.[113]

Currently ignorant of this scheme, the department was pleased with the trend of events. 'We can now rest on our oars a bit,' Cochran told Warren. 'Everything seems to be going along very nicely.' Somoza was less inclined to coast. Having obliged the United States to ignore a formal declaration that he would not stand for the presidency, he felt free to continue manoeuvring. He had told Warren that he would renounce his candidacy publicly at a meeting on 21 December. With less than a week to go, he postponed the meeting until January 1946. Further US pressure was evidently required.[114]

Two days after the postponement, Braden and Cochran invited the Nicaraguan ambassador, Guillermo Sevilla Sacasa, to the State Department. Sevilla tried to argue that Somoza must at least remain head of the National Guard because, if he were to forgo the opportunity to run for the presidency, candidates would emerge from within the Guardia and some of these might be from 'leftist elements'. To Braden, this was unimportant. He delivered a little homily. He told the Nicaraguan ambassador that 'the best way to practice democracy is to practice it and sometimes the way is hard. If leftist or anti-American elements should become active, well, that [is] only part of the difficult progress towards the democratic goal.' He was equally forthright in giving the ambassador his clear views on Somoza's future role in Nicaragua: 'being apart from the presidency, being apart from the National Guard, being apart in general from an active political life, [he] would as an elder statesman continue to exercise great influence upon the development of the political situation in

113 RG 226 XL 34649, report by Morgan, 30 Dec. 1945.
114 817.00/12–1045, Cochran to Fletcher Warren, 10 Dec. 1945; 817.00/12–1145, Fletcher Warren to Stettinius, 11 Dec. 1945; 817.00/12–1545, Fletcher Warren to Stettinius, 15 Dec. 1945.

Nicaragua along democratic and otherwise favorable lines, and thus write his name large on the pages of history.'[115]

In other words, Washington wanted Somoza to be wholly removed from political life. Handing over the presidency was not enough; they wanted him to retire. Warren was following the same line in Managua, telling Somoza's chief aide that neither the Nicaraguan public nor foreign opinion 'could be sold on the idea' of Somoza's remaining *jefe director* of the National Guard if he renounced the presidency.[116] Neither Warren nor his chiefs, however, wanted to see Somoza murdered. Warren had also been active in recent weeks trying to impress upon his contacts in the Guardia that the president's assassination would be reprehensible to Washington.[117] Rumours of a military coup were nonetheless insistent in early December, and the students were back on the streets as in the summer of 1944. They organized a large demonstration outside the US embassy chanting 'viva democracia', 'abajo la reelección', and 'muera Somoza'.[118]

The Independent Liberals and the Conservatives met in León on 16 December and in Granada on 23 December to agree on a joint plan of action. The internal opposition had decided that the best time to attack the government would be after Somoza's speech of 6 January 1946. According to US intelligence, conditions were deteriorating rapidly and would become acute in early January.[119] At the Liberal Party convention of that month, however, Somoza did announce that he would not seek re-election. Under intense American pressure he actually kept his word. With the official abandonment of good neighbourism and a new president in the White House, it seemed that Anastasio Somoza had abruptly reached the end of the road.

---

[115] 817.00/12–1745, Memorandum by Cochran, 17 Dec. 1945.

[116] 817.00/12–645, Fletcher Warren to Stettinius, 6 Dec. 1945.

[117] 817.00/12–445, Fletcher Warren to Cochran, personal letter, 4 Dec. 1945.

[118] 817.00/12–645, Fletcher Warren to Stettinius, 6 Dec. 1945.

[119] 817.00/12–2145, Fletcher Warren to Stettinius, 21 Dec. 1945; 817.00/12–2845, Fletcher Warren to Stettinius, 28 Dec. 1945; RG 226 OSS 34649, report by Morgan, 30 Dec. 1945.

Conclusion

After forty-three years of opprobrium and infamy, at the price of thousands of lives, *los muchachos* have won the day in Nicaragua...As a journalist committed to Our America's cause, I am grateful for having lived to see Sandino's triumph through his children and grandchildren—the people...In them Sandino rides again, shaking off the dust of calculated oblivion with which yesterday's and today's invaders covered him. On horse or mule or foot, he has returned to dwell in his fatherland forever.[1]

The freedom fighters in Nicaragua are the moral equivalent of our Founding Fathers.[2]

Ideologues tend to get things wrong. The empirical approach sees the present as emerging from the past and moving toward the future. Its view of the world is concrete and historical. Ideology is counterhistorical. It lives by models and substitutes models for reality.[3]

The presidency of Somoza's hand-picked successor, Leonardo Arguello, began on 1 May 1947 and lasted for twenty-six days. Somoza had been confident that he could control the new president, but two months before his inauguration Arguello told Fletcher Warren that he intended to remove the *jefe director* from his post. He appointed a cabinet made up largely of opponents to Somoza and announced changes in several Guardia commands. On 25 May he demanded that Somoza leave the country. On 26 May Somocista troops took the national assembly. Congress was convened to remove Arguello and install Somoza's choice, Benjamín Lacayo Sacasa, as provisional president. The United States initially refused to recognize the new government, demanded the return of all arms belonging to the military mission, halted all military aid to the Guardia, and withdrew the American head of the military academy. At the inter-American meeting of foreign ministers in Bogotá in April 1948,

---

[1] Gregorio Selser, *Sandino, General of the Free* (New York: Monthly Review Press, 1981), 205–7.

[2] President Ronald Reagan, speech to the Twelfth Annual Conservative Action Conference, 1 Mar. 1985.

[3] Arthur M. Schlesinger, *The Cycles of American History* (London: Penguin Books, 1989), 56.

however, Washington accepted a resolution that urged the continuity of diplomatic ties within the western hemisphere, and normal relations were re-established in time for Somoza's resumption of the presidency in 1950.[4]

*

The period of good neighbourism was a strange interlude in US policy towards Latin America. A symptom of a nation moving from isolationism to internationalism, of a world moving from depression to war, it was fraught with inconsistencies and contradictions, and beset by a constant tension between established traditions and new principles. A basic problem lay in the definition of the words 'intervention' and 'interference'. What was interference? Where did cooperation end and interference begin? If it could be shown that there was disorder and death because interference was forgone, what value might be placed on non-interference? In the early years of the period, the correspondence from US diplomats in Central America was insistent on such questions. The notion of one's duties in the event of a fire in a neighbour's home was an image that recurred. At the time, viewing the political circumstances in Nicaragua and weighing them against US interests in the rest of the hemisphere, policy-makers in Washington decided that no line could really be drawn between cooperation and interference. If the residents could not resolve the problem, the house would have to burn to the ground.

Any nation's foreign policy must attempt to secure that nation's interests, and it is on such a basis that the good neighbour policy should be judged. Good neighbourism, however, was expounded as something more than a pragmatic method of conducting external relations. It was to be an ethos, based on principles that were hard to criticize: protection of

---

[4] 817.00/3–347, Fletcher Warren to Marshall, 3 Mar. 1947; Richard Millet, *Guardians of the Dynasty* (Maryknoll, NY: Orbis Books,1977), 209–12; *New York Times*, 28 May 1948; Eduardo Crawley, *Dictators Never Die: A Portrait of Nicaragua and the Somoza Dynasty* (London: C.Hurst,1979),107–10. In 1955 the constitution was amended again to allow Somoza to stand for another term, but on 21 Sept. 1956 he was shot by Rigoberto López Pérez in León. Despite treatment in a Canal Zone hospital, he died on 29 Sept. and was succeeded by his older son, Luis Somoza Debayle. Luis Somoza held the presidency until 1963, whereafter he effectively ruled the country through two figurehead presidents, René Schick Gutiérrez and Lorenzo Guerrero. He died of a heart attack in Apr. 1967. His younger brother, Anastasio Somoza Debayle ('Tachito'), then head of the National Guard, assumed the presidency two months later and ceded formal authority to a governing triumvirate in 1972. He resumed the presidency in 1974 for a term that was scheduled to end in 1981, but was forced into exile on 17 July 1979 following a broad-based insurrection. He was assassinated in Paraguay on 17 Sept. 1980.

the weak, liquidation of aggression, absence of fear, respect for sovereignty and independence, the observance of obligations in the international order. For Nicaragua, good neighbourism's *raison d'être* was non-interference, through which Nicaraguans would come to believe that Washington policy-makers meant what they said, and would reciprocate by developing a peaceful democracy in which US interests were respected. It is on the extent to which such expectations and ideals were realized that good neighbour diplomacy in Nicaragua must also be assessed.

As it had to, the good neighbour policy responded at all times to Washington's perceptions of American self-interest. This does not mean, however, that the Roosevelt administration continued US intervention in order to install Somoza as the individual most compatible with American interests. On the contrary, efforts were made to be rigidly non-interventionist. Hence Washington simply did nothing to stop his remorseless ascent. Arthur Bliss Lane, the US minister in Managua during the mid 1930s, did try to stop him but received no official backing from Washington. Conjunctural factors appeared to dictate that this would be the best course. The United States had just withdrawn from an expensive and frustrating war in Nicaragua, a war that had signally failed to secure peace and stability. Intense public and congressional isolationism demanded that the Roosevelt administration strenuously avoid another fruitless entanglement in Nicaraguan instability. Despite the State Department's public pronouncements that tranquillity would prevail, renewed instability after the marine withdrawal of 1933 was probably assumed in Washington. That something like Somoza's ascent might happen must have seemed quite probable. All the more reason, then, that disengagement—graceful or not—should be as absolute as possible.

As it became clearer that the instability was taking the form of confrontation between the elected government and the American-created Guardia, the Central American states were simultaneously organizing a conference to consider the future of the 1923 recognition treaty. When Lane was demanding that the State Department make a public statement of recognition policy in order to forestall Somoza after Sandino's murder, the plans for the conference were nearing completion. Hull did not want to issue a statement at that time, since it might incur for the United States accusations of interference in order to influence the outcome of the conference. Sandino, moreover, was killed in the same month as Hull began negotiations with the Nicaraguan government on the reciprocal trade agreement. The link between non-interference and the trade programme was quite concrete. At the Montevideo conference in 1933, Hull arrived with his trade proposals. The Argentine foreign minister, Carlos Saavedra Lamas, came armed with a non-intervention protocol. The result was a trade-off.[5] The first time that US repudiation of a right of intervention was embodied in inter-American law resulted in part from a negotiating tactic designed to effect acceptance of Hull's reciprocal trade programme. That programme having been accepted, Hull wanted to avoid committing the United States to non-recognition of a future Somoza government, because he was in the midst of negotiating an agreement with the incumbent Sacasa administration and did not want to have to abort the talks if Somoza, as legation reports were constantly indicating, overthrew Sacasa.

When that duly happened, the United States did not immediately pursue the maintenance of Somoza as a policy objective with any great degree of positive action. There was no economic assistance, despite the country's parlous financial situation. There was no military mission to reorganize the Guardia, despite continuing indications of the military's lack of coherence and discipline. Emerging potential threats to the general were viewed with a certain detachment, and there was no diplomatic interference on his behalf.

Towards the end of Somoza's first term, however, as world conditions deteriorated and an external threat emerged, the fact that he was apparently compatible with traditional US security doctrine in the Caribbean did come to seem a clear asset for the United States. With the slow evaporation of isolationism, policy changed. As diplomatic and military thinking converged, the good neighbour policy was partially militarized. Somoza could now be seen as morally objectionable but strategically valuable. US diplomats actively defused political threats. US intelligence agencies monitored the opposition. The US War Department retrained and rearmed the Guardia. This did not require much effort on Washington's part; even the cost of the Lend Lease agreement was relatively minor. The repercussions in Nicaragua, however, were substantial. US plans for hemisphere defence appeared to confirm public perceptions of Washington's commitment to Somoza, perceptions that the general himself astutely encouraged.

---

[5] Irwin Gellman, *Good Neighbor Diplomacy: United States Polices in Latin America, 1933–1945* (Baltimore, Md.: Johns Hopkins University Press, 1979), 24; William Everett Kane, *Civil Strife in Latin America* (Baltimore, Md.: Johns Hopkins University Press, 1972), 122.

The period of direct and active US measures to sustain Somoza, however, was relatively brief: approximately from the fall of France—when the Axis seemed a true global menace—to the Battle of Stalingrad—when it seemed clear that the Axis had lost the military initiative. With the slow dissipation of the external threat, policy changed again. The fact that Somoza was morally objectionable assumed greater significance as military planning disengaged from diplomatic activity. By the war's end, Washington's policy of diplomatic withdrawal from Somoza was hardening into outright opposition, leading to increasingly strong pressure to force him to step down. Throughout the period, Somoza changed very little. US policy altered significantly. The main policy determinant was not the Somoza regime, but the different contexts in which the regime operated.

The prospects for successful implementation of a policy of non-interference were never bright, except for a peculiar period in 1937 when there were no internal threats, no immediate external threats, and an adamant determination on the part of the United States not to engage with the competing powers of Europe and Asia. In 1933, when Sacasa requested US consent to the reorganization of the Guardia, every conceivable response from Washington could have been construed as interference. In context, to decline to make a response could in fact be taken as a response; it simply required more interpretation than a simple yes or no. When the de facto recognition policy was adopted in 1936 it was justifiably announced in the name of non-interference. But in the circumstances that prevailed in Nicaragua in the spring of that year, this too could be construed as interference. When that policy was reversed in the early 1940s, the change was championed in Washington as a strengthening of the policy of non-interference, though by then, in Nicaragua, it could be interpreted as a means of safeguarding the Somoza government.

The instructions to the US legations in Central America embodying good neighbour diplomacy in 1936 stated that the policy was one of 'constructive and effective friendship based upon mutual respect for each other's rights and interests...It would obviously be incompatible with this policy to become involved in the domestic concerns of any of the Central American republics.'[6] But to see non-interference as a panacea for the mistakes of the past and a guarantee of cordiality in the future was a misconception. Implicit even in the term 'good neighbour policy', as

---

[6] US Deparment of State, *Foreign Relations*, 1936, v, 136–7.

Frank Corrigan wrote from El Salvador, was some measure of moral responsibility.[7] From the viewpoint of the constitutional government of Nicaragua at the time, the 'friendly detachment' mentioned in the instructions was quite literally a contradiction in terms.

Good neighbourism failed to convince Nicaraguans that the Roosevelt administration wished their country nothing but good. On the contrary, the majority held the United States responsible for Somoza's failings, and saw his accession as the successful culmination of a long-term plan that Washington had initiated at least as early as 1933. In this they were mistaken, but in the circumstances such a conclusion was understandable. It was a conviction reinforced by a trade agreement that was viewed in Nicaragua as another example of the strong exploiting the weak for its own purposes, the very antithesis of good neighbour theory. Arthur Bliss Lane, who had to deal with situations as they arose, recognized that the austerity of early good neighbourism in Nicaragua, its sheer insistence on non-interference, actively promoted anti-Americanism. Cordell Hull, who expressed policy in terms of abstractions and whose knowledge of Latin America seems to have been inadequate, would consider no alternative. It was Hull, however, who made policy. Lane simply carried it out, often with a reluctance that did not pass unnoticed in Washington.

Two weeks after Lane's transfer to the Baltic republics, Laurence Duggan expressed the opinion that 'the abilities and standing' of US diplomats in Central America varied greatly, and that 'on more than one occasion inept handling of situations by our own representatives has not only served to make these situations worse but has resulted in embarrassment for and intense criticism of the United States.'[8] It would be impossible to prove that Duggan was referring to Lane here, though it seems quite possible. In the end, however, it was Lane who was vindicated. It was his conception of good neighbourism that Hull came to espouse nearly a decade later.

Despite the attempts to cut a new path in inter-American diplomacy, it was the traditional geopolitical considerations of national security that shaped good neighbour diplomacy in Nicaragua as the policy was taken from Hull's hands by events beyond the hemisphere. At the Lima conference the United States had introduced a draft protocol proposing joint action against any western-hemisphere government that had been subverted by 'fascist-oriented' systems. In the nineteenth century the security

---

[7] Ibid., 1937, v, 523.
[8] Ibid., 1936, v, 128–30.

problem had been European governments intent on debt collection. In the early twentieth century the menace was Mexican 'bolshevism'. In mid century the threat was Nazism. Later it would be communism. Only briefly did the United States feel that it could afford to let Nicaragua stand alone. Neither of the two Nicaraguan governments of this period felt that they could afford to let the United States leave them alone.

That the United States did attempt to forgo interference had far-reaching repercussions for Nicaragua. Those repercussions, in the context of the concerns of a later age, were taken to evidence not simply diplomatic interference but also much graver misdeeds: conspiracy to commit murder, the installation of a military dictatorship, the creation of one of Latin America's most enduring regimes. As an American president attempted to overthrow the Nicaraguan government, his predecessor in the White House, half a century earlier, suddenly became a witting midwife to tyranny.

Nevertheless, as was mentioned in the introduction to this study, the present state of US relations with Nicaragua is calmer than it was until recently, and the international debate about those relations is less intense. The current president of Nicaragua has proved himself a staunch ally of Washington, and even sent a small military force to support the US occupation of Iraq. In May 2004 the United States and Nicaragua, as well as the other countries of the isthmus, signed a free trade agreement. As bilateral relations turn cordial, Washington may be able usefully to apply the friendly detachment that it attempted to effect in the early years of the good neighbour period. Absolute non-interference, however, still does not appear to be a viable option.

Three presidents have been elected in Nicaragua in the past fifteen years. President Bolaños of the Constitutionalist Liberal Party is now approaching the end of his term. The FSLN complained bitterly about US interference in the elections that brought him to office. The US embassy in Managua was accused of making unfavourable public comments about the Sandinista candidate, and the State Department was said to have called for a Liberal–Conservative alliance to forestall an FSLN victory. The elections that brought Bolaños to the presidency were held less than eight weeks after the attacks on New York and Washington in September 2001. In the final stages of the campaign, therefore, identifying themselves with the world outlook of the United States, the Liberals sought to capitalize on the ensuing mood by arguing that the Sandinista candidate was associated with 'terrorists'. Once again, following the interlude of the 1990s, the United States had to worry about un-American ideologies, and the present US administration does not seem to view non-interference as a practical policy objective with which to engage in global war.

Bibliography

PRIMARY SOURCES

Most of this study is based on primary source material from various departments of the US government, housed in the National Archives in Washington DC and College Park, Maryland. The greater part of such material is from Record Group (RG) 59, the general records of the Department of State.

Within the decimal files of RG 59, the 817.00 file deals with general political conditions in Nicaragua. The sub-files of this series contain material on specific issues. Of particular value were the 817.001 file, 'Somoza, Anastasio', and the 817.00 file, 'Revolutions'. For the period of the war the 817.00 file, 'Nazis' was helpful. The 817.20 series deals with defence matters. Papers relating to economic and trade relations are contained in the 600 series, most extensively in file 611.1731.

Details of inter-state relations are contained in the 700 decimal series of RG 59, but there is little information here. The 711.17 file deals with US–Nicaraguan relations. The files for the other Central American republics were also consulted: Guatemala (814.00), Honduras (815.00), El Salvador (816.00), and Costa Rica (818.00).

All such decimal files referred to in the footnotes are from RG 59. Other Record Groups used are marked by their corresponding RG number in the footnotes whenever they appear. They are as follows:

RG 38: Records of the Office of the Chief of Naval Operations.

RG 46: Records of the Senate Committee on Foreign Relations.

RG 94: Records of the Office of the Adjutant General.

RG 165: Records of the War Department, General and Special Staffs. See in particular the records of the Military Intelligence Division, the Military Intelligence Service (Latin American Branch), and the Director of Plans and Operations, Pan-American Group.

RG 226: Records of the Office of Strategic Services.

The Department of State *Press Releases* and the Executive Agreement Series (for details of specific treaties) are available in the Library of Congress, Washington DC.

The most used newspaper source was the *New York Times*.

SECONDARY SOURCES

Adams, Frederick C., *Economic Diplomacy: The Export-Import Bank and American Foreign Policy, 1936–1939* (Columbia: University of Missouri Press, 1976).

Adler, S., *The Uncertain Giant, 1921–1941: American Foreign Policy between the Wars* (New York: Macmillan, 1965).

Aguirre y Fierro Harris, Enrique, *La no intervención y la quiebra de la soberanía nacional* (Mexico City: Universidad Nacional de México, 1946).

Alexander, Charles C., *Nationalism in American Thought, 1930–1945* (Chicago: Rand McNally, 1969).

Allen, William R., 'Cordell Hull and the Defense of the Trade Agreement Program, 1934–1940,' in Alexander de Conde (ed.), *Isolation and Security: Ideas and Interests in Twentieth-Century American Foreign Policy* (Durham, NC: Duke University Press, 1957), 107–32.

American Assembly, *The United States and Latin America: Background Papers and the Final Report of the Sixteenth American Assembly, Arden House, Harriman Campus of Columbia University, Harriman, New York, October 15–18,1959* (New York: s.n., 1959).

Atkins, G. Pope, *Latin America in the International Political System* (Boulder, Colo.: Westview Press, 1995).

Bain, David Harward, 'The Man who Made the Yanquis Go Home', in Andrew C. Kimmens (ed.), *Nicaragua and the United States* (New York: H. W. Wilson, 1987), 16–35.

Barahona Portocarrero, Amaru, 'Estudio sobre la historia contemporánea de Nicaragua', Avances de Investigación, 24 (San José, Costa Rica: Universidad de Costa Rica, Facultad de Ciencias Sociales, Instituto de Investigaciones Sociales, 1977).

Barnett, Correlli, *Engage the Enemy More Closely: The Royal Navy in the Second World War* (London: Hodder & Stoughton, 1991).

Beals, Carleton, *The Coming Struggle for Latin America* (London: Cape, 1939).

Beard, Charles A., *The Idea of National Interest: An Analytical Study in American Foreign Policy* (New York: Macmillan, 1934).

—— (ed.), *America Faces the Future* (Boston: Houghton Mifflin, 1932).

Bemis, Samuel Flagg, *The Latin American Policy of the United States* (New York: Harcourt, Brace and Company, 1943).

Blandón, Miguel Jesús, *Entre Sandino y Fonseca Amador* (Managua: s.n., 1980).

Bresler, Robert J., 'The Ideology of the Executive State: Essays on New Deal Foreign Policy', in Leonard P. Liggio and James J. Martin (eds.), *Watershed of Empire* (Colorado Springs, Colo.: R. Myles, 1976), 1–18.

Brogan, Hugh, *The Pelican History of the United States of America* (Harmondsworth: Penguin, 1987).

Brownlee, Roland, *Cooperación económica de los Estados Unidos con Nicaragua* (Managua: Imprenta Democrática, 1945).

Buell, Raymond Leslie, 'Getting Out of Central America', *The Nation*, 135/3479 (13 July 1932), 32–4.

Bullock, Alan, *Hitler and Stalin: Parallel Lives* (London: Fontana, 1993).

Bulmer-Thomas, Victor, *The Political Economy of Central America since 1920* (Cambridge: Cambridge University Press, 1987).

Cancino Troncoso, Hugo, *Las raíces históricas e ideológicas del movimiento sandinista: Antecedentes de la Revolución Nacional y Popular Nicaragüense, 1927–1979* (Odense: Odense University Press, 1984).

Carter, John F., *The New Dealers: By the Unofficial Observer* (New York: Surion and Schuster, 1934).

Cerdas Cruz, Rodolfo, 'Nicaragua: One Step Forward, Two Steps Back' in Giuseppe Di Palma and Laurence Whitehead (eds.), *The Central American Impasse* (London: Croom Helm, 1986), 175–95.

Chase National Bank of the City of New York, *The Countries of Central America: An Economic and Financial Review* (New York: Chase National Bank, 1943).

Christian, Shirley, *Nicaragua: Revolution in the Family* (New York: Vintage Books, 1986).

Clark, Lew B., 'One Year of War, and United States Trade with Latin America', *Foreign Commerce Weekly*, 1/2 (12 Oct. 1940), 47–50.

Colindres, Juan, *Anastasio Somoza: Fin de una estirpe de ladrones y asesinos* (Mexico City: Editorial Posada, 1979).

Collector General of Customs and High Commission *Report for the period of January 1, 1932 to December 31, 1932* (Managua: *s.n.*, 1932).

—— *Report for the period of January 1, 1934 to December 31, 1934* (Managua: *s.n.*, 1935).

Commercial Pan America, 58–60 (Mar.–May 1937).

Commercial Pan America, 70–2 (Apr.–May 1938).

Commercial Pan America, 4–6 (Apr.–June 1941).

Commercial Pan America, 11–12 (Nov.–Dec. 1941).

Conn, Stetson, and Fairchild, Byron, *The Framework of Hemisphere Defense* (Washington: Department of the Army, Office of the Chief of Military History, 1960).

Connell-Smith, Gordon, *The Inter-American System* (London: Oxford University Press, 1966).

Cordero Reyes, Manuel, Castro Wassmer, Carlos, and Pasos, Carlos, *Nicaragua bajo el régimen de Somoza* (San Salvador: Imprenta Funes, 1944).

Crassweller, Robert D., *The Caribbean Community: Changing Societies and US Policy* (London: Pall Mall Press, 1972).

Crawley, Eduardo, *Dictators Never Die: A Portrait of Nicaragua and the Somoza Dynasty* (London: C. Hurst, 1979).

Dallek, Robert, *Franklin D. Roosevelt and American Foreign Policy, 1933–1945* (New York: Oxford University Press, 1979).

Davis, Horace B., 'The Influences of the Second World War', in Latin American Economic Institute, *The Economic Defense of the Western Hemisphere* (Freeport, NY: Books for Libraries Press, 1942), 5–43.

Denny, Harold N., *Dollars for Bullets: The Story of American Rule in Nicaragua* (New York: L. MacVeagh, The Dial Press, 1929).

De Santis, Hugh, *The Diplomacy of Silence: The American Foreign Service, the Soviet Union and the Cold War, 1933–1947* (Chicago: University of Chicago Press, 1980).

Dickens, Paul D., *American Direct Investment in Foreign Countries*, US Department of Commerce, *Information Bulletin*, 731 (Washington DC: US Government Printing Office, 1930).

Diederich, Bernard, *Somoza and the Legacy of US Involvement in Central America* (New York: Dutton, 1981).

Dozer, Donald, *Are We Good Neighbors?* (Gainesville: University of Florida Press, 1959).

Duggan, Laurence, *The Americas: The Search for Hemisphere Security* (New York: Holt, 1949).

Dulles, F. R., *America's Rise to World Power, 1898–1954* (New York: Harper, 1955).

Dunkerley, James, *Power in the Isthmus: A Political History of Modern Central America* (London: Verso, 1988).

Duroselle, J. B., *From Wilson to Roosevelt: Foreign Policy of the United States* (London: Chatto & Windus, 1964).

Edmisten, Patricia Taylor, *Nicaragua Divided* (Pensacola: University of West Florida Press, 1990).

Elliot, A. Randle, 'The Resources and Trade of Central America', *Foreign Policy Reports*, 17/12 (1 Sept. 1941), 150–60.

Escobar Morales, César, *Sandino en el panorama nacional* (Managua: *s.n.*, 1979).

Frye, Alton, *Nazi Germany and the American Hemisphere, 1933–1941* (New Haven: Yale University Press, 1967).

Gardner, Lloyd C., *Imperial America: American Foreign Policy since 1898* (New York: Harcourt Brace Jovanovich, 1976).

Gellman, Irwin, *Roosevelt and Batista: Good Neighbor Diplomacy in Cuba, 1933–1945* (Albuquerque, N. Mex.: University of New Mexico Press, 1971).

—— *Good Neighbor Diplomacy: United States Policies in Latin America, 1933–1945* (Baltimore, Md.: Johns Hopkins University Press, 1979).

Gilbert, Martin, *Second World War* (London: Weidenfeld and Nicolson, 1989).

Goldwert, Marvin, *The Constabulary in the Dominican Republic and Nicaragua* (Gainesville: University of Florida Press, 1962).

Gould, Jeffrey L., *Dangerous Friends: Somoza and the Labour Movement* (Mineographed document, Managua, 1985).

Graber, Doris A., *Crisis Diplomacy: A History of US Intervention Policies and Practices* (Washington: Public Affairs Press, 1959).

Graebner, Norman A. (ed.), *Ideas and Diplomacy: Readings in the Intellectual Tradition of American Foreign Policy* (New York: Oxford University Press, 1964).

Green, Philip Leonard, *Pan American Progress* (New York: Hastings House, 1942).

Greer, Thomas H., *What Roosevelt Thought: The Social and Political Ideas of Franklin D. Roosevelt* (East Lansing: Michigan State University Press, 1958).

Grieb, Kenneth J., 'Negotiating a Trade Agreement with Guatemala,' *Prologue*, Spring 1973, 22–32.

Grow, Michael, *The Good Neighbor Policy and Authoritarianism in Paraguay: United States Economic Expansion and Great-Power Rivalry in Latin America during World War II* (Lawrence: Regents Press of Kansas, 1981).

Guerrant, Edgar O., *Roosevelt's Good Neighbor Policy* (Albuquerque: University of New Mexico Press, 1950).

Guzman Vial, Manuel, 'La intervención y la no intervención', dissertation, University of Santiago Chile, 1948.

Halasz, Nicholas, *Roosevelt through Foreign Eyes* (Englewood Cliffs, NJ: Van Nostrand, 1961).

Harrison, Benjamin T., *Dollar Diplomat: Chandler Anderson and American Diplomacy in Mexico and Nicaragua, 1913–1928* (Washington: Washington State University Press, 1988).

Hartmann, Frederick, *The Relations of Nations* (New York: Macmillan, 1967).

Hawkins, Harry C., and Norwood, Janet L., 'The Legislative Basis of US Commercial Policy,' in William B. Kelly (ed.), *Studies in United States Commercial Policy* (Chapel Hill: University of North Carolina Press, 1963), 69–123.

Herring, Hubert, *Good Neighbors: Argentina, Brazil, Chile and 17 other Countries* (New Haven: Yale University Press, 1941).

Hobsbawm, Eric, *Age of Extremes: The Short Twentieth Century 1914–1991* (London: Michael Joseph, 1994).

Hodges, Donald C., *Intellectual Foundations of the Nicaraguan Revolution* (Austin: University of Texas Press, 1986).

Hull, Cordell, *Memoirs* (New York: Macmillan, 1948).

Humphreys, Robin R., *Latin America and the Second World War* (London: Athlone Press, 1981).

Jenkins, Tony, *Nicaragua and the United States: Years of Conflict* (New York: F. Watts, 1989).

Jinesta, Ricardo, *Confirmación de los derechos de Costa Rica en el Canal de Nicaragua* (San José, Costa Rica: Falco Hnos., 1937).

Jones, Chester Lloyd, *The Caribbean since 1900* (New York: Prentice Hall Inc., 1936).

Jones, Joseph M., 'Good Neighbor, New Style', *Harper's Magazine*, Apr. 1946, 192, 313–21.

Kamman, William, *A Search for Stability: United States Diplomacy toward Nicaragua, 1925–1933* (Notre Dame, Ind.: University of Notre Dame Press, 1968).

Kane, William Everett, *Civil Strife in Latin America* (Baltimore, Md.: Johns Hopkins University Press, 1972).

Kennan, George F., *American Diplomacy, 1900–1950* (London: Secker & Warburg, 1952).

—— *Realities of American Foreign Policy* (London: Oxford University Press, 1954).

Krehm, William, *Democracies and Tyrannies of the Caribbean* (Westport, Conn.: Lawrence Hill & Co., 1984).

Langer, William L., and Gleason, S. Everett, *Challenge to Isolation, 1937–1940* (New York: Harper, 1952).

Langley, Lester D., *The United States and the Caribbean in the Twentieth Century* (Athens: University of Georgia Press, 1980).

Leuchtenburg, William E., 'Franklin D. Roosevelt and the New Deal, 1933–1940', in Arnold A. Offner, ed., *America and the Origins of World War II, 1933–1941* (Boston: Houghton Mifflin, 1971), 79–95.

Macaulay, Neill, *The Sandino Affair* (Chicago: Quadrangle Books, 1967).

Martin, Lawrence and Martin, Sylvia, 'Nazi Intrigues in Central America', *American Mercury*, 53 (July 1941), 66–73.

McWhinney, Edward, 'The "New" Countries and the "New" International Law', *American Journal of International Law*, 60 (Jan. 1966), 1–33.

Mecham, J. Lloyd, *The United States and Inter-American Security, 1889–1960* (Austin: University of Texas Press, 1961).

——*A Survey of United States-Latin American Relations* (Boston: Houghton Mifflin, 1965).

Millet, Richard, *Guardians of the Dynasty* (Maryknoll, NY: Orbis Books, 1977).

Moncada, José María, *Nicaragua: Sangre en sus montañas* (San José, California, 1985).

Morgan, Ted, *FDR: A Biography* (New York: Simon and Schuster, 1985).

Morgenthau, Hans J., *In Defense of the National Interest: A Critical Examination of American Foreign Policy* (New York: Knopf, 1951).

Morison, Samuel E., *History of United States Naval Operations in World War II*, i: *The Battle of the Atlantic, September 1939–May 1943* (London: Oxford University Press, 1948).

Munro, Dana G., *The United States and the Caribbean Area* (Boston: World Peace Foundation, 1934).

Needler, Martin C. (ed.), *Political Systems of Latin America* (Princeton, NJ: Van Nostrand, 1964).

O'Callaghan, D. B., *Roosevelt and the United States* (London: Longmans, 1966).

Parkinson, Roger, *Encyclopaedia of Modern War* (London: Granada Publishing Limited, 1979).

Pastor, Robert, *Condemned to Repetition: The United States and Nicaragua* (Princeton, New Jersey: Princeton University Press, 1988).

Perkins, Dexter, *The United States and the Caribbean* (Cambridge, Mass.: Harvard University Press, 1947).

——*The United States and Latin America* (Baton Rouge: Louisiana State University Press, 1961).

Petrov, Vladimir, *A Study in Diplomacy: The Story of Arthur Bliss Lane* (Chicago: H. Regnery Co., 1971).

Phillips, William, *Ventures in Diplomacy* (Boston: Beacon Press, 1952).

Pratt, Julius W., *Cordell Hull, 1933–1944*, 2 vols., The American Secretaries of State, 12–13 (New York: Cooper Square Publishers, 1964).

'Reciprocal Trade Agreement between Nicaragua and United States Promulgated', *Bulletin of the Pan American Union*, 70 (Oct. 1936), 809.

Rogers, Cleveland, *The Roosevelt Program* (New York: G. B. Putnam's Sons, 1933).

Ronning, C. Neale (ed.), *Intervention in Latin America* (New York: Knopf, 1970).

Rosenman, Samuel (ed.), *Public Papers and Addresses of Franklin D. Roosevelt* (New York: Random House, 1938).

Roucek, Joseph S., 'Minorities: A Basis of the Refugee Problem', in American Academy of Political and Social Science, *Annals*, 203 (1939), 1–17.

Sacasa, Juan Bautista, *Cómo y por qué caí del poder* (Leon, Nicaragua: *s.n.*, 1936).

Sayre, Francis B., *Tariff Bargaining* (Washington DC: US Government Printing Office, 1934).

—— *Glad Adventure* (New York: Macmillan, 1957).

Schlesinger, Arthur M., *The Cycles of American History* (London: Penguin Books, 1989).

Selser, Gregorio, *Sandino, General of the Free* (New York: Monthly Review Press, 1981).

—— *Nicaragua de Walker a Somoza* (Mexico: Mex-Sur Editorial, 1984).

Smith, H. Gerald, 'Economic Ties Linking the United States and Latin America' *Commercial Pan America*, 45 (Feb. 1936), 1–9.

Somoza Debayle, Anastasio, *Nicaragua Betrayed* (Boston: Western Islands, 1980).

Steward, Dick, *Trade and Hemisphere: The Good Neighbor Policy and Reciprocal Trade* (Columbia: University of Missouri Press, 1975).

Stimson, Henry Lewis, *Henry L. Stimson's American Policy in Nicaragua: The Lasting Legacy*, with introduction and afterword by Paul H. Boeker, plus essays by Andrés Pérez and Alain Brinkley (New York: M. Wiener Publishers, *c*.1991).

Strackbein, Oscar R., *American Enterprise and Foreign Trade* (Washington DC: Public Affairs Press, 1965).

Suárez Zambrana, Guillermo, *Los yanquis en Nicaragua* (San José, Costa Rica: Editorial Texto Ltda., 1978).

Tessendorf, K. C., *Uncle Sam in Nicaragua: A History* (New York: Atheneum, 1987).

Tierney, John J., Jr, 'Revolution and the Marines: The United States and Nicaragua in the Early Years', in Belden Bell (ed.), *Nicaragua: An Ally under Siege* (Washington DC: Council on American Affairs, 1978), 8–23.

Trefousse, Hans Louis, *Germany and American Neutrality, 1939–1941* (New York: Bookman Associates, 1951).

Tuchman, Barbara W., *Sand Against the Wind: Stilwell and the American Experience in China, 1911–1945* (London: Macmillan, 1991).

US Department of Agriculture, *General Sugar Quota Regulations*, ser. 1, suppl. 1, 9 Oct. 1934 (Washington DC: US Government Printing Office, 1934).

US Department of Commerce, *A Balance of International Payments of the United States in 1933* (Washington DC: US Government Printing Office, 1934).

—— Bureau of Foreign and Domestic Commerce, *US Trade with the Central American Republics in 1942* (Washington DC: US Government Printing Office, 1944).

—— Bureau of Foreign and Domestic Commerce, *Economic Review of Foreign Countries, 1938* (Washington DC: US Government Printing Office, 1939).

—— Bureau of Foreign and Domestic Commerce, *Foodstuffs Trade with Latin America*, Trade Promotion Series, 214 (Washington DC: US Government Printing Office, 1941).

US Department of States, *The United States and Nicaragua: A Survey of the Relations from 1909–1932* Latin American Series, 6, (Washington DC: US Government Printing Office, 1932).

—— *Press Releases* (Washington DC: US Government Printing Office), 1932, 1933, 1934.

—— *Foreign Relations of the United States* (Washington DC: US Government Printing Office), 1932, v; 1933, iv; 1936, v; 1937, v; 1939, v.

—— *Report of the Delegates of the United States of America to the Seventh Conference of American States*, Conference Series, 19 (Washington DC: US Government Printing Office, 1934).

—— *Nicaragua*, Information Series, 77 (Washington DC: US Government Printing Office, 1935).

—— *Terminating Certain Provisions of the Reciprocal Trade Agreement of March 11, 1936 between Nicaragua and the United States*, Executive Agreement Series, 20 (Washington DC: US Government Printing Office, 1938).

—— *Report of the Delegation of the United States of America to the Meeting of the Foreign Ministers of the American Republics, Panama, September 23–October 9, 1939*, Conference Series, 44 (Washington DC: US Government Printing Office, 1940).

—— *Inter-American Highway Agreement between the United States and Nicaragua*, 8 Apr. 1942, Executive Agreement Series, 295 (Washington DC: US Government Printing Office, 1942).

—— *Reciprocal Trade Agreement and Supplementary Agreement between the United States of America and Brazil*, Executive Agreement Series, 78 (Washington DC: US Government Printing Office, 1942).

—— *Plantation Rubber Investigations Agreement between the United States and Nicaragua*, continuing in force an agreement of 11 Jan. 1941, signed at Managua, 23 and 26 June 1943, Executive Agreement Series, 357 (Washington DC: US Government Printing Office, 1943).

—— *Bulletin*, 10 (1 Jan. 1944).

US Tariff Commission, *Foreign Trade of Latin America*, report 146 (Washington DC: US Government Printing Office, 1942).

—— *Economic Controls and Commercial Policy in Nicaragua* (Washington DC: US Government Printing Office, 1947).

Valle Martínez, Marco Antonio, *La dictadura somocista* (Leon: Comité Político Universitario UNAN, 1980).

Varg, Paul, 'The Economic Side of the Good Neighbor Policy', *Pacific Historical Review*, 45/1 (Feb. 1976), 47–71.

Walter, Knut, *The Regime of Anastasio Somoza, 1936–1956* (Chapel Hill: University of North Carolina Press, 1993).

Watson, Mark S., *Chief of Staff: Prewar Plans and Preparations* (Washington DC: Department of the Army, Historical Division, 1950).

Weeks, John, 'Land, Labour and Despotism in Central America', in Giuseppe DiPalma and Laurence Whitehead (eds.), *The Central American Impasse* (London: Croom Helm, 1986), 111–29.

Wheelock, Jaime, and Carrión, Luis, *Apuntes sobre el desarrollo económico y social de Nicaragua* (Managua: Secretaría Nacional de Propaganda y Educación del FSLN, 1980).

Williams, William Appleman, ed., *The Shaping of American Diplomacy, 1914–1968* (Chicago: Rand McNally, 1973).

'Will Loans by the US Export-Import Bank be a Real Aid to Latin-American Economy', *Congressional Digest*, 19/12 (Dec. 1940), 315–20.

Wood, Bryce, *The Making of the Good Neighbor Policy* (New York: Columbia University Press, 1961).

—— *The Dismantling of the Good Neighbor Policy* (Austin: University of Texas Press, 1985).

Woods, Randall Bennett, *The Roosevelt Foreign Policy Establishment and the 'Good Neighbor': The United States and Argentina, 1941–1945* (Lawrence: Regents Press of Kansas, 1979).

Woodward, Ralph Lee, *Central America: A Nation Divided* (New York: Oxford University Press, 1985).

Zuloaga Z., Jaime A., 'The International Economic Relations of Latin America', *Commercial Pan America*, 10/1 (Jan. 1941), 2–18.

Index